Books by Linda Merinoff

THE GLORIOUS NOODLE

THE SAVORY SAUSAGE

Poseidon Press
New York London Toronto
Sydney Tokyo

The Savory Sausage

. . . .

A Culinary Tour Around the World

ILLUSTRATIONS BY GLENN WOLFF

Published by Poseidon Press
A Divison of Simon & Schuster, Inc.
Simon & Schuster Building
Rockefeller Center
1230 Avenue of the Americas
New York, NY 10020
POSEIDON PRESS is a registered trademark of Simon & Schuster, Inc.
Designed by Karolina Harris
Manufactured in the United States of America

10 9 8 7 6 5 4 3 2 1

Library of Congress Cataloging-in-Publication Data

Merinoff, Linda.
The savory sausage.
Bibliography: p.
Includes index.
1. Cookery (Sausages) 2. Sausages. I. Title.
TX749.5.S28M47 1987 641.6'6 87–21797
ISBN 0-671-62727-9

ACKNOWLEDGMENTS

There are always so many people to thank. Writing a book, especially one involving vast amounts of food, necessitates friends willing to taste your failures as well as your successes. There were some memorable moments, especially the day that David Norton, Brian Murray, Cindy Cable, Alexander Kulli, Larry Strichman, Cindy and Mike Cassutt, Linda Burum, Rosalyn Landor, and I tasted twenty different kinds of commercial hot dogs. It's hard to forget items like the cheese dogs Cindy Cassutt described as tasting like "Velveeta and Spam." Many thanks to all those who helped with all the recipes in this book.

I must also thank Linda Burum for providing information both in person and in her wonderful book, *Cook's Marketplace: Los Angeles,* on where to buy all kinds of exotic ingredients. Janie Rosenthal loaned me some essential books and threw a terrific party for my first book, *The Glorious Noodle.* Kathie Fong Yoneda was very helpful regarding Chinese sausages. Since I forgot to thank Ray Wong for his help on the last book, I'd like to thank him now. The brilliant and talented Bill Hootkins is my inspiration for all things Chinese. Sydny Miner always reminds me that eating and dining should be fun, not pretentious and pompous. Eileen Stukane's friendship and help was invaluable. I call ice skater and opera singer Cyndie Bellen-Berthezene when I want to talk about anything but food.

Ann Patty and everyone at Poseidon Press and Simon and Schuster are generous with their time and support and I think they're terrific. Barbara Torres at the Armour Meat Company was so gracious about providing me with excellent research materials regarding sausage sales and American trends that I was pleased and relieved when Armour hot dogs were in the top three at the hot-dog tasting. Bruce Aidells, one of America's best sausage makers, also provided helpful information.

Many thanks to Val Norwood for the last photo, and to photographer Bernie Boudreau and makeup and hair stylist Victoria Jackson, who made taking the photo for this book lots of fun. The extraordinary gymnastics teacher, Robert Carreiro, and Susan Raper and Dan Isaacson have managed to keep me in excellent shape despite two years of daily sausage intake. Publicists Michael Dougherty and Don DeMesquita were a great help on the noodle book, so I'm taking this chance to thank them. Rona Barrett (that excellent and most unappreciated news reporter) and the funny and talented Bill Royce gave me a priceless gift—confidence in my abilities. As always, love and thanks to my family for always being there.

Although this does sound trite, there are five people without whom this book really could not have been written. Mel Berger is the best possible agent, combining humor, a sense of perspective, and great ability. My books must be considered a joint effort with editor Pat Capon, whose understanding, clear thinking, and insightful editing make them possible. The other three people, Larry Strichman, Paul Bogrow, and Rosalyn Landor, know how important they are to me.

This book is dedicated to all my grandparents, who gave me my best qualities and love me despite my worst.

CONTENTS

ACKNOWLEDGMENTS 7

FOREWORD 11

1. AN INTRODUCTION TO SAUSAGES 13
   - FRESH SAUSAGES 13
   - SMOKED SAUSAGES 14
   - DRIED SAUSAGES 14
   - MAKING SAUSAGES AT HOME 15
   - HOW TO FRY SAUSAGES 20
   - HOW TO POACH SAUSAGES 20
   - HOW TO BAKE SAUSAGES 21
   - HOW TO SMOKE SAUSAGES IN A MANUAL SMOKER 21
   - HOW TO PRESERVE SAUSAGES IN LARD 22
   - BASIC HOMEMADE SAUSAGES 24
2. THE HISTORY OF SAUSAGES 34
3. FRANCE 54
4. ITALY 88
5. GERMANY AND SWITZERLAND 118
6. THE AUSTRO-HUNGARIAN EMPIRE 142
7. RUSSIA AND POLAND 170
8. IBERIA 188
9. SCANDINAVIA AND BENELUX 212

10. BRITAIN 230

11. AFRICA AND THE MIDDLE EAST 248

12. ASIA 264

13. THE NEW WORLD 298

14. THE UNITED STATES 320
AMERICAN RECIPES 325
NEW AMERICAN COOKING 344

15. REGIONAL AMERICAN COOKING 358

BIBLIOGRAPHY 385

INDEX 403

FOREWORD

Suddenly Americans everywhere seem to be as enamored of sausages as I am. Some prefer delicate seafood sausages in beurre blanc and the exotic poultry sausages served on New American pizzas. Others go out of their way for the best Cajun hot links, pepperoni pizzas, and sausage gumbos. Lovers of Thai food need their weekly fix of that unbelievably delicious salad made of cold greens topped with warm Chinese sausage slices in a spicy dressing. All across the country German bratwurst, hot Italian and Swedish potato sausages are barbecued along with hot dogs. The nationwide appreciation of southwestern food has popularized the slightly tart, chile-laden Mexican chorizo, which can be used in hundreds of recipes. And the current, revived popularity of the restaurant breakfast has challenged chefs to find alternatives to the simple pork sausage, such as French chicken and apple sausages.

It has been a strange, but wonderful, two years. Cooking and eating sausages for 730 consecutive days was a dream come true. There's such a great variety of sausages, prepared in so many different ways, that eating them was hardly ever repetitive. There were some drawbacks, however. No one was ever allowed to look in my refrigerator or freezer—packed with somewhat unusual items such as various sizes of animal intestines and gallons of blood. I also tend to label my books, as they're being written, with a silly name to keep things in perspective. I called my first book—officially *The Glorious Noodle*—*Remembrance of Things Pasta.* This one was nicknamed *The Offal Truth* by my friend Larry.

My greatest surprise while writing this book was discovering how many elegant sausage dishes there are. I've always thought of them as messy, juicy delights to be devoured in private or only in the company of close, equally greedy and appreciative friends and family. There are, indeed, a lot of simple, family-type recipes in the book for dishes like German simmered sausages and sauerkraut and the British Toad-in-the-Hole (sausages baked in Yorkshire pudding). But there are also dishes that are worthy of the most discerning guests. The French galantine (a duck skin stuffed with truffles and marinated duck meat to form a giant sausage) and the mixed meat and bean cassoulet; Thai crab and pork sausages; Mexican chicken and sausage topped with garlicky bread crumbs; and Portuguese steamed clams and sausages are just a few of my favorites.

I like arranging my cookbooks by countries, rather than types of recipes such as main dishes, desserts, and so on, since I'm always interested in how recipes originated and how they fit into authentic menus. Although I've suggested accompaniments for each dish, I hope you'll experiment to come up with those you like best. I also hope you'll experiment with the sausage recipes themselves, since I'm sure there aren't two butchers in France using the exact same recipe for boudin blanc, for example. Although my recipes are as authentic as possible, sometimes using a slightly exotic ingredient or two, you're not bound by that restriction. I've listed sources for the unusual ingredients, but I've also mentioned easily obtainable substitutes. When I specify vermouth in a recipe, I'm referring to an Italian vermouth such as Martini & Rossi.

If you're interested in large-scale sausage making, building your own smoker, or in making sausages professionally, I strongly recommend the detailed *Great Sausage Recipes and Meat Curing* by professional sausage maker Rytek Kutas. I bought the book at Kitchen Arts & Letters in New York City, a truly outstanding and definitive cookbook bookstore, but it can also be ordered from The Sausage Maker, 177 Military Road, Buffalo, NY 14207; (716) 876-5521. The company also sells casings, cures, grinders, sausage stuffers, etcetera.

CHAPTER 1

AN INTRODUCTION TO *Sausages*

According to the Armour Meat Company, there are approximately 2,100 meat processors in the United States producing 5.2 billion pounds of over 200 different sausages a year. Nineteen billion of those sausages are hot dogs. Obviously America loves sausages, and so does nearly every other country in the world. Sausages vary, sometimes greatly, sometimes minimally, from country to country, but they fall into only a few basic types.

FRESH SAUSAGES

Fresh sausages are raw, ground or chopped meat mixtures, usually highly seasoned. They can be stuffed into casings, formed into sausage shapes (cylinders) without casings, or used in bulk form, that is, crumbled, fried, and added to casseroles or simmered dishes.

In general, fresh sausages are more highly spiced than other meat mixtures, but the lines often overlap. Fresh sausages can be poached, fried, grilled, baked, or simmered. Raw fresh sausages can be refrigerated, loosely wrapped in butcher, freezer, or waxed paper, for up to three days. Cooked fresh sausages either poached at home or commercially cooked (but not cured or dried) can be refrigerated for one week. After that they can be frozen, wrapped in paper, for three months.

Smoked Sausages

Sausages are cured, meaning processed to retard spoilage, by either smoking or drying or a combination of the two. There are two kinds of smoked sausages. Cold-smoked sausages, such as smoked breakfast links, have been smoked over low heat for a very long time to evaporate the moisture and give them a smoky taste. Since the internal temperature doesn't get very high, however, they must be cooked before they're eaten. Hot-smoked sausages, such as mortadella, are smoked at a high temperature for hours rather than days. They are completely cooked through and can be eaten at once. Both sausages can be refrigerated for up to two weeks, wrapped like the fresh sausages, and frozen for four to six months.

Many commercial producers now use something called "liquid smoke" in their sausages rather than smoking them over wood or charcoal. The brand I use, Wright's Natural Hickory Seasoning, lists only water and natural hickory liquid smoke concentrate as ingredients. You add it to the meat mixture, adjusting the amount to get the exact intensity of smoke you like, then poach or bake the sausages like fresh ones. As a rule, I use ¼ teaspoon liquid smoke per pound of meat and fat. Use liquid smoke *or* hot-smoke a batch of sausages, not both.

Dried Sausages

Dried sausages, such as salamis, have had their moisture evaporated to retard spoilage. That's why they're so compact and keep longer than other sausages. They can be stored at cool temperatures rather than cold, but I recommend refrigerating them for up to six weeks. Although there has been a lot of controversy about the dangers of nitrite, so far no study has shown that the amount used in commercially cured meats causes cancer in humans. It can, however, be toxic for some infants, but infants don't usually eat sausages anyway. Botulism, on the other hand, which grows in improperly cured meats, can kill you. Nitr*a*tes, like saltpeter, can be toxic for both children and adults, so should be avoided in home sausage making. Prague Powder #2, a combination salt and nitrite, is the best available curing agent for dried meats.

I don't recommend drying meats at home, since it's impossible to ascertain whether you've done it properly or not. Dried sausages can be imitated by a baking process discussed in specific recipes, then stored like cooked fresh meats. Since I only make small amounts and I'm scrupulous about storing the sausages properly, I don't use preservatives.

Making Sausages at Home

Cures, including Prague Powders, and both natural and artificial sausage casings can be bought from companies listed in the phone book under "Butcher Supplies." Although these companies are used to selling large quantities, I've always found them to be pleased that a nonprofessional was interested in making sausages. If you can't find a butcher supply store, talk to your local butcher. He'll probably be glad to order some casings for you if you buy your meat from him. Retail sausage stores and ethnic markets, like German and Italian delicatessens, often stock or will order casings.

Sausage Casings

Natural sausage casings are usually cleaned animal intestines and come in many sizes. Sheep, the size used for tiny breakfast links, is also called "chipolata." Hog, the casing you see on Italian sausages, is fairly easy to find. A firmly stuffed hog casing will be about 1½ inches wide, a loosely packed casing about 1 inch wide. Caul fat and the larger cases may require some persuasion on your part. Caul, a lacy net of fat that surrounds an animal's stomach and is used to wrap sausage patties, helps to baste the sausage and provides a crispy exterior. Hog bungs (used for liverwurst) are approximately 3½ inches wide, beef middles (used for some salamis) are around 3 inches wide, and beef rounds (which curve, so are used for ring bologna) are about 2 inches wide. These widths all vary within ½ inch in different batches. You will probably have to order more than you'll need since beef middles come in 57-foot-long sets, rounds in 100-foot sets, for example, but it's always good to have extras around in case some tear. I've recommended my preferred casing size in each recipe, but you can substitute any casing ½ inch smaller or larger than my suggestion.

Casings dry-packed in salt will keep indefinitely in the refrigerator, while those in brine can be refrigerated for up to a year. To keep caul, place the pieces in individual mounds on a baking sheet. When they freeze, place them into a plastic bag. The caul can only be refrigerated for two to three days, but can be frozen for a year. Some batches of casings are always going to tear easily, others will be slightly tough, and there's no way to predict. They're all usable, however. Hog bungs, the casings used for liver sausages and salami, often have weak spots, so buy double-walled sewed hog bungs, which are stronger. I don't use artificial casings, since I like the taste and texture of natural casings.

Grinding Meat for Sausages

Manual meat grinders are generally adequate, although your arm can get tired if you're making a lot of sausages. The big electric mixers have grinding attachments that work quite well. The problem with both the manual machines and mixers is their metal funnel attachment, which can easily tear the casings. I grind sausage mixtures in a food processor using the on/off pulse to prevent the meat from becoming too finely ground. The processor is unbeatable at making sausages, such as hot dogs, which require smooth meat mixtures. Then I use an inexpensive Scandinavian manual cookie press with a plastic funnel to stuff the sausages. All of these machines can be found in housewares or cooking equipment stores.

The cut of meat you use for sausages is important for taste, texture, and convenience. I bought inexpensive cuts of pork several times, laboriously cutting out the tendons, separating the fat from the meat, cutting out the many small bones, until I gave up. Now I buy pork loin when it's on sale and freeze the meat and fat separately. Try to find unsalted fatback or use thick, solid pieces of fat from the loin, since they provide a more desirable texture. Most butchers will give you strips of pork fat or chunks of beef suet for no charge if you're a regular customer. If you buy preground meat, take the fat content into account and adjust the recipe accordingly. For example, supermarket ground pork usually has 25 to 30 percent fat, so if the recipe calls for 1 pound lean pork plus ¼ pound fat, you can just buy a 1¼-pound package at the market. If you prefer buying ground meat, ask at your supermarket what percentage of fat is in each kind of ground meat. Ground meat spoils more quickly than larger pieces, so take your schedule into account when deciding which cut to buy.

Once you've tasted or cooked with a particular sausage, you'll be able to figure out substitutions easily. Just look up the recipes, figure out which ingredients give each sausage its unique taste, and compensate by adding some of that to the dish you're cooking the sausages in. If you need smoked, garlic chorizo, for example, and you only have smoked, garlic kielbasa, just add extra chile pepper to the recipe. If you don't have any Chinese sausage, substitute ham and add extra soy sauce and five-spice powder to the dish. Make a tour of the various ethnic groceries in your town or city. Middle Eastern groceries sell Armenian sausages and Indian ingredients; German and Polish butchers offer sausages from all of central and eastern Europe; Mexican markets sell many Latin American chorizos; a Scandinavian smokehouse makes Christmas potato sausages in season. Call an ethnic church, social group, or travel board and chances are you'll find someone there so delighted that you want to try his country's sausages that he'll insist on taking you on a tour of his favorite markets.

How to Stuff Sausage Casings

The first thing you do is cut off the amount of casing you'll need. There are some sections of casing that are very fragile and will tear no matter how careful you are, so always cut off more than you think is necessary. Even herbs that aren't finely chopped enough or a piece of cartilage that has slipped through can tear the casing. You'll also notice that some casings curve a great deal when they're stuffed, others barely, but it doesn't make a difference in taste or cooking, so don't worry about it.

Rinse each casing well, then slip one end over the faucet and run cold water through it to rinse out the inside and reveal any holes. If you find holes, cut the casing at that point and use that as one end. Soak dry-packed casings for two hours in cold water, brined casings for thirty minutes. Just before you're going to use them, remove them from the soaking liquid, and drag them between two fingers to squeeze out any liquid.

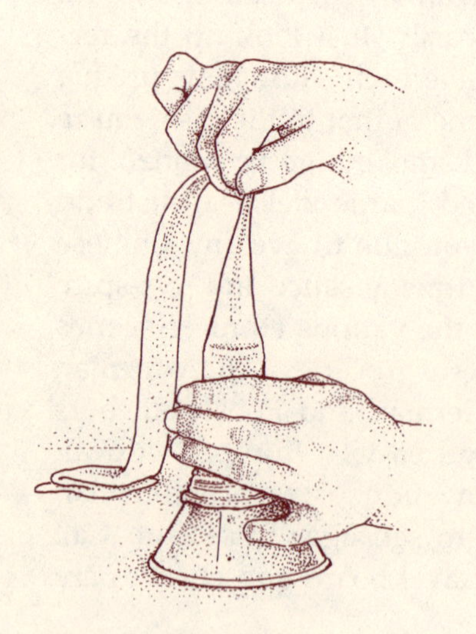

Use a cookie press, meat grinder attachment, pastry bag with a large round tip, or a funnel. Gently open one end of the casing and slip it over the funnel. With the thumb and first finger of one hand, hold the casing out so it stands straight out from the tip of the funnel for about 4 inches. Gently slide the casing onto the funnel with your other hand, guiding with the first hand, until only an inch of casing is hanging off the end of the funnel.

Fill the funnel, cookie press, etcetera, with sausage meat, packing it in as tightly as possible to eliminate air pockets. One way to avoid air pockets is to keep the tip of the funnel slightly poked into the sausage meat that has already entered the casing. If too much air gets into the casing and it begins to balloon, prick the casing with a pin there or cut the casing off at that point and tie off the sausage.

Use your right hand to run the machine. Hold the casing on the funnel lightly with your left hand, letting it slip through your fingers as it becomes filled. Fill 1 inch of the casing. Then twist the casing in the middle of that filling. Tie a double-knotted string tightly around the casing at that point, or you can cut off the casing and tie it into a tight knot. This prevents large air pockets at the end of the sausage. If you cut off the casing, make sure you've left enough at the end, because it's very slippery and can be difficult to tie. If you spot a hole or if the casing tears, just tie off the sausage at that point.

Remove the ½ inch of filling at the end and reuse it. Continue stuffing the sausage, using as steady a motion as possible, following the individual recipe's directions regarding whether you pack the casing loosely or firmly.

The finished sausages should rest on a smooth, flat surface. If you let them fall into a bowl they might tear. When you get to the end of the sausage mixture, use your little finger to push through any sausage left in the funnel. When you've finished stuffing the sausages, methodically look for air pockets. Use a pin to prick them, then very slightly pinch the sausage to force out the air. Once you've removed all the air, gently roll the sausages between your palms to even out their width and push out any remaining air.

Most sausages are better if you store them in the refrigerator, not touching each other, overnight. That dries out the surface slightly, making them brown better when cooked and causing the sausage meat to adhere to the casing. It also gives the flavors a chance to blend. If you're planning to smoke the sausages, this drying process is essential to prevent mold caused by wet casings.

How to Fry Sausages

These are instructions on how to fry the average 1½-inch-wide fresh sausage link. If you're frying the very thin breakfast links, there's no need to simmer them first. If your sausages are 2 inches wide, add 5 minutes additional simmering time. For sausages any wider than 2 inches, check the individual recipes for instructions.

Prick the sausages with a pin in five or six places. Place the sausages in a heavy skillet and pour in cold water to just come to the top of the sausages. Bring to a boil over high heat, skimming if lots of foam rises to the top. If the sausages float, turn them once with tongs while bringing to a boil. As soon as the water comes to a boil, turn the heat to low and simmer, uncovered, for 10 minutes. Turn once, after 5 minutes.

Pour off any remaining water and turn the heat to medium. Prick each sausage again with a pin at about 2-inch intervals on two sides. Enough fat should come out of the sausages to fry them. If not, pour in a thin film of vegetable oil. It will take about 2 to 3 minutes on each side to brown the sausages.

How to Poach Sausages

These instructions are for the average 1- to 1½-inch-wide fresh sausage link. If your sausages are 2 inches wide, add 10 minutes additional simmering time. For sausages any wider than 2 inches, check the individual recipes for instructions. Sausages smaller than 1 inch wide should be fried.

Prick the sausages with a pin in five or six places. Place the sausages in an insert, like a spaghetti cooker, steamer, or colander, then fit the insert into its pot. Pour in enough cold water to cover the sausages by at least ½ inch. Turn heat to high and watch carefully. As soon as one or two bubbles appear on the surface, immediately turn heat to very low and cover. Cook for 20 minutes, making sure the water never comes to a boil.

How to Bake Sausages

These instructions are for fresh sausages about 1½ inches wide. Bake for an additional 10 minutes if the sausages are 2 inches wide. For sausages any wider than 2 inches, check the individual recipes for instructions. Sausages smaller than 1½ inches wide should be fried or poached.

Preheat the oven to 300°. Prick the sausages with a pin in five or six places and place on a rack in a baking dish (I use a round cake rack in a large quiche pan). Bake for 45 minutes, until the juices run clear rather than pale when you prick the sausages.

How to Smoke Sausages in a Manual Smoker

These are instructions on how to hot-smoke sausages, since it is almost impossible to properly cold-smoke sausages without a professional smokehouse. My small smoker, made by Meco, retails for about $70 and can also be used as a barbecue. The temperature inside your smoker is critical. If it's too hot, the sausages will char before they become smoky tasting. If it's too cold, they won't reach the desired interior temperature.

Make sure the sausage casings are thoroughly dry. Place 5 pounds of good-quality, non-self-lighting charcoal in the bottom of your smoker. Douse well with charcoal lighter fluid, let rest for 1 minute, then light your fire. Let the coals burn down until they're uniformly covered with gray ash and the thermometer or gauge on the smoker reads 275° or "ideal."

Place a handful of soaked wood chips on top of the charcoal, then place the empty water bowl in the smoker. Fill two-thirds of the bowl with water, place the cooking grids in the smoker, then carefully lay the sausages on top. If you're cooking fairly short sausages, hang them from metal hooks so that they dangle. They should not come any closer than 2 inches to the water.

Close the smoker and smoke for the amount of time indicated in the individual recipe, or until a thermometer stuck into the sausage indicates 170° interior temperature. If the temperature seems too hot and the sausages are beginning to look grilled, open the louvers. You can also pour more cold water into the water pan. Both should lower the temperature.

HOW TO PRESERVE SAUSAGES IN LARD

Sausage Confit

This method, used in France, Scandinavia, the United States, and Greece, is a terrific way to preserve any fresh sausages you don't want to use right away. Freezing sausages usually changes the texture, if very slightly, and preserving them in fat keeps them very juicy. I like to tie sausages off in shorter lengths, about 3 inches, when I'm going to preserve them, since that makes it easier to fit them into a jar. You can always stand them up if they're too long to lie flat. Whenever you remove any sausages, reheat the top layer of lard and pour over the remaining sausages to reseal.

5 tablespoons coarse, kosher, or sea salt
1 bay leaf, minced or crumbled
3 teaspoons minced fresh thyme, or 1½ teaspoons crumbled dried

1½ teaspoons minced fresh rosemary or ¾ teaspoon crumbled dried
1 pound fresh sausage links
1½ pounds lard
1 whole bay leaf

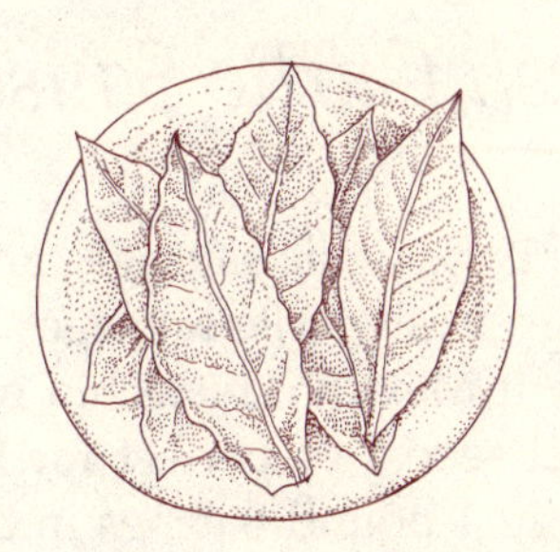

Mix together 3 tablespoons salt, the minced bay leaf, and two-thirds of the thyme and rosemary, then rub the mixture on the sausages as well as possible. Place the sausages in a bowl just large enough to hold them in one layer, then sprinkle on any salt-herb mixture that wouldn't stick to the sausages. Refrigerate for 4 hours, then rinse the mixture off the sausages, dry the sausages well, and prick each with a pin in 4 to 5 places.

Melt the lard in a heavy pot, then add the sausages. If the lard doesn't cover the sausages, add a bit more. Cover and cook over very low heat for 30 minutes. If the temperature is too hot, the sausages will get crispy and browned, which is undesirable. You want them boiled in lard, not fried.

Remove the pot from the heat and let the sausages cool to room temperature in the lard.

Mix together the remaining ingredients and place in an even layer on the bottom of a glazed earthenware cannister large enough to hold the sausages. When the sausages have cooled, remove them from the lard. Strain the cooled lard through a double thickness of cheesecloth. Pour enough lard into the cannister to cover the salt and herbs completely. Refrigerate until the lard has set.

Place a layer of sausages on top of the chilled lard and pour in just enough lard to cover them. Continue until all the sausages and lard are used up. Bang the cannister gently a couple of times to get rid of any air bubbles. The lard must cover the top layer of sausages by at least 1″, since it will contract a bit when cooled. Store in the refrigerator for 1 to 8 weeks.

BASIC HOMEMADE SAUSAGES

Fresh Garlic Sausages

This basic garlic sausage can be quickly adapted to replace any foreign fresh garlic sausages. Ground chile, cumin, and vinegar make it Mexican; pistachio nuts identify it as French; and with fennel seeds it's perfect for Italian dishes. I freeze the sausage meat in 1-pound batches in bulk, not casings, then remove just as much as I need and doctor it to turn it into an authentic ethnic sausage. This also makes delicious breakfast sausage links or patties and can be used as bulk sausage in any American recipe.

4 pounds very lean pork, ground
1½ pounds pork fat, ground
2 large garlic cloves, crushed then minced
1 tablespoon salt
⅜ teaspoon white pepper
½ bay leaf, ground or very finely minced
1 teaspoon minced fresh thyme, or ½ teaspoon crumbled dried
½ cup Cognac

Prepared hog casings

Knead all the ingredients together, then stuff into prepared hog casings or pack tightly into a container. Refrigerate for 1 day before using, then use within 2 more days or freeze for up to 3 months.

Makes approximately 5½ pounds raw sausage

Beef Salami

This is a perfect example of how baked sausages can mimic the texture of commercially dried salamis. You can make it with pork or lamb, but this is closest to the version served in Jewish delicatessens throughout the world. If you don't care whether this is kosher-style, use pork fat rather than suet, since it adds more taste. Make sure everyone in your house knows this is not preserved, since you don't want anyone leaving it out of the refrigerator. It's a wonderful sandwich sausage, especially good thinly sliced with lots of mustard on an onion roll. You can also chop it up and use it in pasta sauces and stuffings or in simmered vegetables or gratins.

. . . .

¼ teaspoon dry mustard
¼ teaspoon ground ginger
1 teaspoon salt
½ teaspoon crushed black peppercorns
1 teaspoon minced fresh oregano, or ½ teaspoon crumbled dried
½ teaspoon minced fresh thyme, or ¼ teaspoon crumbled dried
½ teaspoon sugar
Large pinch of paprika
1 tablespoon white vermouth or other dry white wine
1¼ pounds lean beef chuck, coarsely ground
¼ pound fat from chuck or suet, roughly chopped

Prepared beef middles

Mix together the mustard, ginger, salt, peppercorns, herbs, sugar, paprika, and vermouth.

Knead together the beef and fat, then knead in the spice mixture. Stuff the sausage mixture into 2 lengths of prepared beef middles. Prick any air pockets with a pin. Let sit in the refrigerator for 1 to 3 days, hanging from the shelves or on a rack, to dry the casings.

Preheat the oven to 200°. Place the salamis on a rack on a

baking sheet and cook for 5 hours to produce a semi-dried texture. These cooked sausages can be refrigerated for 2 weeks or frozen for 3 months.

Makes 1½ pounds raw sausage

Basic White Sausages

This is similar to German weisswurst, bockwurst, and bratwurst, French boudin blanc, and English white puddings made with meat, and you can use this as a substitute for any of those. It's lighter and more delicate than other sausages, but the cream and egg also make it more perishable. It's a perfect sausage for clear soups, but I like it best simply grilled or poached and eaten with an interesting mustard on a roll. To make one of the famous upstate New York white hots, add as much ground chile as you can stand.

1 cup heavy cream
½ cup tightly packed white bread with crust, torn into bite-size pieces
⅛ teaspoon grated nutmeg
⅛ teaspoon ground coriander
1½ teaspoons salt
¼ teaspoon white pepper
2 teaspoons minced fresh chives
2 teaspoons minced fresh parsley
½ pound skinless, boneless, raw white meat chicken, ground
½ pound lean veal, ground
½ pound pork fat, ground
1 cup roughly chopped onion
1 large egg
2 large egg whites
Butter and bread crumbs (optional)

Prepared hog casings

Heat the cream in a small saucepan until hot but not boiling. Pour over the bread in a small bowl. Stir a couple of times. Let the bread sit for 5 minutes, then stir in the nutmeg, coriander, salt, pepper, chives and parsley. Set aside.

Place the chicken, veal, fat, and onion in the bowl of an electric mixer or a food processor. Beat or process in one-third of the bread mixture at a time until completely incorporated. Beat in the egg, then the egg whites. You can also do this by hand, but you have to beat it furiously with a wooden spoon. The mixture should be very fluffy.

Stuff loosely into prepared hog casings. The sausages should be 1 inch to 1¼ inch in diameter. Tie off in 6″ lengths. Prick any air pockets with a pin.

Place the sausages in a skillet, cover with cold water, and poach, covered, for 20 minutes. Remove the sausages and pat dry.

You can eat the sausages as is or you can fry them after letting them cool. To fry, gently remove the casings. Roll the sausages in bread crumbs and fry in melted butter in a skillet over low heat until browned all over. Raw sausages can be refrigerated for 2 days, poached for 1 week. Raw or poached sausages can be frozen for 3 months.

Makes approximately 2¼ pounds raw sausage

Smoked Poultry Sausages

Trying to find beef hot dogs in supermarkets years ago was ludicrous. Then it became almost impossible to find all-pork frankfurters. Now poultry hot dogs seem to be taking over the supermarket shelves. Try to find fresh herbs, since there's something particularly succulent about poultry and fresh bits of green. You can use these the way you'd use hot dogs: baked, fried, added to soups, or served with tomato sauce, but to me they're best grilled or steamed and served on a roll, Southern style, with coleslaw.

1¾ pounds skinless raw or cooked chicken, turkey, duck, or goose meat
¼ pound raw poultry fat and/or raw or cooked poultry skin
⅜ teaspoon cayenne pepper
2 teaspoons salt
¼ teaspoon ground cumin
1 teaspoon minced fresh sage, or ½ teaspoon crumbled dried
1 teaspoon minced fresh thyme, or ½ teaspoon crumbled dried
2 tablespoons milk or cream
1 large egg
⅜ teaspoon liquid smoke (optional)
Poultry stock (optional)
Butter (optional)

Prepared hog casings

Grind the poultry and fat and/or skin in a food processor until very smooth. In a cup with a spout whisk together the cayenne, salt, cumin, sage, thyme, milk or cream, egg, and liquid smoke (if used). While the processor is running, pour in the egg mixture and process until completely smooth again.

Stuff firmly into prepared hog casings and tie off into 6″ lengths. Prick air holes with a pin. Poach in stock to cover in a covered skillet for 20 minutes or smoke at 250° for 3 to 5 hours, until the sausages reach an internal temperature of 165°. Don't overcook these or smoke them at too high a temperature or they'll become dry.

Rinse the smoked or poached sausages in cold water, then dry well. They can be refrigerated for 5 days or frozen for 3 months.

To reheat, drop them in a pot of boiling water, cover immediately, turn off the heat, and let them sit for 7 minutes. They can also be browned in butter or grilled.

Makes approximately 2 pounds raw sausage

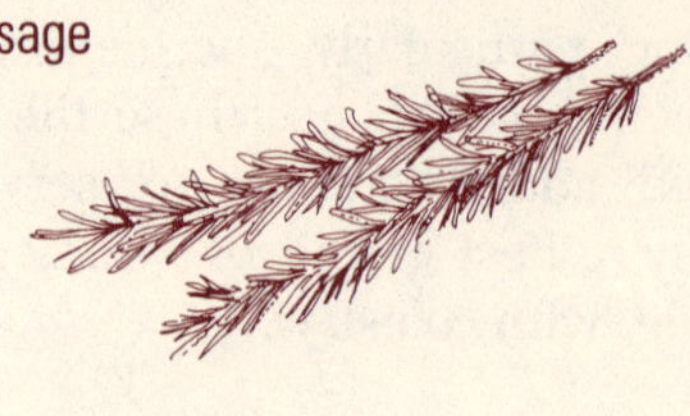

Game Sausages

There has been a welcome, steadily increasing return to game in American cooking, partly inspired by the New American chefs' rediscovery of long-neglected traditional American recipes. Ethnic markets, like German butcher shops, and expensive meat markets have always carried game in the appropriate seasons, but now you can find both birds and larger animals all year round. If your butcher doesn't carry game, he will probably order it for you. It is expensive, though, and if you use poultry, trying to get the meat off tiny birds is extremely tedious. You can, however, make the sausages from cooked meat, rather than raw, which is easier to dislodge from the bones. Venison usually comes in large, solid slabs of meat, often frozen, and wild boar is just beginning to show up occasionally. Don't omit the fat in this recipe, since the sausages will be extremely dry without it. They can also be wrapped in caul fat, rather than casings.

Game sausages can be used in soups and stews, but they are at their best with starches such as rice or potatoes. Try them in jambalayas, fried and served atop a bed of mashed potatoes, or barbecued and served in rolls. If you ever obtain reindeer meat, it makes delicious sausages. Serve strong red wines such as Cabernets or Zinfandels with game meats, spicy white wines like Gewürztraminers with game birds.

. . . .

½ pound game meat, such as venison, coarsely ground
¼ pound pork fat, coarsely ground
½ teaspoon minced fresh thyme, or ¼ teaspoon crumbled dried
½ teaspoon minced fresh rosemary, or ¼ teaspoon crumbled dried
1 garlic clove, crushed then minced
¼ teaspoon salt
Large pinch of black pepper
Large pinch of cayenne pepper
2 teaspoons sweet rice wine (mirin) or orange liqueur

Prepared hog casings

Mix together the meat and fat, then knead in the rest of the ingredients.

Stuff firmly into prepared hog casings and tie off at any length. Prick air pockets with a pin. Let the sausages sit in the refrigerator for 1 to 3 days, loosely covered, before cooking, then poach and/or fry. The cooked sausages will keep for 1 week in the refrigerator. Raw or cooked sausages can be frozen for 3 months.

Makes approximately ¾ pound raw sausage

Headcheese

Also called "sulz," "souse," or "brawn," this is considered a sausage for two reasons. Versions of it originally used the head skin as a casing, and now many professional sausage makers use hog stomachs. Although some people might shudder when they think of this, it's made from muscle meat similar to that in the rest of the hog. Peasants, who could rarely afford meat, made sure they used every part of the pig when they had one. Different countries add their own touches. Greeks flavor it with orange, Vietnamese with fish sauce, Cajuns with chiles, and Austrians add chunks of tongue. I made the headcheese with the leftover head of a suckling pig I had roasted. The best way to eat headcheese is to slice it, lay it on a slice of good, thick peasant bread, top it with pickles, mustard, or Scandinavian horseradish sauce, and drink a glass of spicy Alsatian Gewürztraminer or German lager with it.

. . . .

1 raw or cooked pig's head
4 pig's feet
2 onions, roughly chopped
2 bay leaves
3 sprigs fresh thyme, or ½ teaspoon crumbled dried
4 shallots, roughly chopped

2 tablespoons vinegar
1 cup red vermouth or other semi-dry or dry red wine
1 teaspoon grated nutmeg
1 tablespoon lard or vegetable oil
2 medium onions, finely chopped
2 teaspoons Worcestershire sauce
1 package unflavored gelatin

Place the pig's head, feet, roughly chopped onion, bay leaves, thyme, shallots, vinegar, and wine in a large pot and pour in cold water to cover. Bring to a boil over high heat, turn heat to low, and simmer, covered, for 4 hours. Turn off the heat and remove the meats. Cut the skin off the head in large pieces and line the bottom of a bread pan with them. Strain the broth.

Cut or tear the meat into bite-size pieces and place in a smaller pot with 3 cups of strained stock and the nutmeg. Simmer for 20 minutes more over low heat. As soon as you've begun simmering the meat, heat the lard or oil in a large skillet over low heat and sauté the finely chopped onions for 10 minutes. Remove them with a slotted spoon and add to the simmering meat.

Remove the meat and onions with a slotted spoon and fill the bread pan with them. Stir the Worcestershire and gelatin into the stock, then pour in enough stock to come just to the top of the meat. Cover with foil, then place a light bread pan on top of the foil. You don't want to weight the headcheese, but you do want to keep the top even. Chill in the refrigerator overnight.

Makes one 8½″ × 4½″ × 2½″ loaf

Blood Sausage

Blood sausages take a lot of getting used to, and if you don't like liver, don't bother trying them. That's what they smell like when they're cooked. But if you like liver, you'll love blood sausage. The additives identify a blood sausage's country of origin. If it's oatmeal, it's Scotland; kasha means Russia; and apples or chestnuts point to France. Substitute different cereals for the bread until you find the one you like best. Pork blood is used in most countries, but it's illegal to use or sell it here. A friendly butcher or sausage shop will order beef blood for you, but usually a minimum of a gallon. Try to get fresh blood, not frozen, since the taste deteriorates slightly. Sliced and fried blood sausage is a supper dish, best accompanied by a glass of dark beer and mashed potatoes and gravy. You could also serve red or black beans and rice, or the German apple-and-potato puree Himmel und Erde.

. . . .

1½ cups finely chopped white bread
½ cup heavy cream
2 cups beef blood
1½ tablespoons finely chopped fresh chives
1 tablespoon coarse, kosher, or sea salt
¼ teaspoon black pepper
2 tablespoons gin
⅛ teaspoon grated nutmeg
⅛ teaspoon ground allspice
½ teaspoon minced fresh thyme, or ¼ teaspoon crumbled dried
¼ pound thickly cut smoked bacon, roughly chopped
1 large onion, finely chopped
2 pounds lean pork, coarsely ground
Butter (optional)

Prepared hog casings

Toss the bread and cream together in a large bowl and set aside. Mix together the blood, chives, salt, pepper, gin, spices, and thyme and set aside.

Fry the bacon in a large skillet over medium heat until crisp, then remove with a slotted spoon and stir into the bread. Add the onions to the skillet and fry, stirring often, for 6 to 7 minutes, until they begin to brown around the edges. Remove them with a slotted spoon and stir into the bread. Add the pork to the skillet and fry, constantly mashing with a fork, until cooked through. Pour the contents of the skillet into the bread and mix well. Let cool to room temperature. When the bread mixture has cooled, pour in the blood mixture slowly, stirring constantly.

Place the bowl on a large cookie sheet and stuff the sausages over the sheet since you can't help but drip blood all over the place. The texture of the sausage mixture will be very liquid, so just pour it through a funnel into prepared hog casings. Hold onto the casing carefully to keep it from slipping off the funnel. Tie off into 4″ lengths. Since the mixture is so smooth, there probably won't be any air pockets. If you spot any, prick them with nothing larger than a pin. Even if there aren't any air pockets, prick each sausage at least twice.

Poach for 15 minutes in a covered skillet, then turn off the heat and let the sausages cool in their cooking liquid until room temperature. Pat dry and refrigerate, wrapped, for 1 to 2 days before cooking them. They can also be frozen for 3 months.

When you're ready to serve the sausages, cut into 2″ lengths, prick each once or twice, and fry in butter or grill until lightly browned.

Makes approximately 3 pounds raw sausage

Chapter 2

. . . .

The History of Sausages

Soon after man discovered that meat tasted a lot better when it was cooked, he realized that the animal's stomach was a practical cooking vessel for scraps of meat and blood. It was also good for storing every last piece, since no one could be sure when the next animal would be killed. When man began domesticating animals, possibly as early as 9000 B.C., he was able to obtain intestines and stomachs on a regular basis and sausage making eventually became commonplace. Man next discovered that wind-drying or smoking foods could preserve them.

Although it's believed that sausages were eaten in ancient Tyre, Mesopotamia, and China, the first concrete evidence is in Homer's *Odyssey,* written around 850 B.C. Pork was the most common meat in Homer's Greece, and salami may have come from the Greek island of Salamis. At the same time, Middle Easterners were using grape leaves as sausage casings for mixtures of lamb and rice, and the Chinese were making pork sausages. Early sausages, up through medieval times, usually contained chopped meat rather than ground since there were no widely available grinders. If a smooth sausage was required, the meat had to be laboriously pounded by hand.

It was the ancient Romans, the great lovers of excess, who elevated the European sausage to a delicacy. They became fanatical, constantly seeking new sausages, or new spices to enliven old kinds of sausages, to impress their friends. For a while sausages and other pork products from Gaul, ancient France, were the rage. Smoked Lucanian sausages, from the area around Naples, were also highly regarded. The cookbook purportedly written by one of the Roman gourmets called Apicius (there were at least two), and which was probably written at least a couple of centuries later, includes recipes for highly spiced sausages made of porpoise, squid, cuttlefish, mussels, poultry, liver, blood, and pork. The sausages, made in every size from very thin, long sausages to large blood sausages stuffed into animal wombs, were served by themselves or cooked in casseroles with fish or other meats.

The Romans taught their sausage-making and preserving techniques to almost all their conquered territories. Part of the reason for this was the hope their subjects would create new delicacies they could import. Our word *sausage* comes from the Latin *salsus*, meaning "salted." After the fall of the empire, during the Dark Ages, sausage making continued. The Saxons, who invaded Britain in the seventh century, depended on sheep for both clothing and food, so they used every part of the animal, making sausages in the animals stomachs. The Germans, whose woods provided perfect fodder for foraging boars, took up the Roman methods of preserving and salting meats and sausages with great enthusiasm. Their object was subsistence, not elegance, however.

As a rule, meat was scarce, especially for poorer people. Feeding liverstock in winter, when the animals were unable to forage for food, was almost impossible. Out of necessity, a traditional ritual still practiced today in some parts of the world began. Each fall there would be one day set aside for pig killing. Everyone in the village would help. Pieces of fresh meat were eaten within a couple of days. Some of the meat was turned into hams and bacons or stored in brine. The head became headcheese And the rest of the animal—blood, organs, meat scraps —went into the stomach or the intestines to become sausages. The prepared sausages were dried or hung in the chimney and smoked to make them last as long as possible. but since the poor couldn't afford imported spices, these sausages were less flavorful than the Roman versions. It's probably more than coincidence that Lent, which comes at the end of the winter when most people had run out of meat, was declared a meatless period of fasting.

After the Crusades nations began trading for Asian spices, and sausages regained the sophistication they had lost after the fall of Rome. Expensive spices not only provided cachet, they also were considered to aid digestion. Each area of the world developed its own sausages, often proudly named for the city of origin, whose contents included both imported spices and local ingredients. The type of wood each area used to smoke the sausages also added individual flavor. Blood and other pork sausages were commonplace, enjoyed by both rich and poor.

As the feudal system grew stronger and nobles gained more land and money, they began to entertain on a lavish scale. Meat was a symbol of wealth. Haggis, a large oatmeal sausage, was even considered fit for a British king, and headcheese, served with a mustard cream sauce, was mandatory at banquets. Easily stored foods like sausages were sensible provisions for a castle that might be attacked at any time. The poor extended their sausages with local cereals and regional differences became more and more distinct. When times were really bad, sausages were made from cereals and fats alone. Scots used oats, Russians kasha, and Germans bread. Meanwhile the rich ate easily perishable white sausages containing milk or cream to show that they could afford meat all year round.

In the fifteenth and sixteenth centuries cookshops sold various kinds of sausage, but wise buyers knew that these chopped meats and spices could, and often did, disguise meat that had gone bad. European sausages became more highly spiced and sausage mixtures, called "forc'd-meats," were used in hundreds of dishes. There more exotic the spicing, the better the sausage. They were most often rolled into balls or stuffed into casings and used as a garnish for other meat dishes. The huge "great pie" filled with whole birds, eggs, dried fruits, and forc'd-meat (or forcemeat) balls was an aristocratic favorite in Britain. The Spanish preferred their sausages grilled or in soups and stews.

Sausage lovers went to great lengths for their favorite food. When there were no animal casings available, hollowed-out vegetables were stuffed with forcemeat. Devout Christians, who couldn't eat meat on many fast days, made fish sausages. North

American Indians made sausage patties of dried venison, fat, and berries, which they either ate right away or smoked for traveling. Spaniards brought pigs to North and South America and the Caribbean in the late sixteenth century. These fatty animals, rather than the lean game the natives were used to, made excellent sausages.

Forcemeat continued to be popular in seventeenth-century Europe. It was widely used as a poultry, suckling pig, or veal stuffing. Many rich Europeans enjoyed game sausages. European countries began exchanging sausages on a large scale for the first time since the decline of the Roman Empire. In Russia, Peter the Great was bringing his country into modern times, importing cooks from Germany and France who brought their sausages with them. Link sausages became the rule, rather than one long, coiled sausage cooked then cut into pieces. Although sausages were often served in sweet or sweet-and-sour sauces, especially in Spain, savory, sugarless dishes were becoming more popular.

Oysters were so cheap that they were used as extenders in lamb or pork sausages in England. In Colonial America, domesticated animals such as cattle, pigs, sheep, and chicken prospered and all were used in sausages. Many of the sausage dishes eaten today—sausage patties and fried apples, baked sausage casseroles, and breakfast sausage links—were developed during this century.

In the mid-eighteenth century an Englishman named Robert Bakewell crossed the rangy, boarlike European pig with the smaller, fat Chinese pig. The result was a hardy, large, fat pig, perfect for sausage making. Cattle breeding also improved, providing meatier animals. In many towns and cities in Europe and America, pigs roamed the streets, officially acting as street cleaners. That meant poorer people could now afford to keep a pig since there was no need to pay for fodder. Pigs accompanied westbound American settlers, since the hardy animals could fend for themselves if necessary.

Forcemeats remained popular and were still being used as stuffings or to garnish elegant soups or stews. Liver sausages were very popular, especially served on toast. In Britain and France, skinless sausages, which were much less time-consuming to make, were rolled in bread crumbs and fried.

In most countries, housewives could now go to their local butcher shop and buy sausages instead of making them at home.

In the nineteenth and early twentieth centuries sausages and sausage dishes were almost identical to those we eat now. Links had become an integral part of breakfasts all over Europe. Germans stopped by restaurants for their morning wursts. Bread topped with dried sausage slices was a favorite European lunch or appetizer. In America, Creole cooks had become experts at Spanish-inspired jambalaya and French-inspired boudin blanc and andouille. Germans living in Pennsylvania reproduced their native sausages. Primitive refrigeration made it possible to have fresh meat almost all year long. And sausages grew less spicy, perhaps because there was rarely any need to cover up bad meat. Few cooks bothered to make their own sausages anymore, even though manual meat grinders were relatively inexpensive. Pork butchers flourished throughout Europe, and large American meat-packers began producing sausages that could be shipped all over the country.

Elaborate dishes, such as large pies filled with forcemeat and poultry or roast goose with a garland of sausages around its neck, were still served at formal occasions, but now most sausage dishes were accessible to everyone. Queen Victoria's family ate fried sausages at informal lunches, while the poor combined the same sausages enjoyed by royalty with potatoes or Yorkshire pudding to make Sunday dinner. While the rich ate truffled boudin blanc, those less well-off enjoyed the same sausages made with less exalted mushrooms. Oyster sausages, however, eventually became a thing of the past as Europeans and Americans almost wiped out their oyster beds. And in America, President and Mrs. Franklin Roosevelt served hot dogs to the king and queen of England.

Apicius' Sausage-Stuffed Chicken

Pepper was the ancient Romans' favorite spice, and it was used in everything. This dish would probably have been made with the popular smoked Lucanian sausage from southern Italy. Successful Roman banquets often included both sausages and sex, so reformers illogically had sausages banned. Needless to say, Romans continued to buy sausages secretly. This dish is delicious when accompanied by polenta or cornbread and a white wine such as Fumé Blanc. Try a marinated vegetable salad as a first course, then follow the chicken with a creamy dessert such as zabaglione or even rice pudding.

1 cup chicken stock, homemade preferable but canned acceptable
2 teaspoons dry white wine or vermouth
2 teaspoons sweet liqueur like Cranberria, mead, or sweet rice wine (mirin)
Salt to taste
⅛ teaspoon black pepper, plus more for chicken
1 tablespoon minced fresh lovage or lemon balm (optional)
Large pinch of ground ginger
¼ teaspoon minced fresh or crumbled dried oregano
½ pound fresh sausage meat, or 6 ounces smoked
⅜ cup julienned snow pea pods
1 chicken, approximately 4 pounds
1 tablespoon white flour

Preheat the oven to 450°. Mix together the stock, wine, liqueur, salt, pepper, lovage or lemon balm, ginger, and oregano and set aside.

If you're using fresh sausage meat, fry it in a large frying pan, constantly mashing it with a fork, until cooked through. If you're using smoked sausage, just finely chop it.

Place the cooked or smoked sausage in a bowl and toss it with the snow pea pods and 2 tablespoons of the stock mixture. Salt and pepper the chicken well, then stuff with the sausage mixture. Truss the chicken. Place it on a rack which fits into an oven- and stove-proof dish or pot. Put the chicken in the oven and immediately turn the heat down to 350°. Roast the chicken for 80 minutes (20 minutes per pound of unstuffed chicken).

Remove the chicken from the oven and let it rest while you make the sauce. Stir the flour into the pan drippings over low heat, then stir for 1 to 2 minutes, until smooth. Pour in the stock mixture and stir constantly until thickened. Serve with the sauce poured over the chicken and the stuffing.

Serves 6

Basic Forcemeat: "A Good Force'd-Meat for Any Use"

Although I've adapted this from a recipe in Mary Kettilby's *Collection of Receipts,* this and similar forcemeats had been used for almost 400 years when her book was published in 1734. I use half as much suet as Kettilby did and ham instead of bacon to prevent the recipe from being too fatty. She recommended adding the oysters "on extraordinary occasions" or replacing them with the same amount of marrow.

Eighteenth-century nobles did extraordinary things with forcemeat. One cookbook from that period recommends baking the forcemeat in the shape of a hull of a ship, filling it with various fancy foods, and crowning it with a rigging hung with sausages. You can make links and fry them for breakfast; roll the meat into balls, brown them, and add them to soups; or use as bulk sausage.

- ½ teaspoon fresh thyme, or ¼ teaspoon crumbled dried
- ¼ teaspoon fresh oregano or marjoram, or ⅛ teaspoon crumbled dried
- ½ teaspoon salt
- ¼ teaspoon black pepper

¼ teaspoon ground cloves
½ teaspoon ground mace
½ teaspoon grated nutmeg
1 large egg yolk
1 pound veal, ground
½ pound beef suet, finely chopped
2 ounces ham, finely chopped
¼ cup very finely chopped, drained oysters, fresh or canned

Prepared hog casings

Mix together in a bowl the thyme, oregano or marjoram, salt, pepper, cloves, mace, nutmeg, and egg yolk and set aside.

In a food processer, chop the veal, suet, and ham (in batches if necessary) until just slightly more coarse than a puree. Place the meat mixture in a large bowl and sprinkle with the herb mixture. Beat well with a wooden spoon until smooth, then fold in the oysters.

Stuff into casings or roll into 6″-long skinless sausages, then poach, fry, or grill.

Makes approximately 1¾ pounds raw sausage

Stuffed Chicken Neck

One fifteenth-century version of this dish was a capon neck stuffed with organ meats and roasted and served along with the chicken. This version is a terrific way to use up leftover poultry. You can buy chicken necks inexpensively in large quantities, 5 pounds and up, from poultry wholesalers. Use some of the skins for this recipe, then save the rest of the necks for stock.

This is a wonderful, and simple, recipe. Place the sliced neck in the center of a leafy salad and pour a bit of vinaigrette over the whole plate or a line of garlicky mayonnaise down the center of the sausage. Serve a simple white wine, such as a French

Colombard, with it. Follow it with a fairly strong fish (blackened redfish is an unorthodox, but good, choice) or meat dish accompanied by steamed vegetables. Serve a rich and creamy dessert, since the rest of the meal is rather simple.

. . . .

1 raw chicken neck
Large pinch of saffron
1 small egg yolk
¼ teaspoon salt, plus more for sauce if necessary
Pinch of black pepper, plus more for sauce if necessary
⅛ teaspoon mixed ground cloves and mace
1 teaspoon minced fresh parsley
½ cup finely chopped raw or cooked chicken or turkey meat
4 teaspoons finely chopped raw chicken, turkey, or pork fat
2 teaspoons white flour
3 tablespoons chicken stock, homemade preferable but canned acceptable

Preheat the oven to 450°. Roll the chicken skin down the neck as far as it will go, then gently pull it off. Use the neck bones and meat for stock.

Crumble the saffron into the egg yolk, then stir in the salt, pepper, mace and cloves, and parsley. Knead this into the poultry and fat.

Stuff the chicken mixture into the chicken neck and sew tightly closed on both ends. Place the chicken neck in a cast-iron or other oven- and stove-proof skillet or dish and place in the oven. Roast for 30 minutes, turning once after the first 20 minutes.

Remove the pan from the oven and set the neck aside, draped in foil to keep it warm. Place the skillet or baking dish on the stove over low heat. Stir in the flour until well mixed, then the stock. Stir until slightly thickened, then taste and add salt and pepper if necessary.

Serves 1

Veal Collops

♦ ***Allowes***

This dish has been prepared for hundreds of years, from medieval times to the present. You'll rarely find anyone who doesn't like it. Begin your dinner with spicy boiled shellfish or a shellfish salad, then accompany the veal with buttered peas and baked potatoes. Serve an unmolded chocolate pudding for dessert. A light red wine, such as Chinon from the Loire Valley, goes well with this.

2 teaspoons lemon juice
¼ teaspoon mace
⅔ cup dry bread crumbs
1 teaspoon salt, plus more to taste
Pinch of black pepper, plus more to taste
¼ teaspoon cayenne pepper
1 large egg
6 strips of bacon
6 tablespoons butter
6 slices veal scaloppine (about 1 pound)
1⅓ cups Basic Forcemeat (page 40) or other fresh sausage meat
1½ tablespoons white flour
1 cup chicken or veal stock, homemade preferable but canned acceptable

Bring a medium-size saucepan of water to a boil. Mix together the lemon juice and mace in a small bowl and set aside. Mix together the bread crumbs, 1 teaspoon salt, pinch of black pepper, and cayenne pepper in a medium-size bowl and set aside. Crack the egg into another medium-size bowl and set aside.

Add the bacon to the boiling water, blanch for 3 minutes, then drain well. While the bacon is boiling, melt 2 tablespoons butter in a large skillet over low heat. Sauté the veal for about 10 to 15 seconds on each side, in batches if necessary. It should still be very rare. Don't wash out your skillet; you're going to use it again as is.

Lay a strip of bacon on each piece of veal, then spread each veal slice with an even layer of the forcemeat. Leave a ½" border on all sides of the forcemeat. Roll the veal up, forcemeat on the inside, and skewer closed with a toothpick.

Lightly whisk the egg to mix the yolk and white. With your left hand, dip one roll into the egg and rotate it so that it gets an even egg coating. Lift it out with the left hand and drop it into the crumbs without letting your left hand touch the crumbs. Rotate it in the crumbs with your right hand until evenly covered, then remove it with your right hand and place it on a sheet of waxed paper. This two-hand method prevents getting any egg in the crumbs or crumbs in the egg, thereby avoiding lumps. Repeat until all the rolls are breaded.

Add the remaining butter to the skillet and melt over low heat. Add the veal rolls and brown them all over. Remove them and keep them warm.

Add the flour to the skillet and stir over low heat for about 1 minute, until well mixed and lightly browned. Stirring constantly, slowly pour in the stock and mix well. Stir in the lemon juice and mace and taste. Add salt and pepper if necessary. Bring the sauce to a boil, stirring constantly, then remove the skillet from the heat. Pour it over the veal rolls and serve immediately.

Serves 6

Oyster Sausages

These sausages were popular in both England and New England in the seventeenth, eighteenth, and nineteenth centuries when oysters were a lot cheaper than meat. There were many variations of oyster sausages. Some were made only from oysters, others included veal or mutton. In months without an *r* they were sometimes made with dried oysters instead of fresh.

Traditionally the veal and oysters were pounded, but food processors make this much simpler.

I like serving these as a main course after a hearty hot leek and potato soup. Accompany the sausages with steamed green vegetables and a very dry white wine such as the French Sancerre. Chocolate pastries or cake would be a perfect dessert.

- 2 cups chopped raw oysters
- 1 pound lean veal, chopped
- 1 ounce pork fat or suet, chopped
- ½ cup dry bread crumbs
- 2 teaspoons salt
- 1 teaspoon white pepper
- ¼ teaspoon grated nutmeg
- 2 tablespoons unsalted butter

Emulsify the oysters, veal, and fat in a food processor with the steel blade, or chop them as finely as possible by hand, then mash them with a mortar and pestle until smooth. Add the bread crumbs, salt, pepper, and nutmeg and process or knead until well mixed. With damp hands to prevent sticking, roll and shape the mixture into 4 sausage links each about 1″ wide. Set them aside.

Melt the butter over medium heat in a skillet large enough to hold all the sausages. Add the sausages and brown on all 4 sides, turning carefully with a spatula. When browned all over, carefully pour in water to come halfway up the sides of the sausages. Cover, turn heat to medium low, and simmer for 8 minutes until cooked through.

Serves 4

Baked Stuffed Mackerel

This particular recipe, still popular throughout Europe, is adapted from Mrs. Beeton's *Book of Household Management* published in the nineteenth century. It's both a wonderful dish for entertaining and simple enough to make just for one. You can substitute any bulk sausage for the forcemeat. Just make sure it's not so spicy that it overpowers the fish.

This is a very elegant dish, so begin the meal with a simple soup such as wild mushroom consommé. Accompany the fish with a green vegetable and roasted or boiled potatoes or rice, which taste wonderful with the fish's sauce. You can serve almost any dessert with the meal, but you might as well make a chocolate cake since the rest of the meal was fairly low-calorie. Try a dry white wine such as Chardonnay with the fish.

2 mackerel, approximately ½ pound each
¼ pound Basic Forcemeat (page 40) or mild sausage meat
1 tablespoon white flour mixed with ¼ teaspoon salt and a pinch of black pepper
3 tablespoons unsalted butter
1 garlic clove, finely minced or put through garlic press
1 tablespoon white flour
½ cup fish stock or clam juice
1 tablespoon minced fresh parsley
2 pinches of cayenne pepper
1 tablespoon lemon juice
Salt to taste

Grease a baking dish large enough to hold the fish in one layer and set aside. Bone the mackerel and fill each with half the forcemeat. Gently press closed. Dip each side into the seasoned flour and shake off the excess. Place the fish in the greased baking dish and dot them with 1 tablespoon butter. Bake for 25 minutes, then place under the broiler for 1 to 2 minutes until the tops are slightly browned.

After the fish has finished its first 15 minutes of cooking, begin the sauce. Melt the remaining 2 tablespoons butter in a small skillet over low heat. Add the garlic and stir for 2 minutes. Stir in the 1 tablespoon flour until well mixed. Pour in the fish stock or clam juice, stirring constantly until the sauce is smooth and thick. This will take about 2 to 3 minutes. Turn off the heat, but leave the skillet on the burner. Stir in the parsley, cayenne, and lemon juice. Taste and add salt if necessary. If the sauce is finished before the fish, just leave it on the unlit burner and stir every couple of minutes to prevent a skin from forming. Then reheat the sauce over very low heat for a minute or two, without boiling, while the fish is under the broiler.

Serves 2

Mrs. Beeton's Lobster Bisque with Forcemeat Balls

This is quite expensive and extremely luxurious, very rich, and very delicious. Serve it as the main course of a dinner for 4 or the first course for 8 people whom you really like. Removing the lobster meat from the shells is very messy and time-consuming, but the result is definitely worth it. If you haven't got the nerve to kill the lobster yourself, have your fish seller do it, then immediately go home and begin the dish. Don't substitute clam juice for the fish stock, since the taste is too strong for this soup. The roe will turn the soup into a beautiful pink color as it cooks. You can now buy precooked, frozen, vacuum-sealed lobster roe in some gourmet stores under the name "lobster caviar." Fresh is better, but the packaged kind is quite acceptable.

If you're serving this as a first course, follow it with a simple main course such as a roasted leg of lamb, accompanied by rice and steamed vegetables with a meatless tomato sauce. If the bisque is your main course, precede it with a simple first course such as pasta primavera. The perfect wine for the bisque is a bone-dry champagne like Brut Sauvage, but you can also serve a

Chardonnay. Try a fruit-based dessert, such as a tarte tatin, since you'll feel you've had enough cream after the soup.

2 small lobsters, about 1½ pounds each
2 anchovies
1 onion, thickly sliced
3 cups homemade fish or chicken stock
1 bay leaf
2 sprigs fresh tarragon, or ½ teaspoon crumbled dried
1 piece of lemon peel, ¼″ wide × 3″ long, roughly chopped
⅛ teaspoon grated nutmeg
⅛ teaspoon black pepper
½ cup soft fresh bread crumbs (without any crust)
1 cup heavy cream
3 tablespoons unsalted butter
1½ cups milk
½ pound skinless Basic Forcemeat or Bratwurst (page 40 or 124), rolled into ½″ balls
Salt to taste

Remove the lobster meat from the shell, discarding all the organs except for the light green roe if it's there. Crush the shells slightly with a heavy object, like the bottom of a cast-iron pan. Place the shells, roe (if available), anchovies, onion, stock, bay leaf, tarragon, lemon peel, nutmeg, and pepper in a large pot and cook for 45 minutes over low heat. If you're using precooked roe, add it later. Never let the pot boil. Strain the stock and set aside. Discard the shells, but reserve the roe.

Heat the bread crumbs and cream in a small saucepan until warm to the touch, but not hot. Turn off the heat but leave the pan on the burner.

Rinse out the large pot and wipe it dry. Crush the roe, fresh or precooked, and put it in the pot with the butter and milk. Bring the milk mixture to a boil, then slowly and evenly pour the stock into the pot, stirring constantly. Stir in the bread crumbs and cream, then the forcemeat balls. Simmer for 10 minutes, stirring often. Add the lobster meat and simmer for 5 minutes more. Never let it boil. Taste and add salt if necessary. Serve immediately.

Serves 8 as a first course, 4 as a main course

Dickensian Ham and Veal Pie

Today's commercial veal and ham pies are usually made in a bread pan so they can be easily sliced, rather than the authentic, freestanding cylinder popular in the eighteenth century. You'll need a cannister about 6″ high and 4″ in diameter. You can find them anyplace that sells inexpensive kitchenware. This dish is a direct descendant of those medieval "great pies," the ones containing anything from six kinds of cooked poultry to four-and-twenty blackbirds. Charles Dickens, in both *Our Mutual Friend* and *Pickwick Papers,* rhapsodizes over veal and ham pie.

The pie is terrific for company—it looks very dramatic, it's made ahead of time, it's delicious, and it's extremely substantial. It really doesn't need any accompaniment other than tart pickled vegetables such as onions and cucumbers, a piece of fruit, and some Stilton cheese to make a traditional English pub lunch. Although you can drink a rosé or fruity white wine with it, I prefer beer or hard cider.

- 2 cups unbleached all-purpose presifted flour
- ½ cup diced cold lard or unsalted butter
- 2 large egg yolks
- ½ teaspoon salt
- ¼ teaspoon black pepper
- ¼ teaspoon grated nutmeg
- ⅛ teaspoon mace
- 1 tablespoon minced fresh oregano or 1½ teaspoons crumbled dried
- 1 teaspoon minced fresh rosemary, or ½ teaspoon crumbled dried
- ¾ teaspoon grated lemon rind
- ¼ pound skinless Basic Forcemeat (page 40) or mild fresh sausage meat, rolled into ½"-diameter balls
- ¼ pound smoked ham, cut into ½" cubes
- 1½ pounds boneless veal, cut into ½" cubes
- ½ cup roughly chopped, tightly packed fresh mushrooms
- 3 large eggs, hard-boiled, shelled
- 1 large egg, lightly beaten
- 2 cups beef stock, homemade preferable but canned acceptable
- 2 packets unflavored gelatin

In a food processor fitted with the steel blade or with a fork, mix the flour and lard or butter until the dough is crumbly. Stir or process in the yolks, then add a little water only if necessary to form into a smooth, stiff dough. Knead just till smooth.

Roll out the dough into a 16" square. Place the cannister in the center of the square. Cut the dough into an even cross by cutting away a 6" square of dough from each corner. Reserve the dough you've cut away by forming it into a ball, wrapping it in plastic, and refrigerating it. Bring the sides of the dough up to surround the cannister, then pinch together the four adjoining sides in a pretty braided pattern. Refrigerate the pie case, lightly wrapped in plastic, for 2 to 24 hours.

When the pie case is very cold, remove it from the refrigerator. Gently twist the cannister to loosen it, then pull it out of the pie case. If necessary, carefully run a knife between the pastry and the cannister to loosen it. Put the case on a heavy, ungreased, shiny (not black) baking sheet. Preheat the oven to 450°.

Mix together the salt, pepper, nutmeg, mace, oregano, rosemary, and lemon rind. Place a quarter of the forcemeat balls, ham, veal, and mushrooms in the bottom of the case, either in individual layers or after being tossed together. Sprinkle on a quarter of the seasonings. Lay the hard-boiled eggs on top, pressing very gently to pack the filling slightly without breaking the case. Add the rest of the meat and seasonings, half at a time, ending with the seasonings.

Roll half the remaining dough into a 6″ square, then cut into a 6″ diameter circle. Place on top of the pie case, and crimp the edges to seal the pie. Cut a ⅛″-diameter hole in the center of the top to release any steam. Cut the remaining dough into pretty shapes, such as leaves and flowers. Attach them to the case with some of the beaten egg. I like to attach leaves down either side of the braided seams to make them look like vines. I also make a rose (using three-quarter circles for the petals), with the center cut out, to surround the top vent hole. Brush the decorated pie case with the beaten egg.

Circle the sides of the pie with a double thickness of foil and tie with string in 1 or 2 places to hold the foil on. Drape the top with another piece of foil with a hole cut in the center. If you don't have a pie funnel, make a funnel out of foil and insert it through the foil and the vent hole. Place the pie in the oven and bake for 15 minutes. Without opening the oven door, lower the heat to 350° and bake for 40 minutes more, or until lightly browned all over. The pie will brown even though it's wrapped in foil.

As soon as you've put the pie in the oven, heat the stock just until very warm to the touch. Remove it from the stove and stir in the gelatin until completely dissolved. Let cool while the pie bakes. When the pie has finished baking, remove it from the oven, and let it cool on the baking sheet. As soon as the stock has cooled to room temperature, carefully pour about an eighth of it into the pie through the hole in the top. Keep adding the stock, a little at a time, until it comes almost to the top. Don't let the stock reach the top crust or it will get soggy. Pour any leftover stock into a bowl. Refrigerate both the pie and the leftover stock until cold, then remove the foil from the pie. Cut the pie into wedges and serve the slices topped with some of the chopped jellied beef stock.

Serves 6

Boiled Capon with Sausage Stuffing and Celery Sauce

This was originally a turkey dish, but today's capons are the size of Victorian turkeys and it's almost impossible to fit one of today's turkeys into a pot on the stove. Rich English families often served two birds at Christmas, one boiled, the other roasted and presented with a garland of sausages around its neck.

Despite the fact that this dish is boiled, the celery sauce gives it a festive feeling. Accompany the capon with mashed potatoes or potato pancakes and sautéed green vegetables. Try a light red wine, such as a Beaujolais, with the meal. Fruit pie or tart is a good compromise dessert, neither too rich nor too plain. The stock you make from the capon isn't seasoned, so you can use it in other recipes.

- 1 8-pound capon
- 10 ounces spicy fresh sausage meat or Basic Forcemeat (page 40)
- 1 bay leaf
- 3 sprigs fresh thyme, or ½ teaspoon crumbled dried
- 3 carrots, roughly chopped
- 1 onion, halved and stuck with 2 cloves
- 16 celery stalks with leaves, each cut into 5 or 6 pieces
- 2 tablespoons unsalted butter, room temperature
- 2 tablespoons white flour
- 1 cup heavy cream

1½ teaspoons salt
¼ teaspoon black pepper
1 tablespoon lemon juice

Remove any excess fat and skin and the giblets from the capon. Loosely stuff the capon with the sausage meat, then truss it. Place the capon in a large pot, scatter the giblets, bay leaf, thyme, carrots, and onion around it, then cover it with cold water. Turn the heat to high, bring the water to a boil, then reduce heat to low. Simmer the pot, covered, for 2 hours, adding the celery after 1½ hours. Just before the capon is finished cooking, knead together the butter and flour to make a roux and set it aside.

Remove the capon and all the celery from the stock. Puree the celery in a food processor or blender. Put the celery puree and 2 cups of strained capon stock into a small saucepan and turn heat to low. Bring the puree just to a simmer, then stir in the roux. Simmer, stirring often, for another 5 minutes. Stir in the cream, salt, and pepper. Simmer for 10 more minutes, stirring often.

While the sauce is simmering for the 10 minutes, carve the capon. Stir the lemon juice into the sauce and immediately remove it from the heat. Serve the sauce in a sauceboat alongside the capon and the stuffing.

Serves 8

CHAPTER 3

. . . .

France

The very first foods that gave France its reputation for brilliant cuisine were cured meats—sausages and hams, often exported to ancient Rome. Boarlike pigs roamed the French forests, and when the practical French realized that they could use every part of this self-sufficient animal, they began creating inspired recipes. The early French preferred smoking links to just drying them, and this made the sausages easily exportable. After the fall of the Roman Empire, the French continued to make sausages for themselves.

The first of two events which improved French sausage occurred in the early seventeenth century when *charcuteries,* "cooked meat stores," were officially granted the right to sell all kinds of pork products, raw or cooked. Sausage makers then had the freedom to create many new and different sausages. The second event was in the late eighteenth century when the fat, hardy, crossbred English and Chinese pig became common.

The rich tradition of charcuterie continues today. Every town has at least one charcuterie, and the good ones make many of their own sausages instead of buying them from large manufacturers. Sausages vary from region to region depending on local ingredients. As a rule larger sausages, usually smoked or dried, are called *saucissons,* while smaller sausages, often fresh, are *saucisses. Crépinettes* are lumps or patties of sausage, wrapped in caul fat (*crépine* in French). *Caillettes, gayettes,* and *boulettes* are similar to crépinettes but rounder or more bullet-shaped. All these sausage cakes often include liver and/or greens like spinach. Grilled *andouilles* and the smaller *andouillettes* made from hog casings filled with spices and pieces of tripe, stomach, or intestines, are an acquired taste, but their admirers are almost fanatical in their devotion.

Boudins blancs, white sausages, are made from eggs, cream, and white meats, while *boudins noirs,* black sausages, contain blood and perhaps a little pork or spinach or chestnuts. Boudins blancs are usually the most expensive item at the charcuterie since they're made from the most expensive ingredients and are very perishable. Boudins noirs are the cheapest, since their ingredients are the least expensive. Horse- and donkey-meat sausages are sold by horse-meat butchers. Aside from these and a few seafood or poultry sausages, most French sausages are made with pork.

Only a few sausages or sausage dishes are considered part of haute cuisine. *Galantine,* a huge poultry sausage encased in a whole poultry skin, and the striking-looking vegetable, sausage, and game bird bombe called a *Chartreuse* may be the only two. Sausages are more often *cuisine paysanne,* country cooking, though if you ask many haute cuisine chefs what their favorite dish is, something earthy like *cassoulet* is more likely to be the answer than a chateaubriand. Some sausage dishes are eaten throughout France. *Friandes,* sausages wrapped in pastry dough, are in almost every charcuterie. Warm potato salad with smoked or fresh garlic sausage is a bistro staple. So is *assiette charcutière,* a plate of assorted sausages and other cold cuts.

Cassoulet, *garbure,* and many other hearty dishes made with sausages come from Languedoc in southwest France. This is an area that takes pork very seriously. Charcuteries here stock a huge variety of regional sausages. Along with Gascony and Béarn, Languedoc has been influenced by Spain, and spicy Spanish *chorizos* are often used in dishes like cassoulet. Local boudins noirs have red pepper added to them. The French Basques eat *loukenkas,* Middle Eastern sausages brought to Spain by the Moors over 1,000 years ago. The long, coarse, slightly sugared Toulouse sausage is considered one of the best and most versatile fresh sausages in France. It's usually skewered into a coil and grilled or included in soups and stews.

Chestnuts here are often added to sausage soups or stews, mixed with the sausage meat or blood before it's stuffed into the casing, or pureed and served as an accompaniment to grilled sausages. Other common side dishes for sausages are pureed chick peas, mashed potatoes, lentils, cabbage, and sautéed apples. In the Basque country and Bordeaux, on the west coast, cold oysters and hot or warm pork or blood sausages are served together. Basques include sausage in rice dishes similar to the Spanish paella.

Provence, in southeast France, is Italian-influenced and the cuisine is very Mediterranean. Fresh fennel sausages, like those in Italy, are used in stuffings for veal breasts, savory sponge-cake rolls, and stuffed tomatoes. Spicy dried sausages, similar to Italian salamis, are served as snacks.

Saucisson d'Arles, a salami-type sausage, is highly regarded throughout France. Also native to Provence is a rare skinless, boiled beef-and-greens sausage. Stuffed cabbage dishes including a fresh sausage-and-rice-stuffed version and stuffed red cabbage served with smoked sausages alongside are southern favorites.

Lyonnais, Burgundy, and Franche-Comté, in eastern France, are renowned for both elegant, nouvelle cuisine restaurants and those serving cuisine paysanne. These chefs demand, and get, the highest quality sausages. Some are made with truffles, pistachios, or both, others with garlic, most of them quite large and often dried. Goat-meat sausages, common several hundred years ago, can still be found in small Burgundian villages. Salami-type sausages include the dried-peppercorn-and-garlic-filled *saucisson de Lyons* and the smoked *saucisson de Morteau,* also called *Jesus.* Platters piled high with different kinds of sausages, rich stews packed with meats and highly spiced blood sausages, and andouilles are all local favorites.

Alsace-Lorraine, in the northeast corner of France, has been a political soccer ball bounced between France and Germany for hundreds of years. Many of their sausages still bear German names. Smoked or fresh pork sausages, blood sausages which often include apples, and andouillettes are all served with sauerkraut. The native, red-skinned *saucisson de Strasbourg* with a distinct cumin taste is very similar to the equally popular *saucisson de Frankfort,* our hot dog. Sausage salads, pheasant with sauerkraut and sausage, and duck stuffed with sausage are all adapted from German dishes.

Many northeastern sausages are smoked, a remnant of the time when many of the snowed-in Alsatian villages in the Vosges mountains had to live off their autumn-slaughtered pigs all winter. Sausages are such a part of Alsatian life that they are gilded with caramelized sugar and hung on Christmas trees. Liver sausages; headcheese; Swiss hard sausages called *landjager;* German-style *metwurst;* and *colmarettes,* small, smooth-textured veal and pork sausages, are other popular sausages.

Andouillettes are extremely popular in northern France, and those of Troyes in Champagne are famous throughout France. Unlike most andouillettes, they're made with mutton rather than pork. The boudins noirs of Saint-Quentin in Picardy are notorious for the huge amount of onion in them. The cooking of Flanders is closely related to that of Belgium, and they share dishes such as *hochepot*, the soup made from beef, veal, lamb, pork sausages, and lots of vegetables, and dried fruit-filled boudin noir grilled and served with applesauce.

Boudins noirs and blancs inspire fierce competition in Normandy and Brittany, where there is an annual contest to determine which city makes the best version of each. Norman boudins include the famous Normandy cream and apples or chestnuts or are served with sautéed or pureed apples alongside. Smoked andouilles from Vire, in Normandy, are shipped to charcuteries throughout the country and are usually very expensive because they're time-consuming to make. When cut open, they reveal concentric circles formed by placing intestines of different widths inside each other. Popular Brittany dishes include buckwheat crepes accompanied by grilled sausages, and sliced boulettes, eaten cold, with toast.

There's currently a vogue in France for crépinettes, but made with luxurious ingredients such as sweetbreads and truffles. The seafood boudins with pistachio nuts, popular in the nineteenth century, are also making a return in elegant restaurants, served with butter or white wine sauce. Poultry sausages, often made with game such as quail or with duck, can be sliced and served on toast. Many chefs are turning to almost lost, regional sausage recipes, lightening and creating new sauces for them.

Classic French Cooking

Galantine

When this is served warm, it's called a "ballottine." While tradition calls for the cold version, the galantine, to be served surrounded by aspic, I've found that most people find it less intimidating and like it better unadorned. Although it's one of the classics of haute cuisine, it's really just a giant sausage using the duck skin as a casing. There are also versions made with pheasant, turkey, or goose. You can buy loaf-shaped galantine molds, but the original presentation is much prettier.

This is a favorite for picnics and dinner parties. I usually serve cold, cooked marinated shellfish first, then accompany the galantine with either hot or cold stir-fried Chinese vegetables. Try a very dry white wine, like a Sancerre, or a fruity Alsatian Riesling with the galantine.

. . . .

1 5-pound duck
¼ cup orange juice
2 tablespoons brandy
2 tablespoons red vermouth or other semi-dry red wine
1 teaspoon ground allspice
Rind of 1 orange, grated
1 teaspoon finely chopped fresh tarragon, or 2 teaspoons crumbled dried
2 teaspoons finely chopped fresh thyme, or 1 teaspoon crumbled dried
¾ teaspoon salt
¼ teaspoon white pepper
2 canned truffles with liquid
6 tablespoons blanched unsalted pistachios
1 onion, peeled, halved and stuck with 4 cloves
2 carrots, roughly chopped
3 ounces boiled ham, ground, plus 3 ounces cut into ¼" cubes
1 pound raw chicken meat, ground
1 pound pork, ground
½ cup minced shallots
2 large eggs
Vegetable oil

Cut the duck skin down the backbone. Gently remove the skin from the duck in one piece, cutting the wings so that only the tip section remains attached to the skin. You'll have 2 holes where the legs were, so sew them up. Cut the duck meat off the bones in large pieces with a sharp knife. Then cut all the meat into thin strips.

Mix together the orange juice, brandy, vermouth or wine, allspice, orange rind, tarragon, 1 teaspoon thyme, ¼ teaspoon salt, ⅛ teaspoon pepper, and the juice from the canned truffles in a large bowl. Add the duck meat, pistachios, and duck skin and let sit in the refrigerator, covered, for about 6 hours.

While the duck is marinating, place the duck bones, giblets, any poultry bones you've thrown in the freezer for stock, the onion, and carrots in a stockpot. Cover with a lot of cold water, bring to a boil, turn heat to low, and simmer for about 4 hours. If you don't have any extra bones, use half chicken stock and half water. When you have a tasty stock, strain it, return the stock to the pot and let sit, covered, on the unlit burner.

When you're ready to make the galantine, turn the heat under the stock to high. Remove the duck meat, skin, and the pistachios from the marinade and set aside. Mix the ground ham, chicken, pork, and shallots with the marinade and knead to combine well. Knead in the eggs. Dice the truffles and set aside.

Immerse a large piece of cheesecloth in the vegetable oil, then squeeze out the excess oil. Spread the cheesecloth out in front of you. Lay the duck skin out flat on the cheesecloth, the interior facing up. Place one-third of the ground meat in the center of the skin, in a rectangle. The short side, which is facing you, should be half the width of the skin, while the long side should have a 1½″ border on each end. Place half the duck and half the cubed ham in alternating straight lines, running from head to tail, covering the ground meat. Gently cover with half the remaining ground meat. Repeat the duck and ham layer, but this time sprinkle the truffles down the center, running from head to tail. Cover with the rest of the forcemeat.

Bring the sides of the duck skin over the filling, making sure they overlap by 1″. The filling should be compact, but not crushed. Sew the skin closed. Tie string around the roll in 2 to 3 places to ensure it stays shaped like a log. Then tie the cheesecloth around the roll in 2 to 3 places, alternating with the string inside the cheesecloth.

As soon as the stock comes to a boil, add the duck and immediately turn heat to low. Add stock, if necessary, to cover the duck. Simmer, covered, for 2 hours. Turn off the heat and let the duck cool in the stock for 30 minutes. Remove the duck and gently pull off the cheesecloth. Be careful, since the skin tears easily at this point. Wrap it in foil or plastic and refrigerate overnight, then cut into 16 slices.

Serves 16

Chartreuse

Despite the fact that the originally vegetarian chartreuse is still made with the very humble cabbage, it's considered one of the great dishes of haute cuisine. I use quail or squab, although partridge is more classic, because they're easier to find. The original recipes for chartreuse call for roasting the bird, but braising it ensures it will be tender. Don't cook this dish, however, if your object is to show off some terrific game. This is a main course of cabbage with sausage and poultry, not poultry with accompaniments. The easiest way to cut the vegetables into uniform circles is with a doughnut-hole cutter. Unfortunately, you can't put the chartreuse together in advance, since it won't heat through properly if the ingredients aren't already warm when you put it in the oven.

Begin your meal with something simple like oysters on the half shell or a cup of seafood gumbo. White Burgundies, such as a Meursault, are lovely with the chartreuse. For dessert, serve something creamy like zabaglione or hazelnut mousse.

8 ¼-pound quail, or 4 ½-pound squab, cleaned and trussed
Salt and white pepper to taste
6 tablespoons unsalted butter
Poultry stock, homemade preferable but canned acceptable
2 large heads of cabbage, shredded
2 turnips, peeled, cut into ⅛"-thick slices then cut into 1" circles

4 carrots, cut into ⅛″-thick slices
½ pound (about 1½″ wide) Fresh Garlic Sausage (page 24), smoked or poached, skinned and sliced ¼″ thick
¼ pound thickly sliced bacon, cut into 1″-long pieces
1 large onion, finely chopped
2 garlic cloves, crushed then minced
⅓ cup cooked, thawed frozen, or raw peas
1½ teaspoons minced fresh thyme, or ¾ teaspoon crumbled dried
½ teaspoon ground cloves

Begin bringing a large pot of water to a boil. Preheat the oven to 350°.

Sprinkle the quail or squab with salt and pepper. Melt 3 tablespoons butter in a large oven- and stove-proof pot, such as a Dutch oven, and brown the birds, in batches if necessary, all over. Replace all the birds in the pot, pour in stock to cover, place in the oven, and bake for 15 minutes if quail, 25 minutes if squab.

While the birds are cooking, drop the cabbage into the boiling water, cover the pot, turn off the heat, and let it sit until you're ready to use it.

Use the rest of the butter to grease a mold or deep baking dish large enough (about 5 quarts) to hold the birds in one layer. Arrange the turnips, carrots, and sausage in concentric circles or in any pretty pattern. They should just be touching each other. Press them into the butter to adhere them to the sides of the mold, almost up to the top. Refrigerate the mold until you're ready to use it.

Cook the bacon, onion, and garlic in a skillet over low heat for 10 minutes, stirring often. Stir in the peas, thyme, and cloves and immediately remove from the heat and set the skillet aside.

When the birds are done, begin bringing a kettle of water to a boil, turn the oven heat to 400°, and remove the string from the birds. Drain the cabbage well, pressing on it to remove all the water. Stir the bacon mixture and salt and pepper into the cabbage.

Remove the mold from the refrigerator and place half the cabbage in it. Pack it in firmly, but be careful not to disturb the vegetables. Place the birds in, upside down. It's all right if they touch each other, but they shouldn't touch the sides of the dish. Fill the spaces around the birds with cabbage, then pack in the rest of the cabbage. It should reach the top of the vegetables. Place the mold in a pan at least 2″ wider and half as tall as the mold. Pour boiling water into the wider pan almost to the top. Place in the oven and bake for 30 minutes.

To unmold, put an upside down plate on top of the mold, then, holding the mold and plate together, reverse them. The chartreuse should slip out of the mold easily. If any vegetables stick to the mold, just press them back into place.

Serves 4

NATIONAL FAVORITES

Chicken and Pork Sausage

♦ ***Boudins Blancs***

This is one of the most common sausages in France. The better versions have poultry in them as well as pork, and country versions can include rabbit. A truffled version accompanied by mashed potatoes is traditional in many parts of France on both Christmas and New Year's Eve.

Boudin blanc is very delicate, so it shouldn't be accompanied by anything that will overwhelm it. It's best simply grilled, or pan-fried in butter, and served with a salad and sautéed apples, applesauce, mashed potatoes, very good bread, or the German potato-and-apple puree, Himmel und Erde, for lunch or a late supper. Serve a dry white wine, such as Château Olivier.

2 tablespoons unsalted butter
1 small onion, roughly chopped (about 1 cup)
1 cup heavy cream

½ cup white bread with crust, torn into bite-size pieces and tightly packed
¼ teaspoon mixed ground cloves, coriander, and nutmeg
1½ teaspoons salt
¼ teaspoon white pepper
½ pound raw white chicken meat, finely ground
½ pound lean pork, finely ground
½ pound pork fat, finely ground
1 large egg
2 large egg whites
Butter and bread crumbs (optional)

Prepared hog casings

In a medium-size skillet melt the butter over very low heat. Add the onions, cover, and cook for 15 minutes, stirring occasionally, until very translucent. Don't let them brown. Set the onions aside to cool.

Heat the cream in a saucepan until hot but not boiling and pour over the bread in a small bowl. Stir lightly. Let the bread sit for 5 minutes, then stir in the mixed spices, salt, and pepper. Set aside.

Mix together the chicken, pork, pork fat, and cooled onions. Place the mixture in the bowl of an electric mixer or food processor. Add the bread and cream in thirds, mixing well after each addition. Mix in the egg, then the egg whites. The mixture should be very fluffy. You can also do this by hand, but you'll have to beat it very well with a wooden spoon. Stuff loosely into the prepared hog casings. The sausages should be 1″ to 1¼″ in diameter. Tie off in 5″ lengths. Prick any air pockets with a pin.

Poach the sausages in a covered pot for 20 minutes, never letting the water boil. Remove the sausages and pat dry.

If you want to fry the sausages, gently remove the casings. Roll the sausages in bread crumbs, melt butter in a skillet and fry over low heat until browned all over. Raw sausages can be refrigerated for 1 to 2 days, poached for 3 to 4 days. Raw or poached sausages can be frozen for 3 months.

Makes approximately 2¼ pounds raw sausage

Blood Sausage with Spinach

◆ ***Boudins Noirs aux Epinards***

Blood sausages are so popular throughout France that almost every village has its own closely guarded recipe. Additions like spinach, onions, ground pork, rice, liver, chestnuts, or apples depend on what's available and inexpensive. Pork blood is usually used, but some sausages contain rabbit blood. Like boudins blancs, this sausage is often part of Christmas and New Year's Eve celebrations. These are very fragile, so be careful while handling them. I can tell you from experience that they can be extremely messy if dropped. They will also burst if you cook them at high heat, so never let them boil, and fry them over a very low fire.

These go very well with all kinds of pastry, so place thick slices in baked puff or short pastry shells and top with a bit of warm, unsweetened applesauce and a few raisins. It makes a lovely first course for a dinner party, but make sure your guests are amenable to unusual, peculiar-looking foods. Home-fried potatoes, especially with garlic added, are terrific with grilled boudins noirs. Serve a fairly robust red wine, like a Saint-Emilion, with the sausages.

½ pound spinach leaves, torn into large pieces
1 tablespoon orange liqueur
1 cup beef blood
½ teaspoon minced fresh thyme, or ¼ teaspoon crumbled dried
⅛ teaspoon ground allspice
1 teaspoon coarse, kosher, or sea salt
⅛ teaspoon black pepper
2 teaspoons minced fresh chives
¼ cup fine dry bread crumbs
2 tablespoons heavy cream
2 ounces smoked bacon, finely chopped
½ cup finely chopped onion

1 large egg
Butter (optional)

Prepared hog casings

Rinse the spinach in a colander, then toss well to shake some of the water off. Place the spinach and any water remaining on the leaves in a skillet large enough to hold it in a shallow layer. Turn heat to medium and cook, covered, for 10 minutes until very wilted. While the spinach is cooking, mix together the orange liqueur, blood, thyme, allspice, salt, pepper, and chives and set aside. Also toss the bread crumbs with the cream. Remove the spinach and puree in a food processor or blender.

Bring a large pot of water, preferably one with a colanderlike insert such as a spaghetti cooker, to a boil over high heat. Dry the spinach pan, return the puree to it, and add the bacon and onion. Cook, stirring occasionally, for 15 minutes over very low heat. Stir in the bread crumbs and cream and remove the pan from the heat. Pour the contents into a large bowl. Stir in the blood mixture, one-third at a time, mixing well after each addition. Stir in the egg.

Place the bowl on a large cookie sheet and stuff the sausages over the sheet, since you can't help but drip blood all over the place. The texture of the sausage mixture will be very liquid, so just pour it through a funnel into the prepared casings. Hold onto the casing to keep it from slipping off the funnel. The sausages should be 1″ to 1¼″ wide. Tie off into 4″ lengths, since these are very fragile and smaller sausages are easier to handle. Since the mixture is so smooth there probably won't be any air pockets. If you spot any, prick them with nothing larger than a pin. Even if there aren't any air pockets, prick each sausage at least twice, then gently place them in the pot's insert.

Turn the heat under the pot of water to very low and lower the insert into the water. Simmer for 15 minutes, then take the pot off the heat. Let the sausages cool in their cooking liquid until room temperature. Pat dry, wrap loosely in butcher or freezer paper, and let sit in the refrigerator for 1 to 2 days before serving them. They can also be stored in the freezer for 3 months.

When you're ready to serve the sausages, cut into 2″ lengths, prick each once or twice, and fry in butter or grill them until lightly browned.

Makes 1¼ pounds raw sausage

Sausage with Warm Potato Salad

◆ ***Saucisson Chaud Lyonnais***

It's difficult to find a bistro in France, especially around Lyon, that doesn't serve this dish. The potato salad can be served alongside poached sausage (as it is here), with sausage baked in brioche dough, or accompanying slices of dried sausage like salami. The sausage should be spicy to contrast with the salad. Traditionally, the potatoes are peeled after they're boiled, but I like potato skins so I leave them on.

This is a perfect lunch for close friends. Serve a mixed green salad with Roquefort dressing or asparagus with hollandaise sauce as a first course and individual pastries, such as eclairs or Napoleons, for dessert. Cabernet Sauvignon and beer go well with the sausages.

- 2 pounds new potatoes
- 2 pounds Fresh Garlic Sausage, about 1½″ wide and any length (page 24), pricked with a fork at 3″ intervals
- 2 tablespoons dry white wine or vermouth
- 2 tablespoons red wine or cider vinegar
- 6 tablespoons olive oil
- 1 tablespoon chicken stock, homemade preferable but canned acceptable
- 1 teaspoon mustard, Dijon preferable but any good quality acceptable
- Salt and pepper to taste

2 tablespoons minced fresh chives, or 1 tablespoon minced scallion greens
1 tablespoon minced fresh parsley
1 tablespoon finely minced fresh or ½ tablespoon crumbled dried tarragon
2 tablespoons unsalted butter

Bring a large pot of water to a boil, add the potatoes, and boil till tender, about 30 minutes. While you're bringing the potato water to a boil, also bring a large skillet of water to a boil. Turn the heat under the skillet to low, add the sausages, and poach, covered, for 30 minutes, turning once.

While the sausages and potatoes are cooking, place the wine or vermouth, vinegar, olive oil, stock, mustard, and salt and pepper in a small jar with a lid and, after closing tightly, shake well. Add the chives or scallion, parsley, and tarragon to the dressing and shake again.

Slice the boiled potatoes ¼" thick and place in a large bowl. Pour the dressing evenly over them and toss lightly with your hands, being careful not to smash the potato. Set aside.

Quickly sauté the sausages in the butter in a large skillet over medium-high heat until lightly browned all over. Serve the warm salad alongside the hot sausage.

Serves 4

Sausages in White Wine Sauce

♦ ***Saucissons au Vin Blanc***

This is another simple bistro dish, best accompanied by mashed, boiled, or baked potatoes, which taste delicious with the sauce poured over them. With a salad as a first course; a baked apple, or apple pie or tart for dessert; and a bottle of the wine you used in the sauce or even Beaujolais, you have a complete meal.

- ½ cup white vermouth or other dry white wine
- ½ cup chicken stock, homemade preferable but canned acceptable
- ½ cup water
- 1 sprig fresh thyme, tarragon, or parsley
- 1 tablespoon unsalted butter
- 1 tablespoon roughly chopped leek, white part only
- 4 Apple Sausages or Boudins Blancs (about 1 pound) (page 86 or 64)
- 1 tablespoon unsalted butter cut into small pieces
- Salt to taste
- Pinch of white pepper

Mix together the wine, chicken stock, water, and herb sprig. In a skillet large enough to hold all 4 sausages heat 1 tablespoon butter over low heat. Add the leek and sausages and fry until the sausages are browned on all sides. Pour in the wine mixture, stirring and scraping the bottom of the skillet to deglaze it. Bring to a boil over medium heat, then turn the heat to low and simmer, uncovered, for 20 minutes. Turn the sausages after the first 10 minutes.

Remove the sausages and keep them warm. Discard the fresh herb. Bring the skillet liquid to a boil over high heat and reduce by half. This will take about 3 to 4 minutes. Stir in the cut-up butter until it's melted, then season with salt and pepper. The amount of salt will depend on the saltiness of your chicken stock. Let boil for another 1 to 2 minutes, until thickened, stirring often.

Replace the sausages in the pan and turn them in the sauce to reheat them. Serve with the sauce poured over them.

Serves 4

Sausage Roll

♦ ***Saucisse en Croute***

This can be as simple or as fancy as you like. I'm using a short pastry, but you can use homemade or frozen puff pastry or brioche dough if you prefer. You can also use almost any fresh meat sausage, including Chorizo, Boudin Noir, or even Merguez (see pages 192, 66 and 253), the spicy North African beef sausage popular in Paris. It's amazing how an easy pastry dough turns a simple sausage into something appropriate for the fanciest party.

I usually serve a thick slice of this appetizer on a plate covered with a thin film of mustard and cream sauce or with a selection of mustards. You can serve almost any wine with the sausage. I choose one that goes well with a main course like a spicy fish soup, stew, curry, or gumbo, accompanied by sautéed vegetables if there aren't any in the main dish. You need a simple dessert after this, such as cold pears poached in white wine.

- 1 cup unbleached all-purpose presifted flour
- ¼ teaspoon salt
- 4 tablespoons unsalted butter, cut into small pieces
- ¼ cup water
- 1 ¾-pound Garlic, Pistachio (page 24 or 78), or other fresh sausage (1″–2″ wide)
- 1 egg, lightly beaten with 1 tablespoon water

To make the dough in the processor: Process the flour and salt until well mixed. Add the butter and process until the mixture has the texture of bread crumbs. Pour in the water while the processor is running and stop as soon as the dough is well mixed.

To make the dough by hand: Stir together the flour and salt until well mixed. Add the butter and mix with your fingers, a fork, or pastry cutter until it's the texture of bread crumbs. Sprinkle the water over it and mix well with your hands. Turn the dough out onto a cutting board and gather it into a ball. Then slide the heel of your hand across a walnut-size piece of dough, gently pushing the dough away from the ball, smearing it across and into your cutting board. Push another piece of dough into the first and continue until you've done that with the entire ball. This is called "fraisage" and ensures the butter is evenly worked into the dough.

Whichever method you use, place the dough on a sheet of waxed paper or plastic wrap and pat into a rectangle. The dough will be soft but not sticky. Wrap it in the paper and refrigerate until you're ready to use it.

Prick the sausage in 2 to 3 places with a fork. Place in a saucepan or skillet and pour in water to cover. Bring to a boil, then reduce heat to low, and simmer for 10 minutes if it's a 1″-wide sausage, 20 minutes if it's 2″ across.

Preheat the oven to 350°. Remove the dough from the refrigerator. Roll it out on a floured board until ⅛″ thick. You want the rectangle to be long and wide enough to roll the sausage up completely in the dough. Cut away any excess dough and reserve. Roll up the sausage in the dough, pressing to seal well. Cut out 2 circles from the remaining dough and use to close up the open spaces at the ends of the sausage. Crimp them where they meet the rest of the dough to seal well. Turn the sausage so the seam side of the dough is on the bottom, and place on a nonstick baking sheet. Use the rest of the dough to make decorative cutouts. Attach them with the egg and water mixture, then brush the whole roll with the egg glaze. Bake for 45 minutes until browned all over.

The sausage can be served hot or warm, but make sure you cut it with a serrated knife or the dough will get crushed.

Serves 4 as an appetizer

SOUTHWEST FRANCE

Cassoulet

There have probably been more words written, and more impassioned debates, on cassoulet than on any other dish ever created. To sum up the controversy, three cities in Languedoc—Toulouse, Carcassonne, and Castelnaudary—each claim to have originated the dish and that their version is the best. My opinion is that there is no best version. This is such a wonderful dish that, if made with the correct techniques, it's almost impossible to screw it up.

The Castelnaudary version, probably adapted from an ancient Roman recipe and therefore the original French version, is the simplest. Only beans, some fresh and smoked pork, sausage, and confit are mandatory. Carcassonne adds mutton or lamb and occasionally a game bird. Toulouse gets really enthusiastic, adding more lamb, game birds, and salted pork breast. There are also hundreds of variations: cassoulets which include fish, lentils, truffles, hare, and almost anything else you can imagine.

You need a strong red wine to stand up to cassoulet, so I like a French Cahors. Begin the meal with something simple, such as asparagus vinaigrette, serve the cassoulet alone, then finish with fresh fruit soaked in liqueur, fresh berries, or strawberry shortcake.

1½ pounds white beans
2 sprigs fresh rosemary, or ½ teaspoon dried
2 sprigs fresh thyme leaves, or ½ teaspoon dried
1 bay leaf
2 sprigs parsley, plus 3 tablespoons chopped fresh
1 duck or goose, fresh or Confit (page 77), cut into serving pieces
6 cups chicken stock, homemade preferable but canned acceptable
1 peeled onion, stuck with 4 cloves
2 carrots, peeled, thinly sliced
6 tablespoons confit fat, rendered chicken fat, or lard
4 whole garlic cloves
1 pound Fresh Garlic Sausages (page 24), pricked
¾ pound salt pork, rinsed well, blanched for 15 minutes, then cut into 1″ squares
1 pound lamb, cut into 1″ cubes
1 pound pork loin, cut into 1″ cubes
2 large onions, roughly chopped
3 very ripe tomatoes (about 1½ pounds), peeled, seeded, roughly chopped
2 cups finely chopped day-old French, good white, or egg bread

Soak the beans in a bowl of water to cover for 4 to 5 hours.

Tie the rosemary, thyme, bay leaf, and parsley sprigs in a cheesecloth bag to form a bouquet garni. If you're using preserved duck (confit), rinse it with warm water to remove some of the fat and salt and pat dry.

Bring the beans and their soaking water to a boil in a large stockpot, boil for 15 minutes, drain, and rinse. Place the rinsed beans in the rinsed pot and add the stock, the whole onion and cloves, and carrots. Bring to a boil over high heat. Turn heat to low and simmer, uncovered, for about 30 minutes.

Meanwhile, heat the fat in a large skillet over medium heat, add the garlic, and sauté until golden. Remove the garlic and, using a garlic press or after mincing it, add it to the bean pot. Add the sausages to the skillet and brown all over. Remove them and set them aside. Next, brown the salt pork, lamb, and pork loin in the fat, in batches. Remove and set each batch aside. Preheat the oven to 350°. Turn the heat under the skillet to low, add the chopped onions to the fat, and cook for 15 minutes, stirring often.

By now the beans should have been cooking for 30 minutes. Add the sausage, salt pork, lamb, pork loin, sautéed onions, and the tomatoes to the bean pot, stir well, and simmer for another hour. Remove the onion stuck with cloves and the bouquet garni and stir in the duck or goose. Pour the contents of the pot into an ovenproof earthenware casserole (if available). Make sure the stock comes just to the top of the beans. If not, add more until it does. Sprinkle the bread and chopped parsley over the top and pat into an even layer.

Place the stockpot or casserole in the oven and bake for 1½ hours. As soon as a crust forms on the top (after about 30 minutes), stir the pot from the bottom, then smooth the top, making sure all the meats are buried under the beans. Repeat this step about 6 times during the last hour of cooking, making sure to smooth the top every time.

Serves 12

Vegetable Soup

♦ ***Garbure***

Garbure is most popular in Béarn, Gascony, and the Basque country. The chorizos often used show how closely related the cuisines of southern France and northern Spain are. The starchy vegetable in garbure depends on what's in season. Fresh haricot beans and dried beans are common, but I find the chestnut version more interesting. Then again, I find that chestnuts make anything more interesting.

It's almost silly to serve anything else with this huge amount of food except a glass of young red wine such as Pinot Noir, and some fresh fruit for dessert.

1 ¾-pound piece of salt pork, rinsed well then parboiled for 15 minutes and rinsed again
2 bay leaves
3 garlic cloves, crushed then minced
3 sprigs fresh thyme, or ½ teaspoon crumbled dried
1 sprig fresh marjoram, or ¼ teaspoon crumbled dried
3 quarts cold water
1 pound fresh chestnuts, an "X" carved in the flat side of each
1 head of green cabbage, cored, roughly chopped
3 turnips, peeled, roughly chopped
3 carrots, peeled, roughly chopped or sliced
1 onion, roughly chopped
3 celery stalks with leaves, roughly chopped
½ pound green beans, cut into 2" pieces
3 leeks, halved lengthwise, thickly sliced
1 pound Fresh Garlic Sausages or Chorizos (page 24 or 192), pricked
8 small new potatoes (about 1 pound)
1 teaspoon black pepper
8 small pieces of goose or duck Confit (page 77) (optional)

Bring the salt pork, bay leaves, garlic, thyme, marjoram, and water to a boil in a large pot. Lower heat and simmer, covered, for 1 hour. Bring another pot of water to a boil. Drop the chestnuts in, boil for 10 minutes, drain, and peel. Set aside.

After the first hour of cooking, add the cabbage, turnips, carrots, onion, and celery and simmer for another hour. Add the rest of the ingredients, including the peeled chestnuts, and simmer for another 40 minutes. Remove the fresh herbs, if used. Cut the salt pork into bite-size squares and the sausages into a total of 8 pieces.

Serves 8

Preserved Duck

♦ *Confit*

The French genius for cooking isn't creating haute cuisine out of extravagant ingredients. It's the ability to take what appears to be unusable and turn it into a delicacy. The meat from geese specially bred and fed to create foie gras is usually too tough to eat. Turning it into confit makes it extremely tender.

Once you've tasted duck confit and potatoes browned in the confit fat, you'll understand why the French are devoted to it. It's also used in recipes such as Cassoulet and Garbure and other soups and stews. Confit can be very salty, so you will probably want to rinse the pieces slightly before cooking them. You'll also want to avoid using salt in any dish to which confit is added.

Note: Allow 3 days for the duck to marinate.

1 garlic clove, peeled, crushed, and minced
½ cup coarse, kosher, or sea salt, plus extra for crock
1 bay leaf, very finely crumbled or ground
1 4½-pound duck, cut into about 13 pieces including the neck
3 tablespoons water
Approximately ¾ pound lard

Mix together in a large, fairly straight-sided glass bowl the garlic, ½ cup salt, and bay leaf. Cut off the duck's excess skin and reach under the remaining skin and pull out as much fat as possible. Toss the duck with the salt mixture, cover the bowl, and refrigerate for 3 days. Store the excess fat and skin in a plastic bag in the refrigerator.

After the 3 days, cut the fat and skin into small squares, then place in a medium-size skillet with the water. Simmer over low heat for about 45 minutes, until the skin is brown. Remove the browned skin with a slotted spoon and set aside to be used in a salad. Pour the liquid fat from the skillet into a Dutch oven. Add about two-thirds of the lard and melt over low heat. Stir occasionally.

While the lard is melting, rinse the duck well and pat dry. Add the duck to the melted fat and cook, covered, over very low heat for 2 hours. Drop in the remaining lard, about a third at a time, at 10-minute intervals through the first 30 minutes of cooking. This will keep the fat mixture fairly cool, which is important. You don't want fried duck; you want fat-sealed simmered duck. You'll know the duck is done when you stick a skewer into a piece and the juice coming out is clear rather than red-tinted. Remove the duck with a slotted spoon and cook the fat, uncovered, over low heat for about 20 minutes to evaporate any moisture.

Pour a ⅛″ layer of salt into an earthenware crock large enough to contain the duck. This will catch any duck juice that drips down and keep it from spoiling the confit. Gently pour a ½″ layer of the strained cooking fat onto the salt layer, being careful not to disturb it. Place the crock in the freezer until the fat layer is solid.

When the fat is solid, place half the duck pieces in the crock and pour in enough strained cooking fat to reach the top of the duck. Add the rest of the duck, then pour in enough strained fat to cover the duck by at least 1″. Cover the top of the crock with waxed or parchment paper kept on with a rubber band. Store in the refrigerator for 3 to 6 months. It is ready to eat right away, but is better after being kept a couple of weeks.

Makes 1 duck

LYON

Pistachio Sausages

♦ ***Cervelas aux Pistaches***

This is a very versatile sausage that can be used in almost any dish where its taste won't be overwhelmed by other ingredients. It's very good en croute, alongside Warm Potato Salad, or served for breakfast with eggs. The pistachio nuts and brandy, however, make this more elegant than the average pork sausage.

- 1 pound lean pork, coarsely ground
- 6 ounces pork fat, coarsely ground
- 3 ounces unsalted, shelled pistachios, roughly chopped
- 1 garlic clove, crushed then minced
- 2 tablespoons brandy
- 1 teaspoon salt
- ¼ teaspoon black pepper
- ⅛ teaspoon grated nutmeg
- ¼ teaspoon minced fresh thyme, or ⅛ teaspoon crumbled dried

Prepared hog casings

Knead together the pork, fat, pistachios, and garlic in a large bowl. Stir together the brandy, salt, pepper, nutmeg, and thyme, then knead into the meat mixture. Stuff firmly into casings and tie off into 4″ or 5″ sausages. Prick any air pockets. Poach the sausages in a pot of water for 20 minutes or grill them. The raw sausages can be refrigerated for 3 days, the poached sausages for 1 week. Raw or poached sausages can be frozen for 3 months.

Makes approximately 1¾ pounds raw sausage

BURGUNDY

Whole Stuffed Cabbage

♦ ***Chou Farci***

This recipe may date back to at least the early seventeenth century. Because there's not very much meat in it compared to cabbage, it's very delicate-tasting, more like a side dish than a main course. Since it's the presentation that makes this so impressive, bring it to the table uncut. It's perfect with a roast chicken, since chicken and sausage complement each other very well. You can begin your meal with grilled or sautéed wild mushrooms or wild mushroom soup. Try a dry white Muscadet with the meal and a rich dessert such as chocolate mousse cake.

- 1 head of green cabbage (about 2½ pounds)
- 6 ounces skinless Fresh Garlic Sausage (page 24) or other spicy fresh sausage
- 5 ounces bacon, roughly chopped
- 1 large egg
- 1½ cups cooked rice
- 2 tart apples, peeled and grated
- Salt and pepper to taste
- Scant ½ teaspoon grated nutmeg
- ½ teaspoon chopped fresh sage, or ¼ teaspoon crumbled dried
- 1 teaspoon chopped fresh marjoram, or ½ teaspoon crumbled dried
- 2 tablespoons unsalted butter
- 2 tablespoons white flour
- 1 cup white vermouth or other dry white wine
- 2 cups chicken stock, homemade preferable but canned acceptable

Bring a large pot of water to a boil, drop in the cabbage, boil for 15 minutes, drain.

Mix together the sausage, 3 ounces bacon, the egg, rice, apples, salt and pepper, nutmeg, sage, and marjoram.

Gently roll down the outer leaves of the cabbage to expose the center. When you can't roll away any more leaves without breaking them, you should have a ball of cabbage in the center with about a 3″ diameter. Carve that ball out without loosening the surrounding rolled-down leaves. Roughly chop the cutout cabbage and set aside.

Fill the space left by the cutout cabbage with a ball made up of part of the sausage mixture. Roll up just enough leaves to completely cover the sausage ball. Gently pat a layer of meat around the sides of the enclosed ball. Fold up enough leaves to cover that layer. Use the rest of the meat to form another layer, then roll up the rest of the leaves. Pat the cabbage back into its original shape if necessary. Place the cabbage on a large piece of moistened and squeezed-dry cheesecloth. Bring up the sides of the cheesecloth and tie the top shut with string. This will help the cabbage keep its original shape when you cook it.

Fry the remaining 2 ounces bacon in a pot slightly larger than the cabbage until some of the fat has been rendered. Stir in the butter until it's melted, then the flour, then the wine. Bring to a boil, stirring often. Pour in the stock, stir well a couple of times, then place the cabbage, string side up, in the center of the pot. Surround with the chopped cabbage, cover, and simmer over low heat for 3½ hours.

Remove the cabbage from the pot. Then turn the heat under the pot to high and boil down the pan juices for about 10 minutes, stirring occasionally, until thickened. Season with salt and pepper to taste. Unwrap the cabbage and serve it cut into wedges, topped with the sauce.

Serves 8

Sausage and Chestnut Patties

♦ ***Crépinettes aux Marrons***

The French use chestnuts in every course from soup to dessert during the autumn season. You can substitute diced apples or small cubes of boiled potato for the chestnuts if you prefer. Find a sausage without bread or other cereal filler, since the chestnuts are very starchy. If you can't find caul fat, either omit it or wrap the crépinettes in bacon that has been parboiled for 5 minutes.

You can broil crépinettes instead of frying them and top them with a fresh tomato sauce instead of the browned butter. If you're serving these as an appetizer, follow with a seafood main course or something light such as Chinese chicken salad. Don't worry about whether crépinettes are elegant enough for company; even Napoleon ate them. Beaujolais is perfect with these crépinettes.

8 fresh chestnuts, an "X" carved in the flat side of each
1 pound bulk or skinned fresh pork sausage such as Fresh Garlic, Basic Italian, or Luganega (page 24, 96, or 110)
Caul fat
4 tablespoons unsalted butter

Drop the chestnuts into a large pot of boiling water and boil for 10 minutes. Drain, peel, then mince them and knead them into the sausage meat.

Cut the caul into twelve 4" squares. Divide the sausage mixture into 12 pieces and roll each into a 3"-diameter ball. Wrap each ball in caul fat. The ends of the caul should overlap a good deal. Gently press on each ball with the palm of your hand to flatten to a ½"-thick patty.

Over low heat melt 2 tablespoons butter in each of 2 cast-iron skillets, both large enough to hold 6 patties. Fry the sausage patties for 5 minutes, turn, and fry for another 1 to 2 minutes, until the bottom is lightly browned. Place 2 patties on each of 6 heated plates and pour the browned butter from the skillet over them. Serve immediately.

Serves 6

ALSACE

Garnished Sauerkraut

♦ ***Choucroute Garnie***

Garnished sauerkraut is an understatement of a name for a dish that combines so many wonderful ingredients. This began as a winter dish, but it's now served year-round in Alsatian restaurants. The quality of the sauerkraut is very important, so if you can't find a delicatessen that sells fresh sauerkraut, you'll have to either make your own or rinse the bottled variety very, very well to get rid of the excess brine.

There's nothing you can serve as a first course except, perhaps, a few grilled or raw oysters or a green salad with a cream-based dressing. All the choucroute needs is a good loaf of bread to go with it. Don't serve anything more strenuous than fruit for dessert, baked apples if you insist on something warm. Although you can drink an Alsatian white wine like Riesling with choucroute, an Alsatian or German beer is the best accompaniment. If there's any choucroute left over, and there usually is, I cut the meat into bite-size pieces and add it, and the sauerkraut, to stock to make a wonderful soup.

. . . .

4 peppercorns
Handful of fresh parsley
1 bay leaf
2 sprigs fresh thyme, or ¼ teaspoon crumbled dried
10 juniper berries, or ½ cup gin
¾ pound smoked bacon, roughly chopped
3 carrots, peeled, cut into 1″ slices
2 garlic cloves, crushed then minced
1½ cups finely chopped onion
3 pounds fresh or Homemade Sauerkraut (page 131), soaked in cold water for 1 hour then rinsed and squeezed dry
½ teaspoon white pepper
3 cups chicken stock, homemade preferable but canned acceptable
1 cup Riesling or other German or Alsatian white wine
1 1-pound piece of salt pork, blanched in boiling water for 15 minutes then patted dry
1 pound Fresh Garlic Sausages (page 24)
6 Pork Hot Dogs (page 326), saucisson de Strasbourg, or other smoked pork sausage
1½ pounds new potatoes

Preheat the oven to 325°. Tie the peppercorns, parsley, bay leaf, thyme, and juniper berries in a cheesecloth bag to make a bouquet garni. If you're not using the juniper berries, reserve the gin until later.

Cook the bacon in a Dutch oven over medium heat until it's just beginning to brown. Remove with a slotted spoon and drain on paper towels. Add the carrots, garlic, and onion to the bacon fat and fry over low heat for about 10 minutes, until the onion is very wilted. Stir in the sauerkraut, white pepper, and cooked bacon, mixing well. Pour in the stock, wine, and the gin (if used). Pour in enough water, if necessary, so that the liquid comes to the top of the sauerkraut. Bury the bouquet garni and the salt pork in the sauerkraut. Bring to a simmer, cover, and place in the oven for 3½ hours.

After the choucroute has cooked for about 3¼ hours, begin bringing a large pot of water to a boil. After the 3½ hours, bury the garlic and pork sausages in the sauerkraut, cover the pot again, and bake for another 40 minutes. While the sausages are cooking, add the new potatoes to the pot of boiling water and cook for about 30 minutes, until tender.

Mound the sauerkraut in the center of a large platter and surround it with the potatoes and sliced meats.

Serves 6

FLANDERS AND PICARDY

Potée Bourguignonne

This is a northern version of a dish popular throughout France. The name means "potful" and it is. The broth is usually served as a first course, followed by a main course of the vegetables and carved meats. Because this is cold weather food, a California Zinfandel or a good German beer goes well with the meats. I like delicate, flaky pastry after hearty meals and serve a selection of Viennese or French pastries following this.

. . . .

1 4–5-pound chicken, giblets removed and reserved
½ pound fresh pork sausage meat
2 leeks, white and light green sections, finely chopped
½ cup raw short-grain rice
3 cups hot chicken stock, homemade preferable but canned acceptable
1 teaspoon minced fresh thyme, or ½ teaspoon crumbled dried
Salt and pepper to taste
2 tablespoons vegetable oil
1½ pounds pork ribs (in 1 or 2 pieces)
1½ pounds veal neck bones with some meat on them
4 leeks, thinly sliced
3 garlic cloves, crushed but left in 1 piece
6 carrots, quartered
2 parsnips, quartered
¾ cup roughly chopped fresh parsley
1 bay leaf, broken in half
2 sprigs fresh thyme, or ½ teaspoon crumbled dried
1 8″ smoked garlic sausage, such as Kielbasa or Spanish Chorizo (page 173 or 192), cut into 1″ pieces
1 head of green cabbage, cored, cut into 8 wedges

Finely chop the chicken liver and set aside.

Place the bulk pork sausage in a skillet, turn the heat to medium, and fry until cooked through. Remove with a slotted spoon and drain on paper towels. Add the chopped leeks, turn heat to low, and sauté for 5 minutes. Add the rice and sauté until lightly browned, 3 to 4 minutes. Pour in 1 cup stock and simmer, covered, for about 12 minutes, until all the liquid has been absorbed. Stir in the chicken liver, minced thyme, and salt and pepper to taste. Stir the sausage back into the skillet and mix well. Stuff the chicken loosely with some of the sausage mixture, then sew it closed and truss it. Place the remaining sausage in an ovenproof ramekin and set it aside.

Heat the oil in a large pot over high heat, add the pork and veal, in batches if necessary, and sear on all sides. Remove all the pork and veal and set it aside. Turn off the heat. Standing as far away from the pot as possible and wearing an oven mitt, pour 1 cup stock into the pot. It will splatter, so be careful. When it stops splattering, stir well to deglaze the pan. Turn the heat to low, then stir in the rest of the stock.

Place the chicken in the pot and scatter the pork, veal, sliced leeks, garlic, carrots, parsnips, parsley, bay leaf, remaining thyme, and the giblets around it. Pour in enough water to just cover the chicken. Bring the pot to a boil over high heat, reduce heat to low, and simmer, covered, for 1 hour. Add the smoked sausage and cabbage wedges and cook for another 30 minutes. Reheat the extra stuffing in the oven and serve on the side.

Serves 8

NORMANDY

Apple Sausages

♦ ***Boudins Blancs aux Pommes***

This recipe combines Normandy's famous apples, butter, and Calvados. These are terrific breakfast sausages, but they're also good in delicate soups that could use a bit of a tang and late at night when you want a filling, but not very heavy, snack. Just stick the poached sausages under the broiler, turning them a couple of times until lightly browned all over and heated through. I even like them on hot dog rolls with a little mustard.

2 tablespoons unsalted butter
1 small onion, finely chopped (about 1 cup)
½ cup finely chopped peeled tart apples
2 tablespoons Calvados or brandy
½ teaspoon mixed ground cloves, ginger, coriander, and cinnamon

1½ teaspoons salt
½ teaspoon white pepper
½ pound pork with some fat in it, coarsely ground
½ pound skinless, boneless raw chicken breast, coarsely ground
Butter and bread crumbs (optional)

Prepared hog casings

Melt the butter in a large skillet over very low heat. Stir in the onions and sauté for 10 minutes until translucent. Stir in the apples and cook, covered, for 5 minutes. Pour the contents of the skillet into a bowl. Let cool.

Mix together the Calvados, spices, salt, and white pepper in a small bowl. Knead the pork and chicken together in another bowl. Beat the Calvados mixture into the meats with a wooden spoon until fluffy. Gently fold in the apple mixture. Stuff loosely into prepared hog casings and tie off in 5″ to 6″ lengths. The sausages should be about 1″ to 1¼″ wide. Prick any air pockets with a pin. Poach the sausages in a covered pot of water for 20 minutes, never letting the water boil.

If you want fried sausages, gently remove the casings from the cooled sausages. Roll the sausages in bread crumbs, then fry in butter over low heat until browned all over. Never fry the sausages until you're ready to eat them. Raw sausages can be refrigerated for 2 to 3 days, poached for 1 week. Raw or poached sausages can be frozen for 3 months.

Makes approximately 1½ pounds raw sausage

CHAPTER 4

. . . .

Italy

Italy is renowned mostly for dry sausages, like salamis, but that's because the Italians rarely export their excellent fresh sausages. The ancient Romans turned everything from dormice to porpoises into sausages. Although it was chic to prefer imported sausages, the ancient Romans also liked smoked Lucanian sausages from southern Italy. Today *salumerias,* pork and sausage shops, must still sell a large variety of sausages to please discerning Italian buyers.

Almost every region has its own fresh sausage and dried or smoked salami, or at least a unique way of serving them. Italy has stringent regulations regarding labeling, so every salami must indicate where it comes from and what kind of meat it's made of. Although most are made of pork, some contain beef, lamb, or, occasionally, wild boar or horsemeat. Salami is traditionally served in an antipasto, a platter of cold meats and marinated vegetables, just as it is in America. Rustic restaurants are popular again in Italy, and most pride themselves on making their own salamis, which they hang from the ceiling.

Fresh sausages are rarely eaten on their own. Italians prefer to use them in sauces or to liven starchy dishes like stuffings and rice. Every region of Italy prepares some kind of thin dough with topping, called *pizza, focaccia, schiacciata,* or several other names, and fresh sausage is often sprinkled over the top before the bread is baked. *Cotechino,* a large, salami-sized, delicately spiced fresh pork sausage is also popular throughout Italy, especially in boiled or simmered dishes.

Southern Italians created those robustly flavored foods with which most Americans are familiar. Traditional southern dishes include grilled fresh sausages, onions, and peppers; lasagne with sausage in it; and tomato and sausage sauce. Napolitano and Sicilian fresh sausages are the sweet ones widely available here, while Calabrese sausages are the hotter kind. Eggplant baked with sausage or salami is common, as is roasted poultry with a fresh sausage, ham, dried fruit, and bread stuffing.

There are many southern salamis. The thin pork and beef Napolitan salami is heavily spiced with red pepper. *Soprassata* was originally headcheese, but now it refers to large, round, smooth-textured, dried or smoked sausages. Dried Basilicata and smoked Calabria salamis are famous throughout Italy. Sicilian beef rolls are stuffed with hard-boiled eggs and both salami and fresh sausage, while smoked mozzarella cheese comes with a length of spicy dried pepperoni sausage inside.

Southern breads often made with sausage are pizza and *calzone* and *panzarotti,* baked or fried savory turnovers. There's also a Napolitan Easter bread called *casatiello* filled with cheese and salami. Pastas, like the large tubes of cannelloni, also enclose fresh sausage, usually mixed with ricotta cheese or spinach.

Central Italian cooking tends to be fairly simple, although there are some particularly odd liver sausages made with sugar. Because people from all over Italy have moved to Rome, restaurants there represent every region and many cities and towns. Fresh sausages or pepperoni are often added to many pasta dishes like the very spicy Roman *all'arrabiata* and *paglia e fieno,* green and white pasta with cream sauce.

Other areas in central Italy have their own specialties. Abruzzi pork salami, one of Italy's finest, is served with garlic toast, tomatoes, basil, and perhaps some cheese as an hors d'oeuvre. Fresh sausage- or salami-stuffed mushrooms are also popular appetizers. The word for pork butcher, *norcino,* comes from Norcia or Nursia, an ancient town known for its excellent pork and pork sausages. In Rome, pizza and focaccia, sometimes with sausage on top, are often eaten for breakfast.

Tuscany and Emilia-Romagna, north of Rome, are responsible for some of Italy's most interesting sausages. The most well-known are: cotechino; *zampone*—the skin from a pig's leg stuffed with the same ingredients in cotechino; a pork and wild boar salami; a pork, tomato, and mozzarella sausage; and the huge, pink, smooth, smoked *mortadella.* Salamis from this area include the large *Tuscan;* the small, lightly seasoned *Parma;* the round, smoked *Sugo; finocchiona* with fennel seeds; and *salamini di cinghiale,* dried wild boar sausages sold covered with oil. Fried fresh sausages, accompanied by sautéed greens like rapini or combined with black-eyed peas in tomato sauce, are often served with crisp, flat bread similar to pizza. Soft breads are folded over to enclose fresh sausage, salami, or mortadella.

In northwest Italy, fresh sausages are more common than salamis, although the latter are also eaten. *Peverada,* dating back to medieval times, mixes crushed *luganega* sausage and chicken livers in a creamy sauce served on poultry. Fresh sausages are also served with polenta, a cross between corn pudding and corn sticks, or with rice rather than bread or pasta. The area's German-influenced hearty soups, stews, and braised sauerkraut often include Italian luganega or German wurst. *Canederli,* fluffy bread and sausage or salami dumplings similar to those in Germany, are also served in soup or with tomato sauce.

Northwestern Italy has been influenced by France and Switzerland and fresh sausages in thick soups are also common. Blood sausages, not popular in most of Italy, are common in this area. Genoa pork, veal, and garlic salami is one of Italy's most famous exports, but Milano pork, beef, and garlic salami is more popular in Italy. Novara's delicate, soft *salami d'la duja* and Turin's dried cotechino are equally good. On the Italian Riviera, all of these are served as a part of an antipasto that might also include shellfish, marinated vegetables, and fish salad. Country antipasto is salami, raw beans, and Sardo cheese.

Piedmont grows some of Italy's best rice, and risotto is very popular in the northwest. So are polenta and focaccia, and all three can have sausage cooked with them. Braised veal shanks are sometimes garnished with fried luganega. Even Torino breadsticks are baked with salami in them.

Bollito Misto

Ordering bollito misto in an elegant Italian restaurant is a complete floor show. The waiter wheels up a large domed cart, then opens it to reveal separate compartments, each containing one kind of meat surrounded by hot stock. You choose which meats you want and the waiter or a chef will cut as much of them as you like. You will, invariably, end up with too much on your plate, since it all looks so good. Mostarda di Cremona, a mustard oil-based fruit condiment available in Italian delicatessens, and spicy tomato sauce are sometimes served with this, while green sauce and pickled Italian vegetables are a must.

It's a wonderful dish for a large winter dinner party or a casual buffet, and it's extremely easy to make. If you're serving it at a sit-down dinner, carve the meats before you bring them to the table. If it's a buffet, carve a couple of slices of each, then let everyone help himself. Serve a meatless first course, such as pasta with white clam sauce. The bollito needs no accompaniment except a bottle of Barolo or red Burgundy. Almost any dessert is appropriate, but I like rice pudding in pretty, individual bowls and delicate cookies such as tuiles.

- 1 2-pound piece of beef brisket
- 2 veal shanks
- ½ calf's head (optional)
- 1 onion, roughly chopped
- 1 onion, halved and stuck in cut sides with 4 cloves
- 2 carrots, thickly sliced
- 2 celery stalks with leaves, thickly sliced
- 1 green pepper, seeded, roughly chopped
- 1 bay leaf
- 1 large cotechino sausage (about ¾–1 pound), or 1 pound Fresh Garlic Sausage links (page 24)
- 1 small chicken, cut into serving pieces
- 12 small new potatoes (about 1½ pounds)
- 12 pearl onions, peeled and left whole
- 1 recipe Green Sauce (see next page)

Place the beef, veal shanks, calf's head, onions, carrots, celery, green pepper, and bay leaf in a large pot, cover with water, and bring to a boil. Turn heat to low and simmer for 30 minutes. Skim several times.

Add the cotechino, if used (not the garlic sausage) to the pot and simmer for 1 hour more. Add the chicken and cook for another 30 minutes. Add the potatoes, pearl onions, and small garlic sausages (if substituted for the cotechino) and cook for another 30 minutes. Strain off the broth and save for some other meal. Arrange the sliced meats and the vegetables on a large platter and serve, moistened with a little stock, accompanied by the green sauce.

Serves 12

Green Sauce

♦ ***Salsa Verde***

Although this sauce is always served with Bollito Misto, it's also good with other foods. Pour some on top of an omelette or serve it with grilled pork chops or sausages.

- 3 tablespoons red wine vinegar
- ½ cup olive oil
- ½ cup plus 2 tablespoons finely chopped fresh parsley
- 8 cornichons, finely chopped
- 6 anchovies, mashed
- 1 large garlic clove, crushed then minced
- Pinch of black pepper
- 1 teaspoon mustard, preferably Dijon
- 1 teaspoon red vermouth or other red wine

Place all the ingredients in a large jar with a lid. This can be made a few hours in advance and stored at room temperature until you're ready to use it. Shake well just before serving.

Country Pizza Pie

♦ ***Pizza Rustica***

This traditional country dish is more like a quiche than the pizza we're familiar with. Pizza may date back to ancient Greece, since the Romans learned a great deal about breadmaking from the Greeks. This dish is found throughout Italy, and, like quiche, it's an easy standby for lunch or supper. Serve a salad with vinaigrette dressing first, then the pizza with any light white wine, followed by fresh or baked fruit.

. . . .

1¾ cups unbleached all-purpose presifted flour
1 teaspoon salt
½ cup diced cold lard or butter
Cold water (about ⅛–¼ cup)
2 ounces finely chopped prosciutto or other ham
10 ounces thinly sliced salami, cut into ½″ squares
¾ pound smoked mozzarella or provolone cheese, roughly chopped
¼ cup freshly grated Parmesan cheese
1¼ cups ricotta cheese
¼ cup heavy cream
4 large eggs
Pinch of white pepper
1 teaspoon minced fresh oregano, or ½ teaspoon crumbled dried
½ teaspoon minced fresh rosemary, or ¼ teaspoon crumbled dried
1 large egg, lightly beaten

Preheat the oven to 400°. Mix together the flour and salt in a large bowl or your food processor, add the lard or butter, and mix with a fork or process until it's very crumbly and beginning to stick together. Add just enough water to make a firm dough. Form one-third of the dough into a ball, wrap in plastic, and refrigerate. Roll the remaining dough out into a circle large enough to fit into a 9½″-diameter springform pan 2″ to 3″ high. Fit the dough into the pan and refrigerate.

Toss the prosciutto, salami, and cheeses in a large bowl. Mix together lightly the heavy cream, 4 eggs, pepper, oregano, and rosemary, then fold into the prosciutto mixture.

Remove the pan and the ball of dough from the refrigerator. Brush the interior of the pie shell with some of the beaten egg. Pour in the contents of the bowl.

Roll the unused dough into a circle just large enough to fit inside the pan. Lay the circle on top of the filling. Roll down the dough rising above the top and crimp the edges of both pieces of dough to seal them well. The top should look like a shallow dome. Brush the top with beaten egg and place the pie in the oven. Bake for 1 hour until nicely browned. Let it cool for at least 30 minutes, then remove the whole pie from the pan. Serve it warm or at room temperature.

Serves 8

SOUTHERN ITALY

Basic Italian Sausage

♦ ***Salsiccie***

To turn this sweet Napolitano and Sicilian sausage into the hotter Calabrian version, add ½ to 1 teaspoon cayenne. This sausage can be used in almost any dish requiring fresh sausage. Unfortunately, many American makers of Italian-style sausages overdo the fennel, so use restraint. I love the sausage in lasagne or tomato sauce, or crumbled, cooked, and mixed into egg bread dough just before it rises for the last time.

¼ cup red vermouth or other semi-dry red wine
2 teaspoons sugar

1 teaspoon minced fresh thyme, or ½ teaspoon crumbled dried
1½ teaspoons fennel seeds
2 teaspoons salt
½ teaspoon coarse black pepper
1 teaspoon crushed red pepper
2 pounds pork with some fat, coarsely ground

Prepared hog casings

Mix together the wine, sugar, thyme, fennel, salt, and peppers, then knead them into the pork. Stuff the mixture firmly into prepared hog casings and tie off in 4″ to 6″ lengths. Prick any air holes with a pin. These can be refrigerated for 3 days or frozen for 3 months before being fried or added to other recipes.

Makes approximately 2 pounds raw sausage

Sausage, Onions, and Peppers

♦ ***Salsiccie, Cipolla, e Peperoni***

This method creates wonderfully slightly charred onions and peppers just like the kind you get from street carts in New York City and southern Italy. It's amazing how something so easy can be so good. I developed the technique after reading how Paul Prudhomme makes blackened redfish. The pot will smoke like crazy when you add the sausages to it, so make sure all your doors and windows are open.

Just pile the sausage, onions, and peppers onto a fresh, long, crusty Italian or French roll. You can add condiments like mustard, relish, ketchup, or anything else you can imagine, but, believe it or not, mayonnaise is really good. This is very messy, so save it for family and very close friends.

- 1 pound fresh sweet, hot or Basic Italian sausage links (page 96)
- 1 onion, cut into ⅛″-thick slices
- 1 green pepper, seeded, halved crosswise, then cut into ⅛″-wide strips
- 2 tablespoons fresh rosemary, or 1 tablespoon crumbled dried
- 6 crusty Italian or French rolls

Bring some water in the bottom of a steamer to a boil over high heat. Place the sausage, onions, and peppers on a lightly oiled rack and steam for 15 minutes. Cut the sausage into 2″-long pieces.

Place the rosemary in a cast-iron Dutch oven and heat the pot over high heat, about 10 minutes, until it's so hot it begins to smoke. Add the onion slices and cook, turning once, until they are beginning to char on both sides. Remove and set aside. Cook the peppers the same way, then remove and add to the onions. Add the sausages to the skillet and brown all over. Return the onions and peppers to the skillet and mix well, then divide amongst 6 rolls.

Serves 6

BASILICATA

Pasta with Sausage and Cheese Sauce

♦ ***Pasta alla Zampognaro***

This southern Italian dish is also popular in Abruzzi, where there are still many shepherds, and in Rome, where people gather in restaurants for midnight pasta suppers. A *zampognaro* is someone who plays a reed pipe or bagpipe, and the name is also used for the shepherds of Abruzzi, who play the pipes in

Rome at Christmas. The connection between the shepherds and this dish, however, seems to be lost.

Serve this as a first course, preceding grilled fish and sautéed zucchini with butter sauce. You don't want anything creamy for dessert since you've used ricotta cheese with your pasta, so melon and perhaps a few cookies are perfect. I like a semi-dry red wine, like Lambrusco, with the pasta.

- ½ pound small twisty pasta, such as rigatoni, penne, or shells
- 3 tablespoons olive oil
- ½ pound skinned fresh sausage, such as Luganega, sweet or Basic Italian (page 110 or 96), crumbled
- 1 pound ricotta cheese
- 2 tablespoons unsalted butter
- ½ teaspoon salt
- ½ teaspoon black pepper
- ¼ teaspoon crushed red pepper
- Freshly grated Parmesan cheese

Bring a large pot half filled with water to a boil. Stir in the pasta and cook according to package directions until al dente.

While the pasta is cooking, make the sauce. Heat the oil in a large skillet and sauté the sausage, constantly mashing it with a fork to crush it well, over medium heat for 2 minutes. Mix in the ricotta and butter and stir until the butter is melted. Add the salt and peppers and mix well. If the pasta isn't ready yet, turn off the heat, cover the skillet, and let it sit on the burner. Drain the cooked pasta, then stir it into the skillet of sauce. Serve with the grated Parmesan on the side.

Serves 4

CAMPANIA

Chicken and Sausage in White Wine Sauce

♦ ***Pollo alla Casalinga***

"Casalinga" means "home-style," an appellation given to simple dishes. I always keep a large plastic bag in the freezer into which I toss bones, giblets, and any other leftover pieces from various poultry dishes like this one. When the bag is full, I take the frozen contents out and throw them into a pot, add an onion, a couple of leafy celery stalks, a carrot or two, and cold water to cover them, but no salt and pepper, since I prefer to add them to the final recipes. I then freeze the cooked stock in 1-cup portions. That way I usually have homemade stock whenever I need it, and I don't have to worry about it being too salty.

This is so easy to make and so good that I often make it for company when I'm pressed for time. I start the meal with pasta with gorgonzola sauce or polenta made with cheese. The chicken should be accompanied by steamed or sautéed garlicky green vegetables such as broccoli or spinach. You need a dry white wine, like Verdicchio, for the chicken. For dessert, ricotta cheesecake is perfect.

¼ cup dried porcini (cepes), or ⅓ cup roughly chopped fresh mushrooms
1 cup hot chicken stock, homemade preferable but canned acceptable
1 4–5-pound chicken
5 tablespoons olive oil
1 pound sweet or Basic Italian Sausage (page 96), pricked
2 green peppers, seeded, cut into strips 2" long × ½" wide
2 garlic cloves, crushed then minced
½ cup white vermouth or other dry white wine
2 teaspoons minced fresh rosemary, or 1 teaspoon crumbled dried
½ teaspoon salt
⅛ teaspoon black pepper

If you are using the dried mushrooms, soak them in the stock for 30 minutes, then remove and pat them dry. Reserve the stock. Cut the meat from the chicken into approximately 2″ squares. Reserve the bones, wings, and giblets to make stock at a later time.

Heat 3 tablespoons olive oil in a large skillet over medium-high heat. Add the sausages and cook for 2 to 3 minutes, stirring often to turn them, until they're lightly browned. They don't have to be cooked through, however, since they will be cooked again. Add the peppers to the sausages and cook, stirring, for 15 minutes, until lightly browned. Remove the sausages and peppers and drain them on a paper towel.

Begin heating an ovenproof casserole in a very low oven, about 200°. Add the garlic and mushrooms to the skillet and stir for 1 to 2 minutes, until you can really smell the garlic. Add the remaining 2 tablespoons oil, then stir in the chicken. Cook, stirring often, for 3 to 4 minutes, until the chicken is opaque. While the chicken is cooking, cut the sausages into ½″ slices. Add the chicken stock (whether you've soaked the mushrooms in it or not), sausages, peppers, vermouth, rosemary, salt, and pepper to the opaque chicken and mix well. Bring to a boil, then turn heat to low and simmer, covered, for 15 minutes.

Remove the solids with a slotted spoon and place in the heated casserole. Cover with foil and set aside. Turn the heat under the skillet to high and boil down the sauce until reduced by half, about 10 minutes. Pour over the chicken and sausage.

Serves 4

LATIUM

Boiled Cotechino with Lentils

♦ ***Cotechino con Lenticchie***

New Year's Eve in modern Rome would be incomplete without this very simple dish, which dates back to ancient Rome. Lentils with cotechino or other sausages are also served year-round throughout the entire country. Although Italian cotechino is a fresh, large garlic sausage, exported versions from Italy are cured. You can, however, buy very good fresh cotechino made in the United States at Italian delicatessens. These sausages get their unique taste and slightly gelatinous texture from *cotenna,* the pigskin they usually contain. You can substitute Fresh Garlic Sausages for cotechino, adjusting the cooking time to compensate if they're smaller.

This is a rather heavy dish, so you don't need many accompaniments. Start with a tomato, fresh or pickled pepper, mozzarella, and basil salad, then end the meal with a few ice cream–filled profiteroles with chocolate sauce. Surprisingly, a slightly sweet white wine, such as Lacrima Christi, can be served with the sausage.

- 2 tablespoons olive oil
- 1 small onion, finely chopped
- 1 garlic clove, crushed then minced
- 1 cup water
- 2 cups beef or chicken stock
- ½ cup white vermouth or other dry white wine
- 2 celery stalks, roughly chopped
- 2 teaspoons finely chopped fresh basil or oregano, or 1 teaspoon crumbled dried oregano
- 1 bay leaf
- ¾ teaspoon minced fresh rosemary, or ⅜ teaspoon crumbled dried
- ¾ cup lentils, soaked in cold salted water for 2 hours, drained
- 1 1-pound cotechino

Heat the oil in a large skillet over low heat and sauté the onions and garlic for 5 minutes.

While the onion is cooking, heat the water, stock, and wine in a small saucepan until hot but not boiling. Stir the celery and herbs into the skillet, then the lentils. Pour in the heated liquids and bring to a boil over high heat. As soon as you pour the liquids into the skillet, begin bringing a large pot of water to a boil over high heat. When the skillet contents come to a boil, turn heat to low and simmer, covered, for 1¼ hours.

As soon as you've begun simmering the lentils, add the cotechino to the pot of boiling water and turn heat to low. Simmer, uncovered, for 1 hour, then remove and skin the sausage. Cut it into 1″ slices. After the lentils have simmered the 1¼ hours, add the sliced cotechino. Cover the pot and simmer for 15 minutes more. Remove the lentils and cotechino with a slotted spoon and arrange decoratively on a platter or individual plates.

Serves 4

NORTHERN ITALY

Cornmeal Pudding with Sausage

♦ ***Polenta con Salsiccie***

The northern Italians must be the most patient people in the world, since their favorite dishes, like risotto and polenta, require long, slow cooking. Freshly cooked polenta is eaten on its own or with any of a number of savory toppings. Then, after it has cooled, it's sliced and fried in butter, perhaps for breakfast the next day. Though you can now buy a machine to stir your polenta, the method below works just as well as the traditional continual, exhausting stirring. Each region adds its own individual touches. The substitution of tomato liquid for some of the water in this recipe is my heretical addition. I find it makes the finished dish much tastier, but some people might find the tomato taste a little too much for breakfast.

Begin your meal with a rich beef broth or a fish soup, then serve the polenta and sausages. Accompany the dish with a strong red wine like an Italian Barolo or California Zinfandel. Serve something creamy for dessert like profiteroles or zabaglione.

- 1 tablespoon olive oil
- 1 onion, finely chopped
- 1 pound sweet or Basic Italian Sausage (page 96), cut into 2″ pieces with a serrated knife
- 2 cups roughly chopped drained canned plum tomatoes, liquid reserved
- 3 cups liquid from canned tomatoes
- 5 teaspoons fresh oregano, or 2½ teaspoons crumbled dried
- Salt and pepper to taste
- 1 cup water
- 2 cups milk
- 2 cups yellow cornmeal
- ¼ cup finely chopped fresh Italian parsley

Heat the olive oil in a large skillet. Add the onion and sausages and cook, turning the sausages a few times until evenly browned, for 10 minutes over low heat. Add the drained tomatoes, 1 cup of their liquid, the oregano, salt and pepper and mix well. Simmer, uncovered, for 45 to 60 minutes, stirring occasionally.

While the sausages are cooking, heat the water, milk, and 2 cups of the tomato liquid in a large saucepan over high heat. As soon as it comes to a boil, turn heat to low. Immediately begin adding the cornmeal in a light, steady stream, whisking constantly. Wear long mitts since the mixture will probably spatter after most of the cornmeal has been added. As soon as all the cornmeal is mixed in, begin stirring with a wooden spoon. Stir the polenta constantly for the first 5 minutes. Then stir it for about 1 minute, relax for the next 3 minutes, stir for 1 minute, relax for 3. Follow that schedule until the cornmeal begins to leave the sides of the pan. Then stir constantly until it comes away cleanly. The cornmeal should have cooked for about 30 minutes. Remove from the heat immediately and pour into 6 large serving bowls.

As soon as the polenta is in the serving bowls, remove the sausage and tomato mixture from the heat. It doesn't matter whether it's been cooked for 45 or 60 minutes, since the exact thickness of the tomato sauce isn't critical. Stir the parsley into the tomatoes. Make an indentation in each mountain of polenta and place the sausage mixture in it. Serve immediately.

Serves 6

EMILIA-ROMAGNA

Mortadella

The ancient Roman version of this large sausage was made with myrtle berries, hence its name, but they were replaced by peppercorns when those became fashionable. People either find mortadella insipid and bland or they consider it a gastronomic height. This version, somewhat spicier than store-bought American mortadella, is closer to the authentic Italian sausage. Mortadella is the pride of Bologna, and the Bolognese use it in many different dishes. It's added to savory appetizer fritters, meatloaf, pasta stuffings and sauces, sautéed and gratinéed vegetables, and Genoa's incredible tortas—savory pies with vegetable and cheese fillings. If you like cold mortadella, slice it thickly and serve it as part of an antipasto.

Use the largest possible casing, such as a beef bladder, or a muslin bag to make this sausage. I used the smaller 3½"-wide hog bung casings to minimize smoking time, but commercial versions range from 6" to wider than 1'.

12 ounces pork fat, preferably unsalted fatback
34 ounces lean pork, roughly chopped
1 large garlic clove, crushed then minced
1 teaspoon ground mace
¼ teaspoon ground cloves
2 tablespoons salt
3 tablespoons white vermouth or other dry white wine
¾ teaspoon liquid smoke (optional)
1 teaspoon coriander seeds
½ teaspoon aniseed
½ cup unsalted pistachio nuts
1½ teaspoons whole peppercorns

Prepared beef bladder, hog bung casing, or a muslin bag

Cut 3 ounces fat into ¼″ cubes. In a food processor fitted with the steel blade process the rest of the fat with the meat, in batches, until completely smooth. Mix together the garlic, mace, cloves, salt, wine, and liquid smoke (if used), and process or beat into the meat until mixed well. Fold in the cubed fat, coriander seeds, aniseed, pistachio nuts, and peppercorns.

Stuff the sausage mixture into the prepared casing and tie off into 1 large sausage. Make sure there are no translucent spots in the casing or it will tear during cooking. Prick any air holes. Smoke the mortadella at 275° for 4 to 12 hours, depending on the thickness, until the internal temperature reaches 170°. You can also bake it for 5 hours at 200° on a rack on a baking sheet. Refrigerate for 1 to 2 weeks, or freeze for up to 3 months.

Makes approximately 3 pounds raw sausage

Cappelletti and Tortellini

These two dumplings are almost exactly the same, with only one difference; in Florentine cappelletti the dough begins as a square; Bolognese tortellini are originally circles. Legend has it that these were modeled on the navel of either Venus or a woman whose cook was in love with her. They're traditionally served in clear soup, preferably a capon stock, on holidays, or with various sauces that won't overwhelm the fairly delicate filling.

I go a little crazy when I make these since they freeze so well. I just freeze the ones I'm not going to use right away, making sure they don't touch, on lightly oiled baking sheets, then toss them into plastic bags when they're hard. That way I can take out just as many as I need and cook them straight from the freezer. These can take several hours to form, since there are so many, but I usually make them while sitting in front of the television set. That way I can rationalize watching a soapy miniseries or an evening of sitcoms. You can, of course, divide the recipe and make less, but they're so good you might be sorry.

I usually toss the tortellini with steamed slivered green vegetables, then top them with a butter, cream, and Parmesan sauce or with warmed fresh tomatoes, olive oil, and Parmesan. Serve the tortellini with a salad, and have cannolis for dessert. The wine you drink will depend on the sauce.

- 8 large eggs
- ⅓ cup heavy cream
- 4⅔ cups unbleached all-purpose presifted flour
- 2 tablespoons unsalted butter
- ½ pound boneless, skinless chicken breast, coarsely ground
- ¼ pound pork with some fat, coarsely ground
- ⅜ teaspoon finely chopped fresh sage, or ¼ teaspoon crumbled dried
- ½ pound Mortadella (page 105), very finely chopped
- ¼ pound prosciutto, fat and rind removed, finely chopped
- ½ cup ricotta cheese
- 1 cup freshly grated Parmesan cheese
- ¼ teaspoon grated nutmeg
- Salt and white pepper to taste

Whisk together 7 eggs and the heavy cream, then stir them into the flour. Turn the dough out onto a lightly floured board and knead for about 10 minutes, until it is elastic and blisters begin to form. Wrap in plastic and store in the refrigerator while you make the filling.

Melt the butter in a large skillet over low heat, then add the chicken, pork, and sage. Cook, constantly crumbling the meats with a fork, until the pork has completely lost any redness. Remove the contents with a slotted spoon and place in a large bowl. Stir in the Mortadella, prosciutto, ricotta, Parmesan, nutmeg, salt, and pepper. Let cool. As soon as it's reached room temperature, stir in the remaining egg.

Roll out about one-twentieth of the dough to a thickness of about 3/16″. Keep the rest wrapped in the plastic. Cut it into about twenty-four 1″ squares or 1″-diameter circles. Place ⅛ to ¼ teaspoon meat mixture in the center of each. Fold the top part of the dough over, on the diagonal if you've made squares, and press to seal. The edge of the top of the dumpling should not be even with the bottom; the bottom should stick out just a bit. Take the two corners of the dumpling on the ends of the folded-over side and press them together, leaving a hole in the center. The best way to do that is to wrap them around your little finger. The sealed sides of the dumpling will curl up slightly, but that's what they're supposed to do. Check the dumplings for cracks in the dough and just press the cracked edges together to reseal. Continue until all the dough and filling are used up. If you want to stuff these in front of the television, roll out all the dough at once and place the sheets, separated by waxed paper, on a board to carry them into the TV room.

To cook fresh dumplings, drop them into a large pot of boiling water and boil for 6 to 7 minutes, until the dough is tender. Dried ones will take almost 20 minutes. If you're not using them within a day, set them out on a mesh drying rack, not touching, until they're no longer sticky. You'll need to turn them a couple of times. Then store in a plastic bag in the refrigerator for up to a week.

Makes approximately 480

Stuffed Veal Breast

♦ ***Vitello Ripieno***

Most regions in Italy stuff veal, one of their favorite meats, and every cook has a favorite combination of meats and vegetables for the stuffing. This version is cooked both in Emilia-Romagna and in Venice. Using both Mortadella and fresh sausage, rather than all fresh sausage, keeps the stuffing from overwhelming the taste of the veal.

I usually begin this meal with a tomato, saffron and fish soup, then serve rice, sautéed spinach with onions, and a chilled red Lambrusco with the veal. Fresh fruit and Italian cheese are the perfect dessert.

1 2-pound veal breast with bones, a pocket slit lengthwise
3 slices of Mortadella (page 105)
3 ounces skinned Luganega or other fresh Italian sausage (page 110 or page 96)
3 tablespoons finely chopped onion
2 tablespoons dry bread crumbs
3 tablespoons chopped fresh parsley
¼ teaspoon minced fresh rosemary, or ⅛ teaspoon crumbled dried
¼ teaspoon minced fresh oregano, or ⅛ teaspoon dried
⅛ teaspoon salt
Pinch of black pepper
1 tablespoon pignoli (pine nuts)
1 large egg
2 teaspoons plus 1 tablespoon olive oil
1 tablespoon white flour mixed with pinches of salt and pepper
2 tablespoons salted butter
3 tablespoons white vermouth or other dry white wine
1 tablespoon white flour
6 tablespoons chicken stock, homemade or canned

Preheat the oven to 350°. Place the veal breast on your work surface and lay the slices of mortadella along the bottom of the inside of the pocket. Mix together the fresh sausage, onion, bread crumbs, herbs, salt, pepper, pignoli, and egg, then stuff the pocket with it. The pocket should end up gaping open, showing the stuffing. Pack the stuffing in as tightly as possible. Brush the veal with 2 teaspoons olive oil, then rub with the seasoned flour.

Place the veal on a rack in a roasting pan, such as a round cake rack in a Dutch oven. Place in the oven and bake for 1 hour and 40 minutes (50 minutes per pound of unstuffed veal.) If the stuffing starts bulging out, gently push it back in. As soon as the egg sets, the stuffing will keep its shape. Right after you put the veal in the oven, melt the butter and mix with 1 tablespoon wine. Baste the veal with the butter mixture about every 10 minutes, starting after the first 20 minutes.

Remove the rack with the veal on it from the pan and drape the veal with foil to keep it warm. Place the pan on top of the oven over low heat and stir in 1 tablespoon olive oil and 1 tablespoon flour. Scrape the bottom of the pan to deglaze it. Stir for 2 to 3 minutes, until well mixed, then stir in the stock and remaining 2 tablespoons wine. Stir constantly for another 3 to 4 minutes, until thickened. Slice the veal so that everyone gets some veal and some stuffing, and serve the sauce poured over it.

Serves 4

Northeast Italy

Luganega

The name for this sausage comes from *lucania,* the ancient Roman word for sausage derived from the highly favored Lucanian variety made in southern Italy. Unlike southern Italian fresh sausages, and the ones found in America, it doesn't contain the strong-tasting fennel. It's traditionally a long, narrow sausage, but I've used the wider hog casings because they're easier to find. Do use the narrower sheep casings if you can find them. Luganega is used to stuff veal and pasta dumplings, in pasta sauces, and with polenta or risotto. You can substitute any good, fresh pork sausage for luganega, and I like to substitute luganega for fresh pork sausage in many American recipes.

- 26 ounces pork with some fat, coarsely ground
- ½ cup freshly grated Parmesan cheese
- 6 tablespoons white vermouth or other dry white wine
- 1 garlic clove, crushed then minced

1 tablespoon minced fresh oregano, or 1½ teaspoons crumbled dried
½ teaspoon salt
⅛ teaspoon white pepper

Prepared hog or sheep casings

Knead together the pork and Parmesan. Mix together the wine, garlic, oregano, salt, and pepper, then knead them into the pork.

Stuff the mixture firmly into the prepared casings. You can either make very long sausages or tie them off in 4″ to 6″ lengths. Prick any air holes with a pin. Luganega can be refrigerated for 3 days or frozen for 3 months.

Makes approximately 2 pounds raw sausage

Tuna Sausage

♦ ***Polpettone di Tonno***

One of the first rules of Italian gastronomy is that fish and cheese don't go together. This Venetian dish is one of the exceptions. Italians use tuna in several kinds of sausages, but this is my favorite. Whether you use American or imported Italian tuna, don't use water-packed since it has much less flavor. You can use the more expensive albacore tuna, but I like the stronger taste of light tuna.

This is a perfect brunch or lunch dish, since it's not very heavy and it must be made in advance. Serving a green salad with a vinaigrette dressing alongside the sausage adds a nice contrast in flavors and textures. You can either eat the sausage as is or spread it on crusty Italian or French bread and top it with fresh or sun-dried tomatoes. I like a fairly fruity white wine with the tuna, such as Est! Est!! Est!!!.

- 1 12½-ounce can of chunk light tuna
- 2 anchovy fillets
- ¼ teaspoon finely chopped fresh rosemary, or ⅛ teaspoon crumbled dried
- ¼ cup fine dry bread crumbs
- 5 tablespoons freshly grated Parmesan cheese
- 2 large eggs
- ¼ teaspoon black pepper
- ⅛ teaspoon grated nutmeg
- 1 teaspoon dry mustard
- Mayonnaise
- Chopped fresh basil, dill, or fennel (optional)

Drain the tuna and mash it with the anchovies, rosemary, and bread crumbs using a fork or a potato masher. You can also use a blender or a food processor. Beat, blend, or process in the cheese, eggs, pepper, nutmeg, and mustard.

Place the tuna mixture in the center of a double thickness of cheesecloth large enough to enclose the sausage. Then pat into a 9″-long compact sausage shape. Roll the sausage in the cheesecloth, and tie both ends of the cloth closed with string. Tie a piece of string around the center of the sausage if the cheesecloth is gaping there, but be careful not to squeeze the sausage out of shape.

Place the sausage in a large pot (at least a 10″ diameter). Cover with cold water and bring to a boil over high heat. Immediately turn the heat down to low and cook, covered, for 30 minutes. Place a heatproof plate or smaller pot cover on top of the sausage to weight it down if it rises to the surface.

After the sausage has poached for 30 minutes, turn off the heat and let the sausage cool in its cooking liquid. Carefully lift the cooled sausage from the liquid and gently peel off the cheesecloth. Refrigerate, wrapped in plastic wrap, if you aren't going to serve it right away. It can be stored in the refrigerator for 24 hours.

To serve, cut the sausage into 6 slices and arrange, overlapping, on a long serving dish or platter. Pour mayonnaise, preferably homemade, in a pretty design over the sausage and sprinkle with the fresh basil, dill, or fennel.

Serves 6

Cotechino Wrapped in Veal

♦ ***Involtino di Cotechino***

There are several dishes in Italy in which meat encloses a sausage, and this is a Venetian version. There really is no substitute for cotechino in this recipe. Unless you have a very sure hand, ask your butcher to prepare the veal for you. He should slice it, without cutting all the way through, accordion-fashion, so that it opens up into a long, very thin piece of veal. Then have him pound it to even it out. You want the piece of veal slightly longer than the cotechino in one direction and wide enough to overlap itself by almost 2″ when it's wrapped around the cotechino in the other. The veal will shrink as it cooks, so allow for that. But even if it cracks in some places, you can always garnish each slice so that a crack doesn't show.

Begin your authentic Venetian dinner with marinated or baked and stuffed artichoke hearts. Serve polenta, sautéed spinach, and a red Valpolicella alongside the veal, then finish with a flourless chocolate cake.

1 1-pound cotechino
¾ cup dried porcini (cepes) mushrooms, soaked in ½ cup hot water for 15 minutes, then drained and liquid reserved
¾ pound veal scaloppine in one piece
2 ounces thinly sliced prosciutto
1 tablespoon white flour seasoned with a pinch of white pepper
3 tablespoons unsalted butter
½ cup finely chopped onion
1 celery stalk, finely chopped
¾ cup chicken or veal stock
¼ cup white vermouth or other dry white wine

Bring a large pot of water to a boil, add the cotechino, and turn heat to low. Simmer, uncovered, for 1 hour, then remove and skin the sausage. Reserve ½ cup of the poaching liquid.

Roughly chop two-thirds of the mushrooms, and finely chop the rest. Spread the veal out and cover with the prosciutto slices. It's all right if the prosciutto overlaps. Then scatter the roughly chopped mushrooms over the prosciutto. Place the cotechino on top and loosely roll the veal around it. You don't want to wrap it too tightly, since the veal shrinks during cooking. Tie the veal in place with a couple of pieces of string. Pat the flour onto the veal.

Heat the butter in a skillet slightly larger than the cotechino. Sauté the onion and celery over medium-low heat for 5 minutes, until the onion begins to wilt. Add the veal-wrapped sausage and brown lightly all over. Scatter the finely chopped mushrooms around it, then pour in the stock, wine, the reserved poaching liquid, and the mushroom soaking liquid. Simmer, uncovered, for 1 hour without letting it boil. Turn it once after the first 30 minutes.

Remove the meat and let it rest, loosely covered with foil, while you prepare the sauce. Boil down the liquid in the skillet over high heat until it's reduced by half. That should take about 10 minutes. Slice the meat with a sharp knife and serve the slices, slightly overlapping, on a platter with the pan juices and mushrooms poured over.

Serves 8

Northwest Italy

Focaccia with Sausage

♦ ***Focaccia con Salsiccie***

Like pizza, focaccia is one of Italy's oldest breads. Italians eat focaccia for breakfast and snacks throughout the day. You can top it with whatever you have handy—tomatoes, garlic, salt, leftover sautéed vegetables, any kind of cheese, tomato sauce, salami, strips of leftover meat or poultry, or pesto. There are even sweetened ones, topped with dried fruits. This version is as crowded as the topping should be. Many Italian delicatessens sell excellent homemade fresh or frozen pizza dough, which is the same as focaccia dough, so you can skip much of the rising process. Just roll it out and let it rise for the last 30 minutes.

Since this is a snack, and has tomatoes which distort the taste of wine, I usually drink a glass of whatever wine I have open in the refrigerator, red, white, or rosé. They're all fine with this dish.

. . . .

½ package (½ ounce) dry yeast
¼ teaspoon white sugar
¼ cup warm water (about 95°)
2¼ cups unbleached all-purpose presifted flour
½ cup room temperature water (70°)
3½ tablespoons extra-virgin olive oil
2 teaspoons salt
⅔ cup ricotta cheese, with the liquid squeezed out
½ pound skinned Luganega or other fresh Italian sausage (page 110 or 96)
3 very ripe plum tomatoes, seeded, drained, and finely chopped
2½ teaspoons chopped fresh rosemary, oregano, and/or sage
¾ cup dried porcini (cepes), soaked in hot water for 15 minutes, then roughly chopped

Dissolve the yeast and sugar in the warm water and let sit at room temperature for 10 minutes, until it's fairly frothy. Place ¾ cup flour in a large bowl. Stir the room temperature water into the yeast mixture, then pour the yeast and water into the bowl containing the flour. Whisk to combine well, then set aside, covered with a towel, in a warm, draft-free place for 1 to 1½ hours, until doubled in bulk.

When doubled, stir 1½ tablespoons oil and 1 teaspoon salt into your dough, then mix in the remaining flour. Knead the dough on a lightly floured board until the dough becomes smooth and elastic and blisters begin to form, about 10 minutes. Place it in an oiled bowl, cover with a towel, and let it rise for another 1½ hours, until doubled in bulk. When doubled, divide the dough in half and roll each into a circle with about an 8″ to 9″ diameter. Cover them and let them rise for another 30 minutes, until puffy.

Preheat the oven to 425°. If you're using a baking stone, heat it in the oven according to the manufacturer's instructions. If you're using baking sheets, place the circles on them as soon as they're rolled out. Spread your fingers out as widely as possible. Using the tips of your fingers, but not your nails or you'll go all the way through, gently press several rows of indentations into the dough. This creates pockets to catch the filling. If you're using a baking stone, remove it from the oven, sprinkle cornmeal on it, and place the dough on it now.

Scatter half of the ricotta, sausage, and tomatoes on top of each circle, then gently press them into the dough. Brush them with the remaining 2 tablespoons olive oil, then sprinkle on the remaining teaspoon salt, the herbs and the mushrooms. Place the focaccia in the oven and immediately lower the heat to 400°. Bake for 20 to 25 minutes, until the crust is golden.

Makes 2

Risotto with Sausage

♦ ***Risotto con Salsiccie***

Rice is as popular in the north as pasta is in the south, and Italy grows over 40 different kinds. In Genoa the popular northern risotto is often cooked with sausage. Arborio rice, from the Po Valley, is the only rice that makes a perfect risotto, because you can cook it until it's creamy, but every grain of rice remains distinct and firm inside. Most Italian delicatessens stock arborio, or you can mail-order it from many gourmet stores.

The name *risotto* is the diminutive and affectionate term for *riso,* "rice." Contrary to its reputation, risotto is not difficult to make. Unlike other starchy dishes, such as pasta, risotto is occasionally served as a side dish rather than as a first course. You can add any good stock to leftover risotto to form a rich, filling soup. Italians cook risotto with everything from strawberries to herbs, which turn it respectively pink or green, so feel free to experiment. I serve this risotto as a first course, followed by a veal dish, a salad, and Italian cheeses. Serve a dry white wine, like a California Chardonnay, with the risotto.

2½ cups chicken stock, homemade preferable but canned acceptable
6 ounces skinned sweet or Basic Italian Sausage or Luganega (page 96 or 110), crumbled
1 tablespoon olive oil
2 tablespoons unsalted butter, room temperature
½ cup finely chopped onion
1 shallot, finely chopped
1 cup arborio rice
3 tablespoons dry white wine or vermouth
Salt and white pepper to taste
3 tablespoons freshly grated Parmesan cheese

Bring the stock almost to a boil in a saucepan, turn off the heat, cover, and leave on the unlit burner. Fry the sausage in its own fat in a large skillet over low heat until all the redness is gone. Drain on paper towels.

In the uncleaned sausage skillet heat the oil with 1 tablespoon butter over low heat. Add the onion and shallot and sauté for 5 minutes. Add the rice and stir for 2 minutes to completely coat the rice with the oil. Pour in the wine and stir for 1 to 2 minutes, until it's completely absorbed by the rice. Pour in ½ to ¾ cup of the hot stock and stir well. Cook over very low heat, uncovered, until the liquid is absorbed. Stir often, especially when the liquid is almost completely absorbed. You'll know the liquid is gone when you can't see any more white lines (formed by the liquid and rice starch) on the bottom of the skillet when you stir.

Continue adding the hot stock, ½ to ¾ cup at a time, stirring each time until it's completely absorbed. When all the liquid is used, the rice should be creamy, not dripping or dry. Stir in the salt and pepper and the remaining tablespoon butter, then the sausage and cheese. Serve immediately.

Serves 4

CHAPTER
5

Germany

and Switzerland

The Germans, who love all kinds of meat, produce some of the greatest white and liver sausages in the world. While the contents of the sausages vary from region to region, as a rule they are served in similar ways throughout the country.

Originally every farmer and his family made their own sausages, smoking those they could not eat right away. Now professional slaughterhouses kill and cut up the animals to the farmer's specifications. Various kinds of sausages including liverwurst, stuffed stomachs, and headcheeses use every part of the animal. A good German butcher produces at least 100 kinds of fresh, smoked, cooked, and dried sausages. The range of colors, shapes, and sizes of the sausages decked throughout butcher shops is staggering. Pork, veal, and beef are all used in sausages, sometimes alone but usually combined. Estimates of the number of different German sausages range from 300 to 1,500.

Butchers categorize sausages in four groups. *Bratwurst* is not only a kind of sausage, but also refers to all fresh sausages. *Bruhwurst* are smoked and can be eaten as is or broiled, grilled, or fried. The cured, smoked *rohwurst* and the cooked, smoked *kochwurst* are eaten cold, spread on bread or cut into thin slices. German sausages tend to be mildly spiced, but heavily smoked, some to the point of reaching a leathery texture similar to jerky. Smooth sausages with cubes of meat or fat, blood sausages made with large pieces of meat, and velvety liver sausages are just a few examples of the interesting textures Germans appreciate.

Germans stop for a quick sausage snack throughout the day, beginning with a late breakfast around 10:00 A.M. It's usually a piece of bread, a hot *wurst* (the German word for sausage) or a selection of sliced sausages, and perhaps a glass of beer. Other traditional sausage accompaniments are mustard, white radishes, and pretzels. Children and those who can't leave their offices bring a sausage sandwich with them for their morning break.

Lunch can also include several kinds of salami-type sausages, but restaurants that grill fresh sausages over charcoal are also popular. Family lunches are often thick soups or stews with sausages in them, while at dinner cold sliced sausages and bread are set out for everyone to help himself. If company is coming to dinner, the cold-cut selection, called *vorspeisen,* serves as the appetizer. Fried fresh sausages in tart sauces are also common family dishes. In between these meals Germans can buy boiled sausages from street vendors. They can also stop at restaurants attached to breweries for sausages and a stein of beer.

At meals, sausages are accompanied by sauerkraut, potato salad, or a hot potato dish or added to soups, casseroles, or simmered vegetables like lentils. In the colder months large platters of sauerkraut and several kinds of hot smoked or fresh meats are popular.

Most Americans are familiar with Germany's most popular snacking sausages, the delicate, herbed, white sausages such as *bratwurst, weisswurst,* and *bockwurst.* Unadorned steamed sausages are often served with mustard alongside rather than being included in other dishes. White sausages are usually made from veal or veal and pork and lightened with milk or cream. Smoked *pinkel,* one of the only cereal-based sausages, is made from oatmeal or groats moistened with pork fat.

Not content with simple liver sausages, Germans have created a great many variations. Sautéed onions, anchovies, pickled tongue, truffles, pistachio nuts, pork meat, eggs, and milk all give *leberwurst* distinctive flavors. Some, like *braunschweiger,* are smooth and spreadable. Others, like *kassler,* are coarser. All are eaten cold with bread. Some are smoked, while others are only poached. Some leberwurst is made with liver other than pork. *Ganseleberwurst* is a goose liver and truffle sausage, while *kalbsleberwurst* includes both calf and pork liver.

Blood sausages, *blutwurst,* are almost as varied as leberwurst in size, texture, and flavor. Some are smoked and eaten cold, while others are sold raw to be poached, sliced, fried, and served hot. *Blut zungenwurst,* made with pork fat and blood and pickled tongue, is mosaiclike, while *speck blutwurst* reveals solid pieces of pork fat when sliced. Most are made with pig's blood.

Many German pork sausages, which come in every shape from pear-shaped (*birnenformige*) to the very thinnest links (certain kinds of *jagerwurst*), contain coarsely ground meat and are heavily smoked. The resulting hamlike taste is very popular.

Some, like *bierschinken,* have pieces of ham in them. *Knoblauchwurst* are smooth with chunks of meat embedded in them. Smoked pork salamis range from almost round to long, 3-inch wide sticks. There are only a few all-beef or veal sausages. *Frankfurter wurstchen* is the ancestor of our thick, kosher hot dogs. *Regensburger,* or *knockwurst,* are short, wide sausages often grilled. And veal *gschwollne* are atypically skinless grilled or fried sausages.

The majority of German meat sausages contain mixed meats, mostly beef or veal and pork. Of the smoked sausages, some, like *mettwurst* or *teewurst,* are spreadable, while others, like *fleischwurstring* (rings similar to bologna), are sliced. There are also many pork and beef salami-type sausages like *edel,* the mustard-flavored *cervelat,* and the hamlike *plockwurst. Pfeffer plockwurst* is an unusual pepper-covered rectangular sausage.

Although Swiss cuisine has been equally influenced by France and Italy, their sausages are most similar to those of Germany. Fresh, dried, and smoked sausages are made from pork, beef, veal, or a combination. Like those of Germany, platters of a variety of hot or cold sausages are served for lunch or as an appetizer before dinner. Every Swiss canton has its own local sausages, which are included in these assortments along with national favorites. Some sausages, like *landjager* or *schubli,* are dried or smoked until quite chewy, so they can be grabbed and eaten on the run. Beer halls and other restaurants serve both sausage meals and snacks to help the Swiss get through the cold winter days. Headcheese, fresh and smoked cervelat, mettwurst, and knockwurst, similar to those of Germany, are very popular.

Some sausages are served as part of meals. Italian polenta is topped with fried sausage links. Fried sausage and potatoes is a typical family dinner. Swiss bratwurst, made from pure veal, is often rolled into balls rather than stuffed into casings, poached in stock, and served with rice or noodles. The meat can also be baked with sweetbreads in a pastry shell or simmered with kidneys and tomatoes. *Kalberwurst* is another veal sausage, but, unlike German sausages and Swiss bratwurst, it contains bread or cracker crumbs. Quite a few German and Swiss sausages are traditionally found in American butcher shops and delicatessens, since German immigrants often opened shops like these to supply their neighbors with sorely missed sausages.

GERMANY

Bockwurst

For years butchers wouldn't sell bockwurst in the warmer weather since they're so perishable. With modern refrigeration, they're now available year-round. In upstate New York very spicy bockwurst called "white hots" are eaten instead of hot dogs. There is also a larger, redder, coarser beef and pork bockwurst popular in Berlin, and I don't know how these two very different sausages received the same name. Perhaps it's because they both complement bock beer. Serve these as a snack or lunch with German mustard on a sourdough roll and pickled vegetables on the side. While you can serve bock beer, I must confess it reminds me of molasses. I prefer a German lager.

- ½ pound veal, coarsely ground
- ½ pound pork with some fat, coarsely ground
- ½ cup milk
- 1 large egg
- 2 tablespoons finely chopped onion
- 1 tablespoon finely chopped fresh chives
- 2 teaspoons finely chopped fresh parsley
- ¼ teaspoon mace
- ½ teaspoon salt
- ¼ teaspoon white pepper
- 1 teaspoon sugar

Prepared sheep or hog casings

Mix the veal and pork together in a large bowl. Lightly beat the milk, egg, onion, chives, parsley, mace, salt, pepper, and sugar together, then knead into the meats until well combined.

Stuff into prepared sheep or hog casings and tie off at 4″ lengths. Prick any air pockets with a pin.

Poach the narrower sausages for 15 minutes, the wider for 20 minutes. They can be eaten as is, cut into pieces and added to sauce just to heat through, or browned in butter just before serving. The raw sausages can be refrigerated for 1 to 2 days, poached for 3 to 4 days. They can be frozen, raw or poached, for 3 months.

Makes 22 ounces raw sausage

Bratwurst

This may be the most popular sausage in Germany. While usually fresh, there are excellent smoked versions such as *krainerwurst* and the salami-size *geraucherte*. There is also a less common "red" bratwurst, made without milk. Americans fry these, but they are even better barbecued. In Germany *Nurnberger bratwurstglockl*, so small that average eaters order anywhere from 6 to 18, are served at restaurants featuring wood fires to cook them on. Slashed barbecued bratwurst, horseradish mustard, warm German potato salad, really good braised sauerkraut, and a glass of German Riesling or lager is a perfect summer meal. Cold poached apples are a simple and delicious dessert.

- ¼ cup white bread with no crust
- ¾ cup milk
- 10 ounces veal
- 22 ounces pork with some fat
- 1 teaspoon salt
- ¼ teaspoon white pepper
- ¼ teaspoon mace
- ½ teaspoon minced fresh marjoram, or ¼ teaspoon crumbled dried
- Prepared hog casings

Soak the bread in the milk for 10 minutes. Then drain, reserving the milk.Grind the bread, veal, and pork in a food processor, in batches if necessary, until emulsified. They can also be coarsely ground in a meat grinder for a more unusual, but still authentic, bratwurst. Stir the salt, pepper, mace, and marjoram into the milk, then stir or process the milk into the meats.

Stuff firmly into prepared hog casings and tie off in 4″ lengths. It is easier to stuff the casings if you let the mixture stiffen, covered, in the refrigerator for 1 to 12 hours, but not essential. Prick any air pockets with a pin.

Poach the sausages for 20 minutes. You can eat them right away, or you can fry them in butter over low heat until browned all over. You can also barbecue them raw. Never fry the sausages until you're ready to eat them. Raw sausages can be refrigerated for 2 to 3 days, poached for 1 week. They can also be frozen, raw or poached, for up to 3 months.

Makes 2½ pounds raw sausage

Liverwurst

♦ ***Leberwurst***

There's a world of difference between the sometimes dull commercial kinds and this spice-laden homemade version. If your casing splits, as mine did the first time I tried this and cooked it at too high a temperature, immediately take the pan off the heat. Since this usually happens near the very end of the cooking time, you can then place the liver mixture into a crock and call it pâté. Either way it's a perfect canapé and sandwich spread. I often add lightly browned onions to it for a *zweibelwurst*. If you aren't going to serve a large number of people, make smaller ones and freeze them. You can also hot-smoke it for about 5 hours.

- 1 tablespoon milk or cream
- ½ teaspoon light corn syrup
- 2 teaspoons salt
- ¼ teaspoon white pepper
- ½ teaspoon ground ginger
- ⅛ teaspoon grated nutmeg
- ¼ teaspoon ground cardamom
- ¼ teaspoon minced fresh marjoram, or ⅛ teaspoon crumbled dried
- ⅛ teaspoon minced fresh sage, or large pinch of crumbled dried
- Large pinch of dry mustard
- ¼ cup roughly chopped onion
- 1 pound pork liver, roughly chopped
- ½ pound pork with some fat

Prepared cow bung casing

Begin heating a large pot of water to 175° to 180°. In a cup with a spout mix together the milk or cream and corn syrup, then stir in the salt, pepper, spices, herbs, and mustard. Puree the onion, liver, and pork, in batches if necessary, in a food processor. Return all the meat to the processor if you've pureed it in batches. While the machine is running, pour in the milk mixture.

Tie one end of a prepared soaked cow bung casing very tight, then stuff the sausage into the casing. Before you tie the second end, hold the sausage vertically, untied end up. Gently push the sausage mixture toward the bottom until your sausage is 10″ to 11″ long and 3″ wide. You want it compact, but you don't want to overstuff it. Tie the second end well.

Gently place the sausage in the hot water. Put a heatproof plate or a glass pot lid on top of the sausage to keep it submerged if necessary. The sausage will have lowered the temperature of the water to about 160°. You don't want the temperature to rise above 170°, so turn the heat down as low as possible. If the heat rises despite that, pour in about ½ cup cold water whenever the heat hits 171°.

Poach the sausage for 1½ hours. The internal temperature will reach 160° when it's completely cooked through and the juices will run clear when you prick it. Remove the sausage from the hot water, preferably with tongs, and plunge it into cold water. Let it cool to room temperature, then wipe dry and refrigerate overnight. It will keep in the refrigerator for 1 to 2 weeks, but shouldn't be frozen.

Makes 1½ pounds raw liverwurst

Bread Sausages

♦ ***Brotwurstel***

Like other cereal-based sausages, these were eaten in hard times or at the end of winter when there wasn't very much meat. They can either be absolutely delicious or deadly dull, depending on the quality of the bread you use. I prefer the blackest possible pumpernickel since it has the strongest taste, but very good rye bread will give you equally good, lighter sausages. Double-smoked bacon can be found at German delicatessens. I serve the sausages instead of stuffing alongside poultry, or for a winter breakfast alongside eggs.

2 tablespoons heavy cream
6 tablespoons meat or poultry stock, plus enough to poach the sausages
¼ teaspoon caraway seeds (if none in the bread)
¼ teaspoon fennel or celery seeds
3 cups very coarsely crumbled rye or pumpernickel bread
½ cup tightly packed diced salt pork, blanched for 15 minutes and drained, or ½ cup diced smoked bacon, preferably double-smoked
¾ cup roughly chopped onion
1 large egg
¼ teaspoon black pepper
2 tablespoons unsalted butter or bacon, sausage, or other meat drippings
Prepared hog casings

Mix together the cream, 6 tablespoons stock, caraway seeds (if used), and fennel or celery seeds in a large bowl, then stir in the bread. Let sit in the refrigerator for 1 hour.

Put the bacon or salt pork and the onions in a large skillet, turn the heat to medium-low, and sauté for about 10 minutes until the onions are just beginning to brown. Pour the contents into the bread bowl and stir well. (Don't clean the skillet since you'll use it again soon.) Stir in the egg and mix well. Stuff loosely into prepared hog casings and tie off into 4 sausages. Prick each sausage in 2 or 3 places.

Poach the sausages for 1 hour. When ready to serve them, melt the butter or drippings in a skillet over low heat and fry the sausages until lightly browned all over. The poached sausages can be refrigerated for 1 week, but will develop a mushy texture if frozen.

Makes 1¼ pounds raw sausage

Sausage Dumplings

♦ ***Wurstknödels***

*B*read-based dumplings are a staple in Germany and Austria. Farmers used to bring the cold dumplings to the field with them to keep up their energy. They could eat with one hand while continuing to work with the other. I prefer the dumplings hot, served in soup or poached, then fried in butter or drippings until crispy on the outside and soft on the inside. If you're serving the dumplings in soup for a first course, follow them with roast chicken or broiled fish, sautéed spinach, and meatless Himmel und Erde. Try baked chocolate pudding for dessert and a good Liebfraumilch with the meal. You might want to make a couple of extra dumplings to fry the next morning and serve with eggs.

½ pound white bread or rolls, torn into pieces about 3″ wide or 2″ square

2 large eggs, lightly beaten
2 tablespoons sugar
¾ cup milk
2 slices of smoked bacon, preferably double-smoked, finely chopped
2 tablespoons salted butter
¼ pound smoked sausage, finely chopped
¼ cup finely chopped onion
6 tablespoons white flour
2 teaspoons finely chopped fresh parsley
⅛ teaspoon white pepper
¼ teaspoon crushed caraway seeds
½ teaspoon minced fresh marjoram, or ¼ teaspoon crumbled dried

Begin bringing a large pot half-filled with water to a boil. In a large bowl toss the bread with the eggs, sugar, and milk until all the liquid has been absorbed, then set aside.

Fry the bacon in a large skillet over low heat until it leaves a thin film of fat. Stir in the butter, sausage, and onions, turn heat to medium, and cook for about 10 minutes, stirring often, until the onions are golden. Remove the contents of the skillet with a slotted spoon and mash into the bread with a wooden spoon. Stir in the flour, parsley, pepper, caraway seeds, and marjoram.

With damp hands or 2 damp spoons form 6 egg-shaped dumplings. As soon as each is formed, drop it into the boiling water. When the last dumpling has been added, begin timing them. Boil for 15 minutes until the center is dry and fluffy, not sticky.

Makes 10

Munich-Style Mustard for Sausages

♦ ***Münchener Wurstsenf***

This mustard is both hot and sweet to perfectly complement hot or cold German sausages. You can also serve it alongside other meats, add it to salad dressings, use it in deviled eggs, or brush it on meats or poultry before grilling them. If you like really hot mustard, stir some freshly grated or drained prepared horseradish into the mustard ½ teaspoon at a time, tasting constantly. Homemade mustards are lovely gifts, and you can make an assortment by varying the proportion of seeds to dry mustard, adding different herbs, and changing the texture.

- 6 tablespoons mustard seeds, black preferable but yellow acceptable
- ½ cup dry mustard
- ¼ cup cider vinegar or white wine vinegar
- ½ cup water
- ¾ cup pale German beer, preferably Bavarian, or dry white wine
- ¼ cup brown sugar
- 1 teaspoon salt
- 2 medium garlic cloves, finely chopped
- ⅛ teaspoon ground allspice
- ⅛ teaspoon ground cloves
- ¼ teaspoon fresh tarragon, or ½ teaspoon crumbled dried
- 1 tablespoon honey

Place the mustard seeds and dry mustard in your food processor or blender. In a small saucepan bring the vinegar, water, ¼ cup beer or wine, sugar, salt, garlic, allspice, cloves, and tarragon to a boil. Immediately pour the liquids into the processor or blender and process or blend for about 1 minute until well mixed. Let the mixture sit for about 3 hours so the flavors blend. Then stir in the honey and the remaining ½ cup beer or wine. Process the mustard again until it's the desired texture (I prefer it just slightly grainy).

It can be stored in a lidded jar in the refrigerator for several months. If it becomes dry, stir in a little white wine to moisten it.

Makes just over 1½ cups

Homemade Sauerkraut

It's impossible to think of sausages without sauerkraut, and if you don't have a European grocer near you who sells homemade kraut, you should make your own. It's very simple, and it tastes much fresher and much less salty than the bottled variety. You can be very imaginative, adding juniper berries, caraway seeds, or other flavorings. I prefer to add the seasonings after the sauerkraut has fermented since I might want to use different seasonings for dishes from different countries. You must allow 2 to 4 weeks for the cabbage to ferment.

Sauerkraut is one of the most important staples in all of central and eastern Europe and Alsace, still often the only vegetable available during winter months in some countries. Food historians are still debating whether the Germans learned to make sauerkraut from the ancient Romans or whether it came with the Mongols who invaded Europe 700 years ago. They are said to have learned it from the Chinese, who lived on it while building the Great Wall. Sauerkraut can be eaten raw, braised or baked, alone or mixed with meats and/or vegetables.

2 pounds green cabbage, shredded
2 tablespoons coarse, kosher, or sea salt
1 teaspoon sugar

Toss the cabbage, salt, and sugar together in a large bowl. Let sit at room temperature for 10 minutes to 1 hour, until the cabbage has released a lot of water. If there's not enough brine, the sauerkraut will go bad before it ferments.

Place the cabbage in a large glass or glazed earthenware jar or cannister, first squeezing the liquid from each handful back into the bowl. After you've added all the sauerkraut, push it down with your fist to make it more compact. Then pour in enough brine to cover the cabbage by at least 1″. Insert a small plate large enough to cover all the cabbage inside the jar to keep the cabbage submerged. Drape the cannister with a cloth and let sit at room temperature for 2 to 4 weeks. Check the plate after a couple of days. If it's floating on the brine, place another plate on top of the first to create more weight. It's ready when it tastes like sauerkraut.

Makes about 5 cups

Pureed Potatoes and Apples with Blood Sausages (Heaven and Earth)

♦ ***Himmel und Erde***

The *himmel* (heaven) is the apple, while the *erde* (earth) is the potato. Some versions include pureed turnips, but I like this better. Although it tastes like mashed potatoes, the puree has an underlying sweet aftertaste that is intriguing.

Himmel und erde, without sausage, can be served with rich poultry like goose and duck. If I have any left over, I chop up the fried blood sausage or any other cooked sausage I have on hand, mix it into the puree, then form it into patties. I then press an even layer of bread crumbs onto the patties, place them on a baking sheet, dot with garlic butter, and bake for 15 minutes in a preheated 350° oven. They make a lovely appetizer, a wonderful side dish, or even a terrific breakfast.

- 2 pounds potatoes, peeled, cut into ½″ cubes
- 1½ pounds crisp apples, peeled, cored, cut into ½″ cubes
- 2 tablespoons unsalted butter
- 1 pound Blood Sausage links (page 31), poached, thinly sliced
- 1 tablespoon sugar
- 1 teaspoon salt
- ¼ teaspoon white pepper
- 2 tablespoons unsalted butter at room temperature, diced

Bring a large saucepan of water to a boil, drop in the potatoes and boil for about 25 minutes, adding the apples after the first 10 minutes.

While the apples and potatoes are boiling, melt the 2 tablespoons butter in a skillet and fry the sausage slices until lightly browned on both sides. Turn the heat off under the skillet, cover it, and let it sit on the burner.

Drain the potatoes and apples, then mash or whisk them together with the sugar, salt, pepper, and diced butter until smooth. The whisk attachment of an electric mixer is perfect for this. Don't use the food processor, however, since it will make the mixture gummy. Serve the sausage slices laid on top of the potato and apple puree.

Serves 6

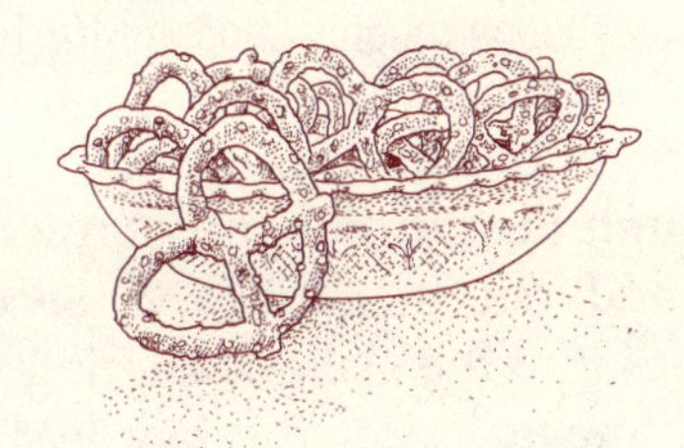

Sausages in Curried Tomato Sauce

♦ ***Curry Tomatensosse***

Traditionally this is made with small red bockwurst, but I like it just as well with the sausages suggested below. Surprising as it may sound, curry powder is very popular in Germany. This appetizer or snack food, sold by Berlin street vendors, is most popular at night after theater or a movie. You can eat it hot dog–fashion, hollowing out a crusty roll to make a container. The sauce is also good over noodles or vegetables.

If the sausage is cut into bite-size pieces, this can be served as the appetizer at a dinner party, garnished with fresh coriander. Follow it with a simple grilled main course like leg of lamb or veal, steamed asparagus, and roasted new potatoes. You can serve any dessert, but cheese-filled strudel is my favorite. Serve a spicy wine like Alsatian Gewürztraminer with the sausages.

- 2 tablespoons unsalted butter
- 1 pound Bockwurst, Bratwurst, knackwurst, or Pork Hot Dogs (page 123, 124, or 326), each pricked in 2–3 places
- 3 cups seeded and chopped canned tomatoes, liquid reserved
- ¾ cup juice from canned tomatoes
- 1 bay leaf
- 1 teaspoon salt
- ¼ teaspoon black pepper
- ½ teaspoon paprika
- 1 tablespoon curry powder or Garam Masala (page 286)
- 1 onion, halved, stuck with a total of 3 cloves
- 2 tablespoons roughly chopped fresh parsley

Heat the butter in a large skillet and fry the sausages over medium-high heat until lightly browned all over. Remove the sausages and cut them into 2" slices. Set them aside. Stir the tomatoes into the skillet, scraping the bottom to mix well. Stir in ½ cup tomato juice, the bay leaf, salt, pepper, paprika, curry powder, and onion. Mix well, bring to a boil over high heat, then turn heat to low and simmer, uncovered, for 20 minutes.

After the sauce has simmered for 20 minutes, remove the onion and bay leaf, then add the sausages and remaining ¼ cup tomato juice. Stir well, then simmer for 30 minutes more. Sprinkle with parsley and serve.

Serves 8 as an appetizer, 4 as a main course

Bratwurst in Beer Gravy

♦ ***Bratwurst in Bier***

This Berlin favorite is a great way to use up any leftover flat beer. If you can't find or make bratwurst, you can use any fresh pork sausage, including sweet or hot Italian or American breakfast. Sausages with gravy are delicious with any kind of potatoes—roasted, French fried and mashed potatoes, or Himmel und Erde. The next time you need to throw a dinner together quickly, try this dish, French Sausages in White Wine Sauce, or English Sausages Braised in Ale, all variations on the same theme. All you need with the sausages and potatoes is a crisp green salad with a creamy dressing and ice cream and cookies for dessert. Serve the same kind of beer you've cooked with or a simple white wine, such as a California Chenin Blanc.

. . . .

8 white Bratwurst (about 2 pounds) (page 124), each pricked in 3–4 places
1 tablespoon unsalted butter
6 pearl onions, or ½ small yellow onion, minced
2 cups pale German beer
¼ teaspoon salt
Pinch of black pepper
1 tablespoon white or brown sugar
2 tablespoons white flour
1 tablespoon minced fresh parsley

Bring a large pot of cold water to a boil, turn heat to low, gently drop in the bratwurst, and cook for 5 minutes. Carefully remove the sausages with tongs and pat dry. Discard the cooking liquid.

Melt the butter in a large skillet, preferably cast iron, add the sausages and onions, and cook over low heat until the sausages are browned on all sides. The onions can get slightly brown, but they shouldn't burn. Remove the sausages. Pour in the beer, scraping the bottom of the pan, then stir in the salt, pepper, and sugar. Bring to a boil over high heat, reduce heat to low, return the sausages to the skillet, and simmer, covered, for 20 minutes. Turn the sausages after the first 10 minutes.

Remove the sausages again and set aside. Boil the beer sauce for 5 minutes to reduce it. Sprinkle the flour onto the sauce, then whisk until smooth. Stir or whisk for about 3 minutes, until the gravy is thickened. Return the wurst to the skillet and heat through. Sprinkle with parsley and serve.

Serves 4

Bratwurst in Currant Sauce

♦ ***Bratwurst in Korinthesosse***

Germany is known for slightly exotic dishes combining fruits and meats. Here the sweet and sour sauce balances the rich taste of the sausage. You can use any fresh white sausage such as French Boudins Blancs, Smoked Poultry Sausage, or German weisswurst or Bockwurst. It's such an easy recipe, but it turns simple sausages into an interesting supper. I serve a cucumber salad, mashed potatoes or meatless Himmel und Erde, and beer with the sausages. For dessert, I like two or three kinds of cheese.

1 cup cold water
½ cup pale beer or white wine
¼ teaspoon salt
Pinch of white pepper
¼ teaspoon ground allspice
1 bay leaf
1½ teaspoons sugar
4 teaspoons lemon juice
1 lemon or lime leaf (optional)
4 white Bratwurst (about 1 pound) (page 124), each pricked in 2 or 3 places
1½ tablespoons currants or raisins
2 tablespoons unsalted butter
2 tablespoons white flour

Bring the water, beer or wine, salt, pepper, allspice, bay leaf, sugar, lemon juice, lemon or lime leaf (if used), bratwurst, and raisins or currants to a boil over high heat in a very large saucepan or pot. Turn heat to low, cover, and simmer for 25 minutes. Turn off the heat, remove the bratwurst and the leaves, cover the pot, and let sit on the unlit burner.

Melt the butter over medium heat in a large skillet while you pat the sausages dry. Brown the sausages all over in the butter, then remove and drain on paper towels. Turn heat to low and add the flour to the butter, stirring constantly, for about 5 minutes, until golden brown. Gradually stir in the sausage cooking liquid, then simmer, stirring often, for about 5 minutes, until thick and smooth (except for the currants).

While the sauce is cooking, slice the sausages into ½″-thick pieces. Stir the sausages into the smooth sauce and cook for another 30 seconds to heat the sausages through.

Serves 2

Simmered Barley and Sausage

♦ ***Eintopf***

One-dish meals are as popular in Germany as they are in every other cold climate. Eintopfs are either soups or stews, served in both homes and casual restaurants, and are best with a view of the snow so you can see how the warm eintopf shields you from the cold outside. Eintopfs are also made with potatoes instead of barley, and cabbage, turnips, dried beans, and other winter vegetables. I love the taste of barley and the way it absorbs flavors like stock. The best wine for an eintopf is a tart German apple wine. For an unorthodox starter, I like fried mozzarella cheese with marinara sauce, then warm stewed fruit for dessert.

- 3 slices of smoked bacon, preferably double-smoked, roughly chopped
- 1 large onion, roughly chopped
- 2 celery stalks, roughly chopped
- 2 carrots, roughly chopped
- 1½ cups rinsed and drained pearl barley
- 1½ teaspoons fresh thyme, or ¾ teaspoon crumbled dried
- 4 cups chicken stock, homemade preferable but canned acceptable
- ½ teaspoon salt (if stock is not salty enough)
- ¼ teaspoon black pepper
- 4 old-fashioned thick Hot Dogs (page 326) or knackwurst (about 1 pound), cut into 2″ slices

Cook the bacon in a large pot over medium heat for about 2 minutes, until some of the fat has been rendered. Stir in the onions and celery and sauté over low heat for 10 minutes. Stir in the carrots, barley, thyme, stock, salt, and pepper and bring to a boil over high heat. Turn heat to low, cover, and cook for 1 hour. Don't uncover the pot to check the barley during this hour since it's being both simmered and steamed.

After the barley has cooked for the hour, uncover the casserole and stir in the sausages. Cook for another 30 minutes, stirring every 10 minutes to prevent the barley from sticking to the bottom.

Serves 8

Potato and Sausage Salad

♦ ***Wurstsalat***

German potato salad makes a nice change from the American mayonnaise-laden version. Cooking the onions in the stock before adding them gets rid of the sharp raw onion taste, but if you like raw onions you can just chop and add them without boiling them first. This is better than American potato salads for picnics, since it won't spoil as quickly. I use Kielbasa, as many Germans do, in the salad, but you can use any smoked sausage. If you make the salad without the sausage in it, you can serve it alongside fried or grilled sausages accompanied by a green vegetable such as braised cabbage.

- 6 cups chicken or beef stock, homemade preferable but canned acceptable
- 2 medium onions, halved
- Salt to taste (depending on saltiness of stock)
- 1 pound (about 8) small red boiling potatoes
- ½ cup diced celery or celeriac
- ½ cup diced smoked garlic sausage

¼ cup vegetable oil
3 tablespoons wine vinegar
2 teaspoons prepared mustard, preferably German (page 129)
1 tablespoon minced fresh parsley
¾ teaspoon minced fresh thyme, or ⅜ teaspoon crumbled dried
⅛ teaspoon black pepper

Bring the stock and onions to a boil over high heat in a large saucepan. Add the salt and potatoes. If there isn't enough stock to cover the potatoes, add more. Once the pot returns to a boil, cook for 20 minutes, until the potatoes are tender. Remove the potatoes with a slotted spoon and peel as soon as you can. (If you tear the skin off in large enough pieces, you can toss the pieces of skin with butter and bake them in a hot oven until crisp for a wonderful snack.)

Remove the onion from the stock with a slotted spoon. Halve the peeled potatoes lengthwise, then cut into ¼"-thick half-circles. Return the potatoes to the stock and let them cool to room temperature. Cooling them in the stock lets them absorb a lot of wonderful flavor. When the potatoes and stock are room temperature, remove the potatoes with a slotted spoon and place in a salad bowl with the celery and sausage. Remove the onions with a slotted spoon, finely chop, and add to the bowl.

Place the oil, vinegar, mustard, parsley, thyme, pepper, and 2 tablespoons of the stock into a jar, screw on the lid, and shake well. Pour over the potatoes and toss gently, being careful not to crumble the potatoes. Serve warm or at room temperature.

Serves 6

SWITZERLAND

Gypsy Salad

◆ ***Zigeunersalat***

The name probably comes from the fact that the salad is full of bright colors. Try to find a German or Swiss salami or cervelat, since their intensely smoky taste makes the salad unusual. It's also good with Italian salami, but more common. Serve the salad at lunch or supper, preceded by a cup of thick soup such as fish or corn chowder. Accompany the salad with rye or pumpernickel bread or rolls and butter and a glass of beer. For dessert try cream puffs, eclairs, or ice cream–filled profiteroles.

½ pound smoked salami, cut into ½" cubes
½ cup thinly sliced dill pickle
¼ cup pearl onions, parboiled for 5 minutes, drained, and thinly sliced
1 large very ripe tomato, diced
¼ pound Gruyère cheese, cut into ½" cubes
2 eggs, hard-boiled, thinly sliced
2 tightly packed cups of salad greens torn into bite-size pieces
¼ cup fresh peas, parboiled for 2 minutes, drained, or thawed frozen
2 anchovy fillets, minced
¼ cup vegetable oil
2 tablespoons red wine, sherry, or cider vinegar
1½ teaspoons prepared mustard, preferably German (page 129)
Pinch of paprika
2 teaspoons minced fresh dill (optional–don't use dried)
⅛ teaspoon salt
⅛ teaspoon white pepper

Toss the salami, pickles, onions, tomato, cheese, eggs, greens, peas, and anchovies in a salad bowl.

Place the oil, vinegar, mustard, paprika, dill, salt, and pepper in a jar, screw on the lid, and shake well. Immediately pour over the salad and toss well. Refrigerate, covered, for 2 to 24 hours. Toss again just before serving.

Serves 4

CHAPTER
6

The Austro

Hungarian Empire

Austria, Hungary, Czechoslovakia, Yugoslavia, and Romania have a common cultural and political heritage. They were all constantly being invaded by Europeans, Turks, and nomadic Asians such as the Tatars, and in peacetime they were the crossroads for traders traveling between Asia, Africa, and Europe for hundreds of years. Their food reflects all these influences and, coupled with native ingredients such as superior pork and the ever-present sour cream, unique and marvelous cuisines have evolved.

The American frankfurter may sound like it comes from Germany, but it might also be a descendant of Czech *parkys*, Austrian *wurst*, or Hungarian *virsli*. People in this part of the world snack on these sausages all day long, especially at the 10:00 A.M. morning break and in late afternoon. In sausage-only restaurants patrons order the number they want—the sausages come in pairs—then eat them standing up, with a glass of beer. Hungarians use horseradish or mustard on these sausages, respectable Czechs only mustard, while Austrians often eat them unadorned.

Although many of the sausages of these countries are unique, the way they are served is very similar. Cold cuts are served first thing in the morning. Thick soups with sausage in them are served midday or in the evening. They all excel in braised or baked dishes combining sausages (usually smoked), other kinds of meat, vegetables, and often sauerkraut. Open-faced sausage sandwiches are often served to after-dinner guests. A sign of the sausage's popularity is the prevalence of very realistic, imitation sausages made from chocolate, dried fruits, marzipan, or cookie dough, which delight both children and adults.

In Hungary, sausages made with organ meats, blood, or cereals like bread or cornmeal are called *hurka*, while *kolbász* is a sausage made mostly from muscle meat, usually pork, although pork and beef are sometimes combined. Hungary's famous dried salami, made with large pieces of pork, is eaten throughout central and eastern Europe. Debrecen in southeastern Hungary produces outstanding spicy, strongly smoked pork sausages. Nearby Gyula is known for smoked, sweet paprika-flavored sausages tied into a ring.

In the not-so-distant past when every town had its fall pig-killing day, the day ended with a huge dinner where many different kinds of sausages were served. The pigs' livers, lungs, and heart were transformed into the spicy *májas hurka* or combined with rice and some of the head meat in *fehér hurka.* The blood was cooked, then thickened with bread and a small amount of ground pork for *véres hurka.* Caul-wrapped meat sausages were baked. Seasonings, like lemon peel, caraway seeds, and invariably paprika, enhanced both large and small pork link sausages. Hungarian Jews, who didn't eat pork, stuffed goose-neck skin with ground goose meat, goose liver, onions, and bread, then fried it in goose fat and served it hot or cold. Non-Jews added pork and hard-boiled eggs to the goose sausages and fried them in lard.

Historically, Hungary has used every meat possible in sausages, including poultry, fish, shellfish, and game. Now Transylvania, which has been absorbed into both Romania and Hungary, produces the more unusual sausages. Transylvanians make smoked pork brain and millet or rice sausages and a short, wide veal sausage. The Armenians who emigrated to Transylvania brought recipes for roasted kid's stomach stuffed with kid and veal and for blood sausage.

Romanian cuisine is very close to Yugoslavian. Both countries like skinless sausages, possibly introduced from India or the Middle East. Salami and other dried sausages are included in hors d'oeuvres selections similar to the Middle Eastern meze or Italian antipasto. Sausages, similar to those of Hungary, are made from liver, blood, pork, and/or beef, or lamb for Yugoslavian Moslems. Both Romanian and Yugoslavian restaurants serve a lavish mixed grill, which might include both spicy smoked sausages and skinless sausages.

Austrian cuisine has been equally influenced by Hungary, Germany, the skill of great Austrian chefs, and peasants able to

make delicious meals out of the humblest ingredients. While the Austrian "peasant's feast" combines pork chops, ham, wurst, and sauerkraut, real country people rarely feast that way. They're more likely to eat fried skinless sausages made from pork, beef and bacon, baked tomatoes with sausage stuffing, and smoked sausage slices added to soups. Leftover sauce from a goulash is put to good use, moistening the next day's meal of sausages and potatoes. Real Vienna sausages, which we can only buy canned and usually very gelatinous and unpleasant, are simply wurst stuffed into chipolata casings, tied off into short lengths, and smoked.

The Czechs love their parkys so much, they make several different versions, some shorter and wider, another with bacon, a third with lots of paprika. Unfortunately national factories now produce the parkys, and the recipe being used is one that will offend the fewest people. Many cooks rescue the sausages by surrounding them with a potato dough and baking them. There are still some good country sausages, like the smoked pork or veal *klobásy*; the wide, pork liver, head meat and rice or bread *jaternice*; blood and bread or barley *jelita; bachor,* a blood sausage boiled in a pig's stomach; and *tlačenka,* made with large pieces of pork. For company dinners, a large, smooth, smoked beef and pork sausage called *uzenice* is sliced and fried to form bowls to hold individual hors d'oeuvres or vegetables.

Lemon Sausage

These can be used in any recipe that calls for fresh pork sausage. They're often cooked with eggs, combined with apples in goose stuffing, and added to soups and stew. I especially like these in a sliced potato, hard-boiled egg, and sour cream casserole. You can also top fried sausage patties with tomato sauce and grated cheese, accompanying them with mashed potatoes and a light Hungarian red wine for a simple Transylvanian supper.

. . . .

½ cup white bread with crust, torn into small pieces
¼ cup milk
Pinch of ground cloves
1 teaspoon salt
¼ teaspoon black pepper
½ teaspoon paprika
1 tightly packed teaspoon finely grated lemon peel
1 pound pork with some fat, coarsely ground

1 long prepared hog casing

Preheat the oven to 300°. Mix together the bread and milk in a small bowl, stirring occasionally for 2 minutes to soften the bread completely. Stir in the cloves, salt, pepper, and paprika with a fork. Knead together the lemon peel and pork, then knead in the bread mixture. Stuff into the prepared hog casing, tying off both ends. Prick any air pockets with a pin.

Coil and place on a rack in a roasting pan. Bake for 45 minutes, until juices run clear. The raw sausage can be refrigerated for 2 days, the baked sausage for 1 week. They can be frozen, raw or baked, for 3 months.

Makes approximately 18 ounces raw sausage

Potato and Sausage Goulash

♦ ***Goulasch***

Although goulash was originally Hungarian, it's now common throughout eastern Europe. Some versions of this dish omit the tomatoes, and it's equally good either way. Along with the sour cream, paprika and caraway seeds give goulash an authentic, distinctive taste. (I was once so desperate, having run out of caraway seeds right before company was expected, that I actually sat there and picked seeds out of a loaf of rye bread.)

In eastern Europe this dish is served to family, not to company, because it contains what is considered very little meat. I think that's silly, and my guests have always loved it, especially in winter. Begin your dinner with a spinach and shellfish salad. The goulash doesn't need any accompaniments, although bread is often served alongside. You can serve beer or a Hungarian red Lake Balaton Cabernet, then a flourless chocolate torte for dessert.

- 2 tablespoons lard, bacon drippings, or vegetable oil
- 2 cups roughly chopped onions
- ¼ teaspoon minced fresh marjoram, or ⅛ teaspoon crumbled dried
- 2 teaspoons paprika
- ½ teaspoon caraway seeds
- 1 teaspoon vinegar
- 2 very ripe or canned tomatoes, peeled, seeded, and chopped
- 2 carrots, cut into ½″-thick slices
- 2 pounds boiling, not baking, potatoes, peeled, halved lengthwise, then cut into ½″-thick half-circles
- Salt and pepper to taste
- 3 cups beef stock, homemade preferable but canned acceptable
- 4 Pork and/or Beef Hot Dogs (page 326 and 328), cut into ½″-thick slices
- ½ cup sour cream (optional)

Heat the fat over medium-high heat in a Dutch oven or other large pot. Add the onions and sauté until they're just beginning to brown around the edges, about 6 minutes. Add the marjoram, paprika, caraway seeds, vinegar, tomatoes, carrots, potatoes and stir well until the potato is well coated with the onions and fat.

Stir in the stock, add salt and pepper, turn the heat to high, and bring to a boil, stirring once or twice and scraping the bottom of the pot. Turn heat down to medium-low and boil the goulash for 20 minutes. Stir in the frankfurters and cook for an additional 10 minutes. Add the sour cream, if used, stir well, and immediately remove the pot from the heat. If you're planning to reheat the goulash, bring the sour cream to the table separately and let everyone stir in as much as he likes, since it's difficult to reheat sour cream without curdling it.

Serves 4

Meatloaf

Adding sausage to meatloaf makes it more festive, and it's a dish country people in eastern Europe serve to company. Treat meatloaf with the same respect accorded to French terrines, a very close relative. Something this good shouldn't be looked down on.

I begin the meal with warm goat cheese on a bed of interesting greens. The meatloaf is accompanied by mashed potatoes and large chunks of zucchini brushed with butter and put under the broiler just until heated through. An Alsatian red wine, like Pinot Noir, is just right for the meatloaf, not too formal nor too wishy-washy. For dessert, I serve a pie made with a graham cracker crust topped with frozen chocolate pudding, coffee ice cream, and frozen whipped cream sprinkled with grated chocolate.

- ¾ cup good-quality white bread, torn into pieces
- ½ cup milk
- 1 pound pork with some fat, ground
- 1 pound regular, not lean, ground beef
- 1 large egg
- 1 medium onion, finely chopped
- 1 teaspoon salt
- ¼ teaspoon black pepper
- ½ teaspoon paprika
- 1 tablespoon roughly chopped fresh marjoram, or ½ tablespoon crumbled dried
- 8 strips of smoked bacon
- 1 straight, not curved, piece of Debreceni, Kielbasa (page 173), or other smoked garlic sausage about 1" shorter than the length of your meatloaf pan

Preheat the oven to 350°. Toss the bread with the milk and let it sit until the milk has been absorbed, about 5 minutes. Knead the bread with the pork, beef, egg, salt, pepper, paprika, and marjoram.

Cover the bottom of a standard-size bread pan (8½" × 4½" × 2 ½") with half the bacon strips. Cover with half the meat mixture, then lay the sausage down the middle, leaving a ½" border on either end. Top with the rest of the meat, lightly pressing on it to make the loaf more compact. Cover with the remaining bacon. Bake for 1¼ hours. Pour off any excess fat, then remove the meat from the pan and cut it into thick slices.

Serves 8

HUNGARY

Lecsó

Lecsó is as much a staple of Hungarian cooking as paprika. Similar to the French ratatouille, it's used as the base for many baked or simmered dishes or eaten on its own. Hungarians often can lecsó so they have a constant supply throughout the winter. All you need to do to produce a delicious main course is to brown some meat, add lecsó, a little stock and some seasonings, then braise until the meat is tender. It's also a good soup base, dip, or side dish. If you find you like lecsó, make double the amount here, cooking half of it in a second pot without sausage. Can the extra batch or refrigerate it in a covered jar for up to 2 weeks.

This dish is a perfect family supper, needing only a cup of noodle soup, some bread, a simple dessert like warm cherry strudel, and a glass of beer.

3 tablespoons lard or vegetable oil
3 onions, finely chopped
2 tablespoons paprika
3 pounds green, yellow, and/or red bell peppers, seeded and cut into thin strips
2 26-ounce cans tomatoes, drained well, roughly chopped
2 pounds Debreceni, Kielbasa (page 173), or other smoked garlic sausage, cut into ⅛"-thick slices
¼ cup sugar
Salt and pepper to taste

Heat the fat over medium heat in a Dutch oven or other large pot. Add the onions and sauté for 10 minutes, until they're very wilted. Stir in the paprika, then immediately add the rest of the ingredients. Stir well, cover, and cook over medium heat for 10 minutes. Uncover, stir well, and cook for 20 minutes longer.

Serves 16

Partridge, Cabbage, and Smoked Sausage

♦ ***Fogoly, Káposzta, és Kolbasz***

Game has always been a staple for the Hungarian aristocracy. You can substitute game hens for the partridges if you can find ones small enough. Serve this dish to friends who have a sense of humor, since it appears at first that you're serving cabbage, and only cabbage, as your main course. A wild mushroom soup is an excellent first course. Rice, especially wild rice, baked in timbales goes well with the partridges. Serve an interesting German Riesling with dinner. This calls for an elegant dessert such as *palatschinken*, crepes filled with fruit preserves and sprinkled with toasted nuts and sugar.

1 large head Savoy or Chinese cabbage, halved through the core
2 partridges, each about ½–¾ pound, cleaned, trussed
2 tablespoon melted unsalted butter
Salt and pepper to taste
8 slices of smoked bacon, plus 1 slice roughly chopped
2 ounces smoked Hungarian sausage or Kielbasa (page 173), cut into a total of 8 pieces
1 carrot, thickly sliced
8 pearl onions, peeled
2 cups chicken or other poultry stock, homemade preferable but canned acceptable

Preheat the broiler and broiler pan. Bring a large saucepan of water to a boil, drop in the cabbage halves, and boil for 5 minutes. Drain, rinse until cool, then squeeze out extra water. Detach all the leaves, but leave them whole. Discard the core. Set aside the 4 largest leaves of each half.

Brush the partridges with the melted butter and sprinkle with salt and pepper. Broil them for 10 minutes, 5 minutes on each side. Remove the birds from the broiler and cut off the trussing string. Preheat the oven to 350°.

Wrap each partridge, spiral-fashion, in 2 strips of bacon. Lay one partridge on its side on 2 of the largest cabbage leaves. Cover with 2 other large leaves. Wrap in string so that it looks like a whole head of cabbage. Repeat with the other partridge.

Line a small roasting pan or 3-quart baking dish with the rest of the cabbage leaves. Place "cabbages" on top, lying on their sides. Drape 2 slices of bacon over each "cabbage." Surround them with the roughly chopped bacon, the sausage, carrot, and pearl onions. Pour the stock around the "cabbages" and place the dish in the oven. Bake for 1¼ hours, until the cabbage is tender. Remove the string and serve the whole "cabbages" with the rest of the cabbage and its accompaniments.

Serves 2

Stuffed Cabbage Simmered with Sausage

♦ ***Töltött Káposzta***

Middle Easterners introduced stuffed grape leaves, but since the leaves were often scarce, cooks began using available vegetables like cabbage. Every country, and every cook, has strong preferences as to what goes into the cabbage. Unlike Middle Easterners, Hungarians always use meat, but it can be pork, beef, veal, lamb, or a combination. In some countries the cabbage is soured just like sauerkraut before being used.

Traditionally this dish is served by itself, occasionally with bread. Start with a slightly sweet salad, such as French cucumber salad made with a little sugar, and serve beer with the cabbage.

- 8 large green cabbage leaves
- 2½ tablespoons lard or vegetable oil
- ¼ cup plus 1 medium onion, finely chopped
- ¼ cup rinsed rice, cooked until al dente
- ½ pound regular, not lean, ground beef
- ½ pound pork, ground
- ¼ teaspoon salt
- Pinch of black pepper
- 1 large egg yolk
- Large pinch of dried marjoram
- ½ teaspoon paprika
- 2 tablespoons white flour
- ¼ pound smoked bacon, preferably double-smoked, roughly chopped
- 1½ pounds fresh or Homemade Sauerkraut (page 131), lightly rinsed
- 2 smoked pork chops, each halved
- ½ pound smoked sausage, such as Kielbasa (page 173), cut into a total of 4 pieces
- Unsalted chicken or beef stock or water
- ⅓ cup sour cream

Bring a large pot of water to a boil. Drop the cabbage leaves into the boiling water, boil for 10 minutes, then drain well.

While the cabbage is cooking, heat ½ tablespoon lard or oil in a small skillet over low heat, add the ¼ cup onions, and sauté for 10 minutes, until softened but not browned. Remove the onion with a slotted spoon and toss it with the rice, beef, pork, salt, pepper, yolk, and marjoram.

Place a cabbage leaf with the stem end facing you. Cut out the hard part of the leaf at the stem end, which would break if rolled. Take one-eighth of the filling and place it about ½″ from the end nearest you. Form it into a rectangle, the shorter ends of which are about 1″ from either side of the leaf. Push it into a fairly compact tube. Fold the sides of the cabbage leaf over the filling, then roll the leaf up beginning at the end near you. Make the remaining 7 rolls the same way.

Heat the remaining 2 tablespoons lard or oil in a Dutch oven, preferably cast iron, or any other large heavy pot over low heat. Sauté the remaining onion for 5 minutes, then stir in the paprika, flour, and bacon. Stir for 2 to 3 minutes more. Stir in the sauerkraut until the bacon and onion mixture is distributed evenly throughout the kraut. Turn off the heat, but leave the pot on the burner.

Remove two-thirds of the sauerkraut from the pot. Place the cabbage rolls on the remaining kraut, seam side down, in one layer. Top with the rest of the sauerkraut, then pour in just enough stock or water to come to just below the top of the sauerkraut. Lay the pork chops and sausages on top. Cover, turn heat to low, and cook for 1½ hours. Turn off the heat.

Uncover the pot and hold a mesh colander over it with one hand. With the other hand use a slotted spoon to remove the solids in batches, placing them in the colander. When all the liquid has drained back into the pot, arrange the solids on 4 large plates, evenly dividing the meats and cabbage rolls. When all the solids have been removed, turn the heat to high and stir the sour cream into the liquid. Bring to a boil, turn heat to low, and simmer, stirring often, for 5 minutes or until the gravy is as thick as you like.

Serves 4

TRANSYLVANIA

Beef and Sausage Stew

♦ ***Tokány***

This is considered one of Transylvania's, and Hungary's, greatest dishes. The combination of ingredients creates a stew with a complex, unusual flavor that is extraordinarily good. It's one of those dishes that evolved as people added whatever was available to the kettle. There are many versions of this dish, so feel free to experiment.

If I'm serving this to company, I usually serve smoked salmon or trout canapés with drinks before dinner. Serve the stew with a strong red wine, like the famous Hungarian Eger Bikavér, and *csipetke,* the Hungarian version of spaetzle, or other noodles to absorb the delicious gravy. The best dessert for this meal is cream puffs and eclairs.

. . . .

- ¼ pound smoked bacon, roughly chopped
- 1 onion, finely chopped
- 1 garlic clove, crushed then minced
- 2 green peppers (about ¾ pound), seeded and cut into ½″-wide strips
- ¼ teaspoon paprika
- 1½ pounds flank or skirt steak, cut into 2″–3″-long × ¼″-wide strips
- ¾ cup beef stock, homemade preferable but canned acceptable
- 2 very ripe or canned tomatoes, seeded, drained, roughly chopped
- ¼ cup white vermouth or other dry white wine
- ½ teaspoon minced fresh marjoram, or ¼ teaspoon crumbled dried
- 1 teaspoon salt
- ⅛ teaspoon black pepper
- ½ pound smoked Hungarian sausage, Kielbasa, or Pork Hot Dogs (page 173 or 326), cut into 2″–3″-long × ¼″-wide strips

Heat the bacon in a Dutch oven, preferably cast iron, or other large pot over medium-high heat until some of its fat has been rendered. Turn heat to medium-low, add the onion and garlic, and cook for 5 minutes, stirring occasionally. Add the green peppers and paprika and cook for another 5 minutes, stirring occasionally.

Stir in the beef, stock, tomatoes, wine, marjoram, salt, and pepper. Turn heat to low, cover the pot, and cook for 1 hour, until the meat is tender. Stir in the sausages and cook, uncovered, for another 5 minutes to heat them through.

Serves 8

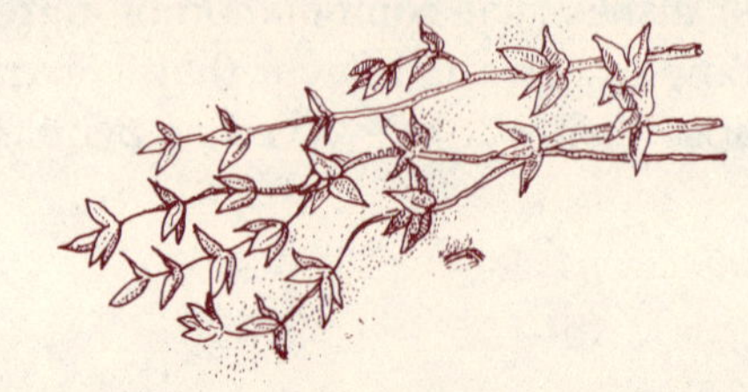

Sauerkraut, Rice, and Sausages

♦ ***Rakott Káposzta***

Pork without sauerkraut seems to be almost heretical in eastern Europe, from Alsace in France to the Asian borders of Russia. There's a good reason for this. By the time this dish has finished cooking, the ingredients have melded to create an entirely new taste.

The rice makes this a complete course, and I usually make it a complete winter meal. It's best accompanied by beer or a spicy white wine like a California Gewürztraminer. Baked apples are an appropriate dessert.

2 pounds fresh or Homemade Sauerkraut (page 131), rinsed and drained
1½ teaspoons caraway seeds
¼ teaspoon black pepper
4 slices of smoked bacon, roughly chopped
1 large onion, roughly chopped
1 teaspoon paprika
1 tablespoon lard or vegetable oil
1 pound spicy fresh sausage, such as Lemon Sausage (page 147), pricked with a pin at 2" intervals
1 cup raw rice
2 cups unsalted or low-salt chicken or meat stock
1 pound boned smoked pork, such as ham, shoulder or chops, cut into 1" cubes
1 cup sour cream

Preheat the oven to 350°. Toss the sauerkraut, caraway seeds, and pepper in a large bowl and set aside.

Place the bacon and onions in a large, cold stove- and oven-proof pot such as a cast-iron Dutch oven. Cook over medium heat for 5 to 6 minutes, stirring often, until the bacon is cooked through but not crisp. Stir in the paprika and mix well. Turn off the heat. Remove the ingredients with a slotted spoon and toss with the sauerkraut.

Turn the heat under the pot to low and stir in the lard or oil. Add the sausages and brown all over. Remove the sausages with a slotted spoon and set aside. Stir the rice into the pot. Stir for about 2 minutes, until the rice is coated well with the fat. Using your slotted spoon, remove 2 spoonfuls of sauerkraut from the bowl and stir into the rice. Pour the stock into the pot and stir well. Cover with one-third of the remaining sauerkraut, top that with the sausages and pork cubes, then add the rest of the sauerkraut.

Cover the pot, place in the oven, and bake for 40 minutes. Then turn up the heat to 450°. Spread the sour cream on top of the sauerkraut, smoothing it with a spatula. Bake, uncovered, for another 15 minutes.

Serves 6

Wrapped Pork Cutlets and Sausages

♦ ***Hargitai Töltött Káposzta***

Wrapping the pork chops elevates this from a simple dish to a dinner party centerpiece. I like to begin the meal with a pasta course, something as unorthodox as cold Chinese noodles in sesame sauce. The main course doesn't need any side dishes except, perhaps, some pickled vegetables and Eger Bikavér wine. Since there's sour cream with the pork, serve something without a lot of cream for dessert. The very chocolate Rigó Jancsi torte is my favorite.

4 1″-thick pork chops
½ cup diced plus ½ cup thinly sliced smoked sausage, such as Kielbasa (page 173)
6 tablespoons raw rice
8 large green cabbage leaves
3 tablespoons lard
1½ cups finely chopped onion
½ teaspoon paprika
½ teaspoon minced fresh marjoram, or ¼ teaspoon crumbled dried
4 teaspoons caraway seeds
Large pinch of salt
Large pinch plus ½ teaspoon black pepper
1 pound fresh or Homemade Sauerkraut (page 131), rinsed well and drained
2 cups unsalted or low-salt beef stock
½ cup sour cream

Bring a large pot of water to a boil. Remove the bones from the pork chops to form cutlets. Set the bones aside, since you'll need them later.

Toss the diced sausage and rice in a bowl and set aside. Drop the cabbage leaves into the boiling water and boil for 3 minutes. Drain the leaves and set them aside.

Heat the lard over high heat in a cast-iron Dutch oven or other large heavy pot. Add the pork cutlets and sear well on both sides. Remove them with a slotted spoon and turn heat to low. Add the onion, paprika, marjoram, and 2 teaspoons caraway seeds and sauté for 2 minutes. Turn the heat off, but leave the pot on the burner. Remove 2½ tablespoons of the onion mixture and add it to the rice bowl. Stir the salt and pinch of pepper into the bowl.

Place 2 long pieces of string on a cutting board, forming a cross. Place two cabbage leaves end to end, with their stem ends overlapping, centered on the string. Place a cutlet in the center of the cabbage leaves and top with one-quarter of the rice mixture. Fold the cabbage leaves over the cutlet to completely enclose the filling, then tie the leaves closed with the string. The package should look like a tied parcel. Repeat with the rest of the cutlets.

Turn the heat under the pot to medium, stir in the sliced sausage, and lightly brown on both sides. Stir in the sauerkraut, remaining 2 teaspoons caraway seeds, and the ½ teaspoon pepper. Turn the heat to low and remove half the sauerkraut. Place the packages and pork bones on top of the remaining sauerkraut, then return the rest of the kraut to the pan. Pour in the stock, cover, and cook for 2 hours.

Remove the packages and the pork bones from the pot and set aside, keeping the packages warm. Turn the heat to high, stir in the sour cream, and bring to a boil. Immediately remove the pot from the heat. Make a nest of sauerkraut on each of 4 plates, then place the packages, with or without the string, in the center of each.

Serves 4

ROMANIA

Grilled Skinless Beef and Pork Sausages

♦ ***Mititei***

These sausages are as ubiquitous in Romania as hot dogs are in America. Vendors line streets with portable charcoal grills, cafés do a brisk business in them, and they can precede the soup course at a formal dinner. Refrigerating the meat mixture for 12 to 36 hours helps the flavors blend. Throw a few sausages on the grill the next time you barbecue, or mix up a batch and freeze on a baking sheet. Place the frozen sausages in a plastic bag and seal tightly. Then, the next time you're in the mood for a hamburger, take a few of these out instead, broil them, and eat with hot peppers and sour pickles. You'll be very pleased you did.

½ pound regular, not lean, ground beef
¼ pound pork with just a small amount of fat, finely ground
3 tablespoons hot beef stock
¼ teaspoon minced fresh rosemary, or ⅛ teaspoon crumbled dried
½ teaspoon minced fresh marjoram, or ¼ teaspoon crumbled dried
1 garlic clove, crushed then minced
1 teaspoon baking soda
Salt to taste
¼ teaspoon black pepper
Large pinch of ground cloves

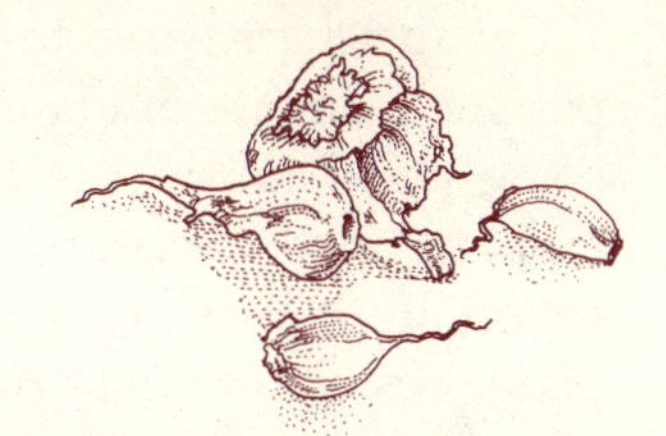

Mix together the beef and pork in a large bowl. Mix together the stock, rosemary, marjoram, garlic, baking soda, salt, pepper, and cloves, then knead them into the meat. Wrap tightly in plastic and refrigerate for 12 to 36 hours.

When you're ready to cook the sausages, divide the meat into 16 pieces. With damp hands, shape each portion of the meat into a 2"-long sausage. If you're cooking these inside, place them on a greased pan and broil fairly close to the heat. If you're cooking them over charcoal, place them in a long-handled, metal wire hamburger holder so that they won't fall into the fire. That way you can also turn all of them over at once. Using either method, cook the sausages for 6 minutes, turning once, until cooked through.

Makes 16

YUGOSLAVIA

Grilled Skinless Beef Sausages

♦ ***Cevapcici***

These are very similar to the beef and pork Romanian Mititei. Some cevapcici connoisseurs insist you need to grind several cuts of beef together to obtain the proper taste and texture, but it seems unlikely that most people, if any, will be able to tell the difference. These were originally grilled over vine cuttings, but now charcoal is most commonly used.

Cevapcici are served with pita bread, chopped raw onion, hot peppers, and tomato salad. I usually slit the bread, spoon in some Ajvar relish (see the recipe in this chapter), raw onions, and chopped tomatoes, then add the sausage. Kids love this, especially if you don't tell them that Ajvar is made from eggplant. It's also perfect picnic food if you bring along a portable hibachi.

1 pound regular, not lean, ground beef
2 garlic cloves, crushed then very finely minced

½ teaspoon paprika
½ teaspoon salt
⅛ teaspoon black pepper
1½ tablespoons white flour

Place the beef in a bowl and knead in the garlic, paprika, salt, and pepper. Divide the meat into 20 pieces. With damp hands, shape each into a 2″-long sausage. Roll them in flour, shaking off any extra. Refrigerate, draped with plastic, for 1 hour, until they're very firm.

These are traditionally placed on flat metal skewers and broiled or grilled over charcoal, turned once, for a total of 6 minutes. I usually place them in a long-handled, metal wire hamburger holder so I can turn all of them together.

Makes 20

Eggplant Relish for Grilled Sausages

◆ ***Ajvar***

This is adapted from either the Indonesian or Malaysian *atjars* or the Indian *aachar,* the word for pickles. There are Asian atjars made from mangoes (popular in South Africa), cauliflower, and many other fruits and vegetables. It's also similar to a Middle Eastern spread called *baba ghanouj*. Ajvar is a terrific dip, a wonderful addition to sausage or grilled meat sandwiches, and a nice gift. It can be eaten at once or stored in lidded jars in the refrigerator for at least 2 weeks. There's also very little oil, less than 1 tablespoon per cup, which makes it less fattening than many other dips.

- 1 large eggplant (about 2 pounds), halved lengthwise through stem end, then stem discarded
- 3 green bell peppers, halved through stem end, then stem and seeds discarded
- 1 small (about 2″ long) fresh, hot chile pepper, halved through stem end, then stem and seeds discarded
- 2 very ripe fresh tomatoes (about 1 pound), halved and seeded
- 2 medium onions, each roughly chopped into about 6 pieces
- 2 garlic cloves, roughly chopped
- 2 tablespoons vinegar
- 2 teaspoons mustard seeds
- 1½ teaspoons salt
- ¼ teaspoon black pepper
- 6 tablespoons olive oil
- 2 tablespoons finely chopped fresh parsley

On a lightly oiled baking sheet place the eggplant, bell and chile peppers, and tomatoes, skin side up. Broil them with the top of the eggplant halves 3″ or 4″ away from the heat. Watch them carefully, and as soon as the skin has charred on each piece, remove it. The green peppers will take anywhere from 10 to 25 minutes, depending on how large they are; the chile pepper 15 to 20 minutes; the tomatoes about 20 minutes; and the eggplant about 25 minutes. Don't overcook the chile pepper or it will turn to mush.

Peel each piece as soon as you can after it's removed from the broiler. Use the point of a knife to loosen the blackest part of the peel, then pull the skin off from that point. If it's hard to get the peel off, place that vegetable in a paper bag, close it, and let it sit for about 3 minutes. Then try again. It's all right if a little bit of peel is left on.

While the vegetables are cooking, puree the onions, garlic, vinegar, mustard seeds, salt, and pepper in a food processor or large, powerful blender. Stop often to scrape down the sides. When the mixture is completely pureed, keep the machine running as you pour in the oil. Stop the machine when the oil is incorporated.

As the vegetables are peeled, add them to the processor. You can process the mixture each time you add a vegetable, or you can wait until you've added a few pieces. When all the vegetables have been processed, add the parsley and process with 2 pulses just to mix it in.

Makes 6½ cups

Simmered Pork Chops and Sausages

♦ ***Svinjski Kotlet sa Kobasica***

You can substitute 3 cups meatless Lecsó (page 151) for the tomatoes, green peppers, onion, and garlic in this recipe. Even without Lecsó, this is easy enough to make even after a hard day at work. It's a very satisfying dish, one that makes you feel you've had real food for dinner.

I begin the meal with a spinach salad with blue cheese dressing and croutons, serve the braised meats with applesauce and a glass of Cabernet Sauvignon or Zinfandel, then end with a small slice of strudel.

2 teaspoons white flour
Salt and pepper to taste
Pinch plus ¼ teaspoon paprika
2 ½-pound pork chops
2 strips of smoked bacon, cut into 2″-long pieces
¼ pound Hungarian salami or Kielbasa (page 173), cut into 1″-wide slices
2 ripe tomatoes (about ½ pound), roughly chopped
1 green pepper, cut into thin strips
½ medium onion, finely chopped
1 garlic clove, crushed then minced
½ cup water

Mix together the flour, salt and pepper, and pinch of paprika, then flour the pork chops lightly. Set them aside.

Fry the bacon in a large skillet over medium heat until it's crisp. Remove it with a slotted spoon and drain it on paper towels. Add the chops and sear on both sides. Remove them and set them aside. Brown the sausage lightly on both sides in the bacon fat, then add to the bacon. Turn the heat to very low, add the tomatoes, green pepper, onion, and garlic to the skillet and cook, covered, for 10 minutes. (*Note:* Omit this last step if you're using Lecsó instead of the raw vegetables.)

Stir the sausage, bacon, salt and pepper, and ¼ teaspoon paprika (and Lecsó, if used) into the skillet, pour in the water, then add the chops. Cover and simmer for 30 minutes over medium-low heat, until the chops are tender.

Serves 2

AUSTRIA

Roast Beef Larded with Sausages

♦ ***Wurstbraten***

Austria's citizens eat more pork per capita than those of any other country in Europe, yet Austrians make this dish with beef while Hungarians use a pork roast. The sausages not only look pretty when you slice the meat, they also lard it, providing internal basting. Make sure you buy very good quality hot dogs, preferably from a butcher, since packaged hot dogs develop an unpleasant texture when cooked like this. You can also use any other slightly spicy, very smooth cooked sausage, since a coarse sausage will fall apart. The sausage should also be pink to add a nice color contrast.

Serve this at a dinner party, beginning with a rich consommé. Savory cabbage strudel, broccoli sautéed in butter, and a Hungarian Cabernet can be served with the main course. Go all out for dessert with a marble cheesecake or chocolate torte, or be sensible with baked apples.

. . . .

1 2-pound rump roast of beef
1 good-quality Pork Hot Dog (page 326), ¼" piece at each end cut off and discarded, the remaining sausage quartered lengthwise
3 large garlic cloves, cut into slivers
1 tablespoon white flour
⅜ teaspoon salt
¼ teaspoon paprika
1 cup apple juice
1 cup dry white wine or white vermouth
1 bay leaf
1 teaspoon minced fresh thyme, or ½ teaspoon crumbled dried
2 tablespoons vegetable oil
2 carrots, roughly chopped
½ turnip, peeled, roughly chopped
1 celery stalk, roughly chopped

Preheat the oven to 350°. Plunge a thin, sharp knife into the roast, cutting straight down through to the bottom. Remove the knife and plunge it in again, crossing and perpendicular to the first cut. You will have formed an "X." Make 3 more holes evenly spaced in the roast. Thread the frankfurter quarters through the holes until they are even with the bottom of the roast. Cut off any excess frankfurter coming out of the top of the roast. Cut shallow slits all over the roast—top, bottom, and sides—and stick in pieces of garlic. Mix together the flour, salt, and paprika and rub the roast all over with it. Mix together the apple juice, wine, bay leaf, and thyme and set aside.

Heat the oil over high heat in a Dutch oven, preferably cast iron, or other large oven- and stove-proof pot. Brown the roast on all sides in the oil, then remove it. Add the carrots, turnips, and celery to the pot and fry for 2 minutes, stirring often. Return the roast to the pot and pour in the apple juice mixture. Place the pot in the oven and cook for 1½ hours, covered.

Remove the pot from the oven, take out the roast, and let it stand for 10 minutes before you carve it. Meanwhile, remove the bay leaf from the pot. Then either puree the ingredients left in the pot in a blender or a food processor or push them through a wide-meshed sieve. Serve this sauce alongside the meat.

Serves 4

CZECHOSLOVAKIA

Lentil Soup

◆ ***Čočka Polévka***

Czechs serve thick soups with a bit of sausage in them for supper when they've had a large midday meal. There's no better winter supper (except a bag of Wise potato chips and a container of sour cream) than a large bowl of this soup, a glass of dry white wine, and a homey dessert such as warm apple pie, cobbler, strudel, or brown Betty.

Don't discard the garlicky bacon fat. Strain it after you've added the bacon to the lentils and store it in a jar in the refrigerator. Use it to fry potatoes or toss it with hot pasta.

- 5 cups water
- 1 cup lentils
- 1 onion, roughly chopped
- 3 slices of smoked bacon, roughly chopped
- 1 large garlic clove, crushed then minced
- 4 good-quality Pork Hot Dogs (page 326), cut into 2"-wide pieces
- Salt and pepper to taste
- 1 celery stalk, thinly sliced
- 2 carrots, thinly sliced
- Croutons

In a large pot bring 4 cups water, the lentils, and onion to a boil over high heat. Turn heat to low and simmer, covered, for 1½ hours.

After the lentils have simmered about 1¼ hours, begin cooking the bacon in a large skillet over low heat until some of the fat has been rendered. Add the garlic and cook for 5 minutes, stirring often. Set aside.

When the lentils have simmered for 1½ hours, leaving the heat on under the pot, remove half the lentils and a bit of the water. Puree them in a blender or food processor and return them to the pot. Remove the bacon and garlic from the skillet with a slotted spoon and add them to the lentil pot. Stir in the remaining 1 cup water, the frankfurters, salt and pepper, celery, and carrots. Without bringing to a boil, simmer, covered, for another 15 minutes.

Serve with croutons on top.

Serves 4

CHAPTER 7

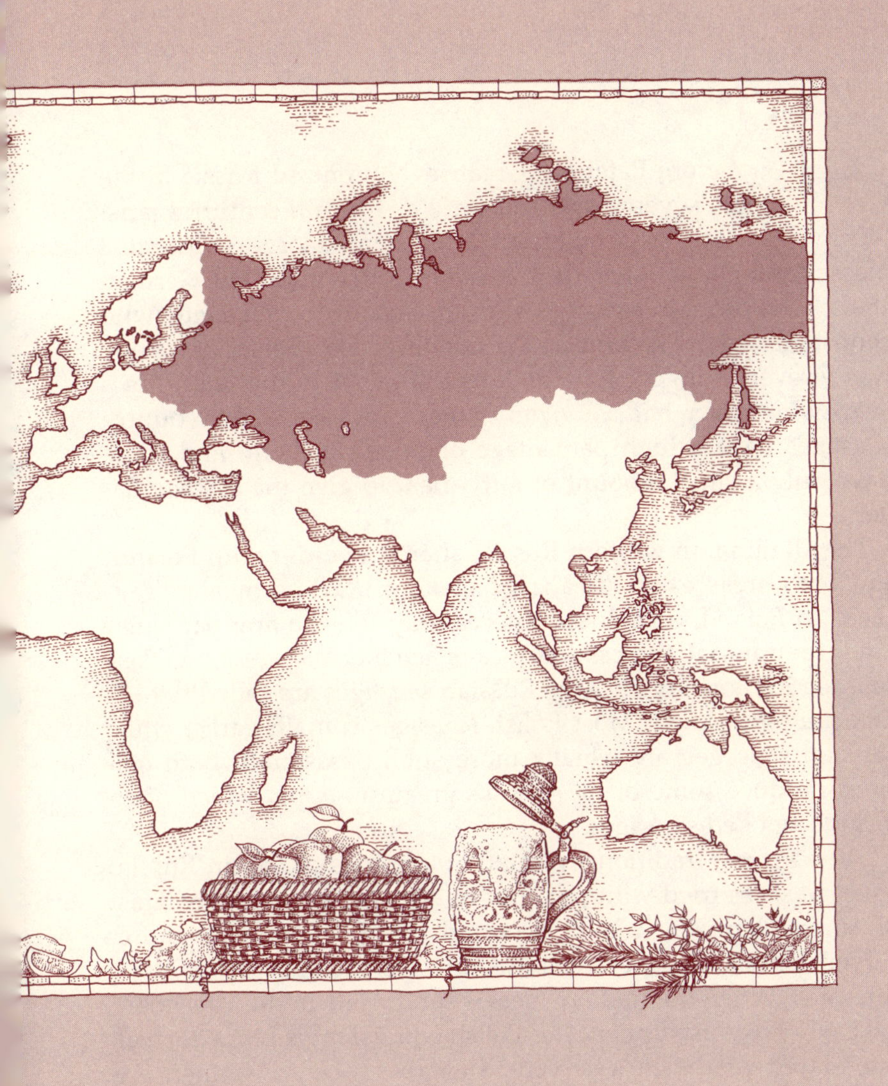

and Poland

Before Peter the Great revolutionized Russia in the late seventeenth and early eighteenth centuries, aristocrats rarely ate chopped meats. They wanted large, substantial pieces, and that's what they got. But Peter imported German chefs, who brought sausages with them, and French chefs, who contributed more sophisticated cooking, and Russian cuisine was forever changed. It made little difference to the poor, however, who never had very much meat anyway. Many country sausages have a high percentage of cereal in them, and some have only a small amount of fatty meat to give them some flavor.

The Ukraine, in western Russia, shares a border with Poland, and both areas excel in sausage making. *Kielbasa* means "sausage" in Poland, and doesn't necessarily refer to any particular kind; the sausage we call kielbasa is actually *krakowska,* smoked sausage Krakow-style. Large Russian sausages are called *kolbásy,* link sausages *sosiski.* Most Polish sausages contain garlic, while Russian sausages are usually more subtly seasoned. Both cuisines produce some of the world's greatest soups, which often include smoked sausages.

Sausages are traditionally eaten at all times of day in Russia. Sausage slices fried with potatoes or eggs are a typical breakfast or simple supper. *Zakuski,* a wonderful hot and cold buffet served before the evening meal, always includes salami-type sausages. When the midday meal is served late in the afternoon, zakuski serves as supper. The Polish equivalent is *kanapki,* small open-faced sandwiches served to company before dinner. Zakuski may also include hot sausage dishes such as fresh sausages or frankfurters in tomato or other sauces. Sausage salads, adapted from the Germans, are also common.

Smoked and fresh sausages are part of Easter dinner, the most elaborate holiday meal in Russia and Poland. In some areas, the sausages, and other foods for the holiday dinner, are brought to the priest for a blessing the night before. Stuffed goose necks, filled with goose liver and kasha, are also holiday and special occasion treats. Blood sausages, always the food of the poor, are common in both countries. There's a Ukrainian Christmas blood sausage with lingonberries. Onion and kasha *kishka* may or may not include blood. *Kaszanka,* from southern Poland, is a national favorite. In both countries' rural areas, animal stomachs, usually those of sheep, are still used as casings for sausage stuffings made of organs and various other odd-size pieces of meat. Polish sausage makers really excel at headcheese, making dozens of different kinds, which are sliced and eaten on black bread.

Moscow salami is popular in Russia and Poland. So are the best Ukrainian sausages: *mazurka,* made with ham and caraway seeds; the thin, juniper-smoked "hunter's sausage"; and a white sausage similar to German bratwurst. Some Polish specialties are a smooth liver sausage similar to liverwurst; *kabanos,* a narrower version of the smoked krakowska; and *pozhanska kabanos,* dried rather than smoked. There are also many coarse, fresh, garlic pork sausages, as well as those that are dried or smoked over juniper.

Many of the countries now incorporated into the U.S.S.R. have their own specialties. Byelorussian skinless sausages, usually made from beef and salt pork, are fried, then served with sour cream and potatoes. Byelorussians also make breaded or battered deep-fried sausages, some made from liver, others smoked ham. Asian Russians smoke horsemeat sausages. Armenians, who have a Middle Eastern cuisine, prefer lamb sausages baked in casseroles and make a delicious dried beef and garlic sausage called *soujouk. Luleh kebab,* lamb sausages threaded onto skewers and grilled, are eaten throughout southern and eastern Russia. Lithuanians like their beef and pork garlic sausages seasoned with sweet spices like nutmeg and served in tomato sauce. Bulgarian mixed grills include sausages and various cuts of pork served with a very spicy sauce. The Latvian "farmer's breakfast" is a pork, beef, fresh sausage, potato, and sour cream casserole.

Smoked Garlic Sausage

♦ ***Kolbásy/Kielbasa***

This is the most commonly used country sausage in Russia (kolbásy) and Poland (kielbasa). To prepare the equally authentic, smooth version that is better known in America, grind the meats until they're emulsified. You can use these sausages in any recipe that calls for a smoked garlic sausage. Unlike commercial sausages, which are cold-smoked to preserve them without cooking them, these are hot-smoked, so they're already cooked. Most of the large, commercial sausage companies make fairly good kielbasa, but you can adjust homemade to accommodate your own tastes. Add more garlic if you really love it, as I do, and make it coarser or smoother, depending on whether you want to cook with it or slice it and eat it cold.

I like to cut off a 3″ piece, braise it, and serve it alongside pancakes, waffles, French toast, or eggs for breakfast. It's equally good when added to any kind of meat, poultry, or vegetable stew, giving them a slightly smoky flavor. And if you can't find andouille sausage for a Cajun gumbo, use kielbasa instead.

2 pounds lean pork, ground
1¾ pounds regular, not lean, ground beef
3 garlic cloves, crushed then minced
2 tablespoons salt
¾ teaspoon black pepper
2 teaspoons light corn syrup
½ teaspoon minced fresh marjoram, or ¼ teaspoon crumbled dried
2 tablespoons milk
¾ teaspoon liquid smoke (optional)

4 prepared beef round casings

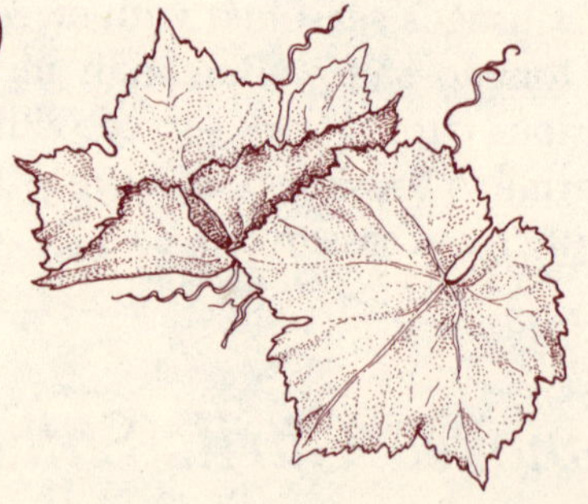

Mix together the pork, beef, and garlic in a large bowl. Mix together the salt, pepper, corn syrup, marjoram, milk, and liquid smoke (if used), then knead into the meat mixture until evenly distributed.

Stuff the meat firmly into the prepared casings. Prick any air pockets with a pin. Tie the ends of each sausage together to form a ring. Refrigerate the sausages for 1 day before baking or smoking, preferably hanging from the shelves to dry the casings.

If you're baking the sausages, preheat the oven to 200°. Place the sausages on a rack placed on a baking sheet. Bake them for 1½ hours, then turn heat to 275° and bake them for 30 minutes more. If you're smoking the sausages, wipe the casings as dry as possible, then smoke at 275° for 4 to 5 hours, until they reach an internal temperature of 170°. They can be refrigerated 3 days if raw, 2 weeks if cooked or smoked. They can be frozen raw, cooked, or smoked for 3 months.

Makes four 1-pound raw sausages

Winter Borscht

This is Russia's and Poland's most widely discussed national food treasure. Poles and Russians can debate for hours about what should go into the perfect borscht. It may include several different kinds of meats, or none at all. Completely vegetarian versions are made with mushroom stock instead of beef. Tomatoes, cabbage, potatoes, and the other vegetables are optional. The only mandatory item in winter borscht—as opposed to the green summer borscht made with spinach—is beets. There are also regional differences. Ukrainian borscht is packed with meat and vegetables. The version from Moscow has lot of tomatoes and no meat. The slightly tart Polish *barszcz* is invariably served on Christmas Eve and Easter. What the Russians call *borscht Polsky* contains roast duck.

Even if you don't like cold borscht or beets, try this dish. You can't even tell it contains beets; there's just a slightly sweet flavor you can't define. All you need for supper is a large bowl of the borscht, some *pirozhki* (Russian turnovers) or black bread, a glass of white wine or beer, and a delicious Russian dessert such as a slice of honey-raisin-nut cake.

2 tablespoons unsalted butter
3 pounds meaty beef bones
2 bay leaves
Salt and pepper to taste
6 cups homemade beef stock plus 2 cups water, or 2 cans concentrated beef stock (consommé or bouillon) plus 8 cups water
2 carrots, roughly chopped
2 leeks, halved lengthwise, thinly sliced
2 large potatoes, cut into bite-size chunks
6 fresh or canned tomatoes, roughly chopped
½ head of green cabbage, shredded
½ cup white, red wine, or sherry vinegar
4 fresh beets, peeled and julienned
1 pound smoked sausage, such as Kielbasa (page 173), cut into 1″ lengths

Melt the butter in a Dutch oven or stockpot, add the beef bones, and brown any meat left on them on all sides. Add the bay leaves, salt, pepper, stock and water, carrots, leeks, potatoes, tomatoes, cabbage, and vinegar. Bring to a boil over high heat, turn heat to low, and simmer, covered, for 1½ hours.

Remove the bones with a slotted spoon, letting the soup continue to simmer. Remove any meat from the bones, discard the bones, and return the meat to the soup. Add the beets and sausage to the soup and simmer for 10 minutes more.

Serves 8

Kielbasa Smothered in Cabbage

♦ ***Kielbasa z Kapusta***

This is a quick and easy dish, made more luxurious by the dried mushrooms. It's still a family dish, a bit too casual for company, especially since many people don't like cooked cabbage. I do, and this is one of my favorite ways of preparing it. The cabbage picks up the taste of the mushrooms and sausage and the sausage is kept juicy by its cabbage blanket.

I usually serve baked, roasted, or garlicky hashed brown potatoes with this, and a young red wine like California Zinfandel. Cherry cobbler is the perfect dessert.

- 1 cup beef stock, homemade preferable but canned acceptable
- 2 tablespoons dried porcini (cepes) mushrooms broken into small pieces, or ¼ cup roughly chopped fresh mushrooms
- 1 cup dry red wine
- 1 teaspoon salt
- ¼ teaspoon black pepper
- 1 tablespoon sugar
- 2 tablespoons tomato paste
- 2 tablespoons unsalted butter
- 1 2-pound head of red cabbage, cored and shredded
- 1 onion, roughly chopped
- 1 tablespoon wine or sherry vinegar
- 3 carrots, cut into ½″-thick slices
- 4 sprigs fresh tarragon, or ½ teaspoon crumbled dried
- 1 bay leaf
- 1 pound Kielbasa (page 173) or other smoked garlic sausage, cut into 6 pieces

Bring the stock to a boil, then pour over the mushrooms in a large bowl. Let sit for 30 minutes, then stir in the wine, salt, pepper, sugar, and tomato paste. Set aside.

Melt the butter in a large skillet over low heat and fry the cabbage and onion for 10 minutes, stirring occasionally. Stir in the vinegar, then the carrots, herbs, and the mushrooms and their liquid. Bring to a boil over high heat, turn heat to low, and simmer, covered, for 50 minutes. Bury the sausage in the cabbage, cover, and simmer for 10 minutes more over very low heat, until the sausage is heated through.

Serves 6

RUSSIA

Cold Cucumber and Sausage Soup

♦ ***Okroshka***

Whenever I serve this soup, I picture Russian aristocrats lunching in a gazebo on a beautiful day in June. Actually, okroshka was, and is, eaten by all Russians, rich or poor. It's amazing how something this simple can taste so sophisticated. The beer in the recipe is used as a substitute for the grain-based alcoholic beverage, *kvas*, which can only be found in the rare Russian food store in the United States. Southern Russians use yogurt, northerners sour cream, so take your choice. Use the best possible stock, since the taste is very important in this recipe.

This is a lovely summer first course, served with beer, kvas, or a light white wine, and I usually follow it with a salad made with every kind of green and hard cheese I can find in the market. Obviously you don't want to use a creamy dressing after the soup, so serve a simple, herb-packed vinaigrette. A bowl full of berries is a typically Russian dessert.

¾ cup sour cream or plain yogurt
1½ teaspoons prepared mustard
1½ teaspoons sugar
¼ teaspoon white pepper
3 cups homemade beef or chicken stock, room temperature
2 cups flat pale beer
½ pound smoked Kielbasa (page 173), cut into ½″ cubes
1 large cucumber, peeled, cut into ½″ cubes
3 scallions, white and green sections, thinly sliced
3 eggs, hard-boiled, finely chopped
Salt to taste
3 tablespoons chopped fresh dill

Stir together the sour cream, mustard, sugar, and pepper in a pitcher, bowl, or soup tureen. Mix together the stock and beer in a separate bowl. Slowly pour ½ cup of the stock and beer into the sour cream, stirring constantly until smooth. Then, continuing to stir, slowly mix the rest of the stock and beer into the sour cream. Stir in the sausage, cucumber, scallion, eggs, and salt. Chill, covered, for 1 to 24 hours.

Sprinkle individual bowls with some of the dill just before serving.

Serves 8

Mixed Meat Soup

♦ ***Myasnaya Solyanka***

Borscht, Okroshka, and solyanka are considered Russia's greatest soups. There is also a casserole called solyanka, basically a less soupy version of this dish. The olives, capers, pickles, and lemon slices in the soup cut the rich taste, adding a pleasant tartness. Although it looks like there's a lot of meat in this dish, much of it is bone to give the soup flavor.

This is a main course soup. I usually begin the meal with a vegetable dish such as asparagus with hollandaise sauce. There are all kinds of Russian breads and dumplings which go with soup. I usually serve a coffee-cake–like bun made with ricotta or other soft cheese, or cheese-stuffed pirozhki or *vareniki* dumplings. The tart taste of the soup will ruin the taste of a good wine, so serve beer or vodka. Dessert can be any kind of Russian cake, such as a chocolate sponge cake with walnut buttercream icing.

- 2 pounds beef short ribs
- 2 quarts water
- 1 onion, peeled and stuck with 2 cloves
- 2 bay leaves
- 3 sprigs parsley
- 2 carrots, halved
- 1½ pounds bony chicken parts
- 1 onion, thinly sliced
- 2 tablespoons unsalted butter
- 4 very ripe or canned plum tomatoes, seeded, cut into ½″ cubes
- 1 tablespoon capers
- ½ cup halved pitted black olives
- ¼ cup thinly sliced dill pickles
- ¼ pound smoked ham, cut into ½″ cubes
- 4 thin, good-quality Hot Dogs (page 326 or 328), cut into ½″ cubes or slices
- Salt and black pepper to taste
- 2 tablespoons plus 2 teaspoons chopped fresh dill
- 2 scallions, white and light green sections, finely chopped
- 16 thin lemon slices

Place the meat and water in a large stockpot and bring to a boil over high heat, skimming until it's fairly clear. Add the whole onion, bay leaves, parsley, and carrots, turn heat to low, and simmer, covered, for 45 minutes. Add the chicken and simmer, covered, for another 1¼ hours.

While the soup is simmering, melt the butter in a small skillet and sauté the sliced onion for 10 minutes over low heat, then set the skillet aside. (If you want to defat the soup overnight, sauté the onions the next day.)

Take the beef and chicken out of the pot, which should continue to simmer, covered. Remove all the meat from the bones and discard the chicken skin and bones. Cut the meat into 1″ squares and set aside. Take the pot off the heat and strain the broth, discarding all the remaining solids. Rinse out the pot. *Note:* If you want to defat the soup, refrigerate it overnight at this point. Remove the fat the next day and continue, sautéing the onions.

Replace the meat and the strained stock in the pot and add the sautéed onions, tomatoes, capers, olives, pickles, ham, hot dogs, and salt and pepper. Simmer over low heat, stirring often, for 30 minutes. If you're reheating the soup, begin timing the 30 minutes when you see the first bubble appear on top of the soup.

Pour the soup into 8 large bowls and sprinkle each with some of the dill and scallions. Serve 2 lemon slices floating in each bowl.

Serves 8

Scrambled Eggs and Sausage

♦ ***Yaitsa-Boltun'ya z Kolbásy***

Just like in America, this is a Russian breakfast dish. This typically French method of scrambling eggs with long, slow cooking, which makes them smoother and more creamy, was probably brought by the French chefs so chic in eighteenth- and nineteenth-century Russia. To serve two people, rather than one, just double the ingredients and use a skillet twice as large. The cooking time is the same. To serve four people, use two skillets.

2 large eggs
2 teaspoons heavy or light cream
⅛ teaspoon salt
Pinch of black pepper
¼ cup loosely packed diced Kielbasa or skinned, crumbled Fresh Garlic Sausage (page 173 or 24)
1 tablespoon unsalted butter

Lightly stir the eggs, cream, salt, and pepper together with a fork, mixing well without letting it get foamy. Stir in the sausage.

Melt the butter in a small skillet over the lowest possible heat. Don't let it brown or get foamy. As soon as the butter melts, pour in the eggs. When the bottom begins to set, begin constantly stirring the eggs from the bottom. They will take 10 to 15 minutes. Remove the pan from the heat when the eggs look slightly underdone, since they will continue to cook for a moment. Turn out onto a heated plate.

Serves 1

Beef and Mushroom Sausages

♦ ***Zrazy***

Russians serve zrazy for breakfast, lunch, or as part of the zakuski table. These sausages can also be made with horseradish or liver instead of mushrooms. Mushrooms, however, are a Russian passion. Many Russians know how to identify edible varieties, and they go out mushroom hunting even in the cold Russian winter.

These sausages were probably introduced to Russia from the Middle East. Serve them as a first course, topped with browned butter or a mushroom-cream or tomato sauce. Serve a very light red wine, like Beaujolais, with them. Grilled or poached sturgeon, Russia's favorite fish, can follow, accompanied by peas and egg noodles. Try thick pureed apricot kissel for dessert.

½ cup dried wild mushrooms, such as cepes, porcini, or morels
½ cup roughly torn pieces of crustless white bread
Hot chicken or beef stock to cover
5 tablespoons unsalted butter
¾ cup finely chopped onion
1 pound lean, but not extra lean, ground beef

½ teaspoon salt
¼ teaspoon black pepper

Soak the mushrooms and bread in the stock for 30 minutes, squeeze them dry, finely chop them, and set aside.

Melt 3 tablespoons butter in a large skillet over low heat, add the onions, and sauté, stirring occasionally, for 5 minutes, until they're just turning golden. Stir in the mushrooms and bread and remove from the heat. Don't clean the skillet, since you'll use it again soon. While the onions are cooking, knead together the beef, salt, and pepper and form into 8 very thin patties, each about 5″ in diameter.

Sprinkle one-eighth of the mushroom mixture on each patty and roll up like a jelly roll. Seal the end by pressing it closed and smoothing it with your thumb. Roll the sausage between your palms, compressing it slightly but not enough to poke the mushrooms through the beef.

Add the remaining 2 tablespoons butter to the skillet and melt it over medium heat. Brown the sausages well on all sides. Carefully use tongs or a spatula to turn them, since they're very fragile. Serve with the browned butter from the skillet poured over them.

Serves 4

Kasha and Salt Pork Sausages

Kasha comes already roasted. If you can't find whole-grain, buy the smaller kind and follow the directions on the box regarding how long you should let the kasha cook in the stock. This is delicious with eggs in the morning, very comforting and very cheap. Like oatmeal, it provides a sort of comfortable fullness. It's also easy to fry—you don't have to worry about cooking everything through since the interior is already cooked.

2 cups chicken stock, homemade preferable but canned acceptable
1 cup roasted whole-grain kasha
1 large egg, lightly beaten
¼ pound salt pork, rinsed well, parboiled for 10 minutes, then finely chopped
¾ cup finely chopped onion
⅛ teaspoon black pepper
4 tablespoons unsalted butter

Prepared hog casings

Begin bringing the stock to a boil over high heat, preferably in a saucepan with a spout.

Mix the kasha and egg, making sure every grain of kasha gets coated with egg. Place the coated kasha in a dry skillet, preferably cast iron, and turn heat to medium. Stir constantly, breaking up any lumps, until each grain of kasha is separate and there's a definite toasty smell, about 4 minutes. By now the stock should be boiling. Wearing long oven mitts and standing as far back as possible, pour one-quarter of the stock into the kasha skillet. When it stops sputtering, pour in the rest of the stock. Stir well, turn heat to low, cover, and cook for 30 minutes.

While the kasha is cooking, heat the salt pork in another skillet over low heat until some of the fat has been rendered. Stir in the onion and sauté for 10 minutes. Turn off the heat and let sit on the burner until the kasha is done.

Uncover the kasha after 30 minutes and stir well to break up any lumps. It should be light and fluffy. If it's still soggy, cover the pan and let it continue to cook until it's done. Check every 3 minutes to see if it has absorbed all the liquid yet. When the kasha is done, stir in the contents of the salt pork pan, then stir in the pepper.

Loosely stuff the mixture into prepared hog casings and tie off into 6″ lengths. Prick the air pockets with a pin. Melt the butter in a large skillet and brown the sausages well. Serve the sausages with melted butter poured over. These can be refrigerated for 1 week before being fried. They cannot be frozen or they will become mushy.

Makes approximately 1 pound raw sausage

POLAND

Hunter's Stew

♦ ***Bigos***

This has been a Polish staple for hundreds of years, made with whichever meats are available. There are two versions as to how it got its name. Both agree it was eaten by rich people on hunting parties. But one version says it was popular because it used up all the leftover meat from the ball the night before. The other says that the hunters just added whatever they caught to the pot each night. There's probably some truth in both. In other central and eastern European countries it's called "Stew, Polish-style."

This is a very rich dish with a flavor you'll remember long after the stew is gone. It's one of my favorite dishes. I make a huge pot of it once a year, on the first cold day in November, and freeze individual portions. That way I'm guaranteed something comforting and savory on those chilly nights when it's just too much effort to cook. California Cabernet Sauvignon is the perfect wine for the stew. I usually start the meal with a salad or some bread and cheese, then finish with baked pie and fresh walnuts straight out of the shell.

- ½ cup tomato paste
- 1 cup hot beef stock, homemade preferable but canned acceptable
- ¼ pound bacon, coarsely chopped
- ¾ pound stewing pork, cubed
- 1 pound green cabbage, shredded
- 1 onion, coarsely chopped
- 1 large tart apple, cored, quartered, thinly sliced
- ¾ pound Kielbasa, (page 173), cut into 1" slices
- 6 dried porcini (cepes) mushrooms, soaked in 1 cup hot water for 1 hour, drained, and roughly chopped
- ½ pound fresh or Homemade Sauerkraut (page 131), rinsed well
- Salt and pepper to taste
- 2 bay leaves
- ½ cup dry red wine

Dissolve the tomato paste in the stock. Set aside.

In a Dutch oven or stockpot fry the bacon until cooked but not crisp. Remove the bacon, leaving the drippings. Fry the pork in the drippings, then remove and add to the bacon. Add the cabbage to the bacon drippings and cook over low heat for 10 minutes, stirring 2 or 3 times. Add the onion to the cabbage and cook for another 10 minutes, stirring occasionally. Stir in the apple and cook for 5 minutes, stirring occasionally. Add the kielbasa, bacon, and pork, then stir in the rest of the ingredients including the broth and tomato paste. Cover the pot and simmer over low heat for 30 minutes. Uncover and cook for another 30 minutes. It can be served right away or reheated.

Serves 6

Bread Soup

♦ ***Zupa Chlebowa***

I thought I was going to hate this since it sounded like it was going to be soggy mush. It's absolutely delicious. The seasonings in the bread, which dissolves completely, richly flavor the soup. This was obviously a poor man's dish, although richer Poles soon caught on and began enjoying it too. I usually serve it to friends for a late supper, accompanied by several kinds of cheese, coleslaw, pickles, dark beer, and honey cake for dessert.

3 tablespoons unsalted butter
6 slices of very good quality pumpernickel bread, roughly chopped
6 cups beef stock, homemade preferable but canned acceptable
6 ounces smoked Kielbasa or Hot Dogs, (pages 173, 326, 328), thinly sliced
Salt to taste
⅛ teaspoon black pepper
2 tablespoons chopped fresh chives

Melt the butter in a large pot over medium heat. Add the bread and stir until all the butter has been absorbed. Stir in the stock and bring to a boil over high heat. Turn heat to low and simmer, covered, for 30 minutes. Uncover and whisk well to break up the bread. Stir in the sausage, salt, pepper, and chives and just heat through, about 1 minute.

Serves 6

CHAPTER 8

. . . .

Iberia

Spain and Portugal were once provinces of ancient Rome, from whom the Iberians probably learned sausage-making techniques. Adding their own native ingredients, they created sausages instantly identifiable as Iberian. It's hard to imagine Spanish cooking without *chorizo,* called *chouriço* in Portugal, a smoked or dried paprika-and-pork sausage. In Somerset Maugham's novel, *Catalina,* he describes a sixteenth-century bridal couple's wedding breakfast—bread, cheese, cold chicken, sausage, and a bulging skin of wine. "Who could want anything better?" the hero asks.

Chorizo can be slightly spicy or fairly hot, in which case it's called *chorizo picante.* In Portugal *linguiça, longaniza* in Spain, is the most popular sausage. As a rule it's thinner and slightly milder than chorizo, left long rather than separated into links, has more of an herb-flavored taste, and is often fresh rather than dried or smoked. But since every version of chorizo or longaniza is different, these rules may not apply in all cases. *Morcillas* are blood sausages, some of which can contain rice. They're poached, cooled, added to stews, or sliced and fried.

Since the paprika turns chorizo and longaniza orange, and blood sausages are so dark, other sausages are called "white." *Morcilla blanca,* white morcilla, is made with pork organ meats and occasionally includes chicken. Sausages made from meats other than pork are very rare, despite all the sheep raised in Iberia.

There are certain dishes popular throughout Spain, with slight variations from region to region, such as breads containing sausages and chorizo or morcilla wrapped in pastry. Every region has its *cocido,* a free-for-all stew using every kind of sausage, meat, or vegetable easily obtainable. Sausages are also baked or simmered with just one other kind of meat, such as tripe, chicken, veal, lamb, pickled pork, or duck.

Since the Spanish don't particularly like vegetables, adding chorizo helps make them palatable. Occasionally chorizo is cooked by itself, with just a wine or cider sauce. The most common sausage *tapa* (tidbits served with drinks) is cold sliced chorizo, but some restaurants prepare fancier hors d'oeuvres. Chorizo-stuffed dates or mushrooms, hot canapés with grilled morcilla or chorizo and *tortillas,* delicious potato and chorizo omelettes, are just a few. *Paella* and other rice dishes can also include chorizo.

Two of Spain's best white sausages come from the north, an area known for its excellent cooking. While the northwestern *salchicha blanca* is herb-seasoned, the northeastern *butifarra,* probably influenced by the Moors who ruled Spain 1,000 years ago, contains spices. Bean and sausage dishes abound in the north, especially in Catalan. *A la Catalan* can mean a dish has sausage or chocolate in it, and the beef stew called *estofado à la Catalana* has both. The Basques have long been known as expert shepherds, and northern dishes often combine lamb and sausages in casseroles or stews. One of the best tortillas is the Catalan version made with white beans and butifarra.

Three exceptional northern dishes, rarely found elsewhere, are a Catalan fried pancake made of shredded cabbage and sausage, butifarra cooked in caramelized sugar, and a flat bread, similar to pizza, topped with butifarra. *Fabada Asturiana* is renowned throughout Spain. It's either a bean soup or stew, depending on how much liquid the cook adds, which contains several cuts of pork including morcilla, chorizo, ham, and pig's feet. Sausage turnovers, called *empanadas,* are more popular in Latin America, but they're also found in Asturias.

Madrid, in central Spain, is a cosmopolitan city, and restaurants there serve dishes from all over the country. There are also Madrileño specialties, like snails in chorizo or morcilla sauce. *Cocido madrileño,* also called *olla podrida,* is perhaps Spain's most famous stew. Just like in Portugal, which part of central Spain borders, fish and pork, such as trout and chorizo, is a popular combination. Bean dishes are stretched out and enhanced with small amounts of meat like chorizo or morcilla.

The most famous dish from Valencia, in southeast Spain, is paella, as popular now as it was hundreds of years ago. Though paella contains chorizo, *blanquet Valenciano,* a white sausage similar to butifarra, is used in many other dishes. The southern cocido combines chorizo, blanquet, and morcilla with the white beans. In Murcia, south of Valencia, chorizos are more popular than white sausages, which is hardly surprising since it produces the best paprika in Spain. Andalusia, in southwestern Spain, is famous for *huevos à la flamenca,* eggs baked with brightly colored vegetables arranged in a decorative pattern. It's also known for its pumpkin, chorizo, and paprika cocido. The Balearic Islands, especially Majorca, make an Italian-inspired *sobrassada* sausage, combining the paprika of chorizo with the nutmeg of butifarra.

In Portugal, linguiça are preferred to chouriço, but they're often smoked, unlike Spanish longaniza. The Portuguese also eat red beans, as well as white beans, simmered with linguiça or chouriço. Fresh coriander often distinguishes Portuguese dishes from their Spanish counterparts. Tripe dishes, baked eggs, and Portuguese gazpacho also include sausages. Some Portuguese favorites are a mixed pork grill including linguiça; an open-topped sausage pie; sautéed morcilla slices served with pickled onions; a kale, potato, and linguiça soup; and that absurd-sounding and wonderful-tasting combination of sausage and clams called *cataplana*.

Chorizo or Chouriço

There are hundreds, perhaps thousands, of dishes made in Spain and Portugal with these sausages. Use chorizo in any dish requiring spicy smoked sausage. It's also good sliced and eaten on top of a slice of bread, along with pickled vegetables and a glass of dry sherry. If you can't find the Spanish or Portuguese version, and don't want to make it yourself, substitute Mexican or South American chorizo for the fresh sausage and good pepperoni if you want a hard sausage. If you can only find American breakfast sausage, mix a scant ½ teaspoon hot paprika or ground chiles and 1 small garlic clove into each pound of bulk sausage.

2 teaspoons salt
¼ teaspoon black pepper
1 teaspoon ground chile or cayenne pepper or hot paprika
¼ teaspoon sugar

2 tablespoons red wine
¼ teaspoon liquid smoke (optional)
1 pound lean pork, very finely ground
2 ounces pork, cut into ¼″ cubes
2 ounces pork fat, coarsely ground
2 garlic cloves, crushed then minced

Prepared hog casings

Preheat the oven to 200° if you're baking the sausages rather than smoking them. Mix together the salt, pepper, chile or cayenne or paprika, sugar, red wine, and liquid smoke. Knead the meat, fat, and garlic together, then add the wine mixture and knead until well mixed.

Stuff the sausage mixture firmly into prepared hog casings and tie off into 6″ lengths. Prick any air pockets with a pin.

If you've used the liquid smoke, place the sausages on a rack placed on a baking sheet and bake for 3 hours. Or smoke the sausages at 275° for 3 to 5 hours. The raw sausages can be refrigerated for 3 days, the smoked or baked for 1 week. Raw, smoked, or cooked sausages can be frozen for 3 months.

Makes approximately 1¼ pounds raw sausage

Longaniza or Linguiça

The Spanish longaniza is usually served fresh, while the Portuguese linguiça is frequently smoked. It's traditionally stuffed into the narrow sheep casings, but you can also use the more easily obtainable hog casings. There are several companies in America who make linguiça, especially in New England where many Portuguese immigrants settled. Linguiça are even included in many traditional New England clambakes. If you can't buy and don't want to make these, add 1¾ teaspoons sweet paprika, 1 scant teaspoon fresh rosemary, 4 teaspoons vinegar, and 2 small cloves of garlic per pound of bulk sausage.

1½ teaspoons salt
¼ teaspoon black pepper
2 teaspoons sweet paprika
1 teaspoon minced fresh rosemary, or ½ teaspoon crumbled dried
2 garlic cloves, crushed then minced
1½ tablespoons white vinegar
1 pound lean pork, coarsely ground
¼ pound pork fat, coarsely ground

Prepared sheep or hog casings

Mix together the salt, pepper, paprika, rosemary, garlic, and vinegar. Knead the pork and fat together, then knead in the vinegar mixture.

Stuff the meat firmly into the prepared casings and tie off into any length you prefer. Prick any air pockets with a pin. Refrigerate the sausages for 1 to 3 days before cooking. These can be poached and/or fried or used as bulk sausage. The raw or cooked sausages can be frozen for 3 months.

Makes approximately 1¼ pounds raw sausage

SPAIN

Macaroni with Sausage and Tomatoes

♦ ***Macarrones Español***

Spaniards are avid noodle eaters, influenced mostly by Arab invaders and nearby Italians. In many parts of Spain, especially Barcelona, they like colored macaroni rather than plain. I personally prefer the plain, and as long as you're buying a brand made with all semolina flour you can't go wrong. This is a very easy dish and makes a nice change from typically Italian pastas. If you're serving it as a main course, a salad with a creamy dressing like blue cheese can be served first. A young, Spanish red wine from La Mancha stands up to the tomatoes and sausage. Serve a flan or other kind of custard for dessert.

- ½ pound medium-size macaroni, preferably shells
- 1 28-ounce can tomatoes, drained, seeded, and roughly chopped
- 3 tablespoons chopped pimientos or other pickled peppers
- 6 ounces smoked Chorizo (page 192) or pepperoni, quartered lengthwise, then cut into ¼" slices
- 6 tablespoons blanched slivered almonds
- 3 tablespoons lard or vegetable oil
- 1 green bell pepper, seeded and diced
- 1 onion, finely chopped
- 1 garlic clove, crushed then minced
- ½ pound fresh mushrooms, roughly chopped
- 1 teaspoon salt
- ¼ teaspoon cayenne pepper

Bring a pot of water to a boil, add the macaroni, cook until al dente and then drain. Immediately toss with the tomatoes, pickled peppers, sausage, and almonds in a 3-quart casserole and set aside.

Preheat the oven to 350°. Heat the lard or oil in a skillet over low heat and sauté the green pepper, onion, and garlic over low heat. Add the mushrooms and cook, stirring, another minute. Stir in the salt and cayenne. Pour the contents of the skillet into the casserole and toss everything well. Place in the oven and bake for 20 minutes.

Serves 6

Garlic Soup

♦ ***Sopa de Ajo***

The garlic mellows considerably as it cooks, so the soup tastes piquant, but you don't feel like you have to hold your hand over your mouth every time you talk to someone for the next few hours.

I like this recipe because it turns a dull stock into something special and interesting. Serve it as the first course at an informal dinner. You can follow it with anything, but I like the typically Spanish grilled rack of lamb, served with roasted potatoes and *pisto,* simmered onions, zucchini, green peppers, and tomato, similar to the French ratatouille. A Spanish custard would be a fine dessert.

1 tablespoon olive oil
2 garlic cloves, crushed then minced
½ tablespoon paprika
¼ teaspoon chopped fresh rosemary, or ⅛ teaspoon crumbled dried
3 ounces smoked Chorizo (page 192) or pepperoni, finely chopped
2 cups chicken stock, homemade preferable but canned acceptable
Salt and pepper to taste

Heat the olive oil in a 1-quart saucepan over low heat. Stir in the garlic and paprika and cook for 10 minutes, stirring occasionally. If the garlic begins to brown, immediately remove from the heat before it burns. After the 10 minutes, stir in the rosemary and sausage, pour in the stock, and stir well. Bring to a boil over high heat. Add the salt and pepper and boil for 10 minutes.

Serves 4

CATALONIA

Butifarra

This is an absolutely wonderful sausage. The intriguing combination of pork and spices adds an unusual flavor to any dish into which it's added. I hate to bury it in stews, but it's perfect for clear meat soups or egg dishes. Use it, as the Spanish do, to flavor beans, cabbage, rice, or mushrooms. There is no substitute that will duplicate the unique taste of butifarra, but you can substitute any cooked pork sausage in recipes that call for it.

- 2 teaspoons salt
- ¼ teaspoon black pepper
- ⅛ teaspoon cayenne, ground chile pepper, or hot paprika
- ⅛ teaspoon ground cinnamon
- ⅛ teaspoon grated nutmeg
- ⅛ teaspoon ground cloves
- ¼ teaspoon minced fresh thyme, or ⅛ teaspoon crumbled dried
- 2 tablespoons white wine
- 1½ pounds lean pork, coarsely ground
- ½ pound pork fat, coarsely ground

Prepared hog casings

Mix together the salt, peppers, spices, thyme, and wine. Knead together the pork and fat, then knead in the spice mixture.

Stuff the sausage meat into the prepared hog casings to make two 30"-long sausages. Prick any air pockets with a pin.

Dry the sausages in the refrigerator, uncovered and hung from the shelves or on a rack, for 2 to 3 days before cooking. Then poach and/or fry or cut up and use in recipes. The dried sausage can be frozen for 3 to 4 months.

Makes approximately 2 pounds raw sausage

Galicia

Potato and Sausage Omelette

♦ ***Tortilla Gallego***

It's impossible for me to convey how absolutely delicious this dish is, especially considering that I think eggs are generally quite boring. This is one of my favorite recipes, and I make it as often as I can. It's even better when it's cold, so save some for breakfast. Tortillas are essential to good tapas bars, usually cut into small pieces and often eaten on toast. I like to eat them plain, since it's impossible to improve on them, but if you insist on an accompaniment try an unauthentic but good Mexican *salsa verde*. This is the ideal breakfast, brunch or lunch dish, incorporating eggs, potatoes and sausage into one delicious mass. All you need is a glass of chilled white Rioja or California Chardonnay and a knockout dessert like a rich chocolate torte.

1 cup olive oil
2 red potatoes (about 1 pound), peeled, cut into ½″ cubes
1 medium onion, finely chopped
1 yellow, red, or green bell pepper, seeded and roughly chopped
½ pound Chorizo, Longaniza, or Butifarra (pages 192, 193, or 197), skinned and crumbled if fresh, roughly chopped if smoked or dried
5 large eggs
½ teaspoon grated nutmeg
1 teaspoon salt
¼ teaspoon pepper

Heat the oil in a 9″ ovenproof skillet, preferably cast iron, over medium heat. Add the potatoes, onion, and bell pepper and cook, stirring often, for 10 minutes. Add the sausage and cook for another 5 minutes. While the sausage is cooking, beat the eggs with the nutmeg, salt, and pepper to mix well. Remove the cooked vegetables and sausage from the skillet with a slotted spoon and add to the eggs.

Begin heating your broiler. Pour off all but about 3 tablespoons oil from the skillet. Heat the oil until it's very hot but not smoking. Pour in the egg mixture, stir once to distribute the solid ingredients, and cook for 5 minutes over medium heat, until you can lift up whole sections with a spatula. Place the pan under the broiler for 3 or 4 minutes, until the top is set. Run a knife around the edge of the tortilla, then lay an upside-down serving plate on top of the pan. Holding the pan and plate together, invert them and remove the pan.

Serves 8 as an appetizer, 4 as a main course

CASTILE

Sausage-Stuffed Bread

♦ ***Hornazo***

There are several breads with sausage baked into them in Iberia. In Portugal, a roll baked with linguiça and onions in it is an everyday treat. Wheat and corn breads with chorizo are sometimes wrapped in leaves to steam them as they cook. *Hornazo* (the masculine of *hornaza,* which is both an oven and a yellow glaze, since the baked bread is glazed with egg) is a traditional Easter specialty.

You can make decorative swirls on top of the dough to tell yourself where the eggs and pieces of sausage are, making it easier to cut the bread neatly. Serve the bread with eggs and brandied coffee for a complete, Iberian breakfast.

- ¼ pound smoked bacon
- ½ pound mixed poached or smoked sausages, such as Blood Sausage, Chorizo, Longaniza, and/or Butifarra (pages 31, 192, 193, and 197)
- 1½ cups milk
- 1 package dry yeast
- 4 teaspoons sugar
- 1½ teaspoons salt
- 3-3¼ cups unbleached all-purpose presifted flour
- 2 small eggs, hard-boiled, shelled
- 1 egg, lightly beaten

Fry the bacon in a large skillet over medium heat until crispy, drain on paper towels, then crumble it. Add all the sausages to the skillet and lightly brown all over. Remove the sausages and drain on paper towels. Discard all but 3 tablespoons of the fat from the skillet.

Heat ½ cup milk to 100°, place in a large straight-sided bowl, and stir in the yeast and 1 teaspoon sugar. Let sit for 10 minutes. Mix the remaining 1 cup milk with 3 teaspoons sugar, then stir into the warm milk mixture after the 10 minutes. Stir 1½ cups flour into the milk mixture and beat for about 1 minute with a wooden spoon. Let sit, loosely covered, in a warm, draft-free place for about 1 hour, until doubled.

Stir 2 tablespoons of fat into the bread dough, then beat in the salt and the rest of the flour. Turn the dough out onto a lightly floured board and knead until elastic and blisters begin to appear, about 10 minutes. During the last minute of kneading, knead in the crumbled bacon. Pat the dough into a ball, lightly coat with the remaining fat, and place in a clean, straight-sided bowl. Let rise, loosely covered, another hour, until doubled again. While the dough is rising, wipe off any fat on the sausages and cut them into 1½″-thick slices.

Gently pat the dough out into a 9″- or 10″-diameter circle. Lay the pieces of sausage on their sides on the dough, spaced symmetrically around the circle. If the sausages are curved, their curved sides should be parallel to the circumference of the dough. Lay the hard-boiled eggs on the dough. Gently pull the dough into a ball, covering the sausages completely, and seal the seams well. Turn the ball over and place it seam side down on a lightly oiled cookie sheet. It should have about a 7″ diameter. Let the bread rise, uncovered, for 1 hour. After the bread has risen 45 minutes, place a large cake pan full of water on the floor of the oven. Then preheat the oven to 400°.

Place the bread in the oven and bake for 15 minutes. Remove the pan of water, brush the bread with the egg, and bake for another 10 minutes, until a rich brown. With gloved hands, turn the bread upside down, brush it with more egg, and bake for another 25 minutes.

Makes 1 loaf

MADRID

Madrid-Style Stew

♦ ***Cocido Madrileño***

This was originally called olla podrida, meaning "putrid pot," an affectionate nickname. An *olla* is an earthenware pot taller than it is wide, with a pinched-in neck and a slightly flared top. Traditionally, whatever the cook had around would be added to yesterday's leftovers to create a whole new stew. You should use at least 3 kinds of meat. It is possible that the original cocido was a Jewish dish, made with meats other than pork, that could simmer for a long time over very low heat so no one would have to cook on the Sabbath.

The proper way to eat this cocido is to add the very fine *fideos* noodles to the broth and serve it as a first course, then serve the vegetables, then the meat. This dish can take a strong red wine, so I like a good French Burgundy such as Clos de Tart. Serve fresh oranges for dessert.

- 10 cups water
- 1 cup dried chick-peas, soaked in cold water to cover for 24 hours
- 1 1¼-pound piece of beef chuck or stewing lamb
- 1 ¾-pound piece of salt pork, rinsed well and parboiled for 15 minutes
- 2 whole turkey legs
- 2 garlic cloves, crushed then minced
- 1 large bay leaf, torn in half
- ¼ teaspoon black pepper
- 2 chicken legs with thighs
- 1 ¼-pound piece of smoked ham
- ½ pound smoked garlic sausage, such as Chorizo (page 192), cut into a total of 8 pieces
- 2 large carrots, each cut into 4 pieces
- 2 large leeks, white and light green sections, cut into 1" slices
- 8 small potatoes, or 4 medium, halved (about 1 pound)
- 2 ripe fresh tomatoes, quartered
- 2 tablespoons roughly chopped fresh parsley
- 2 tart apples, cored, each cut into 8 wedges

Bring the water, chick-peas, beef or lamb, and salt pork to a boil in a large pot over medium heat. Skim often as foam rises to the top. Turn heat to low and simmer for 30 minutes, uncovered, skimming occasionally. Add the turkey, garlic, bay leaf, and pepper. Every time you add something new, push the new ingredients to the bottom of the pot. Simmer, covered, for 30 minutes. Stir in the chicken, ham, and chorizo and simmer, covered, for 30 minutes more. Add the carrots, leeks, potatoes, and tomatoes and simmer, covered, for another 15 minutes. Stir in the parsley and apple and cook, covered, for a final 15 minutes.

Serves 8

Chick-Pea and Chorizo Salad

♦ ***Garbanzos con Chorizo***

This salad includes ingredients traditionally baked together in a casserole, but, eaten cold, they make a perfect appetizer as well as a main course. This tapa is a terrific picnic dish since it doesn't have any ingredients that spoil easily. It also makes a lot of salad, so be sure you're serving it to people who like chick-peas. It makes a nice summer main course, preceded by a cup of vichysoisse and accompanied by a cold glass of beer. Serve an almond-based torte for dessert.

- 2 pounds dried chick-peas, soaked in cold water to cover for 5–6 hours
- 2 cups chicken stock, homemade preferable but canned acceptable
- 1 cup virgin olive oil
- 1 medium Spanish onion, minced
- 2 garlic cloves, crushed then minced
- 1 teaspoon minced fresh rosemary, or ½ teaspoon crumbled dried
- 1 bay leaf
- ½ cup sherry, red wine, or cider vinegar
- 1 teaspoon salt
- ½ teaspoon pepper
- ¼ cup finely chopped fresh parsley
- 4 scallions, both white and green sections, thinly sliced
- ½ pound smoked Chorizo (page 192) or pepperoni, cut into ¼″–½″ cubes

Drain the chick-peas and place them in a large pot with the chicken stock. If the stock doesn't cover the chick-peas by 4″, add enough so that it does. Bring the pot to a boil over high heat, then turn heat to low and simmer, covered, for 2 hours. Turn the heat off under the pot and let it sit, uncovered, while you make the dressing.

Heat 2 tablespoons olive oil over low heat in a large pot such as a Dutch oven. Add the onion, garlic, and rosemary and sauté for about 10 minutes, until the onion has softened but not browned. Turn down the heat instantly if the garlic begins to brown. Stir in the bay leaf, vinegar, salt and pepper, and the rest of the oil. Bring to a boil over high heat, then take the pot off the stove. Stir in the parsley, scallions, and chorizo.

Drain the chick-peas and place in a large bowl. Discard the bay leaf, then pour the dressing over the chick-peas and toss well with your hands or a large spoon. Let cool to room temperature. This can be made a day ahead and refrigerated overnight, then brought to room temperature before serving.

Serves 20 as a side dish

VALENCIA

Paella

The Valencia version, perhaps the original, is now a real citified paella. In the country, people put in 2 or 3 different kinds of meat or fish and regard this version as silly and overdone. Those of us who like variety will appreciate it. Every self-respecting Spanish cook has her own version of paella, usually using the best local ingredients.

Serve a warm goat cheese salad first and a dry white Catalan wine with the paella. End the meal with a luxurious, cream-filled cake.

- ¼ teaspoon saffron
- 4 cups chicken stock, homemade preferable but canned acceptable
- 5 tablespoons olive oil
- 2 whole chicken breasts (with skin and bones), cut into a total of 30 roughly square pieces
- 1 red or green bell pepper, seeded, cut into ¼″-wide × 2″-long strips
- 1 onion, finely chopped
- 2 garlic cloves, crushed then minced

2 cups raw short-grain rice
16 medium raw shrimp, shelled
¼ pound spicy smoked sausage, such as Chorizo (page 192), thinly sliced
½ pound ham, cut into ½″ cubes
1 bay leaf
1 cup shelled raw or thawed frozen peas
6 canned tomatoes, squeezed through your hands to almost puree them
8 small clams, washed well
8 mussels, washed well
¼ cup roughly chopped fresh parsley
16 lemon wedges

Crumble the saffron into the stock and set them aside. Heat 2 tablespoons oil over medium heat in a large skillet or paella pan, add the chicken and bell peppers, and stir constantly until the chicken turns white all over. Remove them with a slotted spoon and set aside. Add the remaining 3 tablespoons oil and sauté the onion and garlic for 5 minutes, then the rice, sautéing for 5 minutes more, until every grain of rice is completely coated with oil. Add the shrimp, turn heat to high, and stir for 2 minutes.

Stir in the chicken, peppers, stock, sausage, ham, bay leaf, peas, and tomatoes. Bring to a boil, then turn heat to very low and simmer, covered, for 10 minutes. Remove the cover, stir well, then place the clams and mussels on top. Cover and cook for another 15 minutes, then uncover and cook for 5 minutes more. Remove the pan from the heat and discard any clams and mussels that haven't opened. Strew the parsley over the paella and serve the lemon wedges alongside.

Serves 8

ANDALUSIA

Baked Eggs with Vegetables and Meat

♦ ***Huevos á la Flamenca***

The colors of the vegetables are almost as important as their taste. This is supposed to look as decorative as possible, so if another vegetable's color strikes your fancy, add it in. Spaniards love eggs and serve them as part of a meal or snack, day or night. It's a little too elaborate for breakfast, to my taste, but it makes a terrific light lunch or supper.

If you're serving this dish for supper, begin with a cup of sausageless Caldo Verde (Potato, Kale, and Sausage Soup). You need fresh bread, perhaps even Portuguese cornbread, to go with the soup and eggs. A glass of any light white wine, such as a Vouvray, complements the eggs nicely. Serve melon marinated in medium-dry sherry for dessert.

1 tablespoon olive oil
½ small onion, finely chopped
1 garlic clove, crushed then minced
1 small red or green bell pepper, seeded and julienned
¾ cup drained, chopped canned tomatoes
2 ounces smoked ham, julienned
¼ pound Chorizo (page 192) or other smoked garlic sausage, very thinly sliced
6 tablespoons chicken stock, homemade preferred but canned acceptable
2 tablespoons sherry
⅛ teaspoon hot paprika or cayenne pepper
Salt and pepper to taste
8 stalks asparagus, halved after hard section at bottom discarded
¼ cup cooked fresh or thawed frozen peas

8 medium eggs
4 teaspoons finely chopped fresh parsley

Preheat the oven to 400°. Heat the oil in a large skillet over low heat. When it's hot, add the onion, garlic, and bell peppers and cook, stirring occasionally, for 5 minutes. Stir in the tomatoes, ham, sausage, stock, sherry, paprika or cayenne, and salt and pepper. Bring to a boil over high heat, stir once or twice, then return the heat to low.

Add the asparagus, cover, and simmer for 10 minutes. Stir in the peas, then immediately remove the pan from the heat. Remove the asparagus tips from the sauce. Divide the sauce among four 15-ounce casseroles, making sure each gets approximately an equal amount of sausage, asparagus, and peas.

With a soup spoon, make 2 smooth hollows in the sauce in each dish. Break an egg into each hollow, making sure you don't break the yolk. It's all right if the eggs are almost touching each other. Arrange the asparagus tips decoratively around the eggs and sprinkle each dish with some of the parsley and salt and pepper. Bake the eggs for 10 minutes until the whites are set but the yolks are still slightly runny.

Serves 4

PORTUGAL

Tomato Soup with Sausage

♦ ***Sopa de Tomate***

It's hard to imagine Iberian cooking without tomatoes, but there were no tomatoes in Europe until they were brought back from the New World in the sixteenth century. The Portuguese are great soup lovers, and sausage soups were usually created by peasants for whom they served as an entire meal, accompanied only by bread.

You can serve this clear soup for supper or as the first course at a dinner party. If you're serving it at dinner, float a slice of toast sprinkled with Parmesan cheese on the soup rather than pouring the soup onto the bread. Then follow it with one of Iberia's many meat and rice dishes, such as paella. End the meal with a Portuguese cheese tart, or American or Italian cheesecake, coffee, and port.

. . . .

2 tablespoons lard or vegetable oil
1 medium onion, roughly chopped
1 garlic clove, crushed then minced
¼ pound spicy smoked sausage, such as Chouriço, Linguiça (page 192 or 193), or pepperoni, thinly sliced
¾ cup tomato puree
4½ cups beef or chicken stock, homemade preferable but canned acceptable
1 bay leaf
Salt to taste
1 teaspoon paprika
2 large, very ripe fresh tomatoes, roughly chopped
6 slices of wide French or Italian peasant bread

Heat the lard or oil in a large saucepan over low heat. Sauté the onions, stirring occasionally, for 5 minutes. Add the garlic and sauté for another 3 minutes, stirring frequently so it doesn't burn. Add the tomato puree, stock, bay leaf, salt, and paprika, stir once or twice, then bring to a boil over high heat. Turn heat to medium-low and boil gently for 30 minutes. Stir in the fresh tomatoes and simmer for 15 minutes. Place a slice of bread at the bottom of each of 6 bowls, then pour the soup over it.

Serves 6

NORTHERN PORTUGAL

Potato, Kale, and Sausage Soup

♦ ***Caldo Verde***

Although it originated in the north, caldo verde is one of the most popular soups throughout Portugal. Many people prefer the soup reheated; I find it loses that fresh taste you get from lightly cooked greens. Since Portuguese kale is stronger-tasting than our kale or the closely related collard greens, I've used our stronger sea kale (Swiss chard). Spinach is equally delicious in this soup if you can't find either kind of kale. Serve this as a complete winter supper accompanied by Portuguese cornbread, or as a first course preceding something light like grilled fish. Accompany it with any Portuguese white wine or a California Chenin Blanc.

4 cups water
½ pound Chouriço, Linguiça, Kielbasa (page 192, 193, or 173) or other smoked garlic sausage
¾ pound potatoes, peeled, halved lengthwise, then sliced
1 tablespoon olive oil
1 onion, finely chopped
½ pound kale, cut into very thin strips
Salt and white pepper

Bring 3 cups of water to a boil in a large pot. Add the sausage, turn down the heat, and simmer for 15 minutes over low heat. Remove the sausage, turn up the heat, and add the potatoes to the water. Thinly slice the sausages and set aside. Boil the potatoes for about 12 minutes, until they're tender. Remove the pot from the heat.

Put the cooked potatoes and ½ cup of their cooking water in your food processor or blender. Puree with on/off pulses until fairly smooth. A couple of lumps are better than overprocessing it. You can also mash the potatoes without any cooking water by hand. Stir about a quarter of the potato puree at a time back into the pot, making sure the soup is smooth after each addition. Begin reheating the soup over low heat.

In a small pot bring the remaining 1 cup water to a boil. Heat the oil in a skillet over low heat and sauté the onion for 10 minutes, until soft but not browned. Pour the contents of the skillet into the potato soup, then add the kale, then the boiling water. Simmer for 3 minutes over low heat. Stir in the sausage, salt, and pepper, heat through, and serve.

Serves 4

SOUTHERN PORTUGAL

Steamed Clams and Sausages

♦ ***Almêijoas na Cataplana***

Whoever invented this dish was truly inspired. In Portugal, it's made in a *cataplana*, a large, shell-shaped pan with a hinged lid. I've found that a wok with a lid is the closest approximation, although you can use a skillet. If you can find a cataplana, it's wonderful for steaming and braising, and when you bring it to the table, open the lid and let the savory steam out... let's just say it's worth whatever it costs. I like to use cockles or the smallest possible clams since they closely approximate the Iberian mollusks.

This is an impressive, romantic dinner for two. Make it in the kitchen in an electric wok up to the point where you begin cooking the clams. Add the clams, cover the pan, and bring it to the table. Plug it in, but refuse to say what's in it and inform your dinner companion that it will be ruined if you open the lid. Serve your first course, perhaps a mixed green salad, and by the time you finish, your clams will be ready. A bottle of Dom Perignon champagne, an elegant chocolate torte, coffee, and port round out the meal.

1½ tablespoons olive oil
1 large onion, halved then thinly sliced
1 garlic clove, crushed then minced
2 ounces prosciutto, cut into ¼″ dice
½ yellow, red, or green bell pepper, seeded, cut into ¼″ dice
3 ounces Chouriço, Linguiça (page 192 or 193), or pepperoni, cut into ¼″ dice
½ teaspoon paprika
Pinch of ground chile pepper or cayenne
Pinch of black pepper
2 very ripe plum tomatoes, fresh or canned, seeded, finely chopped
¼ cup dry white wine
1 bay leaf
16 cockles or small clams, washed well
2 tablespoons finely chopped fresh parsley

Heat the oil over medium-high heat in a cataplana, wok, or a large skillet. Add the onion and garlic and cook, stirring occasionally, for 5 minutes. Add the prosciutto, bell pepper, and sausage and stir for 3 minutes. Stir in the paprika, ground chile or cayenne, black pepper, tomatoes, wine, and bay leaf. Bring to a boil, then turn heat to low and simmer for 5 minutes, until just a thin film of liquid appears in the bottom of the pan when you move aside the solids.

Place the cockles or clams on top of the tomato mixture, cover the pan, and cook over moderate heat until the clams open. It should take about 10 to 20 minutes. Discard any that haven't opened after 20 minutes. Remove from the heat and sprinkle with parsley.

Serves 2

CHAPTER
9

Scandinavi

and Benelux

While some Scandinavian sausages have European counterparts, many of them are unique. There are several kinds of sausages made with grated, cubed, mashed potatoes or potato flour and usually equal amounts of pork and beef. When the sausages don't include potatoes, then potatoes are served alongside. Some sausages are smoked over maple or juniper, which also adds flavor to them. The third distinguishing characteristic of Scandinavian sausages is unusual spices such as cardamom. The sausages are also baked as often as they are fried, alone or in a casserole. *Korv* is Swedish for sausage, *polse* is Danish and Norwegian, and *makkara* is Finnish.

Reindeer sausages, made with meat imported from Lapland, are widely available throughout Scandinavia, and some taste like extremely rich hot dogs. Fish forcemeats, rolled into balls or baked in puddings, are common. Sausages are included in the famous Scandinavian buffets like smorgasbord; cold, sliced salamis are eaten as part of the second, cold course, while small cocktail sausages are included in the hot course, served third. A thick yellow pea soup often contains smoked sausages.

Swedish cooks prepare for weeks for Christmas, making sausages, picking out the right ham, baking the appropriate breads and cookies. On the day before Christmas there is a custom called *doppa i grytan*, "dip in the kettle." Everyone gathers around the stove, dips a piece of bread into the broth in which the Christmas cabbage, meat for the headcheese, ring-shaped sausages, and ham have been cooked, and eats it along with some of the sausage.

It's not surprising that many Swedish sausages combine pork and beef or veal, since they are all favorites. Lamb is rarely used in Swedish sausages, the well-known exception being Göteborg mutton salami. Fried blood and rye meal sausages are part of the traditional Swedish breakfast, and liver sausages are usually eaten cold on sandwiches. Goose liver, rice, and raisins in goose skin casings are served in a blood soup. The strong-tasting *hackkorv* is made from pork organ meats mixed with barley and onion. Casseroles often include sausages, especially the small *prinskorv.*

It was always easy for Swedes to keep sausages over the

winter, since it gets very cold. To ensure that sausages would stay in good condition, however, they were often stored in a sugar and salt brine, sealed in fat like the French confit, dried like *pickekorv,* or smoked like *medvurst.*

The quality of Danish sausages is due to the excellent pork and beef, raised under strict supervision and quality-control standards. Sausages are rarely made from lamb, because it's so expensive. The fame of Danish salami, exported all over the world, is second only to Italian. The Danes add sugar to many foods including their sausages. Smorrebrod, beautifully decorated open-faced sandwiches, are made with sliced salami or liver sausage. These sandwiches and hot sausages in rolls, like frankfurters, are topped with fried onions or accompanied by red cabbage. Onions, allspice, and cloves season many sausages. Fruit preserves, especially lingonberries, are served with sausages to balance the rich meat with an acidic taste. Poached blood sausage, made with barley, apples, or ground pork, is either eaten cold or fried in butter. *Medisterpolse,* a fine-textured pork sausage, and *spegepolse,* a smoked beef summer sausage, are two of Denmark's best.

Norway's main meats are lamb and mutton, since sheep are perfectly suited to the mountainous terrain, but pigs and cattle are now readily available. Lamb is often combined with reindeer, which are raised in the north, in salamis. Blood sausage, liver sausage, and headcheese have remained popular here while losing ground in the rest of Scandinavia. Generally, sausages in Norway contain more herbs, while other Scandinavian sausages are spiced. Smoked pork and lamb sausages are considered company food, served to unexpected guests or at parties. Open-faced Norwegian sausage sandwiches, accompanied by raw onions, are served for breakfast or lunch. Fried fresh sausages served with porridge, potatoes, or cabbage are a common supper dish.

Finland borders Russia in the east and Sweden in the west and Finnish cuisine has been influenced by both countries. A Finnish borscht or sauerkraut soup might contain smoked sausage flavored with Swedish-style spices. The west is famous for blood sausages, the east for meat sausages. Pork and beef are the most popular meats, while veal, lamb, elk, and reindeer are sometimes used. There is a great variety of blood and liver sausages. Oddly enough, bologna and hot dogs are two of Finland's favorite sausages. They're baked with cheese, simmered with vegetables, and cooked on the stove with eggs. Chunks of bologna, pork, or pork and mutton sausages used to be grilled over the sauna stones, but now sauna dressing rooms have fireplaces where they're cooked and served with hot Finnish mustard. Fresh pork, beef, and potato sausages *(perunamakkara)* are stored in brine. Smoked versions *(karistysmakkara)* include veal. Rice is the other starch most commonly added to sausages, including *uunimakkara,* which has suet or pork fat and no meat.

Sausages from Belgium, Luxembourg, and Holland reflect the proximity of both Germany and France. Dutch food, however, is also remarkably similar to that of its northern Scandinavian neighbors. Green split-pea soup is as popular in Holland as yellow is in Scandinavia. Other warming, thick soups also contain smoked sausages. Many vegetables, such as cabbage, potatoes, rice, sauerkraut, and Brussels sprouts, are enlivened with smoked or fresh sausages. *Broodjes,* little sandwiches, with smoked or liver sausage are devoured at lunchtime. *Saucijzebroodjes* or *sauseasons* are pigs in the blanket, made with nutmeg-spiced sausage in pastry dough, which Dutch fishermen used to carry as quick snacks. In eastern Holland, bread is baked already enclosing sausage chunks. Three of the best Dutch sausages are a beef and pork cervelat, a blood sausage with raisins, and *rolpens*—beef sausages poached then marinated in vinegar.

The best Belgian pork sausages come from the Ardennes, bordering France. A *collier d'Ardennes* is a chain of sausages tied in a ring, and *potee d'Ardennes* is a stew filled with smoked pork, vegetables, and knockwurst. White sausages, like boudin blanc and weisswurst, are common but somewhat bland, although more interesting boudins made from game or rabbit are currently in vogue. Smoked wild boar sausages and game bird galantines are excellent. Blood sausages are poached, cooled, skinned, beaten with cream, and spread on toast. In Belgium and Luxembourg, just like France and Germany, sausage is accompanied by warm potato salad. Hard-boiled eggs enclosed in beef sausage are called *vogelnestjes,* "birds' nests," since that's what they resemble when they're halved.

Scandinavia

Cold Horseradish Sauce

♦ ***Pepparrotas***

This thick sauce is served alongside all cold meats, but is especially good with sausages or stuffed cabbage. The peppery taste of horseradish balances the richness of the meat. Make Scandinavian open-faced sandwiches with lightly buttered rye bread, a slice of Danish salami, and a small dollop of the sauce. Please note that a recipe for horseradish sauce is included in Norman Douglas's *Venus in the Kitchen,* a book which deals with purported aphrodisiacs.

1 tablespoon unsalted butter
4 teaspoons white flour
¾ cup milk, room temperature
Dash of white vinegar
3–4 tablespoons tightly packed, well drained, freshly grated or prepared horseradish
¼ teaspoon salt
Pinch of white pepper
¼ cup heavy cream

Melt the butter over very low heat in a very small saucepan. Stir in the flour, immediately remove the pan from the heat, and stir until smooth. Pour in ¼ cup milk and stir until the mixture is smooth and there are no lumps.

Return the pan to very low heat. Stir in the remaining ½ cup milk, then stir often for 15 minutes, never letting the sauce boil. Remove the pan from the heat and whisk in the vinegar, 3 tablespoons horseradish, salt, and pepper. Taste and add more horseradish if desired. Press a sheet of waxed paper or plastic wrap onto the top of the sauce to prevent a skin from forming.

Let cool to room temperature. You can now refrigerate it, with waxed paper or plastic wrap pressed into the top, for up to a day. Just before serving, whip the cream until it holds stiff peaks and fold it into the sauce.

Makes 1 cup

SWEDEN

Christmas Potato Sausages

There are almost as many names for potato sausages as there are recipes. Fresh Christmas sausage is *Julkorv* in Swedish, while the ordinary version is *potatiskorv* and the smoked *brackorv.* There's also *Varmlandkorv,* from western Sweden, with cubed potatoes. Danish and Norwegian Christmas sausage is *Julepolse,* and in Finland they're *Joulumakkara* or *perunamakkara.*

Some Scandinavians say that stock should be used, but others insist on milk. Larger versions of potato sausage, about 3" wide, used to be common, but now the smaller size is more popular. The sausages can be eaten right after they're poached, or they can be cut into chunks and fried in butter. Serve the fried sausages alongside eggs for breakfast, or the poached sausages for supper in a creamy soup. Browned under the broiler, they're delicious accompanied by sautéed cabbage or green peas. Beer seems to go better with potato sausages than wine.

1 cup milk
1 tablespoon plus 2 teaspoons sugar
2 teaspoons salt
1 teaspoon black pepper
½ teaspoon ground allspice
½ teaspoon minced fresh marjoram, or ¼ teaspoon crumbled dried
¼ teaspoon minced fresh thyme, or ⅛ teaspoon crumbled dried

1 pound finely ground lean beef
1 pound lean pork, finely ground
1 pound potatoes, peeled, grated
4 teaspoons coarse, sea, or kosher salt

Prepared hog casings

Mix together in a measuring cup with a spout the milk, 1 tablespoon sugar, regular salt, pepper, allspice, marjoram, and thyme. Knead together the beef, pork, and potatoes by hand, or in a food processor using short pulses. You want the mixture mixed well, but not emulsified. Then beat in the seasoned milk with a wooden spoon until the meat is fluffy, or process it just until completely incorporated.

Loosely stuff the sausage mixture into the prepared casings. These are traditionally tied off in 6″ lengths or can be as long as 18″ to 24″. The diameter should be about 1″ to 1¼″. If you decide on the longer lengths, tie the ends of each sausage together to form a ring. Prick any air pockets with a pin.

Mix together the coarse salt and 2 teaspoons sugar and rub the sausages with the mixture. Let the sausages sit, for 12 to 48 hours in a large bowl, covered and refrigerated. Turn a few times after the sausages have released some liquid.

Rinse off the sausages when you're ready to cook them. Poach for 30 minutes. The poached sausages can be refrigerated for 1 week or frozen for 3 months.

Makes just over 3 pounds raw sausage

Smoked Beef and Pork Sausages

♦ ***Medvurst***

Adding smoked sausages to a vegetable soup, like Green Pea (later in this chapter), gives the soup much more complex flavor. The medvurst can also be sliced and served on open-faced sandwiches topped with fried onions and a dab of Cold Horseradish Sauce.

- 2 teaspoons salt
- ½ teaspoon black pepper
- 3 teaspoons sugar
- ⅛ teaspoon ground cloves
- ⅛ teaspoon grated nutmeg
- ¼ teaspoon caraway seeds
- ¼ teaspoon ground coriander
- ⅜ teaspoon dry mustard
- ½ teaspoon liquid smoke (optional)
- 3 tablespoons pale beer
- 1 pound ground very lean beef
- 1 pound lean pork, ground
- ¼ pound pork fat, ground
- 4 teaspoons coarse, sea, or kosher salt

Prepared hog casings

Stir the regular salt, pepper, 1 teaspoon sugar, cloves, nutmeg, caraway seeds, coriander, mustard, and liquid smoke (if used) into the beer. Knead together the beef, pork, and pork fat, then knead in the beer mixture.

Stuff firmly into the prepared casings and tie off into 4″ lengths. Prick any air pockets with a pin.

Mix together the remaining 1 teaspoon sugar with the coarse salt and rub into the sausages. Place the sausages in a bowl and let sit in the refrigerator, covered, for 1 to 3 days. Turn them once or twice a day.

When you're ready to smoke the sausages, rinse them off and wipe them dry. If you can find juniper chips, soak a handful in water, then throw them on the burning charcoal just before you add the sausage. Smoke them at 275° for 3 to 4 hours, or poach them for 20 minutes. The cooked or smoked sausages can be refrigerated for 1 week or frozen for 3 months.

Makes almost 2½ pounds raw sausage.

NORWAY

Ginger Sausages

♦ ***Ingefarapolse***

Some Scandinavian cooks believe using ginger is a butcher's trick to hide the taste of mediocre sausage. Other cooks believe that, in moderation, ginger is wonderful. You can either make your own potato sausage or buy it at Scandinavian markets. The addition of pickle to the sausage adds an unexpected, delicious bite.

These sausages make a lovely appetizer. Serve them with Cold Horseradish Sauce and parsley or watercress or meatless tomato sauce and fresh coriander. Follow them with a Scandinavian fish dish, such as fillet of sole in red wine sauce, potato slices baked with cheese, and sautéed spinach or spinach soufflé. Norwegian apple pudding would be a perfect dessert. I like a fruity white wine with the sausages, like a California Johannisberg Riesling or Gewürztraminer.

1 pound skinless Potato Sausage (page 218)
3 tablespoons minced onion
¾ teaspoon ground ginger
⅛ teaspoon ground cloves
⅛ teaspoon white pepper
⅛ teaspoon salt
2 large egg whites
1 tablespoon minced cornichons or other very tart pickles
¼ cup dry bread crumbs
Vegetable oil

Beat the sausage until fluffy with a wooden spoon, the paddle of an electric mixer, or in a food processor. Then beat in the onion.

In a bowl mix together the ginger, cloves, pepper, salt, and egg whites and whip until it holds stiff peaks. Fold the whites into the sausage meat. Fold in the pickles, then the bread crumbs.

With damp hands form the meat into 18 small sausages, each about 1″ wide. Heat 1″ of vegetable oil in a large skillet until very hot but not smoking. Drop in about 6 sausages and fry until a rich brown all over, 2 to 3 minutes. Drain the finished sausages on paper towels while frying the other batches.

Serves 6 as an appetizer

FINLAND

Stuffed Cabbage

♦ ***Kaalikaaryleet***

If you're wondering why this recipe is included, it's because it's a sausage with a vegetable, rather than animal, casing. You can also stuff this filling into a hog casing if you want to fry it instead of baking it. Stuffed cabbage is a favorite throughout Scandinavia, possibly adapted from Middle Eastern stuffed grape leaves discovered by Viking traders who traveled to Constantinople in the tenth century. Some historians believe that Charles XII, imprisoned in Turkey, became so attached to stuffed grape leaves that he brought the idea back with him when he returned to Sweden. Onion or lettuce leaves can also be used. The Finnish version usually contains barley, while others use rice or bread crumbs.

Serve these rolls on a bed of mashed potatoes, accompanied by a tart relish such as lingonberry or cranberry. Begin the family dinner with a cup of vegetable soup and end with marzipan-filled baked apples. A bone-dry French Sancerre goes well with the rolls.

- ⅓ cup pearl barley, soaked in cold water to cover for 1–4 hours
- 1 cup water
- 1 2–3-pound head of green cabbage
- 1 pound ground regular, not lean, beef
- ¼ pound veal or pork, ground
- 3 tablespoons heavy cream
- 1 teaspoon salt
- ¼ teaspoon black pepper
- ½ teaspoon ground allspice
- 3 tablespoons unsalted butter
- 4 teaspoons molasses
- 1 tablespoon white flour

Drain the barley and put in a saucepan with the water. Turn heat to low, cover the pan, and cook the barley for 30 minutes, stirring once or twice to prevent it from sticking to the bottom of the pan. Pour the barley into a strainer and let it cool.

While the barley is cooling, bring a large pot of water to a boil. Add the cabbage and boil for 10 minutes until the leaves are pliable. Drain the cabbage well. Knead together the barley, meats, cream, salt, pepper, and allspice.

Detach the leaves from the cabbage, being careful not to tear them. Place a leaf with the stem end facing you. Cut out the hard part of the leaf at the stem end which would break if rolled. Take one-twelfth of the filling and place it about ½″ from the end nearest you. Form it into a rectangle, the shorter ends of which are about 1″ from either side of the leaf. Push it into a fairly compact cylinder. Fold the sides of the cabbage leaf over the filling, then roll the leaf up beginning at the end near you. Set the roll aside and make the other 11 rolls.

Preheat the oven to 350°. Melt the butter over medium-low heat in 2 ovenproof skillets, preferably cast iron. Brown the rolls, seam side first, on all sides, then turn them so the seam sides are down again. Pour in enough hot water to come three-quarters of the way up the rolls. Cover the skillets and place in the oven. Cook for 1 hour, then uncover and drizzle the molasses over the rolls. Cook, uncovered, for an additional 30 minutes.

Place the rolls in a serving dish large enough to hold them, cover with foil, and keep warm in the turned-off oven. Pour the pan juices from one skillet into the other. Place the skillet with the juices over low heat and stir in the flour. Bring to a boil over high heat, turn to low, and simmer for 5 minutes, stirring often, until smooth and thick. Serve the rolls with the sauce poured over.

Serves 6 as a large appetizer, 4 as a main course

Rice, Liver, and Raisin Sausages

♦ ***Riisimakkara***

These somewhat exotic sausages add an authentic air to a smorgasbord buffet or tray of canapés. Serve slices on buttered flatbread or crackers, sprinkled with grated raw onion. Or remove the sausage from the casings and lightly beat it with some cream cheese and a few drops of Tabasco sauce to make a spread. Be sure when you're beating it that you don't mash the rice and raisins completely, since the textural contrast between them and the liver is very nice. You can use these in any way you'd use liverwurst.

2¼ cups milk
⅜ cup raw rice
3 tablespoons unsalted butter or beef suet
1 small onion, minced
½ pound beef or pork liver, ground
3 tablespoons corn syrup
½ teaspoon ground ginger
6 tablespoons raisins
1 teaspoon salt
¼ teaspoon black pepper

Prepared hog casings

Bring 1½ cups milk to a boil in a small saucepan, stir in the rice, turn heat to very low, and cook, covered, until the rice has absorbed all the milk. It will take 10 to 15 minutes.

While the rice is cooking, melt the butter or suet in a skillet over low heat and sauté the onion for 5 minutes. Add the liver and stir, crushing it into very small pieces, until it has lost its redness. Pour the contents of the skillet into a bowl. Stir the corn syrup, ginger, raisins, salt, pepper, cooked rice, and the rest of the milk into the liver.

Loosely fill the prepared hog casings. The sausages should be no wider than 1″. Tie off into 4″ to 5″ links. Poach the sausages for 45 minutes, never letting the water boil. Prick them once or twice if they rise to the top.

Makes approximately 1½ pounds raw sausage

Baked Sausage Pancake

♦ ***Makkarapannukakko***

Pancakes and sausage are a favorite Scandinavian combination. This Finnish kind is more like Yorkshire pudding than American pancakes, making this similar to the English toad-in-the-hole. It will rise unevenly, but that won't show very much when you serve it cut into wedges. Feel free to add cheese or onions to the batter.

This is the perfect lunch or brunch dish, accompanied by lingonberries or applesauce, a cooked vegetable salad, and beer. Serve cheesecake or chocolate pudding for dessert.

- 1¼ cups unbleached all-purpose presifted flour
- 2 teaspoons salt
- 2 teaspoons sugar
- 3 large eggs, lightly beaten
- 1 cup milk
- 1 tablespoon unsalted butter
- 1 pound cooked, dried, or smoked Scandinavian sausages (page 218 or 219), cut into ¼" slices

Preheat the oven to 375°. Mix the flour, salt, and sugar in a large bowl, then whisk in the eggs and milk until smooth.

Melt the butter in a 12" ovenproof skillet, preferably cast iron, over medium-low heat and arrange the sausages symmetrically in it. Pour in the batter. Place the skillet in the oven and bake for 30 minutes, until the pancake is golden and set. Cut into wedges and serve.

Serves 6

HOLLAND

Green Pea Soup

♦ ***Groene Erwtensoep***

This soup is rarely called by its full name in Holland; it's usually just affectionately referred to as "snert." It should be thick enough to stand a spoon in it, but that means you'll have to keep checking it to make sure it's not sticking to the bottom of the pot. The soaking, and long cooking, helps to make this a cross between a puree and a soup. You can omit the soaking and increase the cooking time (by about 1 hour) for a good, though not as authentic, soup. Snert actually tastes better reheated, so the soup for Sunday midday dinner is usually made on Saturday. Frozen ice skaters sip it as a pick-me-up before facing the ice again. It also follows an appetizer and precedes the meat course of a more formal meal. I serve it for a winter supper with coarse rye bread, a glass of dry white wine like Chardonnay, and Dutch apple pancakes sprinkled with sugar for dessert.

14 ounces dried split green peas, soaked in cold water to cover overnight, drained
2 smoked ham hocks
5 cups water
5 cups chicken stock, homemade preferable but canned acceptable
3 leeks, white and light green sections, halved, thickly sliced
3 large potatoes, peeled, quartered
Salt and pepper to taste
1 pound smoked sausage, thinly sliced

Bring the peas, hocks, water, stock, and leeks to a boil in a large pot, turn heat to very low, and simmer, uncovered, for 3 hours. Stir occasionally from the bottom of the pot to keep the peas from sticking.

After 3 hours, remove the hocks. Discard the bones and return their meat to the pot. Add the potatoes, salt and pepper, and sausage to the soup and simmer, stirring occasionally from the bottom, until the potatoes are cooked through, 30 to 40 minutes.

Serves 10

Whipped Kale and Potatoes with Sausages

♦ ***Stamppot***

You can use either bacon or smoked sausage in this recipe. Stamppot made with meat drippings, but no meat, is served as a side dish. While it seems a bit exotic, it actually tastes like beautifully seasoned mashed potatoes, similar to the Celtic colcannon and German Himmel und Erde.

Serve this for lunch or supper with a young red wine like Beaujolais or Chinon. Fruit tarts, made with strawberries, peaches, apricots, cherries, or apples, are popular Dutch desserts which would go well with stamppot.

- 2 pounds kale, collard greens, or Swiss chard, tough part of stems discarded, roughly chopped
- 3 pounds potatoes, cut into ½″ cubes
- 2 tablespoons unsalted butter
- 2 pounds Medvurst (page 219) or other beef and/or pork smoked sausage, cut into link size if larger than that
- 1 small onion, minced
- 1 tablespoon sugar
- 3 tablespoons hot milk
- ½ teaspoon salt
- ½ teaspoon white pepper
- ¼ teaspoon grated nutmeg

Bring a large pot of water to a boil, add the greens and potatoes, and boil, uncovered, for 25 minutes. Turn off the water and leave the pot on the heat until you're ready to use the vegetables.

While the greens and potatoes are cooking, melt the butter in a large skillet and brown the sausages over medium heat. Remove the sausages from the skillet and drain on paper towels.

Add the onions to the sausage skillet and sauté over medium-low heat for about 10 minutes, until they're very soft. Turn down the heat if they begin to brown. While they're cooking, dissolve the sugar in the milk.

By hand or in a food processor using on/off pulses, whip the greens, potatoes, contents of the onion skillet, milk and sugar, salt, pepper, and nutmeg until the mixture has the texture of mashed potatoes. Serve with the sausages laid on top.

Serves 8

Chapter 10

. . . .

Britain

British sausages are very idiosyncratic. Many of them contain a large proportion of cereal filler, like oatmeal or bread crumbs, and most Britons wouldn't have them any other way. White puddings, made from only cereal, seasonings, animal fat, and sometimes cheese, are popular in many country districts. A number of skinless sausages are breaded and deep-fried. Few sausages are smoked.

The English have always loved the sausage mixtures called "forcemeat." Since medieval times, and especially in the seventeenth and eighteenth centuries, heavily spiced "forc'd-meat" was rolled into balls and added to soups, dishes like jugged hare or meat pies, or used as stuffing for veal rolls or poultry. The forcemeats were made from game, ham, pork, veal, organ meats, or even fish. Headcheeses were equally popular, made in all kinds of decorative molds. Oysters were used as extenders, substituting for the more expensive meat, in sausages. By the nineteenth century, slices of mortadella, whole German wursts, and canned bologna sausages were common, and "mincing machines" for making sausages could be bought for a reasonable price from the local ironmonger. Instead of the time-consuming process of smoking, cookbooks recommended painting sausages with creosote.

Sausages in casings were called "puddings," whether the large kind made in animal stomachs or the narrower version stuffed into intestines. *Haggis*, the famous Scottish oatmeal and organ meat–stuffed sheep's stomach, has been made in Britain since at least the thirteenth century. Just as in other parts of the world, sausages developed as a way of using up every last scrap of the animals slaughtered in the fall since there was no way to feed them over the winter. A particularly peculiar sausage from a seventeenth-century cookbook is an orange pudding stuffed into hog casings, boiled, and served as a sweet.

Sausages are still popular in modern England, and the famous Harrods Food Halls stock over fifty different kinds of sausages. Pork is the most commonly used sausage meat, while the most popular sausage is a *banger* or *Oxford sausage*. It's made from equal amounts of pork and veal, breaded or stuffed into casings, and too often overseasoned with sage. Some excellent all-pork sausages are the long, coarse *Cumberland,* the herb-scented *Cambridge,* the lemony *Epping,* and the reddish *saveloy.* In Yorkshire, a large, spicy pork sausage is boiled in a pudding cloth, then sliced and eaten cold with pickles.

Every region makes sausages from available livestock. Yorkshire and Lancashire are known for their beef sausages, made longer and narrower to distinguish them from pork sausages, while the Welsh make skinless sausages or links from mutton or lamb. As a rule, pork sausages are fried in pork drippings, beef in beef drippings, and lamb in mutton fat. Venison sausages, a royal favorite hundreds of years ago, are now becoming popular for anyone who can afford them.

In northern England butchers offer a large selection of blood sausages, called "black puddings." Some puddings mix the beef or pork blood with oatmeal, others include barley, rice, a small amount of ground pork, or lots of onions. They're often served at breakfast accompanied by fried apples or included in potato and mutton stews. *Faggots* are caul-wrapped, minced organ meats and bread crumbs shaped into links or little mounds, baked and served cold or reheated in gravy. Aside from oatmeal sausages, the best white puddings are those made in Glamorgan in southern Wales with grated cheese, minced leeks, bread crumbs, mustard, and herbs. These deep-fried skinless sausages can be served hot or cold, but are best just slightly warm. Cornwall's specialty is its version of *toad-in-the-hole,* sausages baked in a nest of mashed potatoes.

English sausages are usually fried or grilled rather than cooked in stews, soups, or casseroles. Potatoes, fried apples, or red cabbage are common sausage companions. The justifiably famous English breakfast can include fried black puddings; white puddings; and pork or beef links along with bacon, eggs, fried bread, grilled tomatoes, grilled kidneys and any number of other filling foods. *Bangers and mash* (fried sausage and mashed potatoes), *Scotch eggs* (sausage-wrapped hard-boiled eggs), toad-in-the-hole (sausages baked in Yorkshire pudding batter), and pastry-encased *sausage rolls* are all British stand-bys.

Pork seems to be Scotland's least favorite meat. When Scots make smoked sausage, they use salt beef and suet rather than salt pork, and their black puddings are as likely to be made with sheep's blood as that of cattle or pork. Very often the black puddings are simply white oatmeal puddings with blood added to them. Scottish breakfasts are similar to the English, and their breakfast links are made with beef.

The Irish subsist on pork, taking pride in their all-meat pork sausage links that are eaten both at breakfast and at tea. Another excellent sausage is *drisheen,* a wide black pudding tied in a ring, made with either sheep or pork blood, lots of cream, and bread crumbs or oatmeal. After it's poached, it's sliced and fried or grilled, often accompanied by potato pancakes. Baked sausages and potato casseroles are popular.

Australian cuisine is almost as great a melting pot as that of the United States. Australians serve typically British foods such as sausage rolls, Scotch eggs, haggis (which they call "haggis baggis"), and sausage-stuffed poultry recipes. There are also Italian restaurants serving antipasto platters filled with several kinds of salami, German butchers selling every kind of wurst, and elegant restaurants serving French galantines of game birds. And then there are the remarkable *Dinkum Dogs.* A machine makes a hole in the center of a roll and fills it with condiments. The sausage follows the condiments into the roll and, *voilà,* a messless hot dog which the Dinkum Dog owners claim is the only fast food sold at the Sydney Opera House.

ENGLAND

Bangers or Oxford Sausages

This recipe is identical to the one that's been prepared in England for at least 200 years except that the cayenne is modern and I've used slightly less fat. The fat content has been a subject of controversy recently in England. An attempt to have it reduced from the common 30 percent was met with universal fury. It's the fat and bread which make this fairly mild sausage taste so good. Bangers are terrific for any meal. You can grill them, broil them, fry them, braise them, or use them as bulk sausage in recipes like Scotch Eggs.

- ½ pound lean pork, ground
- ½ pound lean veal, ground
- 6 ounces pork fat, ground
- 3 slices of white bread with crust, crumbled or finely chopped
- 1 teaspoon salt
- ¼ teaspoon black pepper
- ¼ teaspoon cayenne pepper
- ⅛ teaspoon mixed grated nutmeg and mace
- ¼ teaspoon minced fresh thyme, or ⅛ teaspoon crumbled dried
- ¼ teaspoon minced fresh marjoram, or ⅛ teaspoon crumbled dried
- 2 teaspoons minced fresh sage, or 1 teaspoon crumbled dried
- 1 teaspoon loosely packed finely grated lemon peel
- 1 large egg

Prepared hog casings

Knead together the pork, veal, fat, and bread. Stir the salt, pepper, cayenne, nutmeg and mace, thyme, marjoram, sage, and lemon peel into the egg, then knead into the meat mixture.

Firmly stuff the mixture into prepared hog casings. Prick any air pockets with a pin. Poach, braise, or fry them before serving. The raw sausages can be refrigerated for 3 days, poached or braised sausages for 1 week. They can also be frozen, raw, poached, or braised, for 3 months.

Makes 2 pounds raw sausage

Mixed Grill

Mixed Grill is either a breakfast or supper item in England. I prefer it for dinner, since Americans, including me, prefer their main meat meal at night. It's also a good way to use up any odd pieces of meat in the freezer, like a couple of chicken wings. Let common sense be your guide in cooking this. Put the thinnest or most fragile items—the tomato and mushrooms—farthest from your heat source, while thicker items—the sausage—should be closest to the heat. Traditionally, salt and pepper are added at the table, not during cooking, so everyone can adjust the seasonings to his own taste.

Start dinner with a typically English sorrel or lettuce soup. All the grill needs are fresh peas tossed with a little butter and a small baked potato. Since you're spending time in the kitchen making the grill, choose a dessert you can prepare ahead, such as a frozen hazelnut soufflé. I like a California Merlot with the grill.

- 1 Banger, Bockwurst, or Bratwurst (page 234, 123, or 124), or other German white sausage, pricked with a pin in 4 or 5 places
- 4 large mushroom caps, brushed with melted butter
- 1 lamb kidney, butterflied
- 1 loin lamb chop, about 1" thick
- 1 4-ounce filet mignon, brushed with melted butter
- 1 medium tomato, halved, cut sides brushed with melted butter

Preheat the broiler and the broiler pan for 5 to 10 minutes. Place the sausage, mushroom caps, and kidney, cut side down, on the broiler pan and cook for 5 minutes. Turn the sausage and kidney and add the lamb, beef, and tomato, cut side up. Broil for 4 minutes. Turn the lamb and beef, brushing the filet with more butter, and cook for 5 more minutes.

Serves 1

Sausages Braised in Ale

Ale, with its distinctive taste, can enliven any especially bland sausages you obviously bought by mistake. It's even better with garlic sausages since the two tastes complement each other. Use a very good ale, since the taste is intensified as it boils down.

Mashed potatoes and sautéed cabbage taste delicious with the pan juices poured over them. All you need is a salad, some coarse peasant bread, more ale to drink, and apple brown betty or strudel for dessert.

2 tablespoons unsalted butter
2 fresh sausages (about ¾ pound total), preferably Garlic (page 24), pricked with a fork in 3 places
1–2 bottles of ale
1 bay leaf

Melt the butter over low heat in a skillet just large enough to hold the sausages. Add the sausages and brown well on both sides. Pour in enough ale to cover the sausages by at least ⅛", add the bay leaf, and simmer, uncovered, over low heat for 20 minutes. Turn the sausages and simmer for another 20 minutes.

Serves 2

Toad-in-the-Hole

Children, and those of us who still like silly-looking food, really love toad-in-the-hole. This is a descendant of an old dish called "froise," which began as bacon lightly coated in batter. Later, Yorkshire pudding batter was poured over any leftover pieces of meat. Now sausages are used more often than roast beef. In Kent, they put sugar in the batter rather than salt and pour it over fruit like pitted cherries.

Since this is a family supper, begin the meal with something simple like tomato soup. Serve an interesting salad with several kinds of greens and fresh herbs, Beaujolais or beer with the toad, and trifle for dessert.

- 2 large eggs
- 1 cup milk
- ½ teaspoon salt
- Pinch of black pepper
- 1 cup unbleached all-purpose presifted flour
- 4 small (4″–4½″ long) Bangers (page 234) or pork sausages (about 1 pound total), pricked with a fork in 2–3 places

The easiest way to make the Yorkshire pudding batter is in a food processor, but it can also be done by hand. Process or whisk the eggs, milk, salt, and pepper until frothy. This will take about 15 seconds in the processor, longer by hand. Gradually pour in the flour while the machine is running or while you continue to whisk, in a steady stream. When the batter is well mixed, refrigerate for about 30 minutes.

After the batter has rested for 15 minutes, preheat the oven to 450°. Place the sausages in a 9″ cast-iron skillet and fry on medium heat until browned all over. Using tongs, arrange the sausages in a decorative, symmetrical pattern in the pan. They can be side by side or forming spokes, for example. Gently, without disturbing the sausages, pour the batter around them.

Place the skillet in the oven and immediately turn the heat down to 375°. Bake for 35 minutes, until the top is crisped and browned. Serve at once.

Serves 4

Fidget Pie

Fidget pie is a specialty of northern England where hearty foods help residents cope with cold. You can also make it without the crust, simply layering the ingredients in a casserole. You can use almost any kind of fresh pork or beef sausage in this recipe, avoiding those with cereal filler. I use Garlic, bulk, or fresh Basic Italian sausage, since they add nice seasonings to this otherwise mild dish.

I like to start with potted shrimp or pâté with toast. The acid in the apples overpowers many wines, so drink beer with the pie. For dessert you can either serve something creamy like rice pudding or a selection of English cheeses.

. . . .

1 cup unbleached all-purpose presifted flour
1 teaspoon salt
6 tablespoons diced cold unsalted butter
1 large egg yolk
2 tablespoons unsalted butter
1 medium onion, grated or finely chopped
1½ pounds fresh sausage, preferably Garlic or Basic Italian (page 24 or 96), skinned and crumbled
¾ cup peas, fresh preferable but thawed frozen acceptable
1 pound (about 3) very crisp apples, peeled, grated
1 pound potatoes, peeled, grated
⅛ teaspoon black pepper
¼ teaspoon mace
1½ teaspoons chopped fresh herbs, such as sage, thyme, and/or rosemary, or ¾ teaspoon crumbled dried
1½ tablespoons chopped fresh parsley
1 egg, lightly beaten

Make a piecrust dough from the flour, ¼ teaspoon salt, diced butter, and yolk. (See Dickensian Ham and Veal Pie, page 49, for dough instructions.) Roll into a ball, wrap tightly in plastic wrap, and store in the refrigerator until ready to use.

Preheat the oven to 450°. Melt the butter in a skillet over medium-low heat. Sauté the onion for 5 minutes, until just softened. Stir in the crumbled sausage and cook just until it loses its red color. Stir in the peas and take the skillet off the heat and set aside.

Mix together the apples, potatoes, ¾ teaspoon salt, pepper, mace, herbs, and parsley and set aside.

This dough is somewhat fragile because of the large amount of butter, so pat it quite gently into a rectangular shape on a floured surface. Then, with a floured rolling pin, smooth it out quickly with just 2 or 3 rolls until it's ¼″ thick and large enough to fit into your baking dish. Cut off any ragged edges. Gently lay it in the dish so that it exactly reaches the top rim on all sides. If the dough breaks, just push it back together with your fingers and lightly pinch together to seal. Fold the top ½″ rim of the dough down and crimp the resulting double layer of dough to form a decorative edge. Prick the bottom all over with a fork, then brush the entire inside of the dough with the beaten egg.

Make an even layer of half the apple and potato mixture on the bottom of the baking dish. Cover with an even layer of half the sausage mixture, then repeat the layers. Place in the oven and bake for 10 minutes. Turn the heat down to 350° and bake for 40 minutes more, until the crust is nicely browned. Serve at once.

Serves 6

SCOTLAND

Beef Sausage

This Aberdeen specialty is cooked like a sausage, but served like a meatloaf. The glaze makes it more dressy, but it isn't absolutely necessary. Pinhead oatmeal, used in Scotland for this sausage as well as haggis, can be difficult to find in the United States. It's only made by the Dorsel Company, Erlanger, KY 41018, which will sell it by mail. The oatmeal we normally buy is pressed flat, while pinhead oatmeal is simply ground. You can also use instant oatmeal, which is just chopped-up pieces of regular oatmeal, but the taste of the sausage will be slightly more mealy.

I serve fish first, either a mussel or clam soup or seviche, then the room-temperature sausage with warm, meatless tomato sauce, accompanied by a salad, fried potatoes, and beer or ale. Dessert can be anything from fresh fruit to a treacle tart.

. . . .

3½ quarts unsalted or low-salt beef stock
2 pounds coarsely ground lean beef
1 pound bacon, finely chopped or coarsely ground
1 cup uncooked oatmeal
1 teaspoon salt
½ teaspoon black pepper
¼ teaspoon cayenne pepper
1 teaspoon mace
Vegetable oil

Begin bringing the stock to a boil in a large pot over high heat. Knead together the beef, bacon, and oats, then knead in the salt, pepper, cayenne, and mace.

Dip a large piece of fine cheesecloth into the oil, squeeze it dry, and double it over. Form the meat mixture into a 4½″-wide cylinder and place on the cheesecloth. Roll the sausage in the cheesecloth to encase it, then tie the ends tightly with string.

Lower the sausage into the boiling stock and immediately turn the heat to low. Boil slowly, covered, for 2½ hours. Turn off the heat and remove the sausage. When the cheesecloth is just cool enough to handle, hold it vertically by one end so the slightly shrunken sausage falls toward the bottom end. Retie the top end to tightly enclose the sausage, then replace it in the stock until room temperature.

Remove the cooled sausage from the stock and pull off the cheesecloth. Place the sausage in a small loaf pan lined with foil. Cover the sausage with foil and weight it down to flatten the top and make the sausage firmer. Store the sausage in the refrigerator overnight. Strain the stock well through a double thickness of fine cheesecloth, then refrigerate overnight, removing the layer of fat on top in the morning.

Place 4 cups of the defatted stock in a saucepan just large enough to hold it. Reserve the remaining stock for another recipe. Boil the 4 cups of stock down over low heat until you have 2 cups left. Check it occasionally to make sure it's not burning. When you have 2 cups of stock left, pour it into a saucepan just large enough to hold it. Boil that down over very low heat until 1 cup is left. Pour that into yet a smaller pan and again reduce it by at least half. Watch the stock very carefully this time as it has a tendency to burn and stick to the bottom of the pan. As soon as the stock looks just slightly lighter than molasses, immediately remove the pan from the heat and let cool slightly.

Turn the sausage out of the loaf pan, remove the foil, and paint with some of the glaze. Replace it in the refrigerator until ready to serve cut into thick slices. Save the remaining glaze to use in sauces. The sausage can be stored in the refrigerator for 1 week, but shouldn't be frozen or the texture will be destroyed.

Serves 8

White Pudding

You may think this sounds awful, but it actually tastes like a wonderful poultry stuffing. Similar white puddings are made in Ireland and England's West Country. There's also *sweet marag,* from the Scottish Isle of Lewis, which contains more sugar and can be cooked in a sheep's stomach rather than hog casings. In areas where sheep are raised, mutton fat is used instead of the pork. You can serve fried white puddings as breakfast sausages, but I think they're best accompanying poultry or meat dishes, replacing potatoes or rice.

2¾ cups oats, preferably pinhead (see headnote for Beef Sausage, page 240)
1 cup finely chopped onion
1½ teaspoons salt
¼ teaspoon black pepper
¼ cup sugar

1 cup raisins
1 teaspoon crumbled dried sage
1 teaspoon ground thyme
¼ pound pork fat, finely chopped

Prepared hog casings

Preheat the oven to 350°. Place the oats on a baking sheet and toast for 5 minutes, stirring once or twice. Pour the oats into a bowl and toss with the onion, salt, pepper, sugar, raisins, sage, and thyme. Knead in the pork fat.

Place 1 cup of the sausage mixture in a large funnel to begin stuffing the casings. Push the mixture through with something just slightly larger than the diameter of the bottom of the funnel. You can't help but get air in the sausages, but you can compensate for that later. Tie off into 4″ links. Make sure there's a very tight knot between links so if one bursts, as it inevitably will, the one next to it won't fall apart, too. Prick the sausages very well with a pin, about 10 places on each link. Then roll the sausages between your palms to even out their width.

Poach the sausages for 30 minutes, prick each one a few times, then poach for another 15 minutes. The raw or poached sausages can be refrigerated for 1 week, but can't be frozen.

Makes approximately 1 pound raw sausage

Scotch Eggs

These are extremely popular throughout Britain. Workers eat them at high tea, college students gobble them between classes, and refined shoppers nibble them at Harrods. They've been popular for over 200 years. It's possible that British colonists brought them back from India where lamb sausage is used in a similar recipe. Since they're so simple, the taste of the sausage is extremely important. Spicy English bangers are perfect if you make your own or can find good ones, but hot Italian sausages are preferable to overly bread-filled bangers.

Halved hot Scotch eggs with tomato sauce make a lovely first course at dinner. They're best with a glass of warm English beer or a slightly fruity white wine like a California Gewürztraminer. Follow them with any kind of fish soup or stew or a grilled game bird. I can vouch for the fact that the delicious cold left-overs can be eaten in the car without making a mess.

. . . .

¼ cup dried bread crumbs
½ teaspoon grated nutmeg
Pinch of cayenne pepper
Salt and pepper to taste
6 large eggs, hard-boiled, cooled, shelled
White flour
1 pound skinless Bangers or Basic Italian Sausage (page 234 or 96)
1 large egg
Vegetable oil

Mix the bread crumbs, nutmeg, cayenne, salt, and pepper in a small bowl and set aside. Roll each of the hard-boiled eggs in flour, then shake off the excess. Divide the sausage into 6 pieces. Flatten each into a circle large enough to enclose an egg. Wrap each hard-boiled egg in sausage, making sure that they're evenly covered.

Beat the raw egg lightly in a small bowl. With your left hand pick up a sausage-covered egg, drop it into the raw egg, and turn to coat it evenly. Pick it up and drop it into the crumbs without letting your left hand touch the crumb mixture. Using your right hand, turn the egg until it's evenly coated with crumbs. Set it aside. Use the same procedure to cover the rest of the eggs in the crumbs. This method prevents thick clumps of crumbs.

When all the eggs are coated with crumbs, begin heating the oil in a large skillet over low heat. When the oil is hot, add 3 of the eggs. Cook until browned, turning once or twice, which should take about 7 minutes. Make sure the oil doesn't get too hot or else the sausage mixture will crack, revealing the egg. Repeat with the remaining 3 eggs.

Makes 6

Ireland

Pig's Haggis

The Irish don't make half the fuss over their haggis the Scots do. Bagpipes aren't paraded in with it, odes aren't written to it, and eating it isn't a test of citizenship. It's also less sophisticated than its Scottish counterpart, but it's probably a lot more palatable to Americans. Centuries ago this was the traditional meal served to workers who helped slaughter the household pig. Like its Scottish counterpart, it's a direct descendant of the savory puddings popular in Britain since ancient Roman days.

Pig's haggis is really just well-basted mashed potatoes in a crispy skin. It's traditionally served with gravy and applesauce, which I think is a perfect combination. With a cup of soup and sautéed green vegetables, it's a soothing winter supper. Drink a simple white wine, beer, or hard cider with it.

3 pounds potatoes
¼ cup heavy cream
½ pound onions, finely chopped
1½ teaspoons salt
¼ teaspoon black pepper
2 teaspoons crumbled dried sage
1½ teaspoons grated nutmeg
½ pound toasted white or untoasted pumpernickel bread, cut into ¼″–½″ cubes
½ pound bacon, coarsely chopped

1 prepared pig's stomach
Caul fat (optional)

Cook the potatoes in boiling water until they're tender. Stir the onions, salt, pepper, sage, and nutmeg into the heavy cream and heat it gently just until it feels warm to the touch. Drain the potatoes well, peel them, then mash them with the heavy cream mixture. Fold the bread cubes into the potatoes and set aside.

Preheat the oven to 350°. Fry the bacon in a skillet over low heat for 10 to 15 minutes, until it's just beginning to brown. While it's cooking, rinse the pig's stomach well but leave any fat clinging to the inside in place. Dry the stomach well. Remove the cooked bacon from the skillet with a slotted spoon and fold the bacon into the potatoes.

Stuff the stomach loosely with the potato mixture. Sew the stomach closed with a curved needle and heavy kitchen thread. Wrap it in a double thickness of caul fat (if available). Pour the bacon fat into a baking dish just large enough to hold the stomach. Place the stomach in the baking dish and turn once to coat with the fat. Place in the oven and cook for 2 hours. Baste with any pan juices every 15 minutes.

To serve, gently cut into slices with a serrated knife, being careful not to push the stuffing out as you cut.

Serves 8

Dublin Coddle

A coddle is a dish that is simmered on the stove, and this is Dublin's most popular version. These days it's just as often baked in the oven. The recipe is at least 200 years old, and probably closer to 400. It's the traditional Saturday night family supper, accompanied by soda bread and stout. Serve a salad or sautéed green vegetables alongside, then a fruit dessert such as blackberry cobbler.

2 tablespoons chopped fresh parsley
1½ teaspoons dry mustard
Salt and pepper to taste
½ pound thickly sliced bacon, roughly chopped

¾ pound onions, thinly sliced
1½ pounds potatoes, thinly sliced
1 pound fresh pork sausages, each pricked with a fork in 2–3 places

Preheat the oven to 300°. Mix together the parsley, mustard, salt, and pepper.

Layer the ingredients in a Dutch oven as follows: Begin with half the bacon, top it with half the onions, half the potatoes, all the sausages, half the seasonings, the remaining onions, the remaining potatoes, the remaining bacon, and the rest of the seasonings.

Place your hand, with your fingers spread apart, on the top layer. Hold it in place as you gently pour in water to come just up to the top layer of bacon. Put an ovenproof plate on top of the bacon. This limits the amount of water you'll need to use—you want as little as possible—and keeps the ingredients submerged. Place a sheet of waxed paper across the top of the pot with at least ½″ overhanging on all sides, then put the lid of the pot on. Place in the oven and bake for 1½ hours.

Serves 6

CHAPTER 11

Africa and

the Middle East

While southern Africa adapted European sausage recipes, North Africa and the Middle East created skinless lamb and beef sausages adopted by Europe. The Portuguese brought pigs to Africa, while the English modernized cattle, goat, and sheep raising. The result is occasionally incongruous. Kenyan cookbooks contain recipes for Scottish haggis, sometimes accompanied into the dining room by a bagpiper. The Safari Club serves the traditional English breakfast, including pork sausages. And Carnivore, a barbecue restaurant outside Nairobi, serves beef sausages with béarnaise sauce and Indian raita, a yogurt and cucumber sauce.

In Portuguese areas in eastern Africa you could find stews made with blood sausages, chicken, bacon, potatoes, sweet potatoes, beans, and other vegetables. The Dutch in South Africa would kill a cow and a hog in winter and make long, dried sausages to last through the winter. Malaysian and Indian immigrants also influenced the cuisine, demonstrated by a South African curried headcheese.

Many North African and Middle Eastern sausages are skewered and cooked over an open fire, a practice said to have originated with Turkish or Mongol warriors. When the army traveled, they would stop every night, skewer their meat on their swords, and roast it over the fire. Since most of the North Africans and Arabs are Moslems, pork is almost never used. They more than make up for that omission with their lamb, beef, and goat sausages. Sheep were specially bred for their fatty tails, providing cooking fat until oil became widely available.

One of the best North African sausages is the thin and very spicy Tunisian and Algerian *merguez.* It's not hot enough for many North Africans, however, who add both merguez and fresh chiles to scrambled eggs or serve them in a green pepper sauce spiked with chili paste. Skinless sausages, called *kefta* or *kofta,* are also made with lamb or beef. They're usually threaded onto skewers and grilled, but they can also be fried, used to stuff poultry, or cooked in stews. In Afghanistan, fried kofta, made from cooked curried beef, lamb, camel, or goat and split peas, are served wrapped in soft flat bread.

Split pea, lamb, and rice sausages are popular in the Arab countries bordering the west side of the Arabian Sea. Fried sausage-enclosed hard-boiled eggs are similar to the Indian *Nargisi Kofta*. Stuffed grape leaves, which are just sausage mixtures surrounded by a vegetable, rather than animal, casing are common throughout the area. In Iraq, the same mixture is stuffed into long sheep casings and served in stews. Lebanese make lamb, rice, and chick-pea sausages. Israelis, who adapted European recipes from their country of origin, serve a bread crumb, flour, and onion-stuffed chicken neck sausage.

The Greeks and Cypriots, who suffer from no religious scruples regarding kinds of meat, make many different kinds of sausages. Some are grilled, skinless *keftedakia* (Greek kofta) while others are stuffed into hog or sheep casings. The word *salami,* and perhaps the sausage, come from the Greek island, Salamis. It is believed that the ancient Greeks were experts in preserving meats in a vinegar solution or with salt. They also made forcemeats, called *myma,* from fish, poultry, pork, organ meats, blood, thickeners like cheese or raisins, and herbs and spices. Pork was very popular, since there was a large population of pigs that lived off the street garbage.

Greeks still love sausages. There are stores, called *allantopoleion,* which only sell sausages. Grilled sausages are sold at the Acropolis. Appetizer platters often include salami and grilled keftedakia. Fried sausages are also cooked in omelettes, served for breakfast, and added to stews. It's the spices, like cinnamon, allspice, cuminseed, aniseed, and orange rind, that make Greek sausages unique, and orange-flavored *pitki,* Greek headcheese, is exceptional. Cyprus is especially known for fresh sausages stuffed into casings or wrapped in caul, while Greece is equally known for its keftedakia.

SOUTH AFRICA

Boerewors

Writer Laurens van der Post, known for his superb books about Africa, writes beautifully about his childhood in South Africa in *First Catch Your Eland* and in the Time-Life book on African cooking. He describes *braaivleis,* the annual occasion when Afrikaaners would travel to the veldt or bush for a barbecue to commemorate their defeat of a Zulu king. Others attribute the *braaivleis* to necessity; the Boers traveling to their new homes had to cook over open fires. By van der Post's childhood, it had become more of a backyard affair, but grilled boerewors were still mandatory. Each winter a cow and a pig were slaughtered, and boerewors were made from beef, a little pork, and pork fat stuffed into the hog casings.

These are best grilled, as are most sausages, but they can also be fried or broiled. It's very impressive at a barbecue, however, to produce a beautiful, browned coiled sausage. Let everyone cut off the amount he wants. If you're frying these, you should tie them off into links since each sausage is normally so large you won't want to cook it all at once.

1½ pounds chopped lean beef
¼ pound pork, chopped
6 ounces pork fat, chopped
¾ teaspoon ground cloves
1 teaspoon grated nutmeg
¾ teaspoon coriander seeds
1 teaspoon salt
1 tablespoon sweet sherry or vermouth
1 tablespoon sugar
½ teaspoon paprika

1 long prepared hog casing

Mix together the beef, pork, and fat and further chop or grind as finely as possible by hand or in a food processor. Mix together the remaining ingredients, then knead into the meat mixture.

Stuff the mixture into the prepared casing. Prick any air pockets with a pin. Coil, place on a rack set in a baking dish, and let dry in the refrigerator for 1 to 3 days.

To cook the sausage, place it in a skillet 1″ or 2″ wider than the diameter of the coil. Pour in enough cold water to come to the top of the sausage, turn heat to low, and cook until the water evaporates. Prick the sausage with a pin every 3″ and fry in its own fat until browned, turning it once with a long spatula. Add oil to the pan if the sausage begins to stick. You can also barbecue the sausage, but first place 2 long metal skewers at right angles through the sausage to keep it coiled. Raw sausage can be refrigerated for 1 to 3 days or frozen for 3 months.

Makes just over 2 pounds raw sausage

NORTH AFRICA

Spicy Beef, Lamb, or Goat Sausages

♦ ***Merguez***

These Tunisian and Algerian sausages are very spicy, so add the Harissa a little at a time, frying and tasting the mixture until it satisfies you. You can make one long sausage, but individual links are easier to cook. If you're barbecuing or broiling these, watch them carefully since they cook very quickly.

Serve them as an appetizer with spicy tomato sauce or on a bed of French ratatouille or Hungarian meatless Lecsó, garnished with fresh coriander. Serve a French Bordeaux or a California Cabernet with the merguez. Follow them with an interesting fish dish such as baked sea bass covered with a savory almond paste, a cooked vegetable salad, and rice. A fruit dessert, such as an apricot tart, is authentic.

1 pound ground regular, not lean, beef, or ¾ pound ground goat or lamb mixed with ¼ pound ground beef suet
¾ teaspoon Harissa (page 256) or ¼ teaspoon ground cumin plus ½
½ teaspoon ground chile pepper or cayenne and ½ teaspoon minced garlic
¼ teaspoon black pepper
¼ teaspoon salt

Prepared hog or sheep casings

Knead together all the ingredients.

Firmly stuff into the prepared casings and tie off into 4″ lengths. Prick each in 2 or 3 places.

Fry over low heat, barbecue, or broil them. Raw sausage can be refrigerated for 3 days, frozen for 3 months.

Makes 1 pound raw sausage

Sausage Turnovers

♦ ***Briks***

Most North African countries have a version of this pastry, which is similar to Turkish *boerek*. Two of my favorites are briks filled with feta cheese and a Moroccan *braewat* into which the cook quickly breaks a raw egg, then seals it and bakes it. Use your imagination, since almost any nonwatery filling will work. *Warka* skins, traditionally used for brik, are thicker than phyllo pastry, but thinner than egg roll skins. Use either as a substitute, although I prefer the flakiness of the phyllo. If you're using egg roll skins, place the meat on them, then brush around the edges with egg and press down to seal in triangle shapes.

Hot Cajun sausage (Chaurice or Saucisse) is a good substitute for the Merguez. Serve the briks with Harissa paste or sauce as a dip, or sprinkle them with confectioners' sugar and cinnamon. Briks are lovely appetizers, elegant but easy. You can make the filling a day ahead and you don't have to worry about making sure the pastry and filling are done at the same time since the filling is already cooked. Serve a white French Sancerre, and follow the briks with couscous topped with lamb stew, then fresh fruits and nuts for dessert.

. . . .

½ pound skinned Merguez (page 253) or other spicy fresh sausage
⅓ cup very ripe fresh or canned tomatoes, peeled, seeded, drained well, and roughly chopped
¼ teaspoon salt
⅛ teaspoon black pepper
¼ teaspoon ground cinnamon
Vegetable oil
4 large sheets of phyllo pastry, halved
2 tablespoons unsalted butter, melted

Place the sausage and tomatoes in a large skillet and turn heat to medium. Fry, constantly mashing the sausage with a fork to crumble it well, until the meat is cooked through. Remove the meat and tomato with a slotted spoon and let sit in a sieve for a few minutes, until no more liquid runs out. Then put the mixture in a bowl and stir in the salt, pepper, and cinnamon.

Begin heating 1″ of oil in a large skillet over medium-high heat. Brush 1 piece of the phyllo pastry with melted butter, then fold it into an approximately 5″ square. Place one-eighth of the filling (about 2 tablespoons) in the center of the phyllo pastry, then brush lightly around the filling with more butter. Fold over the pastry to create a triangle and press firmly all around to seal it closed. Continue making the rest of the pastries.

When the oil is hot, drop 2 or 3 of the pastries in. They should have enough room so that they don't touch each other. Fry until golden brown, then drain on paper towels. Don't let these get too dark or they will taste burnt. Cook the rest of the pastries the same way. Serve hot or warm.

Serves 8

Hot Spice Paste

♦ ***Harissa***

If you add 1 cup of stock to this mixture, it becomes a sauce used for couscous and other North African dishes. As is, it's a versatile spice mixture, a little of which can be added to sausages, stews, noodles, rice, and other dishes to liven them up. In a pinch it can even be used in Chinese or other Asian dishes calling for chili paste. It's very hot.

1 garlic clove, crushed then minced
½ teaspoon salt
2 tablespoons olive oil
1 teaspoon cayenne pepper, ground chile, or hot paprika
½ teaspoon ground cumin
¼ teaspoon crushed coriander seeds

Mix all the ingredients in a lidded jar and shake before using. The paste can be stored in a closed container for several months at room temperature.

Makes 3 tablespoons

TURKEY

Beef Sausages in Tomato Sauce

♦ ***Smyrna Koftesi***

Turks don't eat pork since they're Moslems, but these beef kofta are just as tasty. The sugar and vinegar in this sauce from western Turkey create a sweet and sour taste that is especially popular with Sephardic Jews in the Middle East. You can use the sauce for any fresh garlic sausages with equally good results. Make extra sauce, refrigerate the leftovers overnight, and remove the fat the next day. The sauce can be used for noodles, rice, or other meat dishes.

I serve the kofta on a bed of rice or on the macaroni bows popular in Turkey. Complete this family meal with an eggplant salad and a pastry dessert like baklava bought from a good bakery. While Turks serve a yogurt drink with their meals, I prefer a young red wine or beer with the kofta.

. . . .

2½ pounds fresh ripe tomatoes, peeled
1 pound ground regular, not lean, beef
1 large egg
½ cup very fine dry bread crumbs
1 onion, grated
2 garlic cloves, crushed then minced
2 tablespoons finely chopped fresh parsley
½ teaspoon ground cumin
½ teaspoon plus a pinch of ground cinnamon
¼ teaspoon ground allspice
Salt and pepper to taste
About ⅛ cup white flour
¼ cup olive oil
1 onion, very finely chopped
¼ teaspoon paprika
1 tablespoon sugar
½ cup red wine vinegar
¼ cup tomato paste
1 bay leaf

Press the tomatoes through a strainer, then let the pureed tomatoes sit in a fine-mesh colander to drain them. Knead the beef, egg, bread crumbs, grated onion, half the garlic, the parsley, cumin, ½ teaspoon cinnamon, allspice, and salt and pepper together until very smooth. With damp hands roll into 16 sausages, each 4″ long. Mix together the flour, pinch of cinnamon, and a bit of salt and pepper and roll the sausages in it. Dust off any extra flour.

Heat the olive oil in a large skillet until very hot. Add the sausages and fry until browned all over. Don't worry about whether they're done on the inside since they will be simmered in the sauce later on. Remove the sausages and drain on paper towels.

Turn the heat under the skillet to very low, and add the finely chopped onion. Sauté for 5 minutes, add the remaining garlic and the paprika, and sauté for another 5 minutes. Add the tomato pulp and stir until well mixed. Stir in the sugar, vinegar, tomato paste, and bay leaf and simmer for 20 minutes. Don't let the sauce boil. Return the sausages to the skillet and simmer for another 20 minutes.

Serves 4

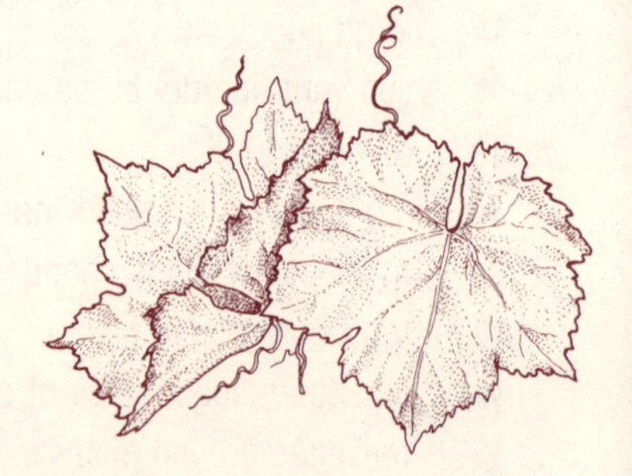

Stuffed Grape Leaves

♦ ***Dolma***

Turkey claims to be the country of origin for these dolma, which have been eaten throughout the Middle East for thousands of years. The meatless version is most popular in Turkey, the lamb in Iran and Iraq, but all Middle Eastern Christians eat the vegetarian grape leaves during Lent. Fresh vine leaves are used in the summer, preserved vine or fresh cabbage leaves in the winter. You can also use Swiss chard. If you're using fresh leaves of any kind, you may have to parboil them for 5 minutes if they seem brittle

When the meat mixture is stuffed into lamb casings, the sausages are called *mumbar.* Dolma are served as part of an appetizer buffet. They also make a perfect party dish since they can be made ahead. The Greek lemon and egg sauce called *avgolemono* and a yogurt and garlic dip are both wonderful with the grape leaves. The vegetarian dolma are best warm, at room temperature, or cold, while the lamb version is best just slightly warmer than room temperature. Wine doesn't go well with these, especially if you're using the lemon sauce, so serve soft drinks, coffee, or beer.

Vegetarian Filling

4 scallions, white section only, minced
¼ cup olive oil
2 cups raw rice, soaked in hot water for 10 minutes, drained, and rinsed
½ teaspoon salt
¼ teaspoon black pepper
1 cup currants, raisins, or roughly chopped dried apricots
¼ cup minced fresh parsley
⅛ teaspoon saffron, dissolved in 1 teaspoon warm water
½ cup roughly chopped pignoli (pine nuts) or unsalted pistachio nuts

Meat Filling

4 medium scallions, white section only, finely chopped
½ cup raw rice, soaked in hot water for 10 minutes, drained, and rinsed
½ teaspoon salt
⅛ teaspoon black pepper
½ pound lamb, ground
2 tablespoons finely chopped fresh parsley
1 tablespoon tomato paste
1 teaspoon finely chopped fresh mint, or ½ teaspoon crumbled dried
2 teaspoons finely chopped fresh oregano, or 1 teaspoon crumbled dried

Approximately 50 grape leaves (1 jar)
Olive oil
Lemon juice
Meat, chicken, or mushroom stock (optional), or water

Rinse the preserved grape leaves and pat dry. Cut off the stems. Toss the vegetarian filling or knead the meat filling well.

Place 1 tablespoon filling on the dull side of a grape leaf near the stem end. Fold the sides of the leaves over the filling, then roll the leaf up, beginning with the stem end, to form a log shape. Set aside, seam side down, while you make the rest.

Place a layer of leaves covering the bottom of a large skillet. Arrange as many dolma as will fit comfortably on top of the leaves. They should be touching, but not crushing, each other. Sprinkle the layer with 1 tablespoon olive oil and 1 tablespoon lemon juice. Place more dolma on top of the first batch, repeating the steps until all the dolma are in the skillet.

Carefully pour in the meat or chicken stock (if meat-filled) or mushroom stock or water (if vegetarian) to just reach the top of the rolls. Cover the rolls with another layer of leaves, then place a plate just smaller than the diameter of the skillet on top to keep the dolma submerged. Turn heat to very low and let cook, undisturbed, for 1½ hours.

Makes 28–30

GREECE

Fried Lamb or Beef Sausages

♦ ***Keftedakia***

These are absolutely delicious hot, warm, or at room temperature, inserted into slit pita bread along with chopped, ripe tomatoes, shredded lettuce, and a yogurt and garlic sauce. Reheat any leftovers in the oven at 350° just until slightly warmer than room temperature. The sandwiches make a nice break from peanut butter or hamburgers.

1 pound lamb or beef, finely ground
¼ cup bread crumbs, soaked in ¼ cup milk for 5 minutes
1 small onion, grated (about ⅜ cup)
1 tablespoon red wine or ouzo
2 teaspoons finely chopped fresh parsley

2 teaspoons finely chopped fresh mint, or 1 teaspoon crumbled dried
1 tablespoon freshly grated Parmesan or kefalotiri cheese
¾ teaspoon salt
Large pinch of black pepper
¼ teaspoon ground cinnamon
¼ teaspoon ground allspice
½ teaspoon whole aniseed
1 large egg, lightly beaten
Vegetable oil
2–3 tablespoons white flour

Knead together the meat, bread crumbs, onion, wine or ouzo, herbs, cheese, salt, pepper, spices, and egg until smooth. Divide the mixture into 8 pieces. With damp hands, roll each into a 5″-long x 1½″-wide sausage. Dry your hands well.

Begin heating ½″ of oil in a large skillet over medium heat until hot but not smoking. While the oil is heating, flour your hands and roll the sausages lightly in your palms until they have a thin coating of flour. Slip the sausages into the oil with a spatula, being careful not to drop them in fast or the oil will splatter. Fry them for 15 to 20 minutes over medium heat, turning 3 or 4 times, until evenly and lightly browned all over. Drain on paper towels.

Serves 4

Cyprus and Greece

Orange-Flavored Pork Sausage

♦ ***Loukanika***

Traditionally the meat is marinated in the wine and spices for several days at room temperature before being stuffed into the casings, but the refrigerator is a lot safer. If your supermarket carries ground pork, just buy 1¼ pounds instead of weighing out the meat and fat.

Loukanika are cooked with green peppers in a stew called *spetsofagi* from eastern Greece, fried and served with eggs, or accompanied by a baked rice pilaf. For a typically Greek lunch, I serve them with a pilaf, pickles or a tart cucumber salad, olives, feta cheese, pita bread, fresh fruit, and a glass of Greek red wine like Castel Danielis.

1 pound lean pork, ground
¼ pound pork fat, ground
2 garlic cloves, crushed then minced
2 tablespoons dry red wine or vermouth
½ teaspoon salt
¼ teaspoon black pepper
½ teaspoon ground coriander
Heaping ¼ teaspoon whole cuminseed
⅛ teaspoon ground allspice
¾ teaspoon grated orange peel

Prepared hog casings

Knead the meat, fat, and garlic in a large bowl. Mix together the wine, salt, pepper, spices, and orange peel, then knead into the meat. Cover and store in the refrigerator for 1 to 3 days.

Stuff the meat firmly into the prepared hog casings and tie off into 6"-long sausages. Prick any air pockets with a pin.

Poach the sausages, then fry them in a little butter until lightly browned all over. They can be refrigerated raw for 3 days, including the marinating period; for 1 week if poached. Raw or poached sausages can be frozen for 3 months.

Makes approximately 1¼ pounds raw sausage

Pork and Lamb Sausages

♦ ***Sheftalia***

The caul fat bastes the sausages and creates a crispy texture on the outside. However, you can add about 2 ounces ground pork fat to the sausages and make sure they're securely placed on the skewers if caul isn't available. If you're using wooden skewers, be sure to soak them in water for at least 30 minutes to ensure they don't catch on fire.

If you're having a barbecue, grill these, shrimp marinated in orange juice and spices, and swordfish steaks for an unforgettable meal. Begin the meal with an eggplant dip (Atjar) and fresh vegetables, accompany the barbecued meats with pickles, olives, yogurt, room temperature rice baked with herbs or Vegetarian Stuffed Grape Leaves, and a white Burgundy. Almond torte or dried fruit fritters are authentic Greek sweets, although usually only served between meals.

. . . .

½ pound pork, ground
½ pound lamb, ground
½ cup finely chopped onion
2 tablespoons coarsely chopped fresh coriander
½ teaspoon salt
Pinch of black pepper
½ teaspoon ground cinnamon
¼ teaspoon cuminseed
2 teaspoons lemon juice
Caul fat

Knead the pork, lamb, onion, coriander, salt, pepper, cinnamon, cuminseed, and lemon juice together until the spices are evenly distributed and the mixture is smooth. Divide the meat mixture into 20 pieces. With moist hands, roll each piece into a 1″-wide × 2″–3″-long sausage

Cut the caul fat into twenty 4″ squares. Place a sausage on each square, then roll up to enfold the sausage completely. Slide the sausages onto flat metal or water-soaked bamboo skewers. There should be 2 to 3 to a skewer. Grill the sausages over charcoal, turning once. They will take about 10 minutes. If you're broiling them, they should be about 3″ to 4″ from the heat source with a pan underneath to catch the drippings.

Serves 4

CHAPTER 12

Asia

Despite Asia's size, its diversity of cultures, and the fact that the Chinese developed a sophisticated pork cuisine almost 500 years ago, one sausage is used more often in Asia than any other. It's called *lop cheong,* known in the United States simply as Chinese sausage, and it's got such an unusual taste that no other sausage can be substituted for it. There are, however, other sausages that are indigenous and unique to the various Asian countries. Almost all Asian sausages are made from pork, since beef only arrived with European traders in the sixteenth century.

The efficient Chinese, who are clever enough to make duck feet, shark's fin, and birds' nests palatable, developed what may have been some of the world's first sausages. Since meat was, and is, not very plentiful, their sausages utilized every last scrap. The three Chinese sausages available in the United States are the red and white lop cheong and the reddish-brown pork or duck liver sausages. All three are dried and are usually attached in pairs.

The Chinese often use exotic casings, like lotus or other leaves. Caul is used to wrap pork sausage patties, or egg-shaped pork and chicken sausages. Duck skin provides a casing for deep-fried duck sausages from Peking. Other traditional sausages are made with beef or shrimp, and there's a delicious long, roasted sausage made with finely chopped barbecued pork, mushrooms, and chicken. Canned pork sausages, salamis, stuffed pig's trotters similar to the Italian zampone, and even British bangers can be found in modern China.

Sausages are often used in *dim sum,* those delicacies served at teahouses. Bread dumplings, called *bao,* enclose chopped lop cheong or tiny duck sausages. Whole sausages are wrapped in bread dough and steamed, and chopped ones are added to spring rolls, pancakes, or flatbread reminiscent of pizza. They're also stir-fried with rice and noodles, added to poultry stuffings, and served, sliced, as part of an appetizer platter.

The Chinese ruled Vietnam for hundreds of years, and high-quality lop cheong, made by Chinese living in Vietnam, are very popular. Usually these sausages are steamed and arranged decoratively with other ingredients like shrimp and chicken atop a mound of rice or glutinous rice. They are also cooked in steamed breads, similar to those in China. Uniquely Vietnamese sausages can be found in some Asian markets in the United States. Skinless, very finely ground, grilled pork or shrimp sausages are served with rice or noodles in lettuce leaves. *Cha*—sausages traditionally steamed in banana leaves, but wrapped in the more easily obtainable foil in the United States—are almost more like pâtés than sausages. Like Vietnamese headcheese, the sausages were probably a result of the French occupation. Served cold and sliced, they can be made from coarse or very finely ground beef or pork, with or without pork skin, and range from heavily spiced to somewhat bland.

Laotian and Cambodian sausages are similar to the Vietnamese, but more heavily spiced. A finely ground pork and chile sausage is stuffed into casings, barbecued, and served with additional chiles on the side. Chile-and-pork-skin–stuffed pig's trotter is simmered in coconut milk.

Although Thais use lop cheong, they also produce some unique sausages of their own. Chicken skin, bean curd skin, banana leaves, and hog casings are all pressed into use. Spicy fillings include ground pork and crab or shrimp, ground chicken and shrimp, and shredded pickled pork and pork skin enclosing a whole fresh green chile. This last sausage is also served raw. Sausages are often steamed, cooled, sliced, dipped into egg, then fried. They can also be eaten cold or stir-fried with rice or vegetables.

Foods in Malaysia, Singapore, and Indonesia are similar, since their histories, politics, and culture have always been intertwined. Both Indian and Chinese immigrants have also influenced their cuisine. Chinese pork sausages, called *lak jiang* here, are eaten in non-Moslem areas. They're usually stir-fried with rice or noodles or steamed with vegetables. Shredded chicken and ham sausages enclosed in caul are fried. Large skinless sausages made with finely chopped pork and small cubes of pork fat are steamed, then sliced and fried or simmered with vegetables. Moslems use banana leaves to wrap large ground beef sausages, and grill kofta, ground beef kebabs, similar to those of India except that coconut is kneaded into the meat mixture. Fish forcemeats are used to stuff whole fish, while skinless turtle sausages are grilled.

Hindus don't eat beef, Moslems don't eat pork, and Jainists don't eat any meat at all. Needless to say, India is not a great sausage-eating country, with the exception of Goa on the west coast, long controlled by the Portuguese. Vinegary and spicy Portuguese chouriço, called *chourisso,* longaniza, and a pork and liver sausage are still popular. Throughout the rest of India lamb kofta, some very spicy, others more subtly seasoned, are grilled over charcoal or simmered in a curry sauce. The English in India ate typically British sausages, but those foods disappeared when the British did.

There are many dietary restrictions regarding meat in Tibet, but beef is acceptable. The most popular sausage is *gyuma,* a blood sausage made with beef or beef organs, barley or wheat, caraway, onions, and a lot of ground chile, stuffed into sheep or goat casings. The same sausage, without the blood, is called *gyukar.* They are fried and served with a cold tomato and chile sauce.

In Japan, meat is expensive, fish is plentiful, and the Shinto religion was once vegetarian. Using what they had, the Japanese created *kamaboko,* a steamed fish sausage, which they add to simmered noodle and rice dishes. Restaurants licensed to sell the potentially poisonous blowfish called *fugu* serve fugu kamaboko. Americans have also made an impact on Japanese cuisine. Hot dogs are sold in the Tokyo park where teen-agers congregate, while bar patrons can get sliced salami with their beer. Korean cuisine, influenced by both Japan and China, includes both dried pork and beef sausages.

Filipino food has been greatly influenced by Spain, the United States, and China. Rice or noodle dishes are as likely to include *chorizo de Bilbao* as lop cheong. While Filipino chorizo is very similar to the Spanish version, their longaniza adds coarsely crushed red chiles, rum, and brown sugar to the traditional pork, vinegar, and garlic. *Dimugan,* a blood sausage, was adapted from the Spanish morcilla. The Filipinos sometimes sauté rather than stir-fry many rice dishes to create versions reminiscent of paella, but coconut milk and/or glutinous rice distinguish the Filipino dish from the Spanish one.

Spaniards also inspired the range of Filipino soups and stews called pucheros or cocidos. One of President Corazon Aquino's cooks took a Spanish soup made with beef, chorizo, and vegetables and added her own distinctive touch; she used liverwurst to thicken it to the consistency of a stew. Meat pies, often with just a top crust, combine ox tongue, fish, or chicken with Filipino chorizo or tiny Vienna sausages. Both hot dogs and empanadas—deep-fried turnovers stuffed with onion, garlic, hard-boiled eggs, tart pickles, shredded chicken, and chorizo—are sold by street vendors. An interesting native Filipino sausage is *embutido,* a large baked foil-wrapped roll made with finely ground Vienna sausage or chorizo, hard-boiled eggs, liverwurst, ground pork, bread crumbs, sweet pickles, and raisins.

European settlers also left their mark on Tahiti, where fried breakfast sausage links are used as a garnish with meat dishes. And legend says a British colonel introduced Indian spice mixtures to the islands, resulting in sausages served in curry sauce.

CHINA

Chinese Pork Sausages

♦ ***Lop Cheong***

This dense, sweet sausage is completely addicting. Of all the sausages in the book, this has to qualify as my favorite. It is closer in taste to ham, which should substitute for it, rather than another kind of sausage. Asian groceries and many supermarkets carry the sausages. The brands made in Canada tend to be slightly leaner, while the American kinds have a bit more taste. If you add the sausages to any kind of Asian noodle, bread, dumpling, rice, stir-fried, braised, or steamed dish or even salad, it's likely you're duplicating a recipe that's popular somewhere in Asia.

2 pounds lean pork, cut into ¼″ cubes
¾ pound pork fat, cut into ¼″ cubes
3 tablespoons sugar
2 tablespoons soy sauce
2 tablespoons sweet rice wine or sherry
2 tablespoons sake or Scotch
2 teaspoons salt
¼ teaspoon five-spice powder

Prepared hog casings

Preheat the oven to 200°. Toss the meat with the rest of the ingredients.

Stuff loosely into prepared casings and tie off in 5″ to 6″ lengths. Prick very well all over.

Place the sausages on a rack placed on a baking sheet. The sausages shouldn't be touching each other. Bake for 5 hours. Turn off the heat and let the sausages sit in the oven for another 2 hours. Don't open the oven door at all. Wipe any excess fat off the exterior of the sausages. Slice and steam for 10 minutes or stir-fry until browned before serving. Homemade sausage keep for 1 to 2 weeks in the refrigerator, store-bought sausages for 2 to 3 months. Both can be frozen for 6 months.

Makes approximately 3 pounds raw sausage

Glutinous Rice and Sausage Dumplings

♦ ***Nor Mai Shui Mai***

This is a common dim sum, served in teahouses throughout China but especially in Canton. Glutinous rice is sold at Asian groceries and, unlike other rice, is supposed to stick together. It's also called "sweet rice." It absorbs flavors better than regular rice, so it picks up much of the sausage taste. Unfortunately, it can't be frozen, so only make as many dumplings as you're going to eat within 2 days.

Refrigerate leftover cooked dumplings in plastic wrap, then reheat them in the steamer. The uncooked dumplings can be stored, covered in plastic and not touching each other, for 3 to 4 hours in the refrigerator, but after that they become too sticky.

This same mixture is also wrapped in lotus leaves and steamed, but these small dumplings are much more impressive. Serve the dumplings on the steamer rack as an appetizer with bowls of dipping sauce made with soy sauce, fresh ginger, garlic, a touch of hoisin sauce, and rice or white vinegar. A good sparkling white wine is perfect for the dumplings. Follow the dumplings with a fish dish such as deep-fried crispy catfish, stir-fried vegetables, and a noodle dish rather than more rice. Finish your meal with fresh fruit, like melon.

---

4 teaspoons soy sauce
2 teaspoons sweet rice wine or sherry
½ teaspoon sugar
Pinch of black pepper
⅛ teaspoon five-spice powder
½ cup glutinous rice, rinsed, soaked in cold water to cover for 30 minutes, then rinsed again
½ cup water
2 teaspoons vegetable or peanut oil
1 tablespoon minced dried shrimp
2 tablespoons dried brown Chinese mushrooms, soaked in hot water for 30 minutes, drained, then finely chopped
1 Chinese Sausage (page 269), finely chopped
20 circular won ton wrappers

Mix together the soy sauce, rice wine or sherry, sugar, pepper, and five-spice powder and set aside. Bring the rice and water to a boil in a medium-size saucepan. Turn heat to very low and cook, covered, for 5 minutes. Remove the pot from the heat and set aside without uncovering.

While the rice is cooking, heat a large wok or skillet over high heat. Add the oil, and when the oil is very hot but not smoking, add the shrimp, mushrooms, and sausage. Stir-fry for 3 minutes. Add the soy sauce mixture and stir for 2 minutes. Uncover the rice and stir in the contents of the wok.

Begin bringing water in the bottom part of a steamer to a boil. Place 2 teaspoons of the filling in each won ton wrapper, then gather the sides around the filling so they pleat naturally, pushing the filling up slightly so that it shows at the top. Press the wrapper close to and around the filling, pinching the edges together if necessary. Place on the steamer rack and steam, covered, for 20 minutes over high heat. Serve hot, warm, or at room temperature.

Makes 20

Turnip Cake

♦ ***Lor Bok Goh***

This is another dim sum, reminiscent of Italian polenta and American scrapple. Be sure to get regular rice flour, not glutinous rice flour, sold in Asian markets, some supermarkets, bakery supply stores, and groceries that cater to a Scots clientele since it's used in shortbread. Turnip cake is a traditional New Year's dish, with the rising of the cake symbolic of rising fortune. I must confess it's rather odd tasting, and I wasn't too crazy about it when I ate it straight from the steamer. But when I let it sit overnight, then sliced and fried it, it was quite enjoyable. You can put other ingredients in the cake, like bacon or chopped water chestnuts, but don't add too much or the cake will fall apart. It's almost impossible to see that the cake is done, since it stays moist while it's in the steamer, so you'll have to rely upon timing it. This is perfect for winter breakfast, and I sometimes gild the lily by frying more sausage slices, then frying the cake in the sausage fat and serving them together.

- 2 tablespoons dried brown Chinese mushrooms, soaked in 4 cups hot water for 30 minutes
- 3 tablespoons dried shrimp, soaked in 4 cups hot water for 30 minutes
- 1½ pounds Chinese or regular turnips, peeled and grated
- ¼ pound sweet potatoes, peeled and grated
- 2 teaspoons grated fresh ginger
- 3 Chinese Sausages (page 269), finely chopped
- ½ teaspoon salt
- 1/16 teaspoon ground black pepper
- 1 tablespoon soy sauce
- 3 cups rice flour
- 1 tablespoon finely chopped fresh coriander

Drain the mushrooms and shrimp and place their soaking liquids in a large pot. Add the turnips, sweet potatoes, and ginger to the pot and bring to a boil over high heat. Turn the heat to low and simmer, uncovered, for 30 minutes. While the turnips are cooking, finely chop the dried shrimp and mushrooms and set aside. After the turnips have simmered for 30 minutes, remove the pot from the heat. Stir in the dried shrimp and mushrooms and the sausage and let the turnips cool.

Begin bringing water in the bottom of a steamer to a boil. Pour the pot contents into a colander placed over a large bowl and drain well. Remove the bowl from under the colander and discard all but 1¾ cups of the cooking liquid. Stir the salt, pepper, and soy sauce into the reserved liquid, then stir in the flour until smooth. Fold the drained ingredients and coriander into the bowl.

Pour the batter into a lightly greased 9″-diameter, 3″-high round cake pan, preferably springform. Place on a rack in the steamer, cover, and steam over medium heat for 2 hours. Remove the cake pan from the steamer and let it cool for 30 minutes to solidify. Remove the cake from the pan, leaving it on the pan bottom if you like. Wrap it in foil and refrigerate overnight. The next day slice and fry the cake as you would Scrapple.

Serves 10

Fried Rice

♦ ***Chow Fan***

It's unfortunate that this dish is representative of mediocre Chinese restaurants pandering to what they consider American taste. It's authentic, it's practical, it's easy, it can be made with ingredients as plebian as chicken or as luxurious as lobster, and it's excellent when made well. I even eat it cold in the morning, which isn't as peculiar as it seems since millions of Chinese eat congee, a rice dish, for breakfast. You can even add just enough egg to hold the leftover rice and meats together, form patties or balls, and deep-fry them to create what seems like a whole new dish.

In China, fried rice is traditionally served at the end of the meal. But if the guests eat it, the host is shamed for not having provided enough food in the earlier courses. I serve it alongside the rest of the meal, most often with dishes like Szechwan spicy green beans and either deep-fried, tea-smoked duck or sweet and sour chicken. Dry white wine or Chinese beer are good accompaniments.

1 cup long-grain rice
1¾ cups water
1 teaspoon salt
5 teaspoons vegetable or peanut oil
2 large eggs, lightly beaten
3 Chinese Sausages (page 269), thinly sliced
⅓ cup green beans, cut into 1"-long pieces
¼ cup shelled, raw peas or thawed frozen peas
¼ cup diced Chinese-style or smoked ham
4 dried brown Chinese mushrooms, soaked in hot water for 30 minutes or 4 fresh oyster or shiitake mushrooms, roughly chopped
2 tablespoons soy sauce
2 scallions, thinly sliced

Place the rice, water, and salt in a saucepan just large enough to hold them and bring to a boil over high heat. Boil for 1 minute, turn heat to very low, cover, and cook for 20 minutes. Turn off heat, and, without ever uncovering, let stand for 10 minutes.

While the rice is standing, heat a wok or large skillet over medium heat. Add 2 teaspoons oil, heat, then stir-fry the eggs until they just lose their liquid look, which will take about 30 seconds. Remove with a slotted spoon and place them in a bowl. Add the sausages to the wok, turn heat to high, and lightly brown on both sides. While the sausage is cooking, use the side of a spoon to break the egg up into smaller pieces. Add the fried sausages to the eggs.

Add the remaining 3 teaspoons oil to the wok and heat for about 10 to 15 seconds. Stir in the rice and beans until well coated with oil. Add the peas, ham, and mushrooms and stir-fry for 2 minutes. Stir in the soy sauce, scallions, sausages, and eggs. Stir for 30 seconds more until everything is hot.

Serves 2 as a main course, 4–6 as a side dish

Steamed Chicken and Chinese Sausage

♦ ***Lop Cheong Jing Gai***

This is simple enough to make after a long day at work and delicious enough to serve to important company. Serve a corn and crabmeat soup first, then this dish accompanied by oysters in black bean sauce, steamed rice, and stir-fried snow pea pods and mushrooms. For a simpler meal, just omit the oyster dish. Chinese toffee apples are a perfect and impressive dessert, but fresh fruit is also good. Serve a Chenin Blanc with dinner.

- 2 teaspoons sesame oil
- 1 tablespoon soy sauce
- 1 teaspoon cornstarch
- ½ teaspoon sugar
- 1 tablespoon minced fresh ginger
- ½ teaspoon salt
- 1 garlic clove, crushed then minced
- 1¾ pounds (about ½) chicken, cut into 2″ squares but not skinned or boned
- 2 scallions, white and light green sections, cut into 1″ lengths
- 3 Chinese Sausages (page 269), cut into 1″ pieces on the diagonal

Mix the sesame oil, soy sauce, cornstarch, sugar, ginger, salt, and garlic in a large bowl. Place the chicken pieces in this marinade and toss them a couple of times to coat well. Marinate for 30 minutes at room temperature. Add the scallions and sausages to the chicken and toss again. Bring water in the bottom part of a steamer to a boil.

Fold over a piece of foil, then turn the edges up to create a circle whose diameter is 1″ narrower than the diameter of your steamer rack. Make sure the foil sides come up at least 1″ high to keep the marinade in. Cut 3 or 4 short slits (not holes, or the marinade will leak) in the foil to let the steam come through. Place the foil "plate" on the steamer rack, then pour the contents of the chicken bowl in it. Place the rack in the steamer, cover, and cook for 30 minutes, until the chicken is very tender. Serve with some of the pan juices poured over.

Serves 4, or 8 with other main dishes

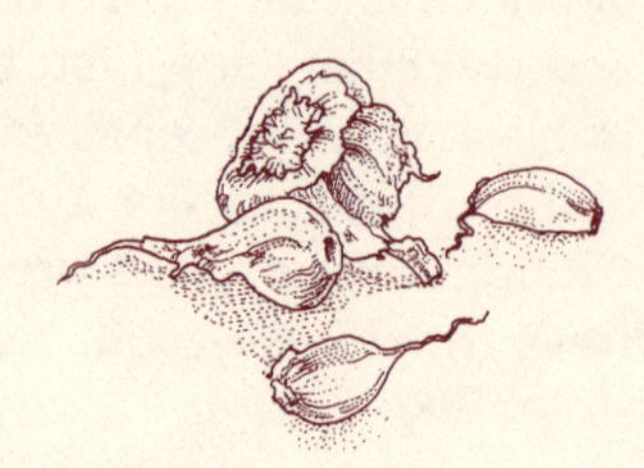

Steamed and Fried Pork, Chicken, and Water Chestnut Sausages

♦ ***Jaau Ng Heungcheung***

These are perfect hot appetizers, delicious accompanied by good-quality plum sauce (duck sauce) or sweet pickled vegetables. They can also be formed into small patties rather than sausage-shaped, especially if served as an appetizer rather than as a canapé. They're very delicate, and tend to fall apart, so handle them carefully. Follow these canapés with shrimp in oyster sauce, cold noodles in sesame sauce, and stir-fried vegetables. A Pinot Noir is a good accompaniment to the sausages.

½ cup white flour
2 tablespoons cornstarch
4 teaspoons sesame oil
2 teaspoons salt
⅔ cup water
¾ pound pork, with some fat, ground
¼ pound boneless, skinless chicken, ground
1 large egg yolk
6 tablespoons finely chopped water chestnuts
1 garlic clove, crushed then minced
¼ teaspoon five-spice powder
½ teaspoon prepared hot mustard, preferably Chinese
1 tablespoon soy sauce
½ teaspoon minced fresh ginger
2 scallions, white and 2″ of light green section, minced
2 cups vegetable oil

Begin bringing water in the bottom part of a steamer to a boil over high heat. Mix the flour, cornstarch, 3 teaspoons sesame oil, and 1 teaspoon salt with the water until smooth and set aside. Knead the pork, chicken, egg yolk, water chestnuts, garlic, five-spice powder, 1 teaspoon sesame oil, 1 teaspoon salt, mustard, soy sauce, ginger, and scallions together. With damp hands form the meat into 1½"-wide sausages of any length that will comfortably fit into your steamer.

Place the sausages on a heatproof plate about 2" smaller in diameter than the steamer rack, then put the plate on the rack. Steam, covered, for 15 minutes. Remove the sausages with a spatula and drain well on paper towels.

Heat the vegetable oil to 350°. While the oil is heating, cut the sausages into 1"-thick slices. Drop a few pieces of sausage into the batter, then lift out with a skewer, letting any excess batter drip off. Push the batter-coated pieces off the skewer and into the hot oil. Fry until golden brown, then drain on paper towels. Repeat with the rest of the sausages.

Serves 6

VIETNAM

Golden Coins

♦ ***Kim Tien Ke***

The unusual ingredients in this dish can be found at Asian groceries and some supermarkets. Golden coins are served with a platter of lettuce leaves, fresh coriander, fresh mint, bean sprouts, grated carrot, and diced apple or pear. Diners then remove the meats from the skewer and place some of each in a lettuce leaf and sprinkle it with herbs, vegetables, and fruit. Roll it up and eat it like a burrito, dipping it into individual dishes of a sauce called *nuoc cham* (made with fish sauce, lime juice, minced fresh chile, garlic, sugar, and a little water). Follow this appetizer with a steamed fish stuffed with transparent noodles, steamed rice, and stir-fried vegetables. A white French Burgundy, such as Meursault, goes well with both the coins and the fish.

1 whole chicken breast, skinned, boned, and cut into 1″ square pieces
2 Chinese Sausages (page 269), cut into ⅓″-thick slices
6 ounces boiled ham, cut into 1″ squares about ¼″ thick
2½ tablespoons Japanese or sweet Indonesian soy sauce
1 tablespoon oyster sauce
1½ tablespoons dry white wine
1½ tablespoons sweet rice wine or sherry
2 tablespoons white vinegar
Pinch of ground cloves
2 pods of star anise
½ teaspoon black pepper
The bottom 3″ of a lemongrass stalk, smashed with the flat side of a large knife or cleaver but left whole (optional)
½″ length of fresh ginger, crushed but left whole

Place the chicken breast, sausages, and ham in a bowl and set aside. Bring the soy sauce, oyster sauce, wines, vinegar, cloves, anise, pepper, lemongrass, and ginger to a boil in a small saucepan and immediately remove from the heat. Pour over the meats and marinate for 1 to 6 hours in the refrigerator, tossing occasionally.

Alternate one-sixth of the chicken, sausage, and ham on a bamboo skewer. Repeat to make 5 other skewers. Don't put sausages on the ends because they will burn. Broil or grill the skewers for about 3 minutes on each of 2 sides until the chicken is white and the edges of the ham and sausage are slightly blackened.

Serves 6 as an appetizer

THAILAND

Spicy Pork and Crab Sausages

♦ ***Si Klok***

These sausages are quite hot, so use less chili paste if you prefer them milder. *Laos,* called "greater galingal" in English, can be found in stores selling Southeast Asian ingredients. Some sausages are made purely from crab, but the pork adds a nice textural contrast and cuts down greatly on the expense. Try to find good-quality crab if you're buying the canned type, since many cans have too much salt . . . and when you rinse the salt off, then they become tasteless. These sausages can be served right after they're poached, or they can be sliced and stir-fried with vegetables. Simple poached sausages are preferred in Thailand, but grilled sausages, hot or cold, are also popular. The grilled sausages are a terrific appetizer at a barbecue. I also like to place cooked chunks of sausage inside Chinese bao, bread dumplings, before they're baked.

2 tablespoons finely chopped fresh coriander leaves
2 teaspoons fish sauce
2 tablespoons coconut milk
¼ teaspoon chili paste, sambal, or ground chile pepper
¼ teaspoon salt
⅛ teaspoon black pepper
⅛ teaspoon ground laos (optional)
½ pound pork with some fat, ground
½ pound shredded cooked crabmeat
3 tablespoons ground roasted peanuts, or 3 tablespoons chunky peanut butter pounded or processed until just slightly coarse
1 garlic clove, crushed then minced

1 long prepared hog casing

Mix the coriander, fish sauce, coconut milk, chili paste, salt and pepper, and laos (if used) together, then knead in the pork, crab, peanuts, and garlic.

Firmly stuff the sausage meat into the prepared casing, prick it to release any air pockets, then coil and poach it for 30 minutes. Serve at any temperature. Raw sausage can be refrigerated 3 days, poached for 1 week. Raw or poached sausages can be frozen for 3 months.

Makes 18 ounces raw sausage

Sausage Salad

This is the first Thai dish I ever ate, and it still remains a favorite. The contrast between the warm, spicy sausage and the cool, crisp greens is outstanding. Each flavor stands out, so you must have very good-quality, authentic ingredients. If necessary, substitute boiled ham fried in tasteless vegetable oil or bacon fat for the sausage. If you can find Thai sausages, like *chiang mai* from the northwest, by all means use them.

The salad is a terrific company dish, since it's both exotic and inoffensive. Serve it as the first course at dinner, followed by shrimp in coconut milk curry sauce, chicken and vegetables in peanut sauce, steamed rice, and an Alsatian Gewürztraminer. Try Thai tangerine sections in sugar syrup for dessert.

- 1 cup fresh lime or lemon juice
- ½ cup sugar
- ¾ cup fish sauce
- 1 teaspoon ground chiles or cayenne pepper
- 4 garlic cloves, crushed then minced
- 2 stalks of lemongrass, white part only, minced (optional)
- 3 heads of romaine lettuce, torn into bite-size pieces
- 3 large cucumbers, very thinly sliced
- 1 large red onion, very thinly sliced, then quartered
- 6 carrots, shredded
- 12 radishes, thinly sliced
- 1 cup fresh coriander leaves
- ¼ cup fresh mint leaves
- 1 pound Chinese Sausages (page 269), thinly sliced

Mix together the lime or lemon juice, sugar, fish sauce, chiles or cayenne pepper, garlic, and lemongrass in a large lidded jar and set aside.

Toss the lettuce, cucumbers, onion, carrots, radishes, coriander, and mint in a salad bowl.

Place the sausages in a large saucepan and turn heat to medium. Cook, stirring often, until the edges are lightly browned. Remove the sausage pieces with a slotted spoon and add to the salad bowl. Shake the dressing well to combine it, then pour it over the salad and toss well.

Serves 16

MALAYSIA

Fresh Spring Rolls

♦ ***Poh Pia***

These same ingredients are stuffed into fried egg rolls. This lighter version can be served as a main course or an appetizer.

You can either mix all the ingredients together, as I do, or cook and serve them individually, letting everyone mix his or her own spring roll. The unusual ingredients are sold at Asian groceries and many supermarkets. If you can't find one of the vegetables, just leave it out, and substitute boiled ham for the sausages if necessary. Follow the spring rolls with fish curry and rice, and serve fruit pudding for dessert. A French Colombard or a Chenin Blanc is perfect with the spring rolls.

- ½ cup bamboo shoots, cut into ½″ cubes
- ¼ cup *daikon* (the long, white Asian icicle radish) or red radish, cut into ¼″ cubes
- 3 Chinese Sausages (page 269), cut into ¼″-thick slices
- 2 garlic cloves, crushed then minced
- ½ pound skinned, boneless chicken, cut into 2″-long thin strips
- ½ pound raw shrimp, then shelled and cut into ½″-thick slices
- 10 water chestnuts, cut into ½″ cubes
- 10 baby corn, cut into ½″ slices
- 1 medium cucumber, peeled, seeded, cut into ½″ cubes
- ¼ pound bean sprouts, roughly chopped
- 1 teaspoon grated fresh ginger
- 1 tablespoon sesame oil
- 1 teaspoon Chinese chili paste, Indonesian sambal, or Harissa (page 256)
- 2 tablespoons sweet Indonesian soy sauce, or 1 teaspoon sugar dissolved in 5 teaspoons Chinese or Japanese soy sauce
- 2 teaspoons cornstarch mixed with 1 teaspoon water
- 1 tablespoon vegetable or peanut oil
- ¼ pound tofu, cut into ½″ cubes
- 2 tablespoons finely chopped fresh chives
- ¼ cup roughly chopped fresh coriander
- 12 large romaine lettuce leaves

Mix together the bamboo shoots, daikon, and sausages in a bowl. Mix together the garlic, chicken, shrimp, water chestnuts, baby corn, cucumber, bean sprouts, and ginger in another bowl.

Combine the sesame oil, chili paste, soy sauce, and cornstarch mixture in a third bowl. Set all 3 bowls aside.

Heat a wok or large skillet over high heat for 1 minute. Add the oil and heat until very hot. Add the contents of the bamboo shoots bowl and cook, stirring constantly, for about 2 minutes, until the fat in the sausages becomes translucent. Add the contents of the garlic bowl and continue to stir until the shrimp is pink all over. If you're using a wok, push the solid ingredients up on the side, letting the liquid accumulate in the bottom. If you're using a skillet, remove the solids with a slotted spoon.

Stir the sesame oil mixture into the accumulated liquid, bring to a boil, and let boil for 1 minute. Stir the tofu into the liquid, carefully so you don't crumble it. Gently stir in the solids. Turn off the heat and stir in the chives and coriander. Pour the contents of the wok in a large bowl and serve with the lettuce leaves alongside. Everyone helps himself to a leaf, fills it with one-twelfth of the meat and vegetables, rolls it up, and eats it.

Serves 6

INDONESIA

Steamed Glutinous Rice and Chinese Sausages

♦ ***Lemper***

This Balinese recipe is a large sausage made from rice and bits of a smaller sausage. Although the method of cooking is Javanese, the inclusion of pork means that it comes from the Hindu Bali rather than the Moslem Java. There are hundreds of variations on this dish made throughout Asia and the South Pacific, using available ingredients and leaves. I've used corn husks, bamboo leaves, banana leaves, waxed paper, and aluminum foil as lemper wrappers. Glutinous rice and coconut milk, which are essential to the recipe, and the other unusual ingredients can be found at Asian groceries and some supermarkets.

While lemper are snack foods, you can also serve them at dinner. Leave them enclosed in the leaves so your guests can unwrap them like tamales. Serve with the slightly sweet, sparkling Italian Asti Spumante. Follow the lemper with Indonesian fried chicken and a *sayur,* vegetables in a soupy curry sauce. Fried banana fritters are perfect for dessert.

. . . .

Pinch of black pepper
½ teaspoon ground coriander
Pinch of ground cumin
⅛ teaspoon turmeric
3 curry plant leaves (optional)
¼ teaspoon ground laos (optional)
1 cup water
1 cup glutinous rice, rinsed, soaked in cold water for 30 minutes, rinsed again, and drained
½ cup unsweetened coconut milk
⅛ teaspoon salt
½ pound Chinese Sausages (page 269)
1 tablespoon vegetable or peanut oil
1 garlic clove, crushed then minced
1 tablespoon minced onion
2 teaspoons sweet soy sauce, or a pinch of sugar dissolved in 2 teaspoons Chinese or Japanese soy sauce
1 teaspoon dried shrimp, soaked in hot water for 10 minutes, drained, and finely chopped, or 1 teaspoon shrimp paste (optional)
Fresh or dried leaves for wrapping

Begin bringing water in the bottom part of a steamer to a boil. Mix together the pepper, coriander, cumin, turmeric, curry plant, and laos (if used). Set aside.

Bring the cup of water to a boil in a saucepan, stir in the rice, coconut milk, and salt and cook over very low heat for 10 to 15 minutes, covered, until all the liquid has been absorbed. The rice is supposed to remain sticky.

While the rice is cooking, steam the sausages over the water for 10 minutes, then dice them. Heat the oil for a few seconds in a wok or small skillet over low heat. Add the garlic, onion, and pepper mixture and stir for 1 minute. Turn off the heat and stir in the sausages, soy sauce, and dried shrimp or paste. Bring the steamer water to a boil again.

If you're using fresh leaves, cut out the tough part of the stem at the bottom. If you're using dried leaves, soak them in hot water until very pliable. Cut the leaves, waxed paper, or foil into 5″-wide × 7″-long rectangles. On one of these, pat one-twentieth of the rice into a 3″ square about 1″ away from either long side, and 1″ from one of the short sides.

Place 1 tablespoon of the sausage mixture in the middle of the rice. With damp hands, using the edge of the leaf to help scrape, push the rice over the filling to form a log of rice with the ends facing the long sides of the leaf. Gently fold the long sides of the leaf over the rice, then, beginning with the end to which the rice is closest, roll up the leaf like a jelly roll. Make the rest of the leaves the same way, letting them rest seam side down while you make the others. You can also make rectangular packages if that's easier. Make sure the filling is completely enclosed. Place the lemper on a rack, in several layers if necessary, and steam for 20 minutes. Serve at room temperature.

Makes 20

INDIA

Sausage Spice Mixture

♦ ***Garam Masala***

Every Indian cook has a repertoire of spice mixtures, some for poultry, others for meat, still others for vegetables. They toast the whole spices before they grind them. If you can't find whole spices, you can toast ground spices, as I do here. This is the masala I prefer for lamb sausages like kofta. It's also good with other meats, so try it anywhere you'd use curry powder. In a pinch, you can certainly use commercial curry powder, which can be reasonably good if fresh and used in moderation. You can also doctor your curry powder by smelling each of the spices below, then adding a bit of the ones that appeal to you. Store your masala at room temperature in a sealed jar out of the light.

¼ cup ground cinnamon
3 tablespoons ground cardamom
2 tablespoons whole cloves
1 tablespoon grated nutmeg
2½ tablespoons ground cumin
1½ tablespoons ground coriander
1 tablespoon black pepper
1 tablespoon turmeric

Preheat the oven to 350°. Mix all the spices well and spread them on a baking sheet. Toast in the oven for 5 minutes, stirring once. Place into a jar and screw on the lid. The spice mixture can be stored at room temperature for 1 to 2 months.

Makes 1 cup

Broiled Lamb Sausages

♦ ***Seekh Kebab***

Besan, chick-pea flour, is one of the ingredients that gives Indian food its distinctive taste. It's available in Middle Eastern and Indian groceries and some health food stores. Cornstarch is the best substitute. Use flattened skewers for these since the sausages often fall off the round ones, although I've used the round wooden ones that look like elongated toothpicks with some success. If a kebab falls off the skewer, just place it back on top.

These make an excellent appetizer, especially if followed by a chicken and rice dish like *biryani*. Try a Beaujolais alongside the kebabs. You can also serve them, as many Indians do, atop a salad of lettuce, onion, and tomatoes or stuff the kebabs, salad ingredients, and yogurt dip into pita bread for an easy-to-handle and delicious sandwich. An Indian rice or vermicelli pudding is an ideal dessert.

- 4 garlic cloves, finely chopped
- 2 cups plain yogurt
- 1 pound lamb with some fat, ground
- 2 tablespoons besan or cornstarch
- 1 cup finely chopped onion
- ¼ cup finely chopped fresh coriander leaves
- ½″ piece fresh ginger, finely chopped
- 2 teaspoons salt
- 1 teaspoon black pepper
- 1 teaspoon Garam Masala (page 286)
- ¼ cup lemon juice

Mix half the garlic with the yogurt and set aside. Knead the remaining garlic with the other ingredients.

Using damp hands since the mixture tends to be sticky, mold into sixteen 3″-long sausages around the skewers like beads on a string. Leave at least 1″ at each end of the skewer uncovered. The ends of the sausages should be just touching each other. You'll probably be able to fit about 4 on each skewer. Brush each sausage with some of the yogurt and garlic. Broil for about 4 minutes, turning as necessary, until they're browned all over. Serve with the remaining yogurt and garlic as a dip.

Serves 4

Lamb Sausage–Wrapped Eggs

♦ ***Nargisi Kofta***

Nargisi means "narcissus," which is what some people think these eggs resemble when they're halved. Historians aren't certain whether the British copied the Indian recipe to create Scotch Eggs or vice versa. In India, these are a festive food, served at banquets and other important occasions. Since this comes from northern India, the onions are not authentic. There they believe onions and garlic have an evil influence on the body, so they're rarely used.

Serve a Merlot with the kofta appetizer, followed by baked chicken that has been marinated in yogurt and spices; onion salad; spicy potatoes and cauliflower; breads; rice; chutneys; and raita, a yogurt and cucumber salad. End the meal with mango ice cream.

3 cups vegetable oil
1 pound lamb, ground
1 medium egg
3 teaspoons grated fresh ginger
1 teaspoon salt
¼ teaspoon black pepper
2 teaspoons Garam Masala (page 286) or curry powder
⅓ cup besan (chick-pea flour) or cornstarch
6 medium eggs, hard-boiled, shelled
2 tablespoons clarified butter or vegetable oil
2 medium onions, finely chopped
¾ pound very ripe fresh tomatoes, seeded and roughly chopped
Large pinch of hot paprika, cayenne pepper, or ground chiles
½ cup plain yogurt
½ cup water
3 tablespoons roughly chopped fresh coriander

Begin heating the oil in a 3-quart saucepan over medium heat to 350°. Knead together the lamb, egg, 1 teaspoon ginger, ½ teaspoon salt, black pepper, 1 teaspoon garam masala or curry powder, and the besan or cornstarch.

Divide this sausage mixture into 6 pieces. With damp hands, gently press 1 piece of sausage between your palms to make a circle large enough to enclose a hard-boiled egg. Place a boiled egg on the sausage and pat the meat around it, pressing on the edges to seal well. Continue wrapping all the eggs.

Add 3 wrapped eggs to the oil. As soon as a crisp layer forms on the meat, which should take 15 to 30 seconds, stir them. Then stir about once a minute until they're golden brown, about 5 minutes. Remove and drain on paper towels while you fry the rest. Don't worry if the meat splits a bit while cooking, since you'll probably be able to disguise the tear when you cut up the eggs.

Heat the clarified butter or oil in a large skillet over medium-low heat. Add the onions and remaining 2 teaspoons ginger and fry for 10 minutes, stirring often. Turn down the heat if they begin to brown. Stir in the tomatoes, paprika or hot pepper, and the remaining ½ teaspoon salt and 1 teaspoon garam masala until well mixed. Cook, stirring occasionally, for 15 minutes, until the tomatoes have softened. Stir the yogurt and water into the sauce and simmer over low heat for a few minutes, until it has a chunky saucelike consistency. Stir in the coriander, then stir in the eggs to coat them with the sauce.

Remove the eggs, halve them (through a tear in the meat if necessary), and serve cut side up on a bed of sauce.

Serves 6

JAPAN

Steamed Fish Sausages

♦ ***Kamaboko***

I really dislike store-bought kamaboko, the kind that are dyed pink along the top or sides. They taste like mediocre bologna. I attempted homemade fish sausages without a lot of enthusiasm, and, much to my surprise, the homemade kind is very good. They're much more delicate and much fresher tasting than the store variety. Kamaboko are often included in *obento*, the individual lacquered lunch boxes that are so much more exciting than their name indicates. Each box has little compartments for sushi, sashimi, pickles, rice, raw vegetables cut into fish shapes or flowers, and other delicacies. At the New Year, kamaboko are made with alternating pink and white squares.

The Japanese usually serve the fish sausages in simmered dishes, similar to sukiyaki, where they absorb the flavor of the stock. They can also be used in "new American" menus since they're similar to the currently popular seafood sausages. Be careful when you're shaping these, so they aren't too lumpy looking on the outside. If they're going to be served sliced, don't worry about a smooth shape; it's only important when they're served whole.

. . . .

2 large egg whites
1 teaspoon salt
2 teaspoons sweet rice wine (mirin) or sherry
1 teaspoon sugar
1 pound fresh halibut or pollack fillets
¼ cup cornstarch

Mix together the egg whites, salt, mirin, and sugar. Puree the fish in a food processor or blender. Put the fish in a bowl and stir in the egg white mixture. Then stir in the cornstarch and mix well.

Begin bringing water in the bottom part of a steamer to a boil. Using damp hands, shape the fish into 4 sausages. Squeeze them to compress them into solid 5″-long × 2″-wide sausages. Then, with very damp hands, smooth the surface. Place them on a lightly oiled plate which will fit into the steamer with at least 1″ to spare on all sides. Cover and steam over high heat for 30 minutes.

Makes 4

Odds and Ends

♦ *Yosenabe*

Any dish with *nabe* in the name is simmered. Since this requires almost no work just before it's served, it's perfect for dinner parties when you want to spend a lot of time with your guests. Children also love it, and you can turn it into a family dish by replacing some of the expensive seafood with less expensive meats or fish.

It's called "odds and ends" because it's a good way to use up small amounts of food. What else can you do with a few shrimp or 1 pork chop, for example? The ingredients below are just a guideline. Japanese stores sell dishes and pots specifically made for nabe dishes (*nabemono*), and if you find yourself making these often you might want to invest in a set. Instant *dashi,* a seaweed and dried fish stock, is sold in Asian groceries. To complete this meal, begin with a vinegary Japanese salad, rounding out the meal with rice, pickles, tea, and seasonal fresh fruit.

6 ounces Japanese noodles, such as udon, soba, shirataki, or harusame
1 whole skinless, boneless chicken breast, cut into 1" squares
1 ½-pound piece of boneless red snapper, cut into 1" squares
1 pound raw shrimp (about 24), then shelled
½ pound sea scallops, thinly sliced into circles
1 cup fresh spinach leaves, torn into 2" squares
12 fresh mushrooms, each cut into 4 slices
1 Kamaboko (page 290), thinly sliced
2 cups chicken stock
2 cups dashi or fish stock, or 1 cup clam juice plus 1 additional cup chicken stock
3 tablespoons soy sauce
1 tablespoon sake or Cognac
4 scallions, white and light green sections, cut into 1"-wide slices
2 carrots, julienned

If you're using harusame noodles, soak them for 20 minutes in hot water to cover. Drain the noodles and refrigerate, tightly wrapped in plastic.

Arrange the chicken, snapper, shrimp, scallops, spinach, mushrooms, and fish sausage in a decorative pattern on a large platter and refrigerate, covered with plastic, if you're not going to use it right away. The platter can be stored in the refrigerator for up to 3 hours before you're ready to serve it.

Just before serving, bring the stock, dashi, soy, sake or Cognac, scallions, and carrots to a boil in an electric pot, such as a wok, in the center of the dining table. As soon as it comes to a boil, turn the heat down to very low and let the mixture simmer. Bring out the platter. Each guest helps himself to one of the ingredients on the platter and holds it, with chopsticks or even a fondue fork, in the simmering liquid until it's cooked.

When everything on the platter is gone, add all the noodles to the cooking liquid. As soon as they're cooked, serve the noodle soup in individual bowls.

Serves 6

PHILIPPINES

Stuffed Beef Roll

♦ ***Morcón***

Morcón, like many other Spanish-influenced foods, is considered appropriate for elegant parties and buffets. The trick is to cook this at a very low temperature so that the meat doesn't split. If it does split, you'll just have to serve this already cut into slices, rather than presenting it whole. The point of carefully arranging the stuffing is to ensure everyone will have a lovely mosaic when the slice of morcón is laid on its side.

Since this shows off the Spanish side of the Philippines, I like to start off with something reflecting its Chinese heritage. Filipino fresh spring rolls, with a soy and garlic dipping sauce, are perfect. A ginger and vinegar cucumber salad, corn relish, rice, and salty shrimp paste called *bagoong* are served with the morcón, along with a good French red Bordeaux or beer. Filipinos often serve flan for dessert.

1 2½-pound piece of flank or skirt steak
2 tablespoons sherry or wine vinegar
3 tablespoons soy sauce
1 tablespoon lemon juice
¼ teaspoon black pepper
2 garlic cloves, crushed then minced
3 eggs, hard-boiled, shelled
12 slices of dill pickles
2 pieces of smoked Chorizo (page 192) or pepperoni, each the length of the short side of the beef, halved lengthwise
2 ¼″-thick slices of smoked ham, cut into ½″-wide strips
2 carrots, quartered lengthwise
2 tablespoons raisins
2 tablespoons lard
½ pound ripe plum tomatoes, roughly chopped
1 cup beef stock, homemade preferable but canned acceptable

Marinate the beef in the vinegar, soy sauce, lemon juice, pepper, and garlic for 1 hour.

Trim any excess meat off the ends to even the piece of meat, then cut the beef in half the long way without cutting through at the end. Open it and press on it to make one double-length flat piece. Be careful not to make any holes in it. If you do make holes, use the trimmed end pieces to patch the holes on the side now facing up. Gently pound the beef to even out the texture. Reserve the marinade.

Place the hard-boiled eggs end to end on the beef, parallel to and 1″ from one short end of the beef. Then arrange the pickles, sausage, ham, carrots, and raisins in alternating rows parallel to the eggs. You should have at least 2 rows of each item except the eggs. Leave a 1″ border when you get to the other short end of the beef. Roll up, being careful not to disturb the filling, beginning with the side where the eggs are. Tie the roll with string in 3 places to keep it closed.

Heat the lard over high heat in a Dutch oven or other large pot. Brown the roll on all sides. Pour in the marinade and add the tomatoes, beef stock, and water to cover. Bring to a boil, turn heat to low, and simmer, covered, for 1½ hours. Turn once, after the first 45 minutes.

Remove the roll from the pot and let rest for 10 minutes before carving. Cut carefully into 8 slices and serve each with some of the pot juices spooned over. Serve the liquid remaining in the pot as soup at another time.

Serves 8

Stuffed Chicken

♦ ***Rellenong Manok***

This appears to be a descendant of the European poultry galantine. The original Filipino version could be very ornate, containing truffles, pâté de foie gras, and pickled tongue, but the simpler kind is preferred today. Boning the chicken is time-consuming but not that difficult if you remember one rule: Always aim the knife toward the bone, not the skin. That way if you slip, you'll nick the bone, not tear the skin.

This is lovely at a buffet if you lay the slices in an overlapping pattern on a pretty platter. It can also be the centerpiece of a formal dinner party. Begin the meal with a spicy fish soup, and serve a Spanish white Rioja, sautéed string beans, and herbed rice with the chicken. End with flaky pastry like Napoleons or baklava.

- 1 pound lean pork, ground
- ½ cup diced bread and butter pickles
- 2 ripe plum tomatoes, seeded and diced
- 1 cup roughly chopped onion
- 1 teaspoon black pepper
- 2 tablespoons lemon or lime juice
- 1½ tablespoons soy sauce
- 2 teaspoons fish sauce, or ½ teaspoon anchovy paste
- ⅓ cup raisins
- 2 garlic cloves, crushed then minced
- 1 4½-pound chicken
- 3 large eggs, hard-boiled, shelled
- 1 piece of spicy smoked garlic sausage such as Kielbasa or smoked Fresh Garlic (page 173 or 24), as long as the chicken from front to back, halved lengthwise
- 1 tablespoon soy sauce mixed with 2 tablespoons unsalted butter, room temperature

Preheat the oven to 350°. Butter a baking dish slightly larger than the chicken.

Mix together the pork, pickles, tomatoes, onion, pepper, lemon or lime juice, 1½ tablespoons soy sauce, fish sauce or anchovy paste, raisins, and garlic and set aside, covered, in the refrigerator.

To bone the chicken I use very sharp kitchen shears, which I find indispensable for tasks like this one. Begin by removing any fat or flesh from the interior of the chicken. Then cut out the tip of the cartilage across from the tail, which should be very easy. When you've removed about 1½" of cartilage you can start loosening the flesh around the bones. Cut out as many bones as you can. When you can't push the meat and skin back any further, turn the chicken over and begin on the back.

Cut off the tail, then cut out the bones just above the tail. Scrape against the backbone with your boning knife or scissors. Keep your eyes on the outside of the chicken, since you don't want to cut through the skin. Also be careful when you turn the chicken, since the cut ends of bones can poke through and tear the skin. You can always sew the skin up, but it's easier not to. Most of the flesh is connected to the skin with just a thin film, so it's easily cut away. As you find pockets of fat in the chicken, discard them. Roll the skin back from the backbone as it's loosened, then cut off as much of the backbone and the surrounding bones as you can. I find I can cut about ¼″ of bone at a time. When you reach the thigh bones, separate them from the rest of the skeleton by cutting through the joint.

When you can't fold back any more skin and flesh in the back, begin working on the breast side again, rolling up the skin and flesh just like in the back. I use my thumbnails to push the meat back from the sides of the cartilage. Keep cutting away the bones on either side of the cartilage as they're exposed. You can keep alternating between breast and back until you're about 1″ from the head end of the chicken. The last inch of bone from the back can gently be pulled out. When you get to the wings, sever them from the breastbone through the joint. Carefully scrape the flesh from the breastbone and wishbone and cut them out. Go back and cut out the first wing bones and the thigh bones. The two other wing bones and leg bones can remain.

Place half the pork mixture in the chicken's cavity, then gently smooth with your hand to form an even layer. Lay the hard-boiled eggs down the center, end to end, from the head to the tail of the chicken. Place a piece of sausage along each side of the eggs. Press the eggs and sausage gently into the filling to cement them into place. Cover with the rest of the pork mixture.

Sew the chicken up to enclose the stuffing completely. Pat it back into shape and truss it so that it looks like a regular chicken. Rub the butter mixture into the chicken skin. Place it in the baking dish and bake for 2 hours, basting 5 or 6 times, turning once after the first hour. Remove the chicken from the oven, cut off the strings, and bring it to the table on a meat board. Slice it crosswise so every piece forms a mosaic of chicken, pork, boiled egg, and sausage.

Serves 8

Chapter 13

The

New World

Before the Europeans landed, South America, Central America, Mexico, and the Caribbean had few domesticated animals. The Europeans imported pigs, cattle, sheep, and goats, and the animals were all greeted enthusiastically—especially the pigs. Pork is now the most popular meat, while only a few areas, like Argentina, Jamaica, Trinidad, Barbados, Puerto Rico, Haiti, and the Dominican Republic, raise large herds of cattle. European and African emigrants brought their native recipes with them, adapting them to fit the available ingredients. Most New World sausages reflect Iberian ancestry. *Chorizo,* a smoked, dried, or fresh pork sausage flavored with red chiles, is eaten throughout this area, with slight variations in many of the countries. However, you can, for example, substitute a Mexican chorizo for a Salvadoran version and vice versa.

There are well over one hundred kinds of chorizo made in Mexico alone, with seasonings varying from region to region and household to household. It's impossible to list all the different ways chorizo is used in Mexican cooking, but here are a few: Most of the tortilla-based dishes, like *tacos, tostadas, enchiladas,* and *quesadillas,* can be stuffed or topped with crumbled, fried chorizo. Chorizos are also stuffed into chiles, turkey, or rolled flank steak. Rice, macaroni, eggs, chick-peas, beans, salads, soups, and stews are all spiced with chorizo.

On the coasts, poached seafood sausages are popular. While some are made from shrimp, others are simply turtle eggs in turtle casings. *Morcilla,* blood sausages, are wider than their Spanish namesakes. There is also a goat's blood sausage, seasoned with fresh herbs and onions, stuffed into a goat's stomach. Liver sausages, often made from either lamb or goat, and poultry sausages are equally spicy. German immigrants brought German-style sausages and sauerkraut. Hot dogs are sold by street vendors in the big cities and used in quickly prepared casseroles and salads.

Central American cooking is similar to that of both Mexico and South America. Iberian *longaniza,* chorizo, and *butifarra* and Italian salami and mortadella are all found there. The Iberian cocido or puchero, a mixed-meat soup or stew depending on the whim of the cook, uses local ingredients such as corn, plantains, lamb, and blood sausages. It might also include the remarkably good Guatemalan chorizo, which is made without the traditional vinegar but with pureed or finely chopped *tomatillos*—tart green vegetables often called "green tomatoes" although they aren't. Salvadoran chorizos are short and fat, while Nicaraguans prefer to fry the chorizo mixture in patties instead of casings.

South American cooking, except for Portuguese-influenced Brazil, is similar to that of Central America. Spanish mixed meat and rice dishes; soups and stews; sausage-stuffed poultry; and dishes combining sausages with lentils, beans, or chick-peas are staples. The dried or smoked chorizo is generally milder than in the northern countries, but varies from recipe to recipe. Argentina, which once had so much meat that it had to throw some of it away, produces international sausages for both immigrants and foreign trade. Salami and sweet Italian sausages are almost as common as chorizo. Many restaurants specialize in mixed grills, sometimes cooked at the table, which can include chorizo and several other kinds of sausages. Blood sausages are popular in countries with large German populations. Chilean blood puddings are made from lamb and cooked in molds rather than casings. Colombia, a predominantly fish-eating country, boils fish sausages in cloth casings, for a native Indian dish.

Brazilian cuisine combines Portuguese, African, and native Indian techniques and ingredients to create sophisticated foods not found elsewhere. Brazilian *cuscuz*—steamed cornmeal, chicken, *chouriço* or *linguiça* (Portuguese chorizo and longaniza), and vegetable pudding—is very different from its North African ancestor, tiny noodles topped with stew. Brazilian stew, cocido, contains linguiça, blood sausage, and sometimes pumpkin and cassava.

The popular mixed grill, *churrasco a gaucho,* from southern Brazil features meats, poultry, shrimp, and fresh sausage grilled over charcoal or wrapped in foil and buried in the coals. The German and Italian immigrants brought salami and German-style sausages, both of which can be served with Portuguese sausages in an antipasto. In São Paulo and Rio you can find American hot dogs, French cassoulets, and Italian bollito misto.

Each Caribbean island's cookery reflects the cuisine of its European conquerers and the ingenuity of the African settlers. Some dishes remain intact, unchanged from their European ancestors. Paella and potato and sausage omelettes are eaten on all the Spanish islands, a mixed grill and Scotch eggs on the English, and turkey galantines on the French. French islands, like Martinique, also stuff chicken with chopped sausage mixed with dried fruits.

Spanish-style smoked or dried chorizo, also called *chaurice,* dried butifarra seasoned with spices like hot chile peppers and cinnamon, and longaniza are staples on the Spanish-speaking islands. The Dominican Republic is especially fond of sausage dishes, like small, fried longaniza. Longaniza and chorizo are also used to stuff suckling pigs and added to vegetable soups and stews. Puerto Ricans and Cubans also eat Spanish-style soups and stews like the bean and sausage *fabada Asturiana. Boliche,* rolled flank steak stuffed with chorizo and hard-boiled eggs, is similar to the Filipino morcón, which is hardly surprising since both recipes came from Spain.

Blood sausages, thickened with rice, sweet potato, or bread and spiked with rum, are considered essential for holiday celebrations. A favorite combination on Barbados is *pudding and souse,* thick blood sausages and spicy headcheese. It seems that many uniquely Caribbean sausages are very large. Puerto Rican *embutidos,* made from ground pork, ham, and bread or from chicken, ham, truffles, and chicken liver, are formed into a log, rolled in crumbs, wrapped in cheesecloth, poached, cooled, and served cold at buffets. Puerto Rican *fiambre Italiano* contains meat and Parmesan cheese. *Carne fiambre,* from the Dominican Republic, is very similar, but made with beef, ham, and shrimp.

Latin American Fresh Chorizo

This is the basic version of the fresh sausage used most often throughout the New World. Be sure to use ground chile peppers, not chili powder which is a mixture of spices. If you can't find dried Mexican chiles, the small red Japanese chiles are a good substitute. There are hundreds of different chorizo, some fresh, others dried or smoked; some plain, some with almonds, tomatillos, wine, or fresh chiles; some made with ground, others with chopped pork. Ground beef can be substituted for all or half the pork. You can also doctor bulk American sausage by kneading in the seasonings in the proportions indicated in the recipe below.

. . . .

4 teaspoons ground dried chile peppers
1 tablespoon paprika
½ teaspoon dried oregano
½ teaspoon ground cinnamon
1 teaspoon ground cumin
½ teaspoon ground cloves
2 teaspoons salt
½ teaspoon black pepper
½ teaspoon ground coriander
2 pounds lean pork, very finely chopped
½ pound pork fat, very finely chopped
4 garlic cloves, crushed then minced
½ cup red wine vinegar

Prepared hog casings (optional)

Mix together the chile, paprika, oregano, cinnamon, cumin, cloves, salt, pepper, and coriander. Mix together the meat, fat, and garlic, then knead in the seasonings. Then knead in a third of the vinegar at a time. Press plastic wrap onto the top of the meat and refrigerate it for 1 day to give the flavors a chance to mingle.

You can leave the chorizo in bulk form or firmly stuff it into prepared hog casings and tie off into 3″ or 4″ lengths. Set the sausages on a rack over a dish in the refrigerator and let them dry for 1 to 2 days. When they've stopped dripping, they're ready to cook or freeze. They can be frozen for up to 3 months.

To cook them, crumble into hot oil or lard and fry over low heat until cooked through.

To smoke them, smoke over 275° heat for 2 to 3 hours, until the interior temperature reaches 170°.

Makes approximately 2½ pounds raw sausage

Sausage Turnovers

♦ ***Empanadas***

Baked or fried sausage-filled turnovers are called *empanadas, empanadillas,* and *empanaditas* in Mexico; *pastelitos, pastelillos,* and *pastechi* in the Caribbean; and *empadas* and *empadinhas* in Brazil. They range from 3″ across to plate-size. Since they are similar to dishes from both Spain and England, either group of settlers could have brought them.

Many kinds of filling are used, with meat and poultry the most common. Cuban empanadas are unique in that they are made in a rectangular pan, then cut into squares. Chopped or shredded meat and vegetables from leftover stews moistened with a bit of the gravy make wonderful fillings. This sausage and potato mixture is an all-purpose filling, used in tacos, quesadillas, enchiladas, tostadas, and many other tortilla-based dishes. The turnovers make great snacks. You can eat them with one hand while you work with the other. Small ones can be served as canapés, accompanied by Brazilian Chile and Lime Sauce.

1 cup plus 2 tablespoons unbleached all-purpose presifted flour
¼ teaspoon salt
¼ cup diced cold lard or butter or room temperature vegetable oil
1 large egg yolk
2 tablespoons cold water
5 ounces skinless Latin American Chorizo (page 302) or other spicy fresh sausage
5 ounces cooked potatoes, peeled, cut into ⅛″ cubes
Vegetable oil
¼ cup chicken or beef stock
Pinch of ground chiles, cayenne pepper, or hot paprika
1 egg, lightly beaten

Stir together 1 cup flour and the salt. Cut in the lard, butter, or oil with a fork or short spurts of a food processor until crumbly. Stir together the yolk and cold water, then mix or process into the flour. As soon as it has formed into a dough, knead it by hand until smooth. Add another tablespoon of water if necessary to make a soft, but not sticky, dough. Form it into a ball, wrap in plastic, and refrigerate for 1 to 24 hours.

When you're ready to make the empanadas, preheat the oven to 350°. Place the sausage in a small skillet, turn heat to low, and sauté, stirring and mashing the sausage, until cooked through. Remove the sausage with a slotted spoon and toss with the potatoes in a small bowl. Add enough vegetable oil to the skillet to make 2 tablespoons fat. Add the 2 tablespoons flour and stir until lightly browned. Add the stock and hot pepper or paprika and stir until thickened and smooth. Remove the skillet from the heat.

Roll half the dough out until 1⁄16″ thick. Cut out five 5″-diameter circles, using a saucer or small dish as a guide. Place 1 heaping tablespoon of filling on each circle and dampen with some of the sauce. Fold the dough over and braid the edges in a pretty pattern to seal them. Continue until you've made all 10 empanadas. Brush them with the beaten egg and bake for 30 minutes until lightly browned all over. Serve hot, warm, or at room temperature.

Makes 10 small empanadas

Tamales

Tamales are native Indian food rather than European-inspired. They're a kind of cornbread, filled with meat, poultry, or something sweet, wrapped in leaves and steamed. Puerto Ricans and Mexicans call them tamales; in Haiti, Venezuela, and other parts of the Caribbean and South America they're *hallacas*, while in Nicaragua they're *nactamales*. In Colombia, Chile, Argentina, and Ecuador these are *tamals*, while *humitas* (green corn tamales) are made with fresh corn kernels. Mexican Christmas wouldn't be Christmas without a constant parade of both savory and sweet, fruit-filled tamales.

Masa harina (corn kernels soaked in lime, then ground into meal) and dried corn husks can be found in Latin American groceries and some supermarkets. If you can't find husks, use 5″ squares of buttered waxed paper. Serve these small tamales as a snack or make them larger and serve them for lunch, accompanied by a salad.

. . . .

½ pound skinless Latin American Chorizo (page 302) or other spicy fresh sausage
2 very ripe fresh or canned plum tomatoes, finely chopped
2 cups masa harina
2 teaspoons baking powder
1 teaspoon salt
6 tablespoons lard or butter
1¼ cups chicken stock

28 fresh or dried corn husks, soaked in hot water for 15 minutes if dried

Heat a large skillet over medium heat, add the sausage and tomatoes and cook, crumbling them with a fork, until the sausage is cooked through. Pour the meat and tomato mixture into a colander and let it drain while you make the dough.

Mix together the masa harina, baking powder, and salt. Using a spoon, food processor, blender, or electric mixer, beat the lard or butter until fluffy. Beat or process in the masa mixture, then the stock.

Begin bringing a lot of water in the bottom part of a steamer to a boil. Place one corn husk on a flat surface in front of you so that it looks like a triangle with the top cut off. Place 1 tablespoon of dough in the center of the husk and smooth it out to form a rectangle that is 3″ long on the side facing you, 4″ long on the side running perpendicular to you. Place 2 teaspoons of filling in the center of the dough rectangle. Bring the long edges of the husk up, the ones running along the 4″ side of the dough.

Use the edges of the husk to scrape the dough down from the sides until the dough covers the filling completely. Fold one long side of the husk over the other. Then fold the other 2 sides up to enclose the tamale. Tuck the small end of the husk into the larger end.

Place the tamales seam side down on the steamer rack or insert. There can be several rows of tamales atop each other. Steam for 1½ hours, adding more hot water to the bottom of the steamer if necessary.

Makes 28

MEXICO

Tortillas and Chorizo in Tomato Sauce

♦ ***Sopa Seca de Tortillas con Chorizo***

Sopas secas, "dry soups," are traditionally served as the third course in the *comida,* the main meal of the day, usually eaten between 1:00 and 2:00 P.M. They often include the same ingredients as *caldos,* soups as we know them, but with a lot less liquid. *Queso fresco* is fresh cheese, which can be found in Latin American markets.

Although this dish may sound plebian, the textural contrast between the sausage, fried tortillas, and cheese creates something truly delicious. Serve this for supper, accompanied by a green salad, Mexican beer, and fresh fruit or rice pudding for dessert.

- 1 tablespoon plus ½ cup lard or vegetable oil
- 12 ounces skinless Latin American Chorizo (page 302) or other spicy fresh sausage
- 1 28-ounce can of plum tomatoes, drained well, roughly chopped
- 2 very ripe, fresh tomatoes, seeded, roughly chopped
- 1 medium onion, finely chopped
- 1 teaspoon chopped fresh oregano, or ½ teaspoon crumbled dried
- 1 teaspoon chopped fresh mint, or ½ teaspoon crumbled dried
- Salt and pepper to taste
- 12 stale tortillas (1–3 days old), cut into thin strips
- 6 ounces queso fresco, roughly chopped, or 3 ounces *each* mozzarella and ricotta cheese

Heat 1 tablespoon lard or oil over medium heat in a large skillet, add the sausage and mash it with a fork until cooked through. Remove the chorizo with a slotted spoon and drain on paper towels. Add the tomatoes, onion, oregano, mint, salt, and pepper to the skillet and cook, covered, for 20 minutes over medium heat, stirring occasionally.

While the tomato sauce is cooking, heat the ½ cup lard or oil in a large skillet with high sides over medium heat. Fry the tortilla strips, one-quarter at a time, until they're soft and just beginning to curl, which should take about 1 minute. Drain them well on paper towels.

After the sauce has cooked for 20 minutes, stir the sausage, tortilla strips, and cheese into it. Cook, stirring, until the cheese has melted, then serve at once.

Serves 4

Chicken, Sausage, and Garlic Bread Crumbs

♦ ***Pollo con Chorizo***

There is a lot of garlic in this dish for the amount of bread crumbs. That's my idea of heaven, but if you're serving this to finnicky company, you might want to omit one of the garlic cloves. Begin your meal with a white (cucumber and almond) gazpacho, then serve the chicken with rice and refried beans. Tortillas accompany both the soup and main course. I like a young red Italian wine, a white Spanish Rioja, or Mexican beer with the chicken. For dessert, try fruit-filled empanadas.

- 1 4-pound chicken, cut into 8 pieces
- ½ cup white wine
- 2 garlic cloves, crushed then minced
- ⅛ teaspoon ground cinnamon
- ⅛ teaspoon ground cloves
- Pinch of grated nutmeg
- 1 teaspoon salt
- ¼ teaspoon black pepper
- 2½ cups chicken stock, homemade preferable but canned acceptable
- 1½ tablespoons unsalted butter
- ⅔ cup bread crumbs
- 2 tablespoons blanched slivered almonds
- 1 tablespoon vegetable oil
- ¼ pound skinless Latin American Chorizo (page 302) or other spicy fresh sausage, crumbled
- ⅔ cup finely chopped onion
- ¼ cup tomato paste

Marinate the chicken in the wine, half the garlic, the cinnamon, cloves, nutmeg, salt, pepper, and ½ cup chicken stock at room temperature for 1 hour. Turn the pieces occasionally. You can also marinate it, covered, in the refrigerator for up to 24 hours.

Preheat the oven to 300°. Put the chicken and its marinade into a large pot and add the remaining 2 cups stock, giblets, and neck. Bring to a boil, turn the heat to low, and simmer for 50 minutes.

While the chicken is simmering, melt the butter and stir in the rest of the garlic. Toss the butter with the bread crumbs and almonds, then rub between your fingers to separate the crumbs. Toast the crumbs and almonds on a baking sheet and toast in the oven for 4 to 5 minutes, tossing once.

After the chicken has simmered for 35 minutes, heat the oil in a large skillet over low heat. Fry the sausage, mashing well with a fork, until cooked through. Add the onion and cook, stirring often, about 8 minutes, until the onion is soft and just beginning to brown. Stir in the tomato paste, then remove ½ cup of stock from the simmering chicken and stir it into the skillet, mixing well. If the chicken isn't done yet, cover the skillet, turn off the heat, and leave the pan on the burner.

When the chicken has finished simmering, remove the pieces and stir into the sausage skillet. Reserve the stock for another use. Place 2 pieces of chicken and some of the sauce on each of 4 warmed plates and sprinkle with the bread crumbs and almonds.

Serves 4

Eggs with Chorizo

♦ ***Huevos con Chorizo***

The spices in Chorizo turn scrambled eggs into a respectably interesting food, just as mustard elevates deviled eggs. You can add diced tomatoes and green peppers, or fresh chiles if you like very hot food, to the skillet when you start cooking the sausage, or you can top the eggs with fresh salsa. I like the tart green tomatillo sauce on top. Mexican breakfasts include refried beans, fresh fruit, coffee, and warm tortillas, which make a nice change from toast.

1 tablespoon vegetable oil
6 ounces skinless Latin American Chorizo (page 302) or other fresh spicy sausage, crumbled
5 large eggs
¼ teaspoon salt
⅛ teaspoon black pepper

Heat the oil in a 9″ or 10″ skillet over low heat. Add the sausage and cook, mashing often with a fork, 3 to 4 minutes, until cooked through.

While the sausage is cooking, lightly whisk the eggs, salt, and pepper together. Add them to the cooked sausage and stir often, constantly scraping the bottom, until set but not dry.

Serves 4

GUATEMALA

Meat and Vegetable Platter

♦ ***Fiambre***

Calling this cold cuts or a salad is like calling cassoulet a pot of beans. Several legends surround fiambre's creation, usually having to do with someone hastily throwing this together when there was nothing else in the larder. I could live very happily with a larder supplied like this. On All Saints' Day, platters of fiambre are exchanged by friends and neighbors.

I try to arrange the platter with an eye toward making pretty designs using the different colored foods. So far I've made a garden of flowers, a man lying on his back (sort of a joke, since *fiambre* means "corpse" as well as "cold meats"), a pseudo-Mondrian painting, and a tropical waterfall (well, *I* knew it was a waterfall). You can, of course, use any other interesting sausages and cold meats as long as you serve the Guatemalan dressing.

Dressing

4 scallions, minced
2 garlic cloves, crushed then minced
½ cup white wine or cider vinegar
½ cup olive oil
1 cup vegetable oil
1½ tablespoons salt
½ teaspoon black pepper
½ cup capers

20 stalks very thin asparagus, tough ends snapped off
1 pound new potatoes, boiled until tender but not falling apart, cut into a total of 20 slices

¼ pound green beans, cut into 2″-long pieces
¼ pound shelled peas, thawed frozen, raw or cooked
2 carrots, thinly sliced
2 celery stalks, thinly sliced
2 heads of soft lettuce, such as Boston or iceberg
½ pound fresh Longaniza (page 193), thinly sliced
¼ pound smoked Chorizo (page 192 or 302), thinly sliced
1 pound Genoa salami, thinly sliced
¼ pound Mortadella (page 105), thinly sliced
1 pound roast beef, thinly sliced
2 cups shredded cooked chicken or turkey
2 medium cans of sardines, drained
4 eggs, hard-boiled, thickly sliced
6 canned hearts of palm, quartered
3 beets, canned or cooked, thinly sliced
1 red onion, thinly sliced
6 radishes, cut into fans or thin slices
2 red bell peppers, seeded, cut into ½″ squares
¼ pound farmer cheese, crumbled or cut into ¼″ cubes
¼ pound young Parmesan or Gruyère cheese, shredded

Place the dressing ingredients in a lidded jar and shake it lightly to mix them. Place the asparagus, potatoes, green beans, peas, carrots, celery, and half the dressing in a large saucepan, bring to a boil, then immediately remove from the heat. Pour into a bowl and store, covered, in the refrigerator overnight. Store the remaining dressing in the covered jar at room temperature.

Line a couple of large platters with the lettuce leaves. Remove the vegetables from the bowl with a slotted spoon and place them on the platter. Arrange the rest of the ingredients in a decorative pattern. Pour the remaining dressing from the vegetable bowl and the jar onto everything but the marinated vegetables.

Serves 20

BRAZIL

Mixed Meats with Black Beans

◆ ***Feijoada Completa***

It is interesting that some of the world's culinary masterpieces, like feijoada, French cassoulet, and Iberian cocidos, are based on the humblest ingredients—beans and chick-peas. Something magical results when beans and meats are combined, so it's not surprising that some of our greatest chefs say that what they really crave are dishes like these. Feijoada is a perfect example of Portuguese food transformed by South American ingredients and African cooks. Brazilians consider it their national dish. Restaurants usually serve it only on weekends, often as a buffet, since no one wants to work after a meal like this. The meats listed in the recipe are only suggestions, but many of them can be found in Latin American, Spanish, or German butcher shops. The important thing is to combine both fresh and smoked meats.

Farofa, also called *manioc* or *farina,* is a flour made from ground cassava out of which the naturally occurring cyanide has been squeezed. It's completely harmless by the time it reaches the table. The proof is the large number of living Brazilians, since they tend to sprinkle it on everything they eat. It's used raw or lightly browned in a dry frying pan. The only other accompaniment necessary for feijoada is a cold glass of rum.

3 pounds smoked beef tongue
2 pig's feet, halved
1 pound dried or jerked beef, in 2–3 pieces, rinsed
4 cups black beans, rinsed
1 pound lean beef chuck
1 ½-pound slab of smoked bacon
1 pound smoked pork chops
1 pound smoked Chorizo (page 192)

1 pound fresh Latin American Chorizo, Longaniza, or Garlic Sausage (pages 302, 193, 24)
3 tablespoons lard or vegetable oil
2 medium onions, roughly chopped
2 garlic cloves, crushed then minced
3 ripe tomatoes, peeled, seeded, and roughly chopped
1 small fresh chile pepper, seeded and minced, or ¼ teaspoon Tabasco sauce
1½ teaspoons salt
2 tablespoons finely chopped fresh parsley
Sliced oranges
Greens, such as kale or spinach, sautéed in butter
Farofa

Place the tongue in a large saucepan, cover with cold water, and bring to a boil over high heat. Turn heat to low and simmer for 1½ hours. Add the pig's feet and simmer for another 2 hours. Discard the skin, bones, and gristle from both meats and replace the meats in the stock. Cool to room temperature, then pour into a bowl and refrigerate overnight. Soak the dried beef and beans in separate bowls of water in the refrigerator overnight.

The next day, drain the beans and place them in a very large pot. Cover them with 2″ or 3″ of cold water and bring to a boil over high heat. Turn the heat to low and simmer, covered, for 30 minutes. Bury the beef chuck and bacon in the beans and simmer for 30 minutes more. Add hot water if necessary to keep the beans moist. Stir from the bottom occasionally throughout the entire cooking process. Bury the pork chops and meat from the pig's feet in the beans and simmer for 1 hour more. Bury the sausages in the beans and continue to cook.

As soon as you've added the sausage to the beans, heat the lard or oil in a skillet, add the onions and garlic and sauté over low heat until softened. Don't let them brown. Stir in the tomatoes, chile or Tabasco, salt, and parsley and mix well. Remove 1½ cups of the beans, as the rest cooks, and stir into the onion skillet. Mash the beans well as you add them. If necessary, stir in about ¼ cup of the bean cooking liquid to smooth the bean and onion mixture. Simmer, stirring often, for 10 minutes, until very smooth and thick. Stir the contents of the skillet into the bean pot, being careful not to mash the beans. Bury the tongue in the beans and continue to cook until the beans have simmered for a total of 4 hours. After the 4 hours, turn off the heat and let the bean pot sit, covered, as you remove the meats one by one, slice them, and place them on the platter.

Traditionally, feijoada is served with the sliced and reconstructed tongue in the middle of the platter, the smoked meats on one side, fresh meats on the other. The beans are served in a tureen. Serve with the oranges, greens, farofa, and Chile and Lime Sauce (recipe below).

Serves 12

Chile and Lime Sauce

♦ ***Molho de Pimenta***

Since this sauce should be very fresh, you can even make it at the table in front of the guests, whisking it in a pretty bowl instead of shaking it in the jar. It begins to lose its fresh taste fairly quickly, so don't make it more than an hour in advance. It won't go bad, and it's still usable, but it tastes different. The fresh, rather than reconstituted, fruit juice also makes a distinct difference in the taste. If you have any leftover sauce, use it as a dip for empanadas or other savory turnovers like Chinese dim sum.

¾ cup minced onion
2 garlic cloves, minced
8 tiny, very hot fresh or pickled chile peppers, seeded if fresh, minced
¾ cup fresh lime (or lemon) juice
½ teaspoon salt

Crush the onion and garlic together in a large mortar with a pestle. There's no other way to get the perfect texture. They should be mashed, but not watery. Add the peppers and crush again. Transfer the mixture to a glass jar.

Pour some of the lime juice into the mortar, swirl it around once or twice to pick up any remaining pepper mixture, and pour it into the jar. Add the rest of the juice and the salt to the jar and screw on the lid. Shake gently until well mixed, but don't let it get foamy. Serve at once.

Makes about 1 cup

CARIBBEAN

Spaghetti with Sausage and Tomato Sauce

♦ ***Espagueti con Salchichas***

This is a direct descendant of Spanish pasta dishes, with a few uniquely Caribbean touches like annatto oil and fresh sweet chile pepper. Similar sauces are used for macaroni or fish in Mexico, while Italian-inspired sausage and tomato sauces flourish in South America. Kale sautéed in butter and garlic, South American cornbread made with fresh corn and cheese, and a young red wine are perfect accompaniments. Try a coconut pudding for dessert.

3 tablespoons lard
1½ tablespoons annatto seeds
¾ pound spaghetti
½ pound salt pork, blanched for 5 minutes, drained, patted dry, and finely chopped
1 pound skinless Latin American Chorizo (page 302) or other fresh garlic sausage
2 cups roughly chopped onion
2 green bell peppers, seeded and roughly chopped
1 large sweet chile pepper, such as Anaheim, seeded, roughly chopped (optional)
12 pitted olives, roughly chopped
1½ teaspoons ground chile or cayenne pepper
5 teaspoons capers
2 cups drained, roughly chopped canned tomatoes
2 cups tomato sauce, homemade preferable but canned or bottled acceptable
1 teaspoon black pepper
½ cup freshly grated Parmesan cheese

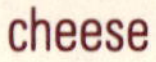

Melt the lard in a small skillet. When it's very hot, but not smoking, add the annatto seeds. Immediately turn the heat to low and stir for 2 minutes. Strain and set aside. Cook the spaghetti in a large pot of water until it's al dente. Drain it and toss with 1 tablespoon of the annatto lard. Set aside.

Heat the remaining annatto lard in a Dutch oven and sauté the salt pork, sausage, and onions over low heat for 10 minutes. Keep mashing the sausage with a fork to crumble it well. Add the peppers and stir for another 2 minutes. Add the olives, ground chile, capers, tomatoes, tomato sauce, and black pepper. Simmer for 10 minutes. Add the spaghetti and stir for 2 or 3 minutes, until the spaghetti is reheated. Serve sprinkled with the Parmesan cheese.

Serves 4

CHAPTER
14

The

United States

The United States is, gastronomically, a very fortunate country. It has a number of climates in which almost every kind of food can be produced. Immigrants and native Americans have provided a world of recipes, while their descendants—observing the typically American willingness to break from tradition—adapt and modify these dishes to create typically American foods. No one says you must serve hot dogs; in America you can throw German bratwurst, Italian luganega, Scandinavian potato sausage, Mexican chorizo, and even Thai pork and crab sausage on the barbecue and everyone will be delighted. Americans taste and test and taste again to create both their own traditional family favorites and bigger and better surprises.

The earliest colonists arrived to find that native Americans, like Europeans, also depended on preserved meat to get through the winter. Native American *pemmican* is simply game, like buffalo or venison, mixed with fat and berries, molded into cakes and smoked—the first American sausage patty. Early colonists brought pigs, sheep, and cattle, which quickly flourished in the New World. To prepare for winter the settlers dried or smoked sausage links or stored sausage meat in a crock or muslin bag sealed with fat.

Later on, German immigrants, who missed their native sausages, opened butcher shops and delicatessens to supply their needs. Other Americans began stopping by, and German sausages became a national staple. The German butchers began producing sausages from other countries to satisfy their growing clientele. It was not unusual at the turn of the century to see a German butcher sell a Portuguese sausage to a proper New England housewife. In farming areas, pigs and cattle were slaughtered at the beginning of winter, with each ethnic community making the sausages from their, or their ancestors', homeland.

It is open to debate whether our hot dog was adapted from the German frankfurter, the Austrian wiener, or the Czech parkys, all of which share a common heritage. The American version is at least 125 years old, and by the 1930s there were hot dog stands from coast to coast. But it was Eleanor Roosevelt's very public love of hot dogs that made them the staple they are today. Aside from the traditional toppings and casseroles, "international" hot dogs—a Greek version with olives and yogurt, the Chinese with sweet and sour sauce, Mexican-style with spicy cheese—are still newspaper food column staples. With all the packaged hot dogs available, it's hard to remember that the original frankfurter was as succulent as any other quality sausage. They can, and have been, added to soups, stews, and casseroles, but are at their best when they are cut into chunks, not finely chopped. If anyone offers you a tofu wiener, that person is not your friend.

Armour and Swift started the first meat-packing plants in the nineteenth century, beginning the standardization of many American sausages. Animal parts that didn't qualify as expensive cuts were ground up and made into sausage. Beef hearts, pork cheeks, and other trimmings were, and still are, made into some very good sausages by both large packers and small butchers alike. The best sausages, unless specifically supposed to contain organs like liver, are made with only the trimmings from the more expensive cuts like pork loin. As a rule, Americans are not fond of sausage made from innards, like blood sausage, with liverwurst the sole exception.

Despite modern refrigeration and the current advice against too much fat in our foods, sausages continue to grow in popularity. Sales have increased by 50 percent in the last fifteen years, with Americans now consuming over 5 billion pounds of sausage a year. That doesn't include homemade sausages or those only sold locally. Each meat packer has its own formula for every sausage, sometimes varying it to appeal to different regions. Most cities also have a variety of markets selling ethnic delicacies including sausages.

American sausage dishes have ranged from the very silly to the very practical to the very elegant. To begin with the silly, a 1941 cookbook recommends serving unmolded scrambled eggs and Vienna sausage timbales at a wedding breakfast and a main course of "crown of frankfurters" on Lincoln's Birthday. Yet at the same time, practical cooks were making lovely canapés with excellent liver sausage, baking savory corn and sausage casseroles, and preparing "Spanish rice"—a cross between Spanish paella and Chinese fried rice. Elegant dishes included crepes accompanied by crispy, fried sausage links and turkey galantines, sliced to reveal a beautiful mosaic of turkey meat, truffles, and ham.

From the 1950s to the early 1980s, sausage dishes tended to be easy and casual. Traditional dishes like "alderman in chains," a roasted turkey with a chain of sausages around its neck, were discarded. Sausages just weren't considered company food. Hot dogs were thrown into every imaginable casserole or soup, bologna or salami sandwiches were lunch-box standbys, and it just wasn't a barbecue without hot dogs. There were street foods, like Italian sausage, onions and peppers, hot dogs and sauerkraut, and, beginning in the early eighties, grilled Middle Eastern sausages served in pita bread. In homes, diners, and "family restaurants," fresh or smoked sausages merged effortlessly and tastily with rice, potatoes, corn, bread, hollowed-out vegetables, and the traditional breakfast eggs, pancakes, waffles, or French toast. But better restaurants rarely served sausages, since customers seemed unwilling to pay restaurant prices for what they considered everyday food. Sausage stuffing for poultry was the lone exception, the only sausage dish considered good enough for the holidays.

Suddenly in the 1980s, the popularity of sausages exploded across America in both very old and very new forms. Restaurants began creating seafood, game, poultry, and mixed poultry and veal sausages to complement their other New American dishes. The sausages were usually poached, then grilled or sautéed in butter and served with herb sauces. Two California chefs, Wolfgang Puck of Spago and Alice Waters of Chez Panisse, produced pizzas topped with exotic sausages made from lamb or duck. Delicious vegetarian sausages, more like sausage-shaped quenelles, also began showing up. Americans were prodded into remembering that they actually liked all kinds of sausages. The Cajun food trend introduced spicy hot links, boudin blanc, and smoked andouille across the country, then the Southwestern restaurants popularized chorizo. Chefs who became addicted to sausages began digging up old recipes or adapting foreign ones. Asian salads combining warm sausage with cool greens, grilled rabbit sausages, mixed grills with veal sausage, and fresh chiles stuffed with game sausage are outstanding examples of today's excellent dishes.

American Recipes

Summer Sausage

Summer sausages, also called "stick sausages," Thuringer, and cervelat, are narrow (about 2½" wide) salamis made from either all-beef or mixed beef and pork. The better ones are almost as spicy as Genoa salami, but less fatty. One explanation for their name is that they were made in the winter, but would keep until summer. The other is that only summer provides the right climate for curing these sausages, which were dipped in wax to keep out the insects. I like to spread some drained coleslaw on a crusty roll, lay the summer sausage slices on top, then add a little relish.

1 pound very coarsely ground lean beef
¾ pound lean pork, very coarsely ground
¼ pound pork fat, very coarsely ground
2 garlic cloves, crushed then minced
½ teaspoon liquid smoke (optional)
2 teaspoons dry mustard
¼ teaspoon grated nutmeg
¼ teaspoon ground cloves
1 tablespoon salt
½ teaspoon black pepper

1 prepared beef middle or hog bung casing

Knead together the beef, pork, fat, garlic, and liquid smoke (if used). Mix together the mustard, nutmeg, cloves, salt, and pepper, then knead into the meat.

Stuff the mixture into the prepared casing and hot-smoke for 4 to 6 hours at 275°, until the internal temperature reaches 170°. You can also bake the sausage on a rack for 5 hours at 200°. Let cool to room temperature, then refrigerate for up to 2 weeks or freeze for 3 months.

Makes 2 pounds raw sausage

Pork Hot Dogs

Pet names for hot dogs include "Hollywood grillburgers," "Coney Island turkey" (which soon became just "Coney Islands"), and "tube steaks." Those of us lucky enough to live in cities enjoyed the privilege of the occasional, steaming, juicy, delicious street vendor hot dog, truly one of the best childhood memories. When *Yankee* magazine ran an article on the best hot dogs in New England, they were deluged with letters from incensed readers, each extolling the unjustifiably ignored, truly best hot dog. Hot dog passions run high.

Americans currently eat 19 billion hot dogs a year. Many commercial hot dogs are acceptable when grilled or broiled. But they're made with artificial casings and skinned before they're packaged. For a really good steamed or boiled hot dog, you need the skin to make it crunchy. Fortunately, there are still butchers who sell the old-fashioned kind, or you can make your own. The only drawback to homemade hot dogs is that they're gray rather than pink since they don't have preservatives.

2 pounds lean pork, roughly chopped
¼ pound pork fat, roughly chopped
½ cup roughly chopped onion
1 tablespoon dry mustard
1 tablespoon coarse salt
½ teaspoon white pepper
¼ teaspoon ground celery seeds
2 teaspoons ground coriander
1 teaspoon ground mace

1 garlic clove, crushed then minced
½ cup milk
2 teaspoons light corn syrup
½ teaspoon liquid smoke (optional)

Prepared sheep or hog casings

Mix together the pork, pork fat, and onion. In a measuring cup with a spout, mix together the mustard, salt, pepper, celery seeds, coriander, mace, garlic, milk, corn syrup, and liquid smoke (if used). Use a food processor with a steel blade to grind the meat mixture until completely smooth. If you have a small processor, grind half the mixture at a time, then return all of it to the processing bowl. Slowly pour in the milk mixture while the machine is running.

Stuff the mixture firmly into prepared sheep or hog casings and tie off in 6″ or 7″ lengths. Prick the hot dogs well with a pin, including any air pockets. Roll them between your palms to press out any trapped air.

Poach them for 15 minutes, weighting them down with an upside-down glass pot cover if they float. Prick them again about halfway through the 15 minutes. This should prevent them from splitting, although one or two always do. Use those for stews. If you're smoking them, they will take about 2 to 3 hours at 275°, until they reach 170° inside.

Place the smoked or poached hot dogs in a colander, rinse with cold water, pat dry, and let cool. They can be refrigerated for 1 week or frozen for 3 months. To reheat the hot dogs, drop them in boiling water, cover immediately, turn off the heat, and let them sit for 7 minutes. They can also be grilled.

Makes approximately 2 pounds raw sausage.

Kosher-Style Beef Hot Dogs

Because these are kosher-style, I haven't used any pork or milk in them. If you don't care about being kosher, but just like beef hot dogs, substitute pork fat for the suet and milk for the water to add a bit more flavor. While pork hot dogs used to be more popular, beef are becoming more and more common. The problem with most commercial hot dogs is that they taste gelatinous rather than dense, so I usually buy my beef hot dogs from a kosher butcher if I don't make them myself. The two best-known beef hot dogs are Nathan's from Coney Island, New York, which are sold in packages, and the Chicago version, topped with fresh hot chile peppers, mustard, ketchup, relish, onions, and tomatoes on a poppy seed roll. Pork hot dogs are better than beef in casseroles, but they're both equally good when eaten on rolls.

- ½ cup roughly chopped onion
- ½ pound beef suet
- ½ pound lean veal, ground
- 1½ pounds ground regular, not lean, beef
- 2 garlic cloves, crushed then minced
- 2 teaspoons dry mustard
- 1 teaspoon prepared mustard
- 2 teaspoons ground coriander
- 1 teaspoon mace
- 1 tablespoon salt
- ½ teaspoon black pepper
- 1 teaspoon corn syrup
- 1 teaspoon sweet paprika
- ½ cup cold water
- ½ teaspoon liquid smoke (optional)

Prepared sheep or narrow beef middle casings

Process the onion and suet with the steel blade of your food processor until well chopped. Add the veal and process until completely smooth. Add the beef and continue to process until smooth again. Mix together the garlic, mustards, coriander, mace, salt, pepper, corn syrup, paprika, cold water, and liquid smoke (if used) in a cup with a spout. Pour the water mixture into the processor as it's running and process until well mixed.

Stuff the mixture firmly into the prepared casings and tie off in 6″ or 7″ lengths. Poach or smoke, rinse, store, and reheat or grill like the Pork Hot Dogs (see above). If in narrower casings, however, they will only take 12 minutes to poach, rather than 15.

Makes approximately 2½ pounds raw sausage

Hot Dog Rolls

The genius who combined hot dogs with the hot dog roll is unsung and unknown. While Europeans eat bread with sausages, the cylindrical roll just long and wide enough to contain both hot dog and condiments in perfect proportions is inspired, to say the least. Legends attribute it to a clever vendor who was trying to convince genteel people that there was a dainty way to eat these somewhat slippery and often messy delicacies. It was obviously a successful attempt, since hot dog aficionados argue over the perfect roll almost as often as they defend the perfect hot dog.

I never had any success making bread until I discovered the *Tassajara Bread Book.* Letting the bread rise in sponge form at first produces a less yeasty, evenly textured, perfect bread. These rolls will look and taste enough like store-bought rolls to avoid frightening any picky eaters. There's one very important difference: Your homemade rolls are very, very fresh, and if you don't normally make bread, you'll be stunned at the difference in flavor. Try it once and see whether you think it's worth the time.

- 2¼ cups milk
- 2 packages dry yeast
- 3 tablespoons light corn syrup
- ¼ cup tasteless vegetable oil
- 2 large eggs, lightly beaten
- 6–7 cups unbleached all-purpose presifted flour
- 1 tablespoon salt
- 1 egg, beaten with 1 teaspoon water

Heat ½ cup milk until about 95°. Stir in the yeast and 1 tablespoon corn syrup. Let sit for 10 minutes at room temperature. After about 2 minutes, use your fingers to mash any lumps of yeast. You want it to be completely dissolved in the milk. In a narrow, straight-sided bowl, mix the rest of the milk with the corn syrup and oil.

After the 10 minutes, stir the yeast mixture into the milk and oil mixture, then beat in the eggs. Stir in 3 cups flour, then beat for 1 minute to mix well. Cover and let rise in a warm, draft-free place until doubled in bulk, about 1 hour.

After the dough has doubled, stir in the salt, then 3 cups more flour. Add just enough more flour to make the dough kneadable. Knead on a lightly floured board until the dough is elastic and blisters form on the surface, about 10 minutes. You can also knead the dough in a food processor with the steel blade until it winds around the rod in the center. Then remove it and knead it for about 30 seconds by hand to form a smooth ball. Rinse out the bowl and pat it dry.

Lightly oil the ball of dough, replace it in the bowl, and let it rise, covered, for about 1 hour, until it's doubled in bulk. Punch it down and cut it into 20 pieces. Keeping the other pieces covered, roll one piece into a 1½″-wide rope. Use your fingers or the side of your fist to pat the rope into a 3″ × 6″ rectangle, smoothing with a rolling pin if necessary. Make the rest of the rolls. Place them on shiny, ungreased baking sheets with their long sides just barely touching. Let them rise, uncovered, in an unlit oven for 45 minutes. Remove them and turn the oven to 375°.

Place a cake pan half-filled with boiling water on the oven

floor, then brush the rolls with the egg wash. If you want soft rolls, bake them for 15 minutes, until lightly browned. If you want crunchy tops, remove the pan of water after 15 minutes and let the rolls cook for an extra 1 or 2 minutes. Immediately remove the rolls from the baking sheet with a long spatula and place on a rack to cool. Pull apart when cool.

Makes 20

Hot Dog Relish

Relishes were created hundreds of years ago to preserve vegetables for long, barren winters. This relish was served alongside cold meats or used as a stuffing for baked ham. Although we have refrigeration today, the texture and vinegary taste of the vegetables is still very appealing. A simpler version, called "Philadelphia pepper relish," is served with both hamburgers and hot dogs. Many people judge a hot dog stand not by its dogs, but by its relish.

Use the relish instead of pickles in deviled eggs, as a salad, on top of tiny rounds of toast with thinly sliced cold roast beef, alongside pork chops, or in falafel sandwiches or omelettes. It's a wonderful standby that can be used to enliven even the quickest meal.

- ½ cup coarse, sea, or kosher salt
- 1 cup sugar
- 1½ cups cider vinegar
- 2 tablespoons mustard seeds
- 1 tablespoon whole allspice
- 2 red bell peppers, diced
- 3 green bell peppers, diced
- 2 medium onions, diced
- 2 cups shredded green cabbage
- 1 cup cauliflower, broken into small pieces
- 1 17-ounce can of corn, not creamed, drained
- 1 cup diced dill pickles
- 1 cup diced bread and butter pickles
- 1 tablespoon prepared mustard

Mix together the salt, sugar, vinegar, mustard seeds, and allspice in a large saucepan. Stir in the peppers, onions, cabbage, cauliflower, and corn and bring to a boil over high heat. Turn the heat down to very low and simmer, uncovered, for 10 minutes. Remove from the heat and stir in the pickles and prepared mustard. Let cool, then pour into jars. Even without being processed and sealed, this relish will keep in the refrigerator for at least a couple of months.

Makes 8½ cups

Corn Dogs

Once again, we pay tribute to an unknown genius. Corn casseroles, corn bread, and polenta are so good with sausage that this cross between corn bread and fried chicken couldn't go wrong. If you've only had greasy corn dogs, you are missing something really special. Those of us who judge hot dogs by the crispy snap of the casing especially love crunchy corn dogs. If you have trouble getting a child (or even an adult in a bad mood) to eat, produce a corn dog on a stick. Petulance is quickly forgotten.

Since the batter can be stored in the refrigerator overnight, with a sheet of plastic pressed into the top to stop a skin from forming, I usually make it a day ahead. That way I can enjoy a solitary corn dog, happily dipping it into a large mound of Dijon mustard while watching TV, the day before everyone else gets them. If I'm feeling really indulgent, I'll grill some onions, then alternate mouthfuls of corn dog and onion. Others prefer ketchup, relish, or sauerkraut with their corn dogs. These have fairly thick coats. If you prefer thinly coated corn dogs, this recipe will make 10 rather than 8.

Vegetable oil
½ cup yellow cornmeal
½ cup unbleached all-purpose presifted flour
½ teaspoon baking powder
½ teaspoon salt
¼ teaspoon cayenne pepper
1 large egg
½ cup milk
⅛ teaspoon dry mustard
8 Pork or Beef Hot Dogs (page 326 or 328)

Begin heating 2″ vegetable oil in a large saucepan or high-sided skillet until it reaches 350°. Stir together the cornmeal, flour, baking powder, salt, and cayenne in a large baking pan or dish. Stir together the egg, milk, and mustard, then stir it into the cornmeal mixture until smooth.

Drop 3 hot dogs in the batter and turn until evenly coated with the batter. Gently lift out the hot dogs with tongs, letting any excess batter drip off. Place the hot dogs into the oil and fry, turning once or twice, until golden brown, about 3 minutes. Remove and drain on paper towels. Make the rest of the corn dogs the same way. If you want to put sticks into them, make a small cut with a knife in one end while the corn dog is draining on the paper towel. Then gently insert a large lollipop or ice cream stick.

Makes 8

Chili for Chili Dogs

Chili dogs have come a long way. Years ago many vendors ladled some fatty, almost meatless, ground beef chili onto a hot dog and we thought it was terrific. Now we've grown more discerning. At one end of the spectrum Cindy Pawlcyn's Fog City Diner sells a $5.50 beef hot dog with homemade pork, beef, and lamb chili on French bread. It's excellent. At the other end is Hormel's Frank 'N Stuff, a hot dog with a vein of beanless chili inside, which is weird, but actually pretty good.

You have two important decisions to make when you prepare chili dogs. The first is whether to degrease the chili overnight or not. The second is whether to peel your hot dogs if you're using those with the natural casings left on. If you leave the skin on, the hot dog stays crunchy. If you remove it, the chili sinks into the hot dog and the tastes become inseparably delicious. Experiment and try it both ways.

My chili is closer to the kind used for Cincinnati five-way chili than to real Texas chili. It's just as good on spaghetti as on a hot dog, so cook enough to freeze some. You can add sharp cheese, chopped raw onions, and/or beans to the hot dog or the spaghetti.

1½ teaspoons ground cinnamon
2 teaspoons ground cumin
1 teaspoon ground cloves
½ teaspoon ground coriander
2 teaspoons finely chopped fresh oregano, or 1 teaspoon crumbled dried
1 bay leaf
1 teaspoon salt
¼ teaspoon black pepper
1½ teaspoons ground chili pepper
1 tablespoon light corn syrup
1½ tablespoons red wine, cider, or sherry vinegar
3 cups drained, roughly chopped, canned tomatoes

½ cup juice from canned tomatoes
5 tablespoons lard or vegetable oil
2 pounds skirt or flank steak, halved with the grain, then cut across the grain into 1″–1½″-wide pieces
2 large garlic cloves, crushed then minced
1 small red or green bell pepper, seeded, julienned
1 cup roughly chopped onion

Mix together the spices, herbs, salt, peppers, corn syrup, vinegar, tomatoes, and juice and set aside.

Heat the lard or oil in a large pot, such as a Dutch oven, over medium-low heat. Add the meat and brown on all sides. Remove the meat with a slotted spoon and add to the tomato mixture. Sauté the garlic, pepper, and onions in the pot for 5 minutes, until just beginning to wilt. Stir in the tomato mixture and bring to a boil over high heat. Stir well, turn the heat to low, and simmer, uncovered, for 3 hours to reduce the liquid. Then cover and simmer for about 1½ hours, until the meat is easily shredded.

Remove the meat from the pot, shred it, and stir it back into the simmering sauce.

Makes approximately 4 cups

Liverwurst Spread

The better the liverwurst, the better the spread. Try replacing the cream cheese with mayonnaise or unsalted butter for a different taste.

This is excellent on sandwiches and classic canapés, but you can also stuff vegetables, like hollowed-out Brussels sprouts, cherry tomatoes, or snow pea pods, with the spread to make more unusual hors d'oeuvres. Place some inside a hamburger before you broil it for a dish that is too good to refer to as ersatz beef Wellington.

6 ounces smooth Liverwurst (page 125), room temperature
3 ounces cream cheese, room temperature
¼ cup finely chopped onion
4 drops of Tabasco sauce
2 teaspoons Cognac, brandy, or dry sherry
Salt and pepper to taste

Mash the liverwurst and cream cheese together with a fork, then beat in the rest of the ingredients.

You can make this in a food processor by first mixing together the liverwurst and cheese with the steel blade, then adding the rest of the ingredients as the processor is running. Stop as soon as they're well mixed.

Makes approximately 1½ cup

Pigs in the Blankets

Tiny sausage links used to be called "little pigs," so that's how these old-fashioned party hors d'oeuvres got their name. In Chicago they used to be called "hog in the wheat." When I was a child looking down on my parents' parties from the top of the stairs, I used to watch the little sausage rolls zealously, cringing when anyone took one, knowing that was one less for me after everyone was asleep. Then, in the era of the quiche, these little gems became passé. But now, with a revived interest in traditional and childhood foods, Americans have returned to the kind of cooking these represent. These aren't, however, uniquely American. Dutch call them *saucijzebroojdes*, while in Brazil a similar recipe is called *enroladinhos Paulistas*.

Although these can be made with Bisquick or refrigerated dough, it's quicker to make your own biscuit dough with staples you're sure to have at home than it is to run out to the grocery store to get the packaged stuff. If you prefer a potato or cream cheese pastry, by all means use it. You can use almost any kind of sausage, parboiling them before wrapping them in dough if they're thicker than the tiny cocktail sausages.

I often improvise with these, replacing the barbecue sauce with mustard, hoisin, or a layer of blue cheese. They're perfect for a buffet since the only correct way to eat them is with your fingers. They can also be frozen before baking and cooked without thawing for an additional 5 minutes at 350°.

- 1½ cups unbleached all-purpose presifted flour
- ¼ teaspoon salt
- 1½ teaspoons baking powder
- ¼ cup finely grated sharp Cheddar cheese
- 2 tablespoons lard or butter
- ½ cup milk
- ½ teaspoon barbecue sauce
- 40 tiny smokies or cocktail sausages
- 1 egg, beaten with 1 tablespoon cold water

Mix the flour, salt, baking powder, and Cheddar together, then cut in the lard or butter. Stir in the milk, then beat for a couple of minutes until smooth.

Preheat the oven to 400°. Grease a baking sheet. Break off about a quarter of the dough and cover the rest. Roll the piece of dough out into a rectangle approximately 6¼″ × 4½″ and brush it with a quarter of the barbecue sauce. Cut it into 10 rectangles, each about 1¼″ × 2¼″. Place a sausage on each rectangle and roll it up. Press the edges together to seal. You should be able to see the 2 ends of the sausage sticking out. Place the finished rolls on the baking sheet, seam side down. Continue making the rolls until you've used up all the dough and sausages.

Brush the top of all the rolls with the egg wash. Bake for 15 minutes, turn down the heat to 350°, and bake for 5 minutes more. Serve hot or at room temperature.

Makes 40

Submarine Sandwiches

The origin of the submarine sandwich isn't certain though sources throughout the east claim the credit. For lack of a more decisive answer, I'll credit the wonderful Manganaro's, a combination Italian delicatessen and café on New York's Ninth Avenue. It claims that one of the original Manganaro brothers created these huge sandwiches to tide him over while fishing. Some food historians believe the New Orleans po'boys and muffulettas are the originals. The sandwiches are most often associated with cities with large Italian populations, probably because they contain several kinds of Italian cold cuts. Grinders, heros, hoagies, blimps, and Cuban sandwiches are several other names for these.

The most impressive way to serve this is to order an extremely long loaf of bread and make one gigantic sandwich. Then let guests cut off just as much as they like. Or you can buy several long loaves of bread, cutting off the rounded ends, and serve them end to end. Although the sandwich is a complete meal, people expect salad with it. I like coleslaw, fresh fruit salad, and Martini & Rossi Asti Spumante with the sandwiches.

The easiest way to demonstrate this recipe is to list the ingredients in the order in which they appear on a sandwich serving 2 people. The slices of each ingredient should overlap each other.

Dressing

2 tablespoons virgin olive oil
2 teaspoons wine or sherry vinegar
½ teaspoon minced garlic
1 tablespoon finely chopped fresh oregano, or ½ tablespoon crumbled dried
⅛ teaspoon finely chopped fresh rosemary, or large pinch of crumbled dried
1 teaspoon coarse mustard

Place all the dressing ingredients in a jar, screw on the lid and shake until mixed.

1 half of a very crusty 10" loaf of French or Italian bread which has been halved lengthwise
Mayonnaise to taste
Very thin slices of 1 very ripe tomato
2 ounces very thin prosciutto
3 ounces Beef Salami or Summer Sausage slices (page 25 or 325)
3 ounces very thin Cheddar cheese slices
3 ounces very thin boiled ham slices
2 ounces thin Provolone cheese slices
3 ounces thin Genoa salami slices
8 thin dill pickle slices
Crunchy sweet pickled peppers to cover the lettuce
Dressing poured on lettuce
Shredded romaine lettuce or cabbage to thickly cover the bread
1 half loaf of bread

Sausage-Stuffed Onions

You can use any fresh sausage for stuffing vegetables, but I prefer spicier ones. Fresh Chorizo, hot Italian sausage, country Kielbasa, and Southern Country Sausage are particularly good. You can also use the sweeter, somewhat expensive, Maui onions to turn this into a first course at a dinner party. In that case, use an exotic sausage like Thai Spicy Pork and Crab and garnish the onions with fresh coriander.

If you're serving these as a main course for a family dinner, begin the meal with homemade chicken or beef noodle soup. A potato, sharp Cheddar cheese, and broccoli casserole goes well with the onions and can be baked at the same time. Very few wines can stand up to onions, so serve a robust red one, like an Italian Nebbiolo, and pear brown Betty for dessert.

- 4 Spanish onions, peeled but left whole
- ½ pound fresh sausage, such as Basic Italian or Chorizo (page 96 or 302)
- 2½ tablespoons toasted bread crumbs
- 4 teaspoons finely chopped fresh parsley
- 4 teaspoons finely chopped fresh oregano, or 1 teaspoon crumbled dried
- 1 garlic clove, crushed then minced
- Salt to taste
- Large pinch of ground chile or cayenne pepper
- 2½ tablespoons freshly grated Parmesan cheese

Place the onions in a large pot of boiling water and boil for 15 minutes, until slightly tender. Remove and drain well. While the onions are cooking, mix together the rest of the ingredients to make the stuffing and set aside. Cut out the inside of the boiled onions, leaving just 3 outside layers. If necessary, you can slit the outer layers slightly near the top to make it easier to remove the centers. Finely chop one-third of the removed onion and add it to the stuffing. Use the rest of the removed onion for another dish.

Stuff the onions and arrange them in a buttered baking dish just large enough to hold them without touching each other. Place in the oven, turn it on to 350°, and bake for 50 minutes.

Serves 2 as a main course

Broccoli, Rice, and Sausage Casserole

While I don't normally like packaged foods, I find Uncle Ben's mixed rice is perfect for this dish. The small amount of wild rice adds interest without overpowering the sausage. When I'm feeling particularly indulgent, I do make this casserole with only wild rice, but usually I prefer the milder and less expensive version below. Use any spicy fresh sausage in the casserole. You can either serve it as a side dish alongside poultry or before or after a bowl of rich, meaty soup.

- 1 box of Uncle Ben's mixed wild and white rice
- 1 cup roughly chopped broccoli
- ½ pound skinned fresh sausage
- 1 small onion, finely chopped
- ¼ pound fresh mushrooms, thinly sliced
- 1 cup chicken or beef stock
- ½ teaspoon ground thyme
- 1 teaspoon minced fresh oregano, or ½ teaspoon crumbled dried
- Salt and pepper to taste
- 2 tablespoons unsalted butter
- 2 tablespoons white flour
- ⅓ cup heavy cream

Preheat the oven to 350°. Cook the rice according to the package directions. While the rice is cooking, put the broccoli in a 2-quart casserole.

Place the sausage in a medium-size skillet and turn the heat to medium-low. Constantly mash the sausage with a fork until browned, then remove it with a slotted spoon and place it in the casserole. Add the onions and mushrooms to the skillet and sauté them for 10 minutes. Remove them with a slotted spoon and add to the casserole along with the cooked rice.

Mix together the stock, thyme, oregano, salt, and pepper. Melt the butter in a small saucepan over low heat, add the flour, and continue to stir until the flour is light brown. Constantly stirring, pour in the stock, then the cream. Stir for another minute, until well blended, then pour into the casserole. Toss everything well. Bake for 40 minutes.

Serves 8

Sausage Strata

That this recipe would fit right into Ernie Mickler's remarkable cookbook, *White Trash Cooking,* is certainly not an insult to the book, the dish, or the people who created it. "White trash" is American for peasants, those wonderful folks who gave us masterpieces like cassoulet, feijoada, and fried rice. It's amazing how such banal ingredients can turn into anything as delicious as this. It may not be cassoulet, but it's a lot cheaper and easier to make. You can even prepare it a few hours in advance and refrigerate it, covered with plastic or foil, until you're ready to cook it. Then bake it for an extra 10 minutes.

The secret of a good strata is the cheese. If the cheese is mediocre, the dish will turn into bland, pasty cafeteria food. You can't serve anything pretentious with a strata or you'll feel very silly. All you need is a fresh green salad with mushrooms, tomatoes, and a garlic vinaigrette. My personal favorite dessert is a lot of Hydrox cookies, but if you've got other people around, they'll probably want something more substantial such as pecan or peach pie.

5–6 slices of egg or white bread, crusts removed
1½ pounds skinned spicy pork sausage

5 large eggs
1 cup milk
¼ teaspoon salt
⅛ teaspoon white pepper
2 drops of Tabasco sauce
½ teaspoon dry mustard
¾ cup grated or shredded Cheddar cheese
¾ cup grated or shredded Swiss cheese

Preheat the oven to 350°. Grease a 9″ or 10″ round baking dish that has 1½″-to 2″-high sides. Arrange the bread slices in one layer to cover the bottom of the dish.

Fry the sausage, constantly crumbling as you stir, in a skillet over low heat until cooked through. Drain the sausage well and place on top of the bread. Beat together the eggs, milk, salt, pepper, Tabasco, and mustard until a uniform color, then pour over the sausage. Sprinkle with the cheeses. Bake for 30 minutes, then cut into 8 wedges.

Serves 8

Sausage Cake

This looks and tastes very much like its close relative, gingerbread. The sausage melts into the cake, adding the necessary shortening. Also called "Cincinnati cake," this pioneer staple comes from northern England. Sausages and salt pork were often the only fats available during the winter, so they were put to use in all kinds of dishes. Butifarra, and other sausages with lots of spices and few herbs, are perfect for this dish. No one will realize the cake has pork in it, so you might not want to tell them. This cake keeps for weeks in the refrigerator and you may get sick of seeing it. It's a solid cake, better for snacks than dessert, and especially good with milk.

- 5 cups unbleached all-purpose presifted flour
- 1½ cups light or dark brown sugar
- 1 teaspoon baking powder
- 1 teaspoon baking soda
- 1½ teaspoons ground cinnamon
- 1 teaspoon grated nutmeg
- 1 teaspoon ground cloves
- 1 cup hot strong black coffee
- 1 cup hot milk
- ½ pound lightly seasoned, skinless, fresh pork sausage
- 1½ cups molasses
- ½ cup raisins
- 1 cup roughly chopped walnuts

Preheat the oven to 350°. Grease a 9″ square pan.

Mix together in a large bowl the flour, sugar, baking powder, baking soda, cinnamon, nutmeg, and cloves. In a separate bowl stir together the hot coffee and milk. Crumble the sausage into a small bowl and pour the coffee mixture over it. Stir well with a fork to break up the sausage into very small pieces, then stir in the molasses. Stir the sausage mixture into the dry ingredients, then fold in the raisins and nuts. Pour into the pan, cover with foil, and bake for 45 minutes. The cake is done when a skewer comes out clean.

Serves 12

New American Cooking

Seafood Sausage

This is my version of a sausage that is now served in every restaurant that claims to serve New American cooking. Many of the cooks don't realize that fish sausages have a long history dating back to ancient Roman times. Mexicans, Hungarians, and central and Eastern European Jews all have unique recipes for fish sausage, most of which have been around for at least hundreds of years. My sausage is much denser than many restaurant sausages. Theirs are more ethereal and quenelle-like, and often quite wonderful, but I like solid sausages, more like fish pâtés. Unfortunately, the only alternative to a food processor is manually pounding the mixture until it's smooth.

I serve these cold with an herb mayonnaise or pesto sauce after a clear soup at formal dinners, before the meat course, which is usually a crown roast of lamb or pork, or steak with a wild mushroom sauce. These sausages can also be served sliced and floating in a hot fish stock. If I want to serve the sausages as a main course, I add them to a predominantly seafood gumbo (see the following recipe) or serve them hot with Himmel und Erde, the German mashed potato and apple puree, both topped with a butter and herb sauce.

1 large egg
2 tablespoons sweet rice wine (mirin)
1 tablespoon fresh or bottled lemon juice
½ teaspoon salt
½ teaspoon white pepper
Large pinch of cayenne or ground chile pepper
1 pound raw skinless, boneless salmon
¼ cup heavy cream
¼ pound smoked salmon, roughly chopped
¼ pound raw, shelled shrimp, chopped into ½″ cubes
1 tablespoon minced fresh dill or fennel leaves (optional—do not use dried)
1 teaspoon minced fresh chives

Begin bringing a large pot of water to a boil. Stir the egg, rice wine, lemon juice, salt, pepper, and cayenne or chile together with a fork to mix well. Puree the fresh salmon in a food processor with the steel blade. With the processor running, add the egg mixture and puree until smooth. Whip the cream until it holds stiff peaks, then fold into the salmon. Fold in the smoked salmon, shrimp, dill or fennel, and chives.

Lay one-sixth of the salmon on a buttered sheet of aluminum foil and pat into a 1½"-wide sausage. Roll the sausage in the foil, pushing on it to compress it a bit. Twist the ends of the foil to seal them. Make the other 5 sausages the same way.

Turn the heat under the boiling water to very low, drop in the sausages, and poach for 20 minutes. Remove the sausages with tongs, cool to room temperature, then refrigerate until you're ready to use them. They can be stored in the refrigerator, still wrapped in the foil, for 3 days, but shouldn't be frozen, since the texture will become unpleasant.

Serves 6 as an appetizer

Seafood and Sausage Gumbo

This is a Cajun gumbo adapted so that it won't overwhelm the more delicate seafood flavors. You can use lobster or crab instead of shrimp, as long as you have the shells. The shells add a great deal of flavor to the gumbo. If you're substituting another kind of fish for the swordfish, make sure it's a strong-tasting fish, not a delicate, white one. You can also add a few other sausages if you have some in your refrigerator or freezer. It's a great way to use up the single leftover bratwurst or the half of the butifarra you didn't eat last night at midnight.

I usually precede gumbo with a salad made with several kinds of greens and tomatoes in a creamy dressing like blue cheese. Gumbo should then be accompanied by white rice. Berry-flavored fruit ices or strawberry ice cream are perfect desserts. You'll need a strong wine to stand up to the gumbo, so I usually drink something unusual like the white Alsatian Riesling.

1 pound medium shrimp with shells
Salt to taste

2 teaspoons black pepper
¼ teaspoon ground chile or cayenne pepper or hot paprika
2½ tablespoons chopped fresh dill, fennel, or parsley leaves
1½ tablespoons chopped fresh chives
½ pound andouille or other smoked garlic sausage, cut into ¼″-thick slices
4 tablespoons unsalted butter
2 tablespoons vegetable oil
½ cup plus 2 tablespoons white or unbleached flour
1 large leek, white and light green sections, roughly chopped
1 large garlic clove, crushed then minced
2 scallions, white and green sections, roughly chopped
1 celery stalk, roughly chopped
1 green bell pepper, seeded, roughly chopped
4 cups fish stock, or 2 cups each clam juice and chicken stock
1 pound poached Seafood Sausages, raw and/or poached Cajun Boudin Blanc, or other white sausage (page 344, 373, 26, or 64)
1 1 -pound piece of boneless swordfish, cut into 1″ squares

Peel the shrimp and set aside. Crush the shrimp shells by placing them in a double thickness of plastic bags and smashing them until flattened but still in large pieces. Set them aside. Mix together the salt, pepper, ground chile or cayenne or paprika, dill or fennel or parsley, and chives and set aside. Heat a large cast-iron pot, such as a Dutch oven, over high heat. When it's hot, add the andouille and cook until browned all over. Remove the andouille and drain on paper towels.

Turn the heat to low, add the butter and oil, and stir until the butter has melted. Then stir in the flour. Continue to stir almost constantly, scraping the bottom, for 20 to 25 minutes, until the flour mixture (the roux) is just slightly darker than milk chocolate. Don't let it burn. Stir in the leek, garlic, scallions, celery, green pepper, and shrimp shells and mix well. Immediately stir in the fish stock or chicken stock and clam juice and bring to a boil, stirring often.

Turn the heat to low and simmer, covered, for 1 hour. Then remove the shrimp shells with a slotted spoon and stir in the andouille, poached sausage, shrimp, and swordfish. Simmer, covered, for 20 minutes, until the swordfish is cooked through. Stir once or twice during this time. Stir in the salt mixture and immediately remove from the heat. Serve at once.

Serves 8

Duck Sausage

Followers of food trends usually think of pizza when they think of duck sausage, but it's much more versatile than that. It's sort of canard à l'orange with the canard and orange completely integrated. If you stuff it into casings and poach it, it's wonderful sliced and added to hot or cold tomato soup. They're also delicious barbecued, but what sausage isn't?

I find I usually serve sautéed duck sausages with traditional roast duck accompaniments such as wild mushroom sauce and mixed white and wild rice. Sometimes I combine everything to make a Chinese-style Fried Rice with duck sausage and wild mushrooms. Sausage-Stuffed Onions, green peppers, or tomatoes should be accompanied by French-fried potatoes. When trying to decide whether to use these sausages in a dish, imagine what that dish would taste like with some orange peel in it. If it sounds good, try it. If not, forget it.

1 5-pound duck
1 garlic clove, roughly chopped
½″ piece of fresh ginger, peeled, roughly chopped
¼ cup white vermouth or other dry white wine
¼ cup orange liqueur
3 strips of smoked bacon, cut into approximately ¼″ squares
1 tablespoon finely chopped fresh chives
½ teaspoon salt
⅛ teaspoon pepper

2 teaspoons grated orange or tangerine peel
¼ teaspoon five-spice powder
⅛ teaspoon ground chile or cayenne pepper or hot paprika

Prepared hog casings (optional)

Remove the skin, bones, and wings from the duck and cut the meat and ¼ cup of the fat into approximately ¼″ cubes. You should have 2 cups of meat. Use the discarded parts of the duck for stock. Mix together the garlic, ginger, wine, and liqueur in a large bowl, then add the duck, duck fat, and bacon and toss well. Marinate in the refrigerator, covered, for 6 to 12 hours. Toss well every couple of hours.

Remove the meat and fat from the marinade with a slotted spoon and place in a large bowl. Stir in the chives, salt, pepper, orange or tangerine peel, five-spice powder, and chile pepper.

You can either stuff it into prepared hog casings or use as bulk sausage. If you stuff it into casings, poach it. This will keep raw or cooked for 3 days in the refrigerator and can also be frozen for 3 months.

Makes approximately 1¼ pounds raw sausage

Duck Sausage Calzone

The Chinese seasonings—ginger, orange peel, and five-spice powder—in the Duck Sausage inspired me to combine it with other Chinese ingredients in this calzone. While calzones and pizzas have become clichés in New American cooking, there's a good reason for their popularity. When chefs use good sense and taste in assembling them, they can be delicious, amusing, and satisfying without being so filling they put you right to sleep.

You can also use this recipe to make pizza or Focaccia. Just roll the dough into two 8″- or 9″-diameter circles, scatter the filling on top and bake until the crust is lightly browned. If necessary, substitute Spanish Butifarra, sweet or Basic Italian Sausage, Fresh Garlic Sausage, or even Country Sausage for the Duck Sausage, by kneading 3 tablespoons orange liqueur and 1 teaspoon grated orange peel into the skinned sausage.

You can serve tiny calzones as appetizers. Since the inside is already cooked, just bake the tiny ones until lightly browned.

½ package (½ ounce) dry yeast
¼ teaspoon sugar
¼ cup warm water (about 90°)
½ cup room temperature water
2¼ cups unbleached all-purpose presifted flour
1½ tablespoons very good quality olive oil
1 teaspoon salt
1 pound skinless Duck Sausage (page 348)
1 cup finely chopped onion
1 green pepper, seeded, diced
10 peeled water chestnuts, diced
10 baby corn cobs, very thinly sliced
2 tablespoons finely chopped fresh coriander or parsley
1 teaspoon Chinese chili paste, Indonesian sambal, or Harissa (page 256)

¼ cup dried cepes (porcini) or brown Chinese mushrooms, soaked in hot water to cover for 10 minutes, drained, and roughly chopped
3 tablespoons oyster sauce
Coarse cornmeal

Dissolve the yeast and sugar in the warm water and let sit at room temperature for 10 minutes, until it's fairly frothy. Place 1½ cups flour in a large bowl. Stir the room temperature water into the yeast mixture, then pour the yeast and water into the bowl containing the flour. Whisk until well mixed, then set aside, covered with a towel, in a warm, draft-free place for 1 to 1½ hours, until doubled in bulk.

Stir the oil and salt into your dough, then mix in the remaining flour. Knead the dough on a lightly floured board until it's smooth and elastic and blisters begin to form, about 10 minutes. Place it in an oiled bowl, cover with a towel, and let it rise again in a warm, draft-free place for about 2 hours, until doubled in bulk.

After the dough has risen for 2 hours, press a sheet of plastic wrap across the top and place the dough in the freezer while you make the filling. Bring water in the bottom part of a steamer to a boil. Mix together the sausage, onion, green pepper, water chestnuts, and baby corn and place in the top section of the steamer. Steam for 10 minutes over high heat, until the sausage is cooked through. Pour into a bowl and stir in the coriander or parsley; chili paste, sambal, or harissa; mushrooms; and oyster sauce.

Preheat the oven to 475°. If you're using a pizza stone, preheat it according to the directions that come with it. Cut the dough into 4 pieces, and keep the unused ones covered as you roll out the rest. Roll 1 piece of the dough out on a floured board into a 9″ or 10″ circle and place one-quarter of the filling in the center. Fold over the dough to enclose the filling, pinching the edges closed in a decorative pattern to seal it completely. Make the rest of the calzones in the same way. Sprinkle cornmeal on a baking sheet or the heated stone and carefully place the calzones on. Bake for 12 minutes. You can also deep-fry the calzones in hot oil to cover. Since the inside is already cooked, you only have to worry about cooking the dough through.

Serves 4

Warm Sausage and Rice Salad

Rice salads gained in popularity when most Americans realized they had eaten one too many pasty pasta salads. Don't overcook the rice, and drain it and rinse it with cold water the second it's done cooking. It should be al dente, soft on the outside with a slight bite on the inside. Luganega, Butifarra, Fresh Garlic, Country, and Swedish Potato are all good sausages to use in this dish. You can also use smoked or dried sausages, but the fresh sausage is more unusual.

The salad can be stored in the refrigerator, covered, for a couple of days, but bring it to room temperature before serving. I usually bring it on picnics along with fried chicken and cold stir-fried vegetables with lots of garlic and ginger. It's also good as a first course before grilled fish served on a bed of sautéed spinach. Cold apple tart and blueberry pie are my favorite desserts for these meals. Serve a spicy white wine, like a California Gewürztraminer, with the salad. I really hate to say this, but it's the absolute truth: Seagram's Peach or Wild Berry Wine Cooler is the ultimate picnic beverage with the rice salad and chicken.

2 cups chicken stock, homemade preferable but uncondensed canned acceptable
1 cup long-grain rice
2 tablespoons unsalted butter, diced, plus 1 tablespoon
½ pound fresh sausage
½ pound very ripe, fresh tomatoes, roughly chopped
4 teaspoons sherry or red wine vinegar
¾ cup crumbled feta cheese
2 tablespoons roughly chopped fresh coriander
⅓ cup julienned snow pea pods
⅓ cup roughly chopped pickled peppers or pimientos
2 tablespoons good-quality olive oil
¼ teaspoon ground chile or cayenne pepper
1½ teaspoons salt

Bring the stock to a boil, stir in the rice and half the diced butter, turn the heat to very low, cover, and cook for 20 minutes. Then uncover and cook, shaking the pan occasionally, for another 5 to 10 minutes, until all the stock has been absorbed. Stir in the rest of the diced butter.

While the rice is cooking, melt 1 tablespoon butter in a medium-size skillet over low heat. Fry the sausage, crushing with a fork to crumble it well, until it has lost its redness. Add the tomatoes and their liquid and 2 teaspoons vinegar to the sausages. Stir well, cover, and cook for about 3 minutes, until the tomatoes are barely softened. Stir once or twice. Remove the pan from the heat.

When the rice is done, toss it with the tomatoes and sausage in a large bowl. Stir in the feta cheese, coriander, snow peas, and peppers or pimientos.

While the salad is cooling slightly, place the olive oil, remaining 2 teaspoons vinegar, hot pepper, and salt in a jar. Screw the lid on tightly, then shake well. Pour the dressing into the salad and toss well. Serve warm or at room temperature.

Serves 6 as appetizer

Salt Cod and Sausage Fritters

This is inspired by both the traditional French and Caribbean salt cod fritters. Salt cod is sold in the refrigerator section of many supermarkets, or in Caribbean, Spanish, and French groceries. Although salt cod fritters are traditionally deep-fried, these are much too fragile since there's no raw egg in them to hold them together. They're delicious topped with a spoonful of finely chopped pickled vegetables, Mexican salsa, tart tomato coulis, leftover gumbo gravy, or an herbed, heavily garlicked mayonnaise.

If I'm serving these as a first course, I follow them with a chicken roasted with a huge amount of fresh thyme, wild rice, and a small cooked vegetable salad. For dessert, I like strawberry shortcake or a génoise cake with a berry liqueur and cream cheese frosting. If I'm serving the fritters as a simple supper, I begin with a small bowl of lentil or mushroom soup, serve a salad with the fritters, and offer fresh fruit for dessert. A Spanish white Rioja or French Vouvray is good with the fritters.

1 pound good-quality salt cod
½ pound potatoes, peeled, cut into a total of 4 2-ounce pieces
½ cup hot heavy cream (110°)
1 large garlic clove, crushed then minced
Large pinch white pepper
⅓ cup hot olive oil (110°)
2 large eggs, hard-boiled, shelled, pressed through a sieve
1 tablespoon sherry or cider vinegar
2 tablespoons finely chopped fresh parsley
2 tablespoons finely chopped fresh chives
½ cup (about 3 ounces) andouille or other smoked garlic sausage, cut into ⅛" cubes
¾ cup fine dry bread crumbs
3 tablespoons butter, room temperature

Soak the cod in cold water to cover for 12 to 24 hours, depending on how salty it is, changing the water at least 6 times.

Drain the cod, place in a skillet, cover with fresh water, and bring to a boil over high heat. The second the water begins to boil, remove the pot from the heat and let it stand for 15 minutes. Don't boil the cod or it will be tough. While the cod is cooking, bring another pot of water to a boil and cook the potatoes until they're tender. Drain them well.

Process the potato and cod together in a food processor with the steel blade, using on-off pulses, just until they're smooth, in batches if necessary. Don't overprocess them. You can also mash them together by hand, but it's very difficult to get it as smooth. Return the cod and potato to the processor if you've mashed them in batches. Mix together the hot cream, garlic, and pepper, then slowly pour them into the running processor. The second you've finished adding the cream, pour in one-quarter of the oil, processing just until incorporated. Keep adding the same amount of oil, making sure it's incorporated each time, until you've used it all.

Scrape the cod mixture into a bowl and fold in the eggs, vinegar, parsley, chives, and sausage. Refrigerate, covered, for 24 hours.

Preheat the oven to 350°. Grease 3 baking sheets. Form the cold cod mixture into 30 patties, each about 2½″ in diameter and ⅛″ thick. Coat with the bread crumbs and place on the sheets. Dot them with the butter and bake for 15 minutes, until nicely browned.

Makes 30

Oyster and Sausage Profiteroles

In southwestern France, bites of sausage are eaten between raw oysters as a matter of course, so this isn't as strange as it seems. I don't know why the combination of the smooth, salty oysters goes so well with the coarse, chewy sausages. It just does.

You can make this dish with or without the profiterole shells. The shells make the presentation prettier and allow you to eat them with your fingers if you choose. (I also really like profiterole shells, and their breadlike taste adds another interesting texture to the dish.) Follow the profiteroles with grilled meat, poultry, swordfish or salmon, steamed Brussels sprouts, and French-fried potatoes or fried potato cakes. Don't serve pastry for dessert since you've used pastry shells in the first course. An ice cream bombe or zabaglione would be appropriate. Serve a young red wine, like the fruity Chinon, with the profiteroles.

12 oysters (in the shell)
½ cup plus 1 tablespoon white flour
⅛ teaspoon salt
½ cup water
5 tablespoons unsalted butter
2 large eggs, room temperature
1 teaspoon minced fresh rosemary, or ½ teaspoon crumbled dried
9″ of fresh sausage links, such as Luganega or Butifarra (page 110 or 197), poached, then skinned and cut into a total of 24 slices, each about ⅜″ thick
1½ cups white wine, such as a California Gewürztraminer
Pinch each of salt and black pepper

Rinse the oysters well under cold running water. Place in a bowl of cold water and let sit for about 45 minutes. Then preheat the oven to 400°. Mix ½ cup flour with ⅛ teaspoon salt and set aside.

Bring the water and 2 tablespoons butter to a boil in a medium-size saucepan over moderate heat. Dump in the flour and salt all at once and quickly begin to beat with a wooden spoon. As soon as the mixture forms a ball and cleanly leaves the sides of the pan, remove the pan from the heat. Set aside for 3 to 5 minutes.

When the bottom of the saucepan is cool enough for you to rest your palm on it without being burned, break 1 egg into a small bowl and stir it just to mix the white and yolk. Pour into the flour mixture and beat very well until it's completely incorporated. It will look as if the mixture has terminally separated into little balls, but if you keep beating it will come together into one large ball again. As soon as that happens, repeat those steps with the second egg. You can also transfer the mixture to a bowl and beat with the paddle of an electric mixer. It's easier, but then you have more to clean. Take your choice. An electric whisk can also be used.

Using a wet tablespoon, drop 12 mounds of the dough onto an ungreased baking sheet. If your mounds are lumpy, dampen your hands and smooth them. Place in the middle of the oven and bake for 10 minutes. Turn heat down to 350° and bake for another 20 to 30 minutes. They should be golden brown all over when they're done.

While they're cooking, melt 2 tablespoons butter in a large cast-iron skillet over medium heat. Add the rosemary and the sausage slices. Brown the sausage on both sides, stirring often so that the rosemary doesn't burn. Remove the sausage and set aside, wrapped in foil. Pour ½ cup of the wine into the skillet and stir well to deglaze the pan. Bring to a boil, then turn heat down to low. Rinse the oysters again and place in the skillet. Cover and cook for 15 minutes.

When the profiterole shells are done, remove them from the oven and transfer to a cooling rack. Cut a small slit about 1″ long across the middle of each, and carefully remove any uncooked portions from inside the shells with a small spoon.

When the oysters have cooked for 15 minutes, turn off the heat and remove the oysters from the skillet. Leave the skillet on the burner. The mixture in the bottom of the skillet will appear burnt, but that's what it's supposed to look like. Immediately pour in the remaining 1 cup wine and stir very well. Cover the pan while you shuck the oysters.

Uncover the pan and turn heat to low. Whisk in a pinch of salt and pepper and the remaining 1 tablespoon butter and flour. Beat well so that you don't have any lumps. Turn off the heat. Dip each sausage slice in the thick sauce, then place two inside a shell. Place an oyster atop the sausage slices inside the profiterole. Then, using a paint or kitchen brush, paint the top of each profiterole with some of the sauce. Serve at once. This will be warm, but not hot.

Serves 12

CHAPTER 15

Regional

American Cooking

American cooking varies from region to region, influenced by the native Americans, immigrants, and the local ingredients. Many regional dishes have been absorbed into the national cuisine thanks to the constant American search for something new. Some regional recipes can be successfully made anywhere, but others still depend on local ingredients expensive or difficult to find elsewhere and the expertise developed by years of cooking the same foods.

The Portuguese fishermen in Massachusetts made a great impact on New England cooking. The red pepper, vinegar, and garlic *chouriços* and *linguiça* are found in traditional New England foods like clam pie, baked beans, and clambakes, while kale, potato, and sausage soup and steamed clams and sausages are almost identical to those served in Portugal. One hundred years ago butchers went from door to door, selling both country sausage and the Portuguese variety. The country sausage varied every day since it was made from whatever small pieces of lamb, beef, and/or pork the butcher had left over. Headcheese; potatoes, game, or poultry stuffed with sausage; and the sausage-filled "field mouse pie" are popular New England dishes.

New York City's gastronomic personality comes from the abundance of cooking styles; you can find almost any kind of food from Ethiopian to Caribbean. Kosher beef hot dogs and salamis were first popular in New York and New Jersey before they became commonplace across the country. White and red hots, which are similar to *bockwurst* and hot dogs, are popular in upstate New York.

Bratwurst, weisswurst, stuffed goose neck, headcheese, and other Swiss and German sausages are very popular in Pennsylvania, home of the Mennonites and Pennsylvania Dutch, a name which everyone now knows is a corruption of *Deutsch*, or German. These groups also devised some of America's most interesting regional dishes. The very wide, smoked, Lebanon bologna created here is a favorite sandwich meat. The bologna and other sausages used to be preserved in brine over the long winter. Sausage patties or links are served with sweet potatoes fried in sausage grease. Turkey sausage, Lancaster sausage, and scrapple (fried cornmeal and headcheese) are three other Pennsylvania specialties.

Southerners don't go in for fancy sausages. They like herb-laden country sausage in patties or links, fresh or smoked. In the eighteenth and nineteenth centuries, the richer you were, the more elaborate your breakfast; but fried sausage and/or ham were mandatory for rich and poor alike. While sausage was packed in crocks and covered in lard throughout the United States, in Tennessee it was formed into cakes and fried before being sealed in the jars. Oyster and veal or pork sausages, similar to those popular in England over one hundred years ago, can still occasionally be found. African slaves also helped create Southern cooking, improvising dishes like Frogmore stew, made with sausage, shrimp, corn, and crab, served on the Carolina Islands. Rice, an important Southern crop, is often baked with sausage meat and sometimes poultry. Florida has a large Cuban population, so dishes such as *platio*—spaghetti with tomatoes, chorizo, and garlic—are common.

Many Cajun and Creole dishes are popular throughout the South, but the Louisiana versions are always bolder and spicier. While Creole cuisine is usually considered more sophisticated and Cajun more rustic, they have become so intermingled that it's hard to tell them apart. Here the word *Cajun* is used to describe both. Spanish, Italian, French, and African influences are obvious in many Cajun dishes like soups, stews, and jambalaya, which efficiently extend the little meat and seafood Cajuns could afford.

Cajun sausages, including headcheese, are especially spicy, adding piquancy to egg dishes and poultry stuffings. Smoked *andouille,* descendant of the French sausage, was traditionally made with strips of casing mixed with seasonings and stuffed into a whole casing. Now it's made with coarse pieces of pork meat and used to flavor vegetables, soups, and stews. *Boudin noir,* also called *boudin rouge,* is a blood and rice sausage rarely found since it became illegal to use pork blood. Chile-doused hot links are essential to Southern barbecue restaurants. The surprisingly uninteresting alligator sausages may owe their popularity to the old Southern belief that alligator meat can cure serious illnesses.

Southwestern cuisine, including the once-underestimated Tex-Mex cooking, has been influenced by both Mexico and Louisiana. *Chorizo,* usually skinless, is cooked in dishes like black bean soup, *huevos rancheros*, omelettes, *tacos*, *gorditas*, *enchiladas*, and *quesadillas*. Barbecue joints serve beef or pork sausages, either the thin, short hot links, or thick sausages cut into short lengths.

Southwestern sausages, however, have been equally influenced by the many German, Czech, Polish, and Alsatian immigrants in the area. Those in New Braunfels and Castroville, Texas, have long battled over the title, "sausage capital of the world," and there is at least one sausage maker in most southwestern towns. Smoked or fresh sausages made from venison or buffalo, sometimes in links, sometimes salami-shaped, are German adaptations of Indian pemmican, and smoked turkey links or rings sometimes include chiles to demonstrate their Texas heritage. White sausages here are closer to German weisswurst than Cajun *boudin blanc*, and smoked pork or blood sausage with sauerkraut is commonly found on restaurant menus.

The northern United States was settled by northern Europeans, including those from Scandinavia, Germany, Poland, Czechoslovakia, and parts of the U.S.S.R. Potato sausages, summer sausages, white sausages, liverwursts, blood sausages, kielbasa, headcheese, and stuffed goose neck are as taken for granted as hot dogs. In a poll taken in the 1930s, St. Louis restaurant-goers declared that their three favorite meals were steak, ham, and bratwurst. The charcoal-broiled, garlicky pork bratwurst served with butter and grilled onions on a crusty roll in Sheboygan, Wisconsin, is particularly delicious.

Cincinnati, Ohio, was proudly called "Porkopolis" years ago, and its sausages were considered superior. Geotta, a breakfast dish unique to Cincinnati, is similar to scrapple and polenta, but made with oatmeal rather than cornmeal. Even Cincinnati five-way chili can include chopped hot dogs along with the spaghetti, onions, beans, chili, and cheese (in which case it's six-way chili) or you can have chili dogs served alongside.

California has been greatly influenced by Asian immigrants. What has become nationally known as California cuisine is often local ingredients cooked in a Japanese, Chinese, or French nouvelle cuisine style. The Californians' obsession with health has inspired nitrite-free, low-fat, and tofu sausages, but traditional sausages are still more popular. Outdoor grills covered with sizzling French, Italian, German, Cajun, and Asian sausages are currently trendy at Los Angeles parties. Breakfast sausages, made from pork or sometimes chicken, have also made a comeback in chic restaurants.

San Francisco's climate is responsible for its unique, dried, Italian-inspired *salame,* while potato sausages are staples for Scandinavian descendants in Washington State. In Alaska, fresh or smoked reindeer garlic sausage is cooked in short thick links or patties, while moose sausages are almost always formed into patties. Chinese, Japanese, Polynesian, and Portuguese-inspired sausages are served in Hawaii. Chinese-Hawaiian batter-fried pork and water chestnut sausages include dried oysters, Japanese *kamaboko* are included in salads, and Chinese *lop cheong* or Portuguese chouriço can be found in fried noodle or rice dishes.

NEW ENGLAND

Stove-Top Clam "Bake"

The pure, simple Indian clambake became an elaborate ritualized extravaganza in the hands of the English settlers. I don't have access to a beach where I can dig a pit, so when I saw an ad for CLAMBAKES TO GO from The Clambake Company in Orleans, Maine, I knew I had to try it. I received a pot already packed with everything I needed, and it was absolute heaven. Now that I have their reusable pot, I buy the ingredients and put it together myself.

The person who sells you your lobster can usually be convinced to sell or give you enough rockweed, or you can go to a nearby beach and pick it up for free. If you have a very large pot, like a steamer, which has closable vents on top, that's perfect. To serve more than 4 people, you'll need 2 pots. Serve a small bowl of thick soup first like Caldo Verde or corn or clam chowder. Accompany the meal with an excellent California sparkling wine such as Piper-Sonoma or Domaine Mumm.

4 small ears of corn
Melted butter or vegetable oil
4 cod fillets
4 teaspoons minced oregano, or 2 teaspoons crumbled dried
4 teaspoons minced fresh parsley
4 Linguiça or sweet or Basic Italian Sausages (page 193 or 96), each pricked in 3 places
8 small new potatoes, halved if larger than 4" diameter
Seaweed, preferably rockweed
4 small lobsters (each under 1 pound)
2 medium onions, halved
12 steamers or other small clams, rinsed well
12 mussels, rinsed well
2 cups water, preferably sea water
1 loaf of French or Italian bread

Husk the corn, and soak the husks in cold water for 15 minutes. Soak a rectangle of cheesecloth in melted butter or oil and squeeze dry. While the husks are soaking, sprinkle the fish with the herbs. Roll up the fillets, then wrap in the cheesecloth.

Add the ingredients to the pot in the following order: corn husks, sausage and potatoes, one-third of the seaweed, 2 lobsters and 2 ears of corn, one-third of the seaweed, 2 lobsters and 2 ears of corn, onions and cod, one-third of the seaweed, clams and mussels. The upper layers—clams, mussels, onions, and fish—will be steamed, while the rest will be boiled.

Pour the water into the pot and bring to a boil over high heat with one vent open. When you begin to see steam coming out of the vent, begin timing. Cook for 30 minutes without opening the pot. Place the pot on a heatproof pad in the middle of the table and give everyone a large bowl. Everyone takes out his own food, then ladles some broth into his bowl. The bread is for dipping in the broth.

Serves 4

PENNSYLVANIA DUTCH

Sausage with Gravy

Gravy always makes a meal seem richer, more filling, more soothing. You can serve the sausage with the gravy or make the sausage for breakfast and the gravy later. Just cool the grease in the skillet, then refrigerate it, covered with foil, until dinnertime. Make the gravy at that point and serve it over mashed potatoes and fried chicken or chicken-fried steak. If you're serving the sausage for dinner, mashed potatoes and a broccoli and cheese casserole can be served alongside. Any light white or red wine can be served with the fried sausages.

- 1 tablespoon unsalted butter
- 1 pound Country Sausage (page 368), formed into 4″ round patties each ½″–¾″ thick
- ½ cup finely chopped onion
- 2 tablespoons white flour
- ½ cup beef stock, homemade preferable but canned acceptable
- ½ cup milk
- ¼ teaspoon white pepper
- Salt to taste

Melt the butter in a large skillet. Add the sausage patties and fry over high heat until the bottoms are browned. Turn the patties and scatter the onion around them. Brown the second side, then remove the sausage with a slotted spoon and keep warm.

Pour off all but 2 tablespoons of fat from the skillet or add butter to compensate if there is less fat than that. Turn heat to low, add the flour, and stir constantly for about 2 minutes, until golden brown. Slowly pour in the stock, then the milk, stirring constantly. Cook until desired thickness, then add salt and pepper.

Serves 4

Sausage-Stuffed Potatoes

I'm always looking for dishes that are perfect for one person, and this is particularly good. Children also enjoy the surprise of finding the sausage in the potato. Use any fresh pork sausage that doesn't have bread or cereal fillers. Traditionally, the potato is stuffed with whole sausage links, but if you remove the casings you don't have to struggle to carve the hole to the exact shape of the sausage. Serve the potatoes with steamed green vegetables or a salad.

- 1 large baking potato
- Salt and pepper to taste
- Paprika to taste
- 2 ounces skinned fresh spicy sausage
- 1 tablespoon melted butter
- 1 slice of smoked bacon

Preheat the oven to 425°. Wash the potato and dry well. With an apple corer or paring knife cut out a thin hole running through the length of the potato. Sprinkle the inside of the hole with salt, pepper, and paprika, then stuff with the sausage. I use a chopstick to pack it fairly tightly since the sausage will shrink as the fat comes out. Brush the potato with the butter, then place it on a rack in a baking dish. Drape the bacon over the potato and bake for 50 minutes.

Serves 1

Scrapple or Ponhaus

Adapted from the German buckwheat *pannhas* and prepared in America for at least 200 years, scrapple was an excellent way to use up leftover headcheese or fresh sausage. Canned scrapple can be mail-ordered from several companies in Pennsylvania, and a frozen version is available in some supermarkets. Many of the brands are decent, although usually not as good as homemade. It's a great breakfast or brunch dish for a crowd since it is made ahead and only sliced and fried at the last minute. Top it with maple syrup, applesauce, or a fried or poached egg.

- 6 cups headcheese cooking liquid or meat or poultry stock
- 2½ cups yellow cornmeal
- 1 recipe Headcheese (page 30)
- Salt and pepper to taste
- ¼ teaspoon paprika
- ½ teaspoon minced fresh sage, or ¼ teaspoon crumbled dried

Chill the headcheese liquid or stock overnight, then skim off the fat. Bring the defatted stock to a boil over high heat in a large pot, then turn heat to low. Stir in the cornmeal, then stir constantly for another 15 to 20 minutes. Continue to cook, stirring well every 5 minutes, scraping from the bottom each time, for another 35 minutes. Then stir constantly for a final 5 minutes.

While the cornmeal is cooking, mash the headcheese until it's the texture of tunafish salad. Stir the headcheese, salt and pepper, paprika, and sage into the cooked cornmeal, pour into loaf pans, and chill until firm, about 6 hours.

To serve the scrapple, cut it into thick slices and fry it in hot butter until crispy on both sides. The loaves will keep in the refrigerator, covered, for 1 week, but can't be frozen or the texture will become unpleasant.

Serves 16

THE SOUTH

Country Sausage

This sausage mixture is typical of traditional Southern sausages made for hundreds of years. Fresh or smoked, it's an essential part of the Southern breakfast and many supper dishes as well. People still love old-fashioned breakfasts, and there's nothing better than fried sausage links, fluffy pancakes with a choice of blueberry or maple syrup or applesauce, homemade biscuits with Red-Eye Gravy, grilled or sliced tomatoes, fresh fruit juice, and strong coffee.

2 pounds lean pork, coarsely ground
¾ pound pork fat, coarsely ground
2 teaspoons salt
½ teaspoon black pepper
1 tablespoon finely chopped fresh sage, or ½ tablespoon crumbled dried
½ teaspoon finely chopped fresh thyme, or ¼ teaspoon crumbled dried
½ teaspoon finely chopped fresh rosemary, or ¼ teaspoon crumbled dried
1 tablespoon brown sugar
½ teaspoon grated nutmeg
½ teaspoon ground cloves
½ teaspoon cayenne pepper

Prepared sheep or hog casings

Knead together the pork and fat, then knead in the rest of the ingredients.

Form into patties or stuff into the prepared casings and tie off to desired lengths. The sausage mixture can be refrigerated for 2 to 3 days, frozen for 3 months.

Makes 3 pounds raw sausage

Fried Country Sausage and Apples

Fried apples are served with pork dishes all over the world. The tartness and sweetness of the apples contrasts with the richness of the meat. Some cooks dip the apple slices in batter, but I like the simplicity of this version. Serve the apples and sausages with hot biscuits for breakfast, or you can fry the apples in butter or meat drippings and serve them with a pork roast, pork chops, or any pork sausage dish at dinner.

16 small Country Sausage links or patties (page 368)
¼ teaspoon ground allspice
¼ teaspoon ground cinnamon
Pinch of ground cloves
1 tablespoon light or dark brown sugar
1 tablespoon white sugar
2 large Granny Smith or other tart apples

Fry the sausages over medium-low heat in a large skillet, preferably cast iron, until browned all over. They can be done in batches if necessary. Drain them on paper towels. While the sausages are frying, mix together the spices and sugars and peel, core, halve, and cut the apples into ¼″-thick slices.

When the sausages are fried, pour off all but about a ¼″ layer of fat from the pan. Heat the remaining fat until it's sizzling. Place the apple slices in the pan in one layer. You can cook them in batches also. Sprinkle with half the sugar and spice mixture, cover, and let cook for about 3 minutes. Uncover, turn the apples over, and sprinkle with the rest of the sugar-spice mixture. Cover and cook for an additional 1 to 2 minutes. Serve the sausage and apples with the pan juices poured over them.

Serves 4

Sausage and Cheese Biscuits

Instead of serving biscuits and fried sausages separately, you can make these. This recipe is for smooth biscuits. If you want more crumbly ones, work the dough as little as possible when you're mixing it. I like both kinds, so I alternate. You must use a sharp cheese or the taste will be flat. You can also use Gruyère, Parmesan, or even blue cheese. The biscuits can, of course, be served at breakfast, but I often serve the smooth kind at dinner instead of bread. They're delicious with stews, main course soups, and roasted poultry. I also reheat 1 or 2 for a quick late-night snack.

- 1½ cups unbleached all-purpose presifted flour
- 6 tablespoons shredded Cheddar cheese
- ¼ teaspoon salt
- 1½ teaspoons baking powder
- 10 tablespoons milk
- ¼ pound skinned fresh sausage, crumbled very well
- 2 tablespoons melted unsalted butter

Preheat the oven to 400°.

Mix together the flour, cheese, salt, and baking powder in a large bowl. Stir in the milk, then the sausage. Mix by squeezing with your hands until you can't see any more unincorporated flour.

Tear the dough into 16 pieces. Roll each into a ball, then pat into 2″-diameter biscuits. Place on an ungreased baking sheet about 1″ apart, brush with melted butter, and bake for 15 to 20 minutes, until golden brown.

Makes 16

Sausage Red-Eye Gravy

While red-eye gravy is usually made from ham, it is sometimes made with sausage or bacon. If you're making it with ham or bacon, however, omit the salt, since it will be salty enough. The coffee should be strong but not bitter. Red-eye gravy is traditionally served with biscuits or grits for breakfast or a light supper, but it's a little too simple for dinner.

¾ pound fresh Country Sausage links (page 368), each pricked in 6 places with a pin
3 tablespoons hot black coffee
Salt to taste

Place the sausages in a small skillet just large enough to hold them. Pour in water so that it comes just to the top of the sausages. Bring to a boil over high heat, then turn heat to medium and cook for about 15 minutes, until the water is gone, turning once. Turn heat to low and brown the sausages in their own fat. Remove the sausages and drain on paper towels.

Pour in 2 tablespoons coffee and stir madly to deglaze the pan. Add the remaining tablespoon coffee and salt, turn off the heat, and stir until well mixed.

Serves 2

Cornbread and Sausage Stuffing

Corn is one of the South's most important staples. This stuffing can be used for poultry or veal or baked by itself. I used it for a suckling pig and it might have been a little too much of a good thing (pork stuffed with pork). There are hundreds of variations on this. Some cooks add raisins, others replace the chestnuts with pecans. If you've made your own sausage you can adjust the herb content of the recipe to compensate. I used bulk pork sausage which was only lightly herbed. Some unorthodox sausages can also be used in this. Mexican Chorizos add a spicy chile taste, and other garlic sausages are also good. Don't use anything too delicate such as white or potato sausages, though. You want something stronger tasting.

1½ cups yellow cornmeal
1 cup unbleached all-purpose presifted flour
2½ tablespoons sugar
2 teaspoons salt, plus more to taste
1 teaspoon black pepper, plus more to taste
1¼ tablespoons baking powder
2 large eggs
1¼ cups milk
2 tablespoons bacon drippings or salted butter
2 tablespoons unsalted butter
1 onion, finely chopped
1 pound skinless fresh sausage
2 celery stalks, roughly chopped
1 tablespoon fresh sage, or 1½ teaspoons crumbled dried
2 teaspoons fresh thyme, or 1 teaspoon crumbled dried
¼ cup chopped fresh parsley
½ cup white wine
½ cup chicken stock
1½ cups (10 ounce can) roughly chopped fresh or drained canned chestnuts

Preheat the oven to 400°. Mix together the cornmeal, flour, sugar, 2 teaspoons salt, 1 teaspoon pepper, and baking powder. Beat the eggs and milk together, then stir into the cornmeal. Mix just until there are no lumps. Heat the bacon drippings or salted butter in a 9″ ovenproof cast-iron skillet. Tilt the pan to coat the sides and bottom with the fat. Pour in the cornmeal mixture and place in the oven. Bake for 30 minutes. Remove from the oven, turn out onto a wire rack, and cool.

Melt the unsalted butter in a skillet over low heat. Add the onion and cook for 10 minutes, until softened. Crumble the sausage into the skillet and fry, constantly mashing it with a fork. Stir the celery, sage, thyme, parsley, wine, stock, chestnuts, and salt and pepper to taste into the skillet, then pour the mixture into a huge bowl or a stockpot. Crumble the cooled cornbread into the sausage mixture and toss well with your hands.

Serves 12

Cajun and Creole

Cajun Boudin Blanc

The French wouldn't recognize this rice and chile–filled boudin blanc. Cajuns are so addicted to it that Broussard, Louisiana, holds an annual boudin festival. The festival's seafood boudin is considered heretical, but *The Picayune Creole Cookbook,* first published at the very end of the nineteenth century, says that boudin blanc can be made with leftover rabbit, chicken, turkey, partridge, other birds, crawfish, or crab. These days boudin competes with hot dogs as the most popular street food. The correct way to eat one is to hold the casing tightly in one hand as you use your teeth to partly scrape, partly inhale the filling out of the casing and into your mouth.

Serve the cold boudin as a summer lunch, accompanied by French-fried potatoes; a tomato, basil, and mozzarella salad; a glass of Alsatian Tokay; and fresh melon for dessert. Or do as I do and grab a boudin when you're in a hurry and have to eat in the car.

- ¾ cup raw long-grain rice
- 1 pound lean pork, ground
- ½ pound pork fat, ground
- ¼ cup finely chopped fresh parsley
- 7 tablespoons finely chopped scallion
- 1 tablespoon salt
- 1 teaspoon black pepper
- ¼ teaspoon ground allspice
- 1 teaspoon cayenne or ground chile pepper

Prepared hog casings or 1½″ wide artificial casings

Cook the rice according to the package directions. Begin bringing a large pot of water to a boil.

Mix the pork, fat, parsley, scallions, and cooked rice together in a large bowl, then knead in the salt, pepper, allspice, and cayenne.

Stuff into prepared hog casings if you're going to eat the casings, or artificial casings if you're not planning to eat them, and tie off in 6″ lengths. Prick any air pockets with a pin and squeeze out the air.

Poach the sausages for 25 minutes, then rinse briefly with cold water. Raw sausages can be refrigerated for 2 or 3 days, poached for 1 week. They shouldn't be frozen or the rice will become mushy.

Makes approximately 2 pounds raw sausage

Chaurice

Try this as a breakfast sausage if you like spicy links. It was originally deep-fried in lard and served for breakfast, lunch, or supper, used in Jambalaya or stuffed cabbage, or added to vegetable dishes. I like to serve chaurice for supper, topped with a spicy Creole tomato sauce and accompanied by the traditional braised cabbage or mashed potatoes. I also make a "Cajun shepherd's pie" by placing cooked, crumbled chaurice and Creole sauce in a casserole, topping them with mashed potatoes and grated cheese, and baking it just until the top is browned. Begin dinner with a cup of seafood gumbo or chowder and serve spinach sautéed in butter and tart pickles with the main course. Try a red wine like a French Chinon or a California Zinfandel. For dessert, and any other time, I like pecan pie.

- 1¼ pounds lean pork, ground
- ¼ pound pork fat, ground
- ½ cup finely chopped onion
- 2 teaspoons minced fresh parsley
- 1 large garlic clove, crushed then minced
- 1 teaspoon minced seeded fresh chile pepper
- ¼ teaspoon ground dried chile pepper
- ½ teaspoon cayenne pepper
- ½ teaspoon salt
- ¼ teaspoon black pepper
- ¼ teaspoon minced fresh thyme, or ⅛ teaspoon crumbled dried
- 1 very finely minced or ground bay leaf
- 1 teaspoon vinegar

Prepared hog casings

Knead together the pork, fat, onion, parsley, garlic, and fresh chile. Mix together the ground chile, cayenne, salt, pepper, thyme, bay leaf, and vinegar, then knead into the meat.

Stuff the mixture firmly into the prepared casings to make 2 sausages, each 14" long. Prick any air pockets and squeeze out the air. Coil and refrigerate for 1 to 3 days to let the flavors meld. Then either fry them, or freeze them for up to 3 months.

Makes approximately 26 ounces raw sausage

Saucisse

The main difference between Chaurice and saucisse is that chaurice are pure pork, while saucisse also contain beef. Louisiana is one of the few Southern states where beef is popular at all. Pork is usually preferred. Saucisse are long sausages, saucisson small links. In the nineteenth and early twentieth centuries, black women selling sausages from large baskets used to roam the streets of New Orleans first thing in the morning, singing out "belle saucisse."

Serve the deep-fried or poached sausages in Creole sauce for supper, accompanied by three kinds of fritters made from rice, eggplant, and banana and a glass of California red or white Zinfandel. Serve oysters on the half shell first and peach pie for dessert.

2 tablespoons plus 1 teaspoon salt
4 cups water
¼ teaspoon ground allspice
¼ teaspoon ground cloves
⅛ teaspoon grated nutmeg
½ teaspoon hot paprika, cayenne, or ground chile pepper
1 bay leaf, finely minced fresh or crumbled dried
¾ teaspoon minced fresh marjoram, or ⅜ teaspoon crumbled dried
1¼ pounds lean ground beef
½ pound lean pork, ground
¼ pound pork fat, ground
½ cup finely chopped onion
2 teaspoons minced fresh parsley
2 garlic cloves, crushed then minced

Prepared hog casings

Mix together 2 tablespoons salt and the water in a large glass or glazed ceramic straight-sided bowl like a soufflé dish; set aside.

Mix together the spices, paprika or cayenne or chile, and the remaining teaspoon salt. Knead the beef, pork, fat, onion, parsley, and garlic together, then knead in the spice mixture.

Stuff the mixture firmly into 2 lengths of prepared hog casings. Each sausage will be about 1½″ wide and 26″ long. Prick any air pockets with a pin and squeeze out the air.

Coil the sausages and place them in the soufflé dish. Place a glass pot top or a plate slightly smaller than the diameter of the bowl on top of the sausages to keep them submerged. Let sit in the refrigerator, covered, for 1 to 7 days. Rinse them off well before cooking and pat dry if they're going to be fried. They can also be frozen for 3 months after being removed from the brine and dried off.

Makes just over 2 pounds of raw sausage

Jambalaya

There are several versions as to how this rice dish got its name, but the most commonly accepted one is that it comes from *jambon,* French for "ham." Some jambalayas are modest dishes of rice with small amounts of whatever meat or seafood are available, an inexpensive meal to feed a large family. Others are lavish restaurant or company jambalayas, more like meat and seafood with rice. Both are descendants of the Spanish Paella. To me the rice, ham, andouille, and at least one kind of seafood are essential. The best andouille I've ever found outside of New Orleans is made by the Aidells Sausage Company in Kensington, California. Bruce Aidells says the secret to good andouille is long, slow, hickory smoking which gives it that deep, rich flavor. Substitute smoked Kielbasa or Spanish Chorizo if absolutely necessary.

Jambalaya is a terrific buffet party dish, since it can be served hot or warm. I serve corn soup first, then accompany the jambalaya with a big salad with blue cheese dressing. Offer guests their choice of a red Beaujolais or white Meursault. Try strawberry ice cream and gingersnaps for dessert.

- 2 pounds andouille sausage, cut into ½″-wide slices
- 4 tablespoons olive oil
- 4 medium onions, finely chopped
- 6 garlic cloves, crushed then minced
- 3 green bell peppers, seeded, finely chopped
- 4 celery stalks, thinly sliced
- 4 cups raw long-grain rice
- 2 pounds smoked ham, cut into ½″ cubes
- 2 28-ounce cans tomatoes, seeded, drained, roughly chopped
- 7 cups chicken broth
- Tabasco sauce to taste
- Black pepper to taste
- 4 teaspoons fresh thyme, or 2 teaspoons crumbled dried
- 4 bay leaves
- 1 cup minced parsley
- 6 scallions, minced
- 2 pounds shelled cooked medium-size shrimp
- 3 8-ounce jars raw oysters

In a very large stockpot brown the andouille in its own fat over medium heat. Remove with a slotted spoon and drain on paper towels. Add the olive oil, onions, garlic, peppers, and celery to the pot, stir until coated with oil, then cook until wilted, about 15 minutes, stirring occasionally.

Add the rice to the pot and stir constantly for five minutes. Add the ham, tomatoes, broth, a few dashes of Tabasco, the pepper, thyme, bay leaf, and sausage. Bring to a boil over high heat, then turn heat to low and simmer for about 40 minutes, just until the rice is tender. Stir in the parsley, scallions, shrimp and oysters and heat just until the oysters are cooked, about 5 minutes.

This can be served immediately or left on an unlit burner on the stove so guests help themselves directly from the pot. In its cooking pot, it will stay warm for at least a couple of hours, especially if covered.

Serves 30

Duck and Sausage Gumbo

Gumbo is one of the most magnificent soups ever created. What makes it unique is the roux, a mixture of fat and flour cooked over very low heat until the color ranges from tan to a rich, deep brown depending on the recipe and the cook. "Gumbo" comes from an African word for okra, often used to thicken the soup. Filé powder, ground sassafras leaves used by Choctaw Indians, serves the same purpose. I don't use either of those since I think the roux makes it thick enough.

Gumbos can be eaten hot, warm, room temperature, cold, or reheated. While it's almost always served over rice, you can also stir the rice into the gumbo itself. Some people like gumbo poured over a baked yam. I serve gumbos at dinner parties, but always make enough to freeze some just for myself. Serve stuffed artichokes first, then the gumbo with rice, pickled cauliflower, okra, cucumbers, and peppers and a good Cabernet Sauvignon or French Bordeaux. Serve flaky French pastries, such as Napoleons, with strong coffee for dessert.

- 8 cups chicken stock, homemade preferable but canned acceptable
- Salt to taste
- ½ teaspoon black pepper
- ¼ teaspoon Tabasco sauce
- ½ teaspon cayenne pepper
- 1 bay leaf
- 1 teaspoon minced fresh thyme, or ½ teaspoon crumbled dried
- ¼ teaspoon ground allspice
- 1 pound andouille, smoked Chorizo, or Kielbasa (page 192 or 173), cut into ¼″-thick slices
- ¼ cup vegetable oil
- 1 duck (4-6 pounds), cut into 16 serving pieces, dried well
- 2 tablespoons unsalted butter
- 1 cup white flour
- 1 onion, roughly chopped
- 2 large garlic cloves, crushed then minced
- 4 scallions, roughly chopped
- 2 celery stalks, roughly chopped
- 2 green bell peppers, seeded, finely chopped

Mix the stock, salt, pepper, Tabasco, cayenne, bay leaf, thyme, and allspice together and set aside. Heat a large cast-iron pot, such as a Dutch oven, over high heat. When it's hot, add the sausage and cook, turning often, until browned all over. Remove the sausage and drain it on paper towels. Add the oil to the pot and heat. Brown the duck pieces well, in batches if necessary. Remove the duck pieces and add them to the sausage.

Turn the heat to low and add the butter to the pot. Stir until melted, then stir in the flour. Stir constantly, scraping the bottom, for 20 to 25 minutes, until the roux is just slightly darker than milk chocolate. Don't let it burn. Stir the onion, garlic, scallions, celery, and green peppers into the roux until mixed well, then immediately stir in the stock mixture. Bring to a boil over high heat, then return the duck and sausage to the pot. Turn heat to low and simmer, covered, for 2 hours.

Serves 8

Red Beans and Rice

Red beans and rice is probably the most beloved dish in Louisiana. It was traditionally made on Monday, using the bone from Sunday's ham, but now it can be eaten any day of the week. The red kidney beans you get in Louisiana can be quite large, but you can either use the ones in your supermarket or send away to Louisiana for the real thing. I like Louisiana popcorn rice in the dish, but any kind of long-grain rice is good. This is also served with fried hot links instead of andouille. Serve with either kind of sausage, cornbread, hot sauce like Tabasco, beer, and fresh fruit.

1½ cups dried red beans, rinsed well and drained
½ pound smoked ham hock or smoked ham bone with some meat on it
1 onion, roughly chopped
2 garlic cloves, crushed then minced
1 green bell pepper, seeded, roughly chopped
1 large celery stalk with leaves, roughly chopped
2 bay leaves
½ teaspoon fresh thyme, or ¼ teaspoon dried
⅛ teaspoon Tabasco sauce
1 cup raw popcorn or long-grain rice
1¾ cups water
½ pound andouille or other hot, smoked garlic sausage, cut into ⅛″-thick slices

Place the beans, ham, onion, garlic, green pepper, celery, bay leaf, thyme, and Tabasco in a large pot and cover by at least 1″ of cold water. Turn heat to low and simmer, uncovered, for about 3½ hours, stirring from the bottom about every 20 minutes.

After the beans have cooked for 2¾ hours, begin making the rice as the beans continue to cook. Place the rice and water in a saucepan just large enough to hold them and bring to a boil over high heat. Boil for 1 minute, turn heat to very low, cover, and cook for 20 minutes. Turn off heat, and, without ever uncovering, let stand for 10 minutes.

As soon as you've added the rice to the water, turn the heat under the bean pot to as low as possible. Remove the ham hock and add the sausage to the beans. Remove the meat from the ham hock, shred, and return to the bean pot. Stir the bean pot every 5 minutes, scraping the bottom each time to prevent the beans from sticking. Mash a bit of the beans every time you stir them. The texture should be a combination of whole and mashed beans. When the rice is cooked, spoon it onto a large platter. Turn the heat off under the beans and spoon the beans and meats onto the rice.

Serves 6

TEXAS

Smoked Venison Salami

Venison is made into large, small, or bulk sausage throughout Texas. The patties or fresh or smoked links are usually served with breakfast. One prizewinning chili recipe is made with both shredded venison and venison sausage. You can buy venison in many butcher shops or have your butcher special-order it. Since it's so lean, you need pork fat to prevent the sausage from being very dry. Serve the venison salami the same way you'd serve Italian salami, such as in sandwiches, casseroles, and salads.

- 2 pounds venison, ground
- ½ pound pork fat, ground
- 2 garlic cloves, crushed then minced
- 1½ tablespoons salt
- 1 teaspoon black peppercorns
- ½ teaspoon ground cumin
- 1 teaspoon minced fresh marjoram, or ½ teaspoon crumbled dried

2 tablespoons brandy, Cognac, or white vermouth
½ teaspoon liquid smoke (optional)

2 lengths of prepared beef middles

Knead the venison and fat together, then knead in the rest of the ingredients.

Stuff the mixture firmly into the prepared beef middles. Prick any air pockets with a pin and squeeze out the air. Roll the sausages gently to even out their width. Let them sit in the refrigerator, hanging from the shelves or on a rack, for 1 or 2 days to let the flavors meld and to dry out the casings.

Wipe the casings dry if necessary and smoke the sausages at 275° for 4 or 5 hours or bake them on a rack in a baking dish for 5 hours at 200°. The smoked or baked sausages can be refrigerated for 2 weeks, frozen for 3 months.

Makes approximately 2½ pounds raw sausage

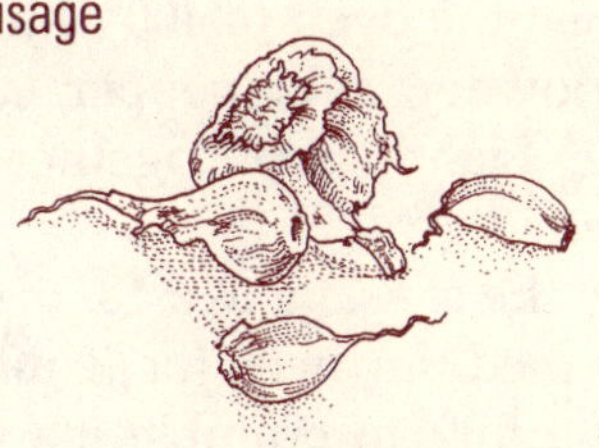

Sausage, Cheese, and Chile Cornbread

This filling, delicious bread is also known as tamale pie. Feel free to vary the recipe, adding whole corn kernels, pimientos, or salsa; substituting cheeses like Monterey Jack or Cheddar; or using pickled chile peppers rather than fresh. If you omit the cheese, you can crumble the bread and use it as stuffing. Serve the cornbread for lunch with a salad and a Texas beer like Rattlesnake or Pearl, or serve it as an alternative to stuffing with roasted poultry.

- 1½ cups yellow cornmeal
- 1 cup unbleached all-purpose presifted flour
- 1¼ tablespoons baking powder
- 2 teaspoons salt
- ½ teaspoon black pepper
- 2½ tablespoons sugar
- 1¼ cups milk
- 2 large eggs
- ½ pound skinless fresh Chorizo (page 302) or other spicy pork sausage
- 1 onion, finely chopped
- ½ small hot chile pepper, seeded, finely chopped
- 2 tablespoons unsalted butter
- ¼ pound Colby or Longhorn Cheddar cheese, grated

Preheat the oven to 400°. Mix together the cornmeal, flour, baking powder, salt, pepper, and sugar in a large bowl and set aside. Lightly mix together the milk and eggs and set them aside.

Fry the sausage in a 10″ ovenproof skillet, preferably cast iron, over medium heat for 3 minutes. Keep mashing the sausage with a fork to crumble it well. Add the onion and chile, turn heat to low, and fry for another 8 minutes, stirring often. Remove the skillet from the heat and pour the contents into a bowl. Lightly wipe out the skillet with a paper towel, leaving a thin film of grease in it.

Melt the butter in the sausage skillet over low heat. Stir the milk mixture into the dry ingredients and mix well. When the butter has melted, tilt the skillet to even the layer of fat. Pour in two-thirds of the batter and scatter the sausage, then the cheese, evenly on top. Carefully pour on the rest of the batter, being careful not to disturb the sausage and cheese. Place the skillet in the oven and bake for 30 minutes, until a skewer inserted in the middle comes out clean. (Don't confuse cheese with raw batter, however.)

Serves 10

Bibliography

Aaron, Jan and Georgine Sachs Salom. *The Art of Mexican Cooking*. New York: Signet, 1982.

Akerstrom, Jenny. *The Swedish Princesses Cook Book*. New York: Albert Bonnier Publishing House, 1936.

Alejandro, Reynaldo. *The Flavor of Asia*. New York and Toronto: Beaufort Books, 1984.

———. *The Philippine Cookbook*. New York: Perigee Books, 1985.

American Express Independent Traveler's Guide to Europe, 1985 (advertising supplement). *Food & Wine*, July 1985.

Ames, Mary Ellis. *Balanced Recipes*. Minneapolis: Pillsbury Flour Mills, 1933.

Anderson, Jean. "Savoring the Algarve." *Travel & Leisure*, October 1985.

Andrews, Colman. "Brussels Is Sprouting French Restaurants and Winning 3 Stars." *Los Angeles Times*, June 16, 1985.

———. "Upstairs, Downstairs Rumors in Beverly Hills." *Los Angeles Times*, August 25, 1985.

Anonymous. *Pennsylvania Dutch Cook Book of Fine Old Recipes*. Reading, Pennsylvania: Culinary Arts Press, 1936.

Anthony, Dawn, Elaine, and Selwa. *Lebanese Cookbook*. Secaucus, New Jersey: Chartwell Books, 1978.

Argy, Josy and Wendy Riches. *A Taste of England*. London: Sphere Books, 1979.

Association for Retarded Citizens—Clay. *Clay County Cooks*. Orange Park, Florida: n.d.

Austen, Howard and Beverly Pepper. *The Myra Breckenridge Cookbook*. Boston and Toronto: Little, Brown, 1970.

Axline, J. Paul. "The Business Trip." *Travel & Leisure*, August 1985.

Aynton, Elisabeth. *English Provincial Cooking*. New York: Harper & Row, 1980.

Bailey, Adrian and the Editors of Time-Life Books. *The Cooking of the British Isles*. Alexandria, Virginia: Time-Life Books, 1969.

Bailey, Freddie. *Aunt Freddie's Pantry*. New York: Clarkson N. Potter, 1984.

Bailey, Lee. *Lee Bailey's City Food*. New York: Clarkson N. Potter, 1984.

———. *Lee Bailey's Country Weekends*. New York: Clarkson N. Potter, 1983.

Barnard, Melanie. "Quick From Scratch: Winter Dinners." *COOK'S*, January/February 1986.

Bates, Caroline. "Specialités de la Maison—California," series. *Gourmet*, June–October 1985.
Beal, Doone. "Gourmet Holidays: Northern Morocco." *Gourmet*, October 1985.
———. "Sardinia." *Gourmet*, June 1985.
Beer, Gretel. *Austrian Cooking and Baking*. New York: Dover Publications, 1975.
Beeton, Mrs. Isabella. *The Book of Household Management*. London: Ward, Lock, 1899.
Benghiat, Norma. *Traditional Jamaican Cookery*. Harmondsworth, Middlesex, England: Penguin Books, 1985.
Bennet, Paula Pogany and Velma R. Clark. *The Art of Hungarian Cooking*. Garden City, New York: Doubleday, 1954.
Bennett, Victor. *The Polynesian Cookbook*. New York: Galahad Books, n.d.
Berolzheimer, Ruth, ed. *Menus for Every Day of the Year*. Chicago: Consolidated Book Publishers, 1941.
Berwick Leo Club. *Home Town Recipes of Berwick, Nova Scotia*. n.d.
Bessunger, Bernard H. *Recipes of Old England*. Newton Abbot, Devon: David & Charles, 1973.
Bethany Women. *Home Town Recipes of Hughesville, Pennsylvania*. n.d.
Beyer, Beverly and Ed Rabey. "A Minnesota City of Parks, Cultural Activities." *Los Angeles Times*, October 6, 1985.
———. "Mexico: Old Iberia." *Los Angeles Times*, September 8, 1985.
———. "Blues and Barbecues." *Los Angeles Times*. August 18, 1985.
———. "Once Again, the Bright Jewel of Eastern Europe." *Los Angeles Times*. July 21, 1985.
———. "Footloose in Ibiza, Spain." *Los Angeles Times*, May 12,1985.
———."Footloose in Padua, Italy." *Los Angeles Times*, April 28, 1985.
Bielefeld, Dr. August Oetker. *German Home Cooking*. Bielefeld, Germany: Ceres-Verlag Rudolph-August Oetker KG, 1963.
Blanch, Lesley. "Afghanistan Remembered." *Gourmet*, October 1985.
Bocuse, Paul. *Paul Bocuse in Your Kitchen*. New York: Pantheon Books, 1982.
Bolotnikova, V. A.; L. M. Vapelnik; I. P. Korzun; L. D. Markova; and D. K. Shapiro. *Byelorussian Cuisine*. Uradzhai, Minsk, 1979.
Borgstrom, Greta and Birgit Danfors. *Scandinavian Cookbook*. Göteborg, Sweden: Wezata Forlag, 1965.
Botafogo, Dolores. *The Art of Brazilian Cookery*. Garden City, New York: Doubleday, 1960.
Boyd, Lizzie, ed. *British Cookery*. London: Helm Ltd., British Farm Produce Council and British Tourist Authority, 1976.
Bradley, Alice. *The Alice Bradley Menu Cookbook: April-May-June*. New York: Macmillan, 1937.
Brady, Jean and Merle Miller. *The Ultimate L.A. Food Guide*. Los Angeles: Jeremy P. Tarcher, 1983.
Brennan, Ella and Dick. *The Commander's Palace New Orleans Cookbook*. New York: Clarkson N. Potter, 1984.
Brennan, Jennifer. *The Cuisines of Asia*. New York: St. Martin's Press/Marek, 1984.

———. *The Original Thai Cookbook.* New York: Coward, McCann & Geoghegan, 1981.

Brissenden, Rosemary. *Asia's Undiscovered Cuisine.* New York: Pantheon Books, 1970.

Brizova, Jova. *The Czechoslovak Cookbook.* New York: Crown Publishers, 1965.

Brobek, Florence and Monika Kjellberg. *Smorgasbord and Scandinavian Cookery.* New York: Grosset & Dunlap, 1948.

de Broglie, Princess Marie-Blanche. *The Cuisine of Normandy.* Boston: Houghton Mifflin, 1984.

Brooks, Patricia. "Bon Voyage, Traveling with Taste: Saratoga Springs." *Bon Appetit,* June 1985.

———. "The Best of Madrid." *Bon Appetit,* January 1986.

Brown, Cora, Rose, and Bob. *America Cooks: Favorite Recipes from 48 States.* Garden City, New York: Garden City Books, 1940.

Brown, Ellen. *Cooking with the New American Chefs.* New York: Harper & Row, 1985.

Bullock, Helen. *The Williamsburg Art of Cookery or Accomplish'd Gentlewoman's Companion.* Colonial Williamsburg, Virginia, 1961.

Burgess, Claudia, comp. *Cooking with Country.* New York: Atheneum, 1978.

Burton, Nathaniel and Rudy Lombard. *Creole Feast: 15 Master Chefs of New Orleans Reveal Their Secrets.* New York: Random House, 1978.

Burum, Linda and Irene Virbila. *Cook's Marketplace: Los Angeles.* San Francisco: 101 Productions, 1986.

Burum, Linda. *Asian Pasta.* Berkeley, California: Aris Books, 1985.

Butel, Jane. "Southwest Christmas." *COOK'S.* November/December 1985.

Cagner, Ewert. *Swedish Christmas.* New York: Henry Holt, n.d.

Caldwell, Mary. "The Readers' Choice: A Restaurant Survey & Guide." *COOK'S,* July/August 1985.

Cameron, Angus and Judith Jones. *The L. L. Bean Game & Fish Cookbook.* New York: Random House, 1983.

Capon, Robert Farrar. *Capon on Cooking.* Boston: Houghton Mifflin, 1983.

Carlisle, Olga. "Oleron: Food Rites Remembered." *The Journal of Gastronomy,* vol. 1, no. 4 (1985).

Casas, Penelope. *Tapas: The Little Dishes of Spain.* New York: Alfred A. Knopf, 1985.

———. *The Foods and Wines of Spain.* New York: Alfred A. Knopf, 1982.

The Celebrity Cookbook. Encino, California: Treasured Publications, 1978.

Chamberlain, Lesley. *The Food and Cooking of Russia.* Harmondsworth, England: Penguin Books, 1983.

Chamberlain, Samuel. *Italian Bouquet: An Epicurean Tour of Italy.* New York: Gourmet Distributing Corporation, 1958.

Chantiles, Vilma Liacouras. *The Food of Greece.* New York: Dodd, Mead, 1975.

Chartraine, Charles. *La Cuisine Chartraine.* New York: M. Barrows, 1966.

Chase, Carter. "Casual Suppers in a Manhattan Loft." *Bon Appetit,* January 1986.

———. "Great Party Recipes from The Silver Palate." *Bon Appetit*, October 1985.

Chelminski, Rudolph. "The Gluttonous Evolution of la Cuisine Française." *Smithsonian*, September 1985.

Cheng-Huei, Yeh. *Chinese Cuisine II.* Taiwan: Huang Su-Huei, 1980.

Child, Julia and Simone Beck. *Mastering the Art of French Cooking, Volume II.* New York: Alfred A. Knopf, 1983.

Child, Julia; Louisette Bertholle; and Simone Beck. *Mastering the Art of French Cooking, Volume I.* New York: Alfred A. Knopf, 1983.

"China Pictorial" Editors. *Chinese Cuisine from the Master Chefs of China.* Boston: Little, Brown, 1983.

Claiborne, Craig. *Craig Claiborne's Favorites.* New York: Quadrangle/New York Times Book Co., 1975.

———. *Craig Claiborne's Favorites, Series II.* New York: Quadrangle/New York Times Book Co., 1976.

———. *Craig Claiborne's Favorites, Volume III.* New York: Quadrangle/New York Times Book Co., 1977.

———. *Craig Claiborne's Favorites, Volume IV.* New York: Quadrangle/New York Times Book Co., 1978.

———. *Craig Claiborne's Memorable Meals.* New York: E.P. Dutton, 1985.

———. *Craig Claiborne's The New York Times Food Encyclopedia.* New York: Times Books, 1985.

Claiborne, Craig; Pierre Franey; and the Editors of Time-Life Books. *Classic French Cooking.* Alexandria, Virginia: Time-Life Books, 1978.

Clark, Phyllis E. *West Indian Cookery.* Edinburgh: Thomas Nelson & Sons for the Government of Trinidad & Tobago, 1960.

Cleveland, Bess A. *Alaskan Cookbook for Homesteader or Gourmet.* Berkeley, California: Howell-North, 1960.

Coffin, Robert P. Tristram. *Mainstays of Maine.* New York: Macmillan, 1944.

Colwin, Laurie. "Nursery Food." *Gourmet*, August 1985.

Connell, Patricia. "All About Sausages." *Bon Appetit*, October 1985.

Conrad, Barnaby. "The Timeless Thames." Traveling in Style. *Los Angeles Times*, October 20, 1985.

Cooking Magic Step-By-Step Cookbook, series. Chicago: Culinary Arts Institute, 1941–56.

Coombs, Anna Olsson. *The Smorgasbord Cookbook.* New York: A. A. Wyn, 1949.

Corey, Helen. *The Art of Syrian Cookery.* Garden City, New York: Doubleday, 1962.

"Correspondents' Courses." Traveling in Style. Los Angeles Times, October 20, 1985.

Cox, Beverly. "Simple Trussing Step by Step." *COOK'S*, November/December 1985.

Craig, Elizabeth. *Court Favorites: Recipes from Royal Kitchens.* London: Andrew Deutsch, 1953.

"Cuisine Courante." *Gourmet*, October 1985.

"Cuisine Courante." *Gourmet*, September 1985.

Cuisines of Europe. New York: Exeter Books, 1982.

David, Claire S., ed. *Pennsylvania Dutch Cookbook of Fine Old Recipes*. Reading, Pennsylvania: Culinary Arts Press, 1972.
David, Elizabeth. *An Omelette and a Glass of Wine*. New York: Elisabeth Sifton Books, Viking Penguin, 1985.
———. *Elizabeth David Classics*. New York: Alfred A. Knopf, 1980.
Davis, Deirdre and Linda Marino. "American Sampler." *Bon Appetit*, September 1985.
———. "Great Duck Dishes." *Food & Wine*, January 1986.
Day, Irene F. *The Moroccan Cookbook*. New York: Quick Fox, 1975.
"Dear Yankee." *Yankee*, October 1985.
Delaplane, Stan. "Feast Fit for a Genoese." *Los Angeles Times*, August 11, 1985.
Dent, Huntley. *The Feast of Sante Fe: Cooking of the American Southwest*. New York: Simon and Schuster, 1985.
Derecskey, Susan. *The Hungarian Cookbook*. New York: Harper & Row, 1972.
DeWit, Antoinette and Anita Borghese. *The Complete Book of Indonesian Cooking*. Indianapolis and New York: Bobbs-Merrill, 1973.
Dille, Carolyn and Susan Belsinger. *New Southwestern Cooking*. New York: Bobbs-Merrill, 1985.
Disrude, Anne. "The Enlightened Sausage." *Food & Wine*, March 1986.
Donovan, Maria Kozslik. *The Blue Danube Cookbook*. Garden City, New York: Doubleday, 1967.
Donovan, Mary; Amy Hatrak; Frances Mills; Elizabeth Shull. *The Thirteen Colonies Cookbook*. New York: Praeger, 1975.
Dorje, Rinjing. *Food in Tibetan Life*. London: Prospect Books, 1985.
Douglas, Norman (under pseudonym of Pilaff Bey). *Venus in the Kitchen*. New York: Viking, 1953.
Dowell, Philip and Adrian Bailey. *Cooks' Ingredients*. New York: William Morrow, 1980.
Dry, Stanley. "One Man's Fast Food." *Food & Wine*, August 1985.
———. "Thanksgivings Past and Present." *Food & Wine*, November 1985.
Dwan, Lois. "Basking in the History and Soul of Italia," *Los Angeles Times*, May 26, 1985.
———. "The Billabong." *Los Angeles Times*, April 21, 1985.
Eckhardt, Linda West. *The Only Texas Cookbook*. New York: Gramercy Publishing, 1981.
Editors of Sunset Books and Sunset Magazine. *Sunset Oriental Cookbook*. Menlo Park, California: Lane Publishing, 1984.
———. *Sunset Scandinavian Cook Book*. Menlo Park, California: Lane Publishing, 1974.
Editors of Time-Life Books. *Pork*. Alexandria, Virginia: Time-Life Books, 1980.
Edwards, John. *The Roman Cookery of Apicius*. Point Roberts, Washington: Hartley & Marks, 1984.
Elder, Mimi. "City Dining—Chicago." *Gourmet*, October 1985.
Ellis, Merle. "Conch Cooking: Best of British, Cubans." *Los Angeles Times*, May 2, 1985.

Elverson, Virginia T. and Mary Ann McLanahan. *A Cooking Legacy.* New York: Walker & Co., 1975.

English Fellowship Church. *Cooking in Equador.* Quito, Equador: n.d.

Exenberger, Maria and Fritz Breit. *Cookbook from Tyrol.* West Germany: Enthaler Verlag, 1982.

Fairchild, Barbara. "Discover the New Cuisine of Spain." *Bon Appetit,* February 1986.

Fantastically Finnish. Iowa City, Iowa: Penfield Press, 1985.

Farah, Madelain. *Lebanese Cuisine.* Portland, Oregon: Madelain Farah, 1982.

Feibleman, Peter. "Catalonia." *Travel & Leisure,* July 1985.

Ferretti, Fred. "Gourmet Holidays—A Finnish Sojourn." *Gourmet,* August 1985.

———. "A Gourmet at Large," *Gourmet,* June–October 1985.

Ferrin, Lynn. "Oaxaca." *Travel & Leisure,* October 1985.

Festive Entrées: The Bon Appetit Kitchen Collection, series. Los Angeles: Knapp Press, 1983.

Field, Carol. *The Italian Baker.* New York: Harper & Row, 1985.

———. "A Bountiful Mediterranean Buffet for Casual Entertaining." *Bon Appetit,* June 1985.

———. "Step by Step to Terrific Party Entrees." *Bon Appetit,* November 1985.

Fire, Rescue, and Police Women's Auxiliary. *Home Town Recipes of Washington, Illinois.* n.d.

Fisher, M.F.K. *The Art of Eating.* New York: Vintage Books, 1976.

Fisher, M.F.K. and the Editors of Time-Life Books. *Provincial French Cooking.* Alexandria, Virginia: Time-Life Books, 1968.

FitzGibbon, Theodora. *A Taste of Ireland.* Boston: Houghton Mifflin, 1969.

Foster, Lee, ed. *The New York Times Correspondents' Choice.* New York: Quadrangle, 1974.

Fox, Margaret and John Bear. *Cafe Beaujolais.* Berkeley, California: Ten Speed Press, 1984.

Fredman, Catherine. "An Italian Feast: New Cookbooks for the Summer Kitchen." *Food & Wine,* July 1985.

Frees, Jeff. "Visiting French Shrine of Good Taste." *Los Angeles Times,* September 8, 1985.

Freiman, Jane Salzfass. "Mexican-Style Lasagna Makes Unusual Entree." *Los Angeles Times,* September 12, 1985.

Friedrich, Jacqueline. "Interview with Alain Dutournier." *The Journal of Gastronomy,* vol. 1, no. 4 (1985).

Frost, Heloise. *Early American Recipes.* Newton, Massachusetts: Phillips Publishers, 1953.

Gaertner, Pierre and Robert Frederick. *The Cuisine of Alsace.* Woodbury, New York: Barron's, 1981.

Garmey, Jane. *Great British Cooking: A Well Kept Secret.* New York: Random House, 1981.

"Gastronomie Sans Argent." *Gourmet,* August 1985.

Geffen, Alice M. and Carole Berglie. *Food Festival.* New York: Pantheon Books, 1986.

Gehman, Richard. *The Signet Book of Sausage.* New York: Signet, New American Library, 1969.

Georgina Majorettes. *Home Cooking Secrets of Georgina Township, Keswick, Ontario.* n.d.

Giusti-Lanham, Hedy and Andrea Dodi. *The Cuisine of Venice.* Woodbury, New York: Barron's, 1978.

Gochman, Alice Rubinstein. "South Street Seaport." *Gourmet,* July 1985.

Gold Star Wives of America, Inc., comps. *Who's Who in the Kitchen.* Washington, D.C., 1961.

Goldstein, Darra. *A La Russe: A Cookbook of Russian Hospitality.* New York: Random House, 1983.

"Gourmet's Menus—Autumn Chicken Dinners." *Gourmet,* September 1985.

Greene, Burt. "Here's a Sausage-Carrot Pie That Even Australian 'Fishies' Would Love." *Los Angeles Times,* July 18, 1985.

Greer, Anne Lindsay. *Cuisine of the American Southwest.* Greenwich, Connecticut: Cuisinart Cooking Club and New York: Harper & Row, 1983.

Grigson, Jane. *The Art of Making Sausages, Pâtés and other Charcuterie.* New York: Alfred A. Knopf, 1985.

Grimm, Michele and Tom. "Time to Drive North for Wild Game Barbecue." *Los Angeles Times,* September 22, 1985.

de Groot, Roy. *Auberge of the Flowering Hearth.* New York: Ballantine Books, 1974.

Guermont, Claude with Paul Frumkin. *The Norman Table,* New York: Charles Scribner's Sons, 1985.

Guy, Christian. *An Illustrated History of French Cuisine.* New York: Bramhall House, 1962.

Hahn, Emily and the Editors of Time-Life Books. *The Cooking of China.* Alexandria, Virginia: Time-Life Books, 1981.

Halliburton, L. N. "A Gust of Nostalgia at Di Stefano's." *Los Angeles Times,* August 30, 1985.

Ham, Marion. *Gifts from a Country Kitchen.* New York: Allen D. Bragdon, 1984.

Hanle, Zack and E.C.K. Read. "A Taste of Philadelphia." *Bon Appetit,* November 1985.

Hanle, Zack. "Bon Vivant." *Bon Appetit,* November 1985.

———. "A Sophisticated Fall Dinner for Friends." *Bon Appetit,* October 1985.

———. "Chinese Classics Made Easy." *Bon Appetit,* July 1986.

Hansen, Barbara. "An Updated Mayan Feast." *Los Angeles Times,* September 19, 1985.

———. "Regent Seafood Restaurant." *Los Angeles Times,* May 2, 1985.

Harland, Marion. *Marion Harland's Complete Cook Book.* Indianapolis: Bobbs-Merrill, 1906.

Hartley, Dorothy. *Food in England*. London: Futura Publications, 1985.
Hauser, Nao. "A Taste of Oxford." *Bon Appetit*, June 1985.
———. "Great Eating in Chicago." *Food & Wine*, September 1985.
Hawaii State Society of Washington, D.C. *Hawaiian Cuisine*. Rutland, Vermont and Tokyo, Japan: Charles E. Tuttle, 1963.
Hazan, Marcella. *The Classic Italian Cookbook*. New York: Alfred A. Knopf, 1979.
———. *More Classic Italian Cooking*. New York: Alfred A. Knopf, 1980.
Hazelton, Nika Standen. *The Art of Scandinavian Cooking*. New York: Macmillan, 1965.
———. *The Swiss Cookbook*. New York: Atheneum, 1967.
———. *American Home Cooking*. New York: Ballantine Books, 1980.
———. *The Belgian Cookbook*. New York: Atheneum, 1970.
Hebbard, Neysa. "Great New England Cooks—Patricia Dunlea, Wellesley, Mass." *Yankee*, January 1986.
Herring, Charlanne F. "Cajun Style on Bayous Plays at Louisiana Festival." *Los Angeles Times*, June 16, 1985.
Hess, Karen. *Martha Washington's Booke of Cookery*. New York: Columbia University Press, 1981.
Hillman, Howard. *Great Peasant Dishes of the World*. Boston: Houghton Mifflin, 1983.
Hillman, James and Charles Boer, eds. *Freud's Own Cookbook*. New York: Colophon Books, Harper & Row, 1985.
Holmes, Buster. *The Buster Holmes Restaurant Cookbook*. Gretna, Louisiana: Pelican Publishing, 1983.
Hughes, Phyllis, comp. and ed. *Pueblo Indian Cookbook*. Santa Fe: Museum of New Mexico Press, 1984.
Hulse, Jerry. "Amish Country." *Los Angeles Times*, July 28, 1985.
ICA Test Kitchen. *Swedish Cooking*. Vasteras, Sweden: ICA-Forlaget AB, 1979.
Jacobs, Jay. "Specialités de la Maison—New York," series. *Gourmet*, June–October 1985.
Jacobson, Max. "Mexican Treasure in East L.A." *Los Angeles Times*, September 22, 1985.
Jaffrey, Madhur. *A Taste of India*. New York: Atheneum, 1986.
"Jeff Smith, the Frugal Gourmet." *Los Angeles Times*, August 1, 1985.
Johnson, Ronald. *The American Table*. New York: Pocket Books, 1984.
Johnston, Mireille. *The Cuisine of the Rose*. New York: Random House, 1982.
———. "Educating a Palate." *The Journal of Gastronomy*, vol. 1, no. 3, Winter (1985).
Jones, Evan. "The American Scene—Cleveland's Farmers' Markets." *Gourmet*, August 1985.
Junior Charity League of Monroe, Louisiana. *The Cotton Country Collection*. 1972.
Junior League of New Orleans. *The Plantation Cookbook*. Garden City, New York: Doubleday, 1972.
Junior League of Omaha, Nebraska. *Amber Waves*. 1983.

Kakonen, Ulla. *Natural Cooking the Finnish Way.* New York: Quadrangle/ New York Times Books, 1974.

Kapetanovic, Alojzije and Ruzica. *Croatian Cuisine.* San Mateo, California: Associated Publishers, 1978.

Kasper, Lynne. "Simple Pleasures." *Bon Appetit,* July 1985.

———. "The Best Restaurants of Belgium." *Bon Appetit,* November 1985.

Kaufman, William I. *Cooking in a Castle.* New York: Bonanza Books, 1965.

Kaye, Dena. "Inside Stuff." *Travel & Leisure,* August 1985.

———. "Tips for Dining at Home Alone." *Food & Wine,* September 1985.

Keating, Bern. "The Wondrous Walled Towns of Europe." *Travel & Leisure,* October 1985.

Kennedy, Diana. *The Cuisines of Mexico.* New York: Harper & Row, 1972.

———. *Recipes from the Regional Cooks of Mexico.* New York: Harper & Row, 1978.

Kershner, Ruth Baudner. *Hungarian Cooking.* Weathervane Books, 1979.

Kettilby, Mary. *A Collection of Above 300 Receipts in Cookery, Physick and Surgery,* 5th ed. London: W. Parker, 1734.

King, Irene Lawrence. *Culinary Gems from the Kitchens of Old Virginia.* New York: Dodd, Mead, 1952.

King, Louise Tate and Jean Stewart Wexler. *The Martha's Vineyard Cookbook.* Chester, Connecticut: Globe Pequot Press, 1971.

Kitchiner, William. *Apicius Redivivus: The Cook's Oracle,* 2nd ed. London: John Hatchard, 1818.

Kolb, Elene Margot. "Fish and Ships: A Look at New Bedford." *COOK'S,* July/August 1985.

Kovi, Paul. *Paul Kovi's Transylvanian Cuisine.* New York: Crown Publishers, 1985.

Krausmann, Pamela. "American Marketplace." *COOK'S,* September/ October 1985.

Krieg, Saul. *The Spirited Taste of Italy.* New York: Macmillan, 1975.

Krochmal, Connie and Arnold. *Caribbean Cooking.* New York: Quadrangle, 1974.

Kutas, Rytek. *Great Sausage Recipes and Meat Curing.* Buffalo, New York: The Sausage Maker, Inc., 1984.

Ladies' Auxiliary Eagles. *Prize Recipes.* Cambridge, Ohio, n.d.

Ladies' Auxiliary of the Hartfield Volunteer Fire Company. *Home Cooking Secrets of Hartfield, New York.* n.d.

Lafayette Suburban Women's Club. *The Art of Cooking in Lafayette, California.* n.d.

Lan, Wang Hui. *Sichuan Recipes.* Hong Kong: Wan Li Book Co., 1984.

Lang, George. *The Cuisine of Hungary.* New York: Bonanza Books, 1971.

———. "Munich's Lively Restaurant Scene." *Travel & Leisure,* October 1985.

Larmoth, Jeanine and Charlotte Turgeon. *Murder on the Menu.* New York: Charles Scribner's Sons, 1972.

Lasky, Michael S. *The Complete Junk Food Book.* New York: McGraw-Hill, 1977.

Latin American Cooking: A Treasury of Recipes from the South American Countries, Mexico and the Caribbean. New York: Galahad Books, 1974.

Lee, Rev. J. Chung Ching. *Father Lee's Chinese Cooking and Culture*. Arcadia, California: Father Joseph Lee, 1983.

Leung, Mai. *The Classic Chinese Cook Book*. New York: Harper & Row, 1976.

Levy, Maxine. "Great New England Cooks—Matheus 'Puddie' Gilmette." *Yankee*, August 1985.

Liberace and Carol Truax. *Liberace Cooks*. Garden City, New York: Doubleday, 1970.

Lie, Sek-Hiang. *Indonesian Cookery*. New York: Bonanza Books, 1963.

Lin, Florence. *Florence Lin's Chinese Regional Cookbook*. New York: Hawthorn Books, 1975.

———. *Florence Lin's Complete Book of Chinese Noodles, Dumplings and Breads*. New York: William Morrow, 1986.

Livingston, Kathryn. "The Transylvanian Kitchen." *Gourmet*, September 1985.

Lo, Eileen Yin-Fei. *The Dim Sum Book*. New York: Crown Publishers, 1982.

Loomis, Susan Herrmann. "French Country Dinners." *Bon Appetit*, October 1985.

Lowe, Wendy. "Historic Inns of Sante Fe." *Travel & Leisure*, August 1985.

Lutes, Della T. *The Country Kitchen*. Boston: Little, Brown, 1936.

Mahnke, Susan. "Great New England Cooks: Terry Flettrich Rohe, Hancock, Maine." *Yankee*, April 1986.

Mallos, Tess. *The Complete Middle East Cookbook*. New York: McGraw-Hill, 1979.

Mama's Favorite Dutch Recipes. Las Vegas: JJ Merchandising Co., n.d.

Mandel, Abby. "Food Processor, The Creative Approach," *Bon Appetit*, September 1985.

———. "Food Processor: The Creative Approach—Breakfast at Campton Place." *Bon Appetit*, November 1985.

Maori Cookbook. New Zealand: Glenfield College Home and School Association, n.d.

Mariani, John. "Eating Out Loosens Up." *Food & Wine*, August 1985.

Marks, Copeland with Mintari Soeharjo. *The Indonesian Kitchen*. New York: Atheneum, 1981.

Marks, Copeland. *False Tongues and Sunday Bread*. New York: M. Evans, 1985.

Marshall, Anne, ed. *Australian and New Zealand Complete Book of Cookery*. Sydney, Australia: Landsdowne Press, 1970.

Marshall, Brenda. *The Charles Dickens Cookbook*. Toronto: Personal Library, 1980.

Martini, Anna. *The Mondadori Regional Italian Cookbook*. New York: Harmony Books, 1982.

Maugham, W. Somerset. *Catalina*. Garden City, New York: Doubleday, 1948.

Mayer-Browne, Elisabeth. *Australian Cooking for You*. New York: Universe Books, 1961.

———. *The Best of Viennese Cuisine*. Chicago, New York, and San Francisco: Rand McNally, 1965.

McCoy, Elin and John Frederick Walker. "To Breathe or Not to Breathe." *Food & Wine*, September 1985.

McDonald, Julie Jensen. *Delectably Danish*. Iowa City, Iowa: Penfield Press, 1982.

McKendry, Maxime. *The Seven Centuries Cookbook*. New York: McGraw-Hill, 1973.

McLaughlin, Michael. "A Fresh Look at Thanksgiving." *Bon Appetit*, November 1985.

Mehren, Elizabeth. "From Whisks to Molds, James Beard's Personal Possessions to be Auctioned." *Los Angeles Times*, September 12, 1985.

Meras, Phyllis with Frances Tenenbaum. *Carry-Out Cuisine*. Boston: Houghton Mifflin, 1982.

Mickler, Ernest Matthew. *White Trash Cooking*. Berkeley, California: Ten Speed Press, 1986.

Miller, Amy Bess and Persis Fuller. *The Best of Shaker Cooking*. New York: Macmillan, 1985.

Miller, Jill Nhu Huong. *Vietnamese Cookery*. Rutland, Vermont and Tokyo, Japan: Charles E. Tuttle, 1968.

Miner, Viviane Alchech with Linda Krinn. *From My Grandmother's Kitchen: A Sephardic Cookbook*. Gainsville, Florida: Triad Publishing, 1984.

Mitchell, Peter Todd. "Castles in Aragon." *Gourmet*, September 1985.

Monaghan, Charles. "Dining out in Sarasota." *Travel & Leisure*, August 1985.

Montagne, Prosper. *New Larousse Gastronomique*. London, New York, Sydney, and Toronto: Hamlyn, 1977.

Moore, Isabel. *Spanish and Mexican Cooking*. Secaucus, New Jersey: Chartwell Books, 1977.

Moore, James. "Trumpet of Death Mushroom Recipes." *COOK'S*, November/December 1985.

Morgan, Jinx and Jefferson. "Cooking for Two," series. *Bon Appetit*, August–September 1985.

Morley, John David. *Pictures from the Water Trade*. Boston and New York: Atlantic Monthly Press, 1985.

Morris, Harriett. *The Art of Korean Cooking*. Rutland, Vermont and Tokyo, Japan: Charles E. Tuttle, 1983.

Mulligan, Tim. "Kingston, New York: Historic Gem on the Hudson." *Travel & Leisure*, July 1985.

Najor, Julia. *Babylonian Cuisine: Chaldean Cookbook from the Middle East*. New York: Vantage Press, 1981.

Neal, Bill. *Bill Neal's Southern Cooking*. Chapel Hill and London: University of North Carolina Press, 1985.

Nelson, Kay Shaw. *The Best of Western European Cooking*. New York: John Day, 1976.

———. *The Eastern European Cookbook*. Chicago: Henry Regnery, 1973.

Neuner-Duttenhofer, Bernd. *Cookbook from Munich and Bavaria*. West Germany: Verlag Wolfgang Holker, 1982.

Ngo, Bach and Gloria Zimmerman. *The Classic Cuisine of Vietnam.* Woodbury, New York: Barron's, 1979.

Nightingale, Marie. *Out of Old Nova Scotia Kitchens.* New York: Charles Scribner's Sons, 1971.

O'Neill, Molly. "Simply Splendid: Fresh Corn," *Food & Wine,* August 1985.

———"Simply Splendid: Soul-Satisfying Soups." *Food & Wine,* October 1985.

Ochorowicz-Monatow, Marja. *Polish Cookery.* New York: Crown Publishers, 1958.

Ojakangas, Beatrice A. *The Finnish Cook Book.* New York: Crown Publishers, 1964.

Ortiz, Elizabeth Lambert. *The Complete Book of Caribbean Cooking.* New York: M. Evans, 1973.

———. "Castles of Scotland, Part II." *Gourmet,* June 1985.

———. "The Cuisine of Mexico, Part IV: Tamales." *Gourmet,* July 1985.

———. "The Cuisine of Mexico, Part VI." *Gourmet,* November 1985.

Ostmann, Barbara Gibbs and Jane Baker, eds. *Food Editors' Hometown Favorites Cookbook: American Regional and Local Specialties.* Maplewood, New Jersey: Newspaper Food Editors and Writers Association, Hammond, Inc., 1984.

Papashvily, Helen and George and the Editors of Time-Life Books. *Russian Cooking.* Alexandria, Virginia: Time-Life Books, 1969.

Patrick, Ted and Silas Spitzer. *Great Restaurants of America.* Philadelphia and New York: J.B. Lippincott, 1960.

Performing Arts Council of the Music Center of Los Angeles. *The Hollywood Bowl Cookbook.* 1984.

The Picayune's Creole Cookbook. New York: Dover Publications, 1971 (facsimile of 1901 edition).

Picower, Warren. "What's New." *Food & Wine,* August 1985.

Pinsuvana, Malulee. *Cooking Thai Food in American Kitchens,* 3rd ed. Bangkok, Thailand: Adul Pinsuvana, 1981.

Polvay, Marina. *The Dracula Cookbook.* New York: Chelsea Publishing, 1978.

van der Post, Laurens. *First Catch Your Eland.* New York: William Morrow, 1978.

van der Post, Laurens and the Editors of Time-Life Books. *African Cooking.* New York: Time-Life Books, 1970.

Puzo, Daniel P. "More Ethnic Dishes Are Headed for Supermarkets." *Los Angeles Times,* May 16, 1985.

Rawlings, Marjorie Kinnan. *The Marjorie Kinnan Rawlings Cookbook: Cross Creek Cookery.* London: Hammond, Hammond & Co., 1960.

Ray, Sumana. *Indian Regional Cooking.* Secaucus, New Jersey: Chartwell Books, 1986.

Reichl, Ruth. "Cajun Cooking—Going Home to the Source." *Los Angeles Times,* April 21, 1985.

———. "Doing Paris Sans Reservations—or a Bad Meal." *Los Angeles Times,* July 14, 1985.

———. "Downhill on a Venetian Gondola." *Los Angeles Times*, July 28, 1985.
———. "Prudhomme Seduces N.Y." *Los Angeles Times*, August 11, 1985.
———. "Haute Dogs: It Ain't the Meat, It's the Potion." *Los Angeles Times*, September 15, 1985.
———. "Carving Chips Off Old Block." *Los Angeles Times*, October 6, 1985.
Renggli, Seppi with Susan Grodnick. *The Four Seasons Spa Cuisine*. New York: Simon and Schuster, 1986.
"Restaurant Recipes—Six American Stars: Len Allison, Huberts, N.Y." *COOK'S*, November/December 1985.
Rhode, Irma. *The Viennese Cookbook*. New York: A.A. Wyn, 1951.
Rice, William. "Eating in Italy." *Food & Wine*, July 1985.
Riely, Elizabeth. "A Catch of Crab." *Gourmet*, June 1985.
Ritchie, Carson I. A. *Food in Civilization: How History Has Been Affected by Human Tastes*. New York and Toronto: Beaufort Books, 1981.
Roalson, Louise. *Notably Norwegian*. Iowa City, Iowa: Penfield Press, 1982.
Roate, Mettja C. *The New Hamburger and Hot Dog Cookbook*. New York: Weathervane Books, 1975.
Rombauer, Irma S. and Marion Rombauer Becker. *Joy of Cooking*. Indianapolis and New York: Bobbs-Merrill, 1975.
Romero, Jose Leopoldo. *Betty Crocker's Mexican Cookbook*. New York: Random House, 1981.
Root, Waverly. *Food*. New York: Simon & Schuster, 1980.
———. *Waverly Root's The Best of Italian Cooking*. New York: Grosset & Dunlap, 1974.
Rosenblatt, Julia and Frederic H. Sonnenschmidt. *Dining with Sherlock Holmes*. New York: Bobbs-Merrill, 1976.
Rosicky, Mary. *Bohemian-American Cook Book*. Omaha, Nebraska: National Printing Co., 1915.
"R.S.V.P.: Letters to the Editor." *Bon Appetit*, February 1986.
"R.S.V.P.: Letters to the Editor." *Bon Appetit*, November 1985.
Ruangkritya, Krissnee and Tim Martsching. *Adventures in Thai Food and Culture*. Bangkok, Thailand: Jonjit Ruangkritya, 1984.
Sampson, Hannah. "Ethnic Foods Are Often Dishes Created Out of Nothing But Bits, Pieces." *Los Angeles Times*, September 5, 1985.
Samson, William. *A Book of Christmas*. New York and Toronto: McGraw-Hill, 1968.
Sarvis, Shirley and Barbara Scott O'Neal. *Cooking Scandinavian*. Garden City, New York: Doubleday, 1963.
Sass, Lorna J. *Christmas Feasts from History*. New York: Irena Chalmers Cookbooks, 1981.
———. *Dinner with Tom Jones*. New York: Metropolitan Museum of Art, 1977.
"Sausages Are Ideal for Outdoor Grilling." *Los Angeles Times*, July 18, 1985.
"Sausages on Grill Perfect for Dad." *Los Angeles Times*, June 13, 1985.
"Tailgate Picnics Celebrate Pregame Football Action with Tasty Festivities." *Los Angeles Times*, September 19, 1985.

Sax, Irene. "Munich." *Food & Wine*, February 1986.

Sax, Richard. "All About Mozzarella." *Bon Appetit*, June 1985.

———. "Delicious Do-Ahead Menus." *Bon Appetit*, August 1985.

———. "New Rules for Game," *COOK'S*, September/October 1985.

———. "Casual Italian Supper." *Bon Appetit*, November 1985.

———. "Great New England Cooks—Rosa Istrail, Cromwell, Connecticut." *Yankee*, December 1985.

Scandinavian Christmas. Iowa City, Iowa: Penfield Press, 1985.

Schell, Orville and Meredith Brody. "Earthly Goods." *California*, September 1985.

Scherer, Francine and Madeline Poley. *The Soho Charcuterie Cookbook*. New York: William Morrow, 1983.

Schmaeling, Tony. *The Cooking of Spain and Portugal*. Secaucus, New Jersey: Chartwell Books, 1983.

Schneider, Elizabeth. "Great Greens." *Food & Wine*, October 1985.

Schoon, Louise Sherman and Corrinne Hardesty. *The Complete Pork Cook Book*. New York: Stein & Day, 1977.

Scicolone, Michele. "Calzone Catches On." *Food & Wine*, October 1985.

Scott, David. *Recipes for an Arabian Night: Traditional Cooking from North Africa and the Middle East*. New York: Pantheon Books, 1983.

Seranne, Ann, ed. *The Southern Junior League Cookbook*. New York: Ballantine Books, 1981.

The Shadows Service League. *The Shadows-on-the-Teche Cookbook*. New Iberia, Louisiana: 1984.

Sheldon, Edena. "The Great Apple Collection." *Bon Appetit*, October 1985.

Sheraton, Mimi. *The German Cookbook*. New York: Random House, 1965.

Shibles, Loana and Annie Rogers, eds. *Maine Cookery Then and Now*. Rockland, Maine: Courier-Gazette, 1972.

Sing, Phia. *Traditional Recipes of Laos*. London: Prospect Books, 1981.

Sis, Vladimir. *Chinese Food and Fables*. Czechoslovakia: Artia, 1966.

Slater, Shirley. "Bon Voyage: Traveling with Taste—Texas Hill Country." *Bon Appetit*, October 1985.

———. "Bon Voyage: Traveling with Taste—The Klondike." *Bon Appetit*, August 1985.

Smith, Gunilla, ed. *Scandinavian Cooking*. New York: Crown Publishers, 1976.

Smith, Michael, ed. *The Duchess of Duke Street Entertains*. New York: Coward, McCann & Geoghegan, 1977.

Snow, Jane Moss. *A Family Harvest*. Indianapolis and New York: Bobbs-Merrill, 1976.

Sokolov, Raymond. *Fading Feast*. New York: E.P. Dutton, 1981.

Solomon, Charmaine. *The Complete Asian Cookbook*. New York: McGraw-Hill, 1982.

Solum, Pat. *Danish Cook Book*. Big Bear Lake, California: Pat Solum, n.d.

Sombke, Laurence. "The Wurst of New York." *New York*, February 3, 1986.

Soniat, Leon E. Jr. *La Bouche Creole*. Gretna, Louisiana: Pelican Publishing, 1983.

Sonnenschmidt, Frederic H. and Jean F. Nicolas. *Art of Garde Manger*, 3rd ed. Boston: CBI Publishing, 1982.
Southwestern Cookery: Indian and Spanish Influences, series. New York: Promontory Press, 1974.
Staples, Radmila Maric. *Yugoslavian Cuisine*. New York: Vantage Press, 1977.
Steinberg, Rafael and the Editors of Time-Life Books. *Pacific and Southeast Asian Cooking*. New York: Time-Life Books, 1970.
Stern, Bill. "Up from a Wurst-Case Scenario." *Los Angeles Times*, July 7, 1985.
Stern, Jane and Michael. *Goodfood*. New York: Alfred A. Knopf, 1983.
———. *Square Meals*. New York: Alfred A. Knopf, 1984.
———. "On the Road: California Cornmeal Pancakes." *COOK'S*, September/October 1985.
———. "On the Road: Cuban Sandwiches." *COOK'S*, January/February 1986.
Stewart, Martha. *Entertaining*. New York: Clarkson N. Potter, 1982.
Stewart-Gordon, Faith and Nika Hazelton. *The Russian Tea Room Cookbook*. New York: Perigee Books, 1981.
Sturgis, Diana, John Robert Massie, and Anne Disrude. "Menus for the Mid-80's Recipes." *Food & Wine*, January 1986.
Su-Huei, Huang, ed. *Chinese Cuisine*. Taiwan: Wei-Chuan Publishing, 1974.
———. *Chinese Snacks*. Taiwan: Wei-Chuan Publishing, n.d.
Taglienti, Maria Luisa. *The Italian Cookbook*. New York: Random House, 1955.
Theroux, Paul. *The Kingdom by the Sea*. New York: Washington Square Press, 1983.
———. *The Old Patagonian Express*. New York: Washington Square Press, 1979.
Thompson, Martha Wiberg, ed. *Superbly Swedish*. Iowa City, Iowa: Penfield Press, 1983.
Thomson, George L. *Traditional Scottish Recipes*. New York: Pentalic/Taplinger, 1978.
Tinne, Rosie, comp. *Irish Countryhouse Cooking*. New York: Weathervane Books, 1974.
Tipton, Toni. "An Invitation to the Cocktail Party." *Los Angeles Times*, May 30, 1985.
———. "Hot Dogs Team with Champagne." *Los Angeles Times*, September 19, 1985.
Tolbert, Frank X. *A Bowl of Red*. Garden City, New York: Dolphin Books, 1972.
"Too Busy to Cook." *Bon Appetit*, July 1985.
"Too Busy to Cook." *Bon Appetit*, September 1985.
Trahey, Jane. *A Taste of Texas*. New York: Random House, 1949.
Trillin, Calvin. *American Fried*. New York: Vintage Books, 1974.
———. *Third Helpings*. New Haven and New York: Ticknor & Fields, 1983.
Troisgros, Jean and Pierre. *The Nouvelle Cuisine of Jean and Pierre Troisgros*. New York: William Morrow, 1978.

Turkbas, Ozel. *The Turkish Cookbook*. New York: Nash Publishing, 1977.

"Twenty-Five Hot New American Chefs." *Food & Wine*, September 1985.

Unity Inn Vegetarian Cook Book. Kansas City, Missouri: Unity School of Christianity, 1923.

Uvezian, Sonia. *The Cuisine of Armenia*. New York: Harper Colophon Books, 1974.

Valldejuli, Carmen Aboy. *Puerto Rican Cookery*. Gretna, Louisiana: Pelican Publishing, 1983.

Van Klompenburg, Carol. *Delightfully Dutch*. Iowa City, Iowa: Penfield Press, 1984.

Vatanapan, Pojanee with Linda Alexander. *Pojanee Vatanapan's Thai Cookbook*. New York: Harmony Books, 1986.

Venesz, Jozsef. *Hungarian Cuisine*. Budapest, Hungary: Corvina Press, 1958.

Verdon, Rene. *The White House Chef Cookbook*. Garden City, New York: Doubleday, 1967.

"Versatile Frankfurters for Graduation Celebrations." *Los Angeles Times*, May 30, 1985.

Viard, Henry and Ninette Lyon. *The Gourmet's Tour de France*. Boston: Little, Brown, 1983.

Viazzi, Alfredo. *Alfredo Viazzi's Italian Cooking*. New York: Vintage Books, 1983.

Vidrine, Mercedes. *Quelque Choses Beaucoup Bon*. Baton Rouge, Louisiana: Claitor's Publishing Division, 1973.

———. *Quelque Choses Piquante*. Baton Rouge, Louisiana: Claitor's Publishing Division, 1966.

Villas, James. "Hooray for Home Cooking." *Food & Wine*, February 1986.

Vincent, Gillain and The National Book League of Great Britain, comps. *Writers' Favorite Recipes*. New York: St. Martin's Press, 1979.

Virbila, S. Irene. "A Spanish Spot Where Past Is Present." *Los Angeles Times*, September 22, 1985.

Visson, Lynn. *The Complete Russian Cookbook*. Ann Arbor, Michigan: Ardis Publishers, 1982.

Volkh, Anne with Mavis Manus. *The Art of Russian Cuisine*. New York: Macmillan, 1983.

Wagner, Candy and Sandra Marquez. *Cooking Texas Style*. New York: Ballantine Books, 1983.

Waldo, Myra. *The Art of South American Cookery*. Garden City, New York: Doubleday, 1961.

———. *The Complete Round the World Meat Cookbook*. Garden City, New York: Doubleday, 1967.

Walker, Sara. *The Highland Fling Cookbook*. New York: Atheneum, 1971.

Wallace, Lily Haxworth. *The Rumford Complete Cook Book*. Providence, Rhode Island: Rumford Chemical Works, 1908.

Walsh, Anne. "Good Fast Food." *Food & Wine*, December 1985.

———. "Good Fast Food." *Food & Wine*, January 1986.

Wason, Betty. *The Art of German Cooking*. Garden City, New York: Doubleday, 1967.

Waters, Alice. *Chez Panisse Menu Cookbook.* New York: Random House, 1982.

Waters, Alice; Patricia Curtan; and Martine Labro. *Chez Panisse Pasta, Pizza and Calzone.* New York: Random House, 1984.

Webster, Mollie E. C. "Racing at Newmarket." *Gourmet,* July 1985.

Weeks, Terry. "Lugano's Vintage Festival." *Gourmet,* October 1985.

Weiss, Edward with Ruth Buchan. *The Paprikas Weiss Hungarian Cookbook.* New York: William Morrow, 1979.

Wells, Patricia. *The Food Lover's Guide to Paris.* New York: Workman Publishing, 1984.

———. "Paris for Food Lovers." *Travel & Leisure,* August 1985.

West, Karen. *The Best of Polish Cooking.* New York: Hippocrene Books, 1983.

Wheaton, Barbara Ketcham. *Savoring the Past.* Philadelphia: University of Pennsylvania Press, 1983.

Willan, Anne. "An Ethnic Mix on the Backyard Barbecue? Now You're Cooking." *Los Angeles Times,* August 29, 1985.

Williams, Chuck. *The Williams-Sonoma Cookbook and Guide to Kitchenware.* New York: Random House, 1986.

Wilmoth, Janet Cook. "Harrods." *Chocolatier,* vol. 1, no. 7, 1985.

Wilson, C. Anne. *Food and Drink in Britain: From the Stone Age to Recent Times.* Harmondsworth, Middlesex, England: Penguin Books, 1973.

Wilson, Marie M. *Siamese Cookery.* Rutland, Vermont and Tokyo, Japan: Charles E. Tuttle, 1965.

Wise, Victoria. *American Charcuterie.* New York: Viking Penguin, 1986.

Witty, Helen and Elizabeth Schneider Colchie. *Better than Store Bought.* New York: Harper & Row, 1979.

Wolcott, Imogene. *The New England Yankee Cookbook.* New York: Coward-McCann, 1939.

Wolfe, Linda. *The Literary Gourmet: Menus From Masterpieces.* New York: Harmony Books, 1985.

Wolfert, Paula and William Bayer. "The Pleasures of Sicily." *Bon Appetit,* October 1985.

Wolfert, Paula. *Couscous and Other Good Foods from Morocco.* New York: Harper & Row, 1973.

———. *Mediterranean Cooking.* New York: Times Books, 1977.

———. *The Cooking of South-West France.* Garden City, New York: Dial Press, Doubleday, 1983.

The World Atlas of Food, series. New York: Exeter Books, 1984.

Wu, Sylvia. *Madame Wu's Art of Chinese Cooking.* New York: Bantam, 1975.

Wyler, Susan. "Food Fantasies of the Rich and Famous." *Food & Wine,* December 1985.

———. "The Ultimate Cookout." *Food & Wine,* July 1985.

Xan, Erna Oleson and Sigrid Marstrander. *Time-Honored Norwegian Recipes.* Decorah, Iowa: Norwegian-American Museum, 1984.

Ykema-Steenbergen, Rie. *The Real Dutch Treat Cook Book.* Grand Rapids, Michigan: Wm. B. Eerdmans, 1949.

Young Ladies Sewing Society. *Young Ladies' Cook Book.* Beloit, Wisconsin, 1896.

Yueh, Jean. *Dim Sum and Chinese One-Dish Meals*. New York: Irena Chalmers Cookbooks, 1981.

Zane, Eva. *Middle Eastern Cookery.* San Francisco: 101 Productions, 1974.

Zeranska, Alina. *The Art of Polish Cooking*. Garden City, New York: Doubleday, 1968.

Zwack, Anne Marshall. "The Florentine Restaurant Scene." *Gourmet*, September 1985.

INDEX

Page numbers in italics indicate recipes.

Afghanistan, 250
African food (*see also* merguez), 144, 163, 248–250, *252–256*, 300–301, 314, 360–361, 379
ajvar, *162–163*, *263*
alderman in chains, 38, 52, 324
ale, sausage braised in, 135, *237*
alligator, 361
almonds, *302*, *309*
American food (*see also* country sausage; hot dogs; Indian, American; specific regions), 13, *22*, *24*, *37–38*, 268, 320–324, *325–343*, 358–363, *363–383*
  New, *29*, 291, 324, *344–355*
anchovies, *47*, *94*, *111*, 121, *140*
andouille, 38, 56–59, 174, 324, *346*, *353*, 361, *377–381*
andouillettes, 56, 58
annatto oil, *317*
apple, *278*
  fried, 37, 57, 59, 64, 233, *369*
  meat and, *185*, *201*, *238*
  potato and (*see* himmel und erde)
  sauces, 59, 66, *166*, 190
  sausage, 31, 58–59, 66, *69*, *81*, *86*, 215
  stuffing, *79*, 147
Armenian food, 17, 145, 173
Asian food (*see also* lop cheong), 34, 36, 131, 144, 163, 173, 243, 250, *256*, 264–269, *269–295*, 316, 322–324, *340*, *348*, *350*, 362–363
asparagus, *206*, *312*
Austrian food, 30, *128*, 142–146, *147–149*, *166*, 322
bachor, 146
bacon, 35, *43*, *62*, *79*, *82*, *128*, *137*, *149*, *152–157*, *165*, *168*, *185*, *199*, *228*, 237, *246*, *272*, *314*, *366*, *371*
  sausage, *31*, *40*, *66*, *81*, *127*, 146, *240*, *245*, *348*

baking sausage, *21*
ballottine, *59*
bangers, 232–234, *234–237*, 243, 266
bao, 266, 269, 280
barley, *137*, 146, 214–215, *222*, 233, 268
barszcz, *175*, 179, 215
Basque food, 57, *75–77*, 191
batter, 173, *277*, *332*, 363
beans (*see also* cassoulet), 92, 137, 191–192, 197, 250, 267, 300–302, 360
  chili, *334*, 362
  feijoada, *314*, 342
  green, *274*, *312*
  rice and, *274*, *381*
  salad, *312*
  soups, *75*, 77, 361
beef, 37, 59, 179, 215, 233, 250, 266–268, 300–301, *314*, 322, *331*, *336*, 360, 362, 376
  chili, *334*, 362
  meatloaf, *149*, *240*
  mixed meats, *92–94*, *236*, *314*
  roast, *166*, *312*
  salad, *312*
  sausage (*see also* specific sausages) 37, 58, 120, 122,

beef *(cont.)*
145, *173*, *182*, 214–217, 233–234, *240*, 250, 266–268, 362, *376*
soups, *175*, *179*, 215, *293*
stews, *155*, 191, *201*, 268
stuffed, 91, *293*, 300, 302
-stuffed cabbage, *153*, 217, *222*
beer, *134–136*, *178*
beets, *175*, 179, 215, *312*
Belgian food, 59, 212, 216
besan, 287
bierschinken, 122
bigos, *185*
"birds' nests", 216
birnenformige, 121
biscuits, *337*, 368, *370–371*
black pudding (*see* blood pudding)
blanquet Valenciano, 191
blood sausage (*see also* blutwurst; boudin noir; morcilla), *31*, 35–36, 59, 92, 121, 144–146, 172–173, 190–192, 214–215, 233–234, 250–51, 268, 301–302, 323, 362
barley, 146, 215, 233, 268
beef, *32*, *66*, 233–234, 268
bread and, 31, 145–146, 190, 199, 216, 234, 302
chestnut, 31, 56–57, 66
cooking, *31*, *66*
dough-enclosed, *71*, 190, *199*
fruit, 31, 58–59, 66, 172, 215, 216
goat, 300
kasha, 31, 172
lamb, 233–234, 301
liver, 66
oatmeal, 31, 233–234
onion, 59, 66, 172, 233, 268, 300
pork, *32*, 36, 56, *66*, 121, 145, 215, 233–234, 361
potato-apple puree and, *132*
puddings, 233–234, 301–302
rabbit, 66
rice, 66, 190, 233, 302, 361
rye and, 214
sauce, 191
sauerkraut and, 58
smoked, 121, 199, 362
soup, 191, 300–301
spinach, 56, *66*
stew, 58, 190–192, 250, 300–301
stuffed stomach, 300
tongue, 121
blood soup, 214
blutwurst (*see also* blood sausage), 120–121, *132*, 301
boar, *29*, 35, 56, 90–91, 216
bockwurst, 26, 121, *123*, *133*, *136*, *236*, 360
boerewors, 250, *252*
boliche, 302
bollito misto, *92–94*, 301
bologna, 16, 122, 216, 232, 324, 360
borscht, *175*, 179, 215
boudin blanc, 26, 38, 56, *64*, *69*, *86*, *136*, 216, 324, *346*, 362, *373*
boudin noir/rouge (*see also* blood sausage), 56–59, *66*, 361
boulettes, 56, 59
brackorv, 218
bratwurst, 26, *47–48*, 120–122, *124*, *133–136*, 173, *236*, 322, *346*, 360, 362
braunschweiger, 121
bread (*see also* biscuits/sandwiches; specific names), 90–92, 95, 120–122, 191, 214, 324
corn-, 199, *305*, 332, *371*, *383*
garlic, with chicken, *309*
meatloaf, *149*
rolls, hot dog, *329*
sausage, *26*, *31*, 36, *44*, *64*, *66*, *111*, 122, *127*, 144, 146, *147*, *182*, 232–234, *245*, 251, *256*, *260*, 302
sausage in, *96*, 190, *199*, 216, 266, 269
soup, *47*, *168*, *187*, *207*, *363*
strata, *342*
stuffings, *108*, *222*, *371*, *383*
breaded dishes, *26*, 37, *43*, *64*, *132*, 173, *221*, 232, *243*, 302, *353*
breakfast, 173
sausage, 14, *20*, *24*, 37–38, *40*, *86*, *127*, *134*, *182–183*, 214, 233–234, *242*, 269, *374*, *382*
briks, *254*
brine, 35, 215–216, *218–219*, 251, 360, *376*
British food, 26, 31, 35–37, *40–52*, 135, 225, 230–234,

234–246, 250, 266, 268–269, 272, 289, 301, 304, 361, 363
broccoli, *341*, 365
brotwurstel, *127*
bruhwurst, 120
buffalo sausage, *29*, 322, 362
bulk sausage (*see* country sausage)
butifarra, 191, *197–199*, 300, 302, *343*, *346*, *350*, *352*, *355*
butter sauce, 59, 81, 182, 345

cabbage (*see also* coleslaw; sauerkraut), 57, 137, 191, 197, 214–216, 233, 237
kielbasa and, *152*, *176*
mixed meats and, *84*, *185*
poultry and, *62*, *152*
relish, *331*
soups, *75*, *84*, 137, *175*, 214
stews, 137, *185*
stuffed, 58, 79, *153*, *158*, 217, *222*, *258*, 374
submarine sandwiches, *338*
caillettes, 56
Cajun food (*see also* andouille; boudin blanc; boudin rouge; gumbo; jambalaya), 30, 38, *254*, 324, 338, 361, *373–381*
cake, 57, *272*, *343*
caldo verde, 192, 206, *209*, 360, 363
calzone, 91, *350*
camel, 250
Canadian food, 269
candy or cookie "sausage", 144
canederli, 92
cappelletti, *106*
capon (*see* poultry)
carne fiambre, 302
carrots, *62*, *75*, *82*, *84*, *92*, *176*, *278*, *312*
casalinga, pollo alla, *100*
casatiello, 91
casings, 15–16, 30, 34–36, 105, 222, 266–267, 284, 326, 334
cassava, 301, *314*
casseroles, 35, 37, 121, *137*, 144, 147, *157*, 173, 179, 191, *194*, 203, 214, 233–234, *246*, 300, 323–324, 332, *341–342*, 374, 382
cassoulet, 57, *73*, 301, 312, 314
Catalan, à la, 191
cataplana, 192, *210*, 360
caul fat, 16, 56, *81*, 145, 233, *245*, 251, *262*, 266–267
celery sauce, *52*
cervelas/cervelat, *78*, 122, *140*, 216, *325*
cevapcici, *162*
cha, 267
chartreuse, 57, *62*
chaurice, *254*, 302, *374*
cheese, 91, 147, 216, *225*, 323, 374
bread and, *338*, *342*, *370*, *383*
calzone/focaccia/pizza, 91, *114*
chili with, *334*, *362*
liver sausage spread, *224*, *336*
pasta with, 91, *98*, *106–107*, *334*
pies, *95*, 105
risotto, *116*
salad, *140*, *312*, *352*
sausage, 91, *110*, 232–233, 251, 260, 302
sausage rolls, *337*
tomato sauce, *307*, *334*
-stuffed vegetables, *340*
chestnuts, 57, *75*, *371*
sausage, *31*, 56–57, *66*, *81*
chiang mai sausage, *281*
chicken (*see* poultry)
chick-peas, 57, *201–203*, 251, 287, 300–301, 314
chile/chili, 161, 250, 311, 324, 328
cornbread, *383*
dogs, *334*, 362
paste, 250, *253–256*, *280*, *282*, *350*
sauce, *163*, 173, *254–256*, 268, *278*, *289*, *304*, *314–317*, 381
stuffed, 300, 324
chipolata sausage, 15, 146
chorizo, 17, 24, 57, 190–191, *192*, 268–269, 300–301, *302*, 303, 322, 324, 360, 362
bread, 190, *199*, *307*, *371*, *383*
chicken and, *309*
clams and, 192, *210*, 360
eggs and, 191–192, *198*, *206*, 302, *311*, 362
feijoada, *314*
meat and, *84*, *293*, 300, 302
pasta and, *194*, 268, 300, *317*, 361
pastry and, *71*, 190, 269, *304*

chorizo *(cont.)*
picante, 190, 300, *302–303*
rice and, 191, *204*, 268, 300, *377*
salad, *203*, 300, *312*
sauce, 191
soup, *75*, 191, *196*, *207*, *209*, 268, 300, 302, *307*, 361, *379*
stew, 190, 192, *201*, 268, 300, 302
stuffings, 190, 300, 302, *304*, *340*, *371*, *383*
tamales, *305*
choucroute garnie, *82*
chou farci, *79*
chouriço (*see* chorizo)
chourisso, 268
chow fan, *274*
Cincinnati food, *334*, *343*, 362
clams, 192, *204*, *210*, 360, *363*
cocido, 190–192, *201*, 268, 300–301, 314
čočka polévka, *168*
cocktail sausages, 214, *337*
coconut, 267–268, *280*, *284*
coleslaw, 27, 325
collier d'Ardennes, 216
collops, veal, *43*
colmarettes, 58
confit:
poultry, *73–77*
sausage, 22, 215, 322, 361
corn (*see also* bread; polenta; scrapple; tamale; tortilla), 144, 300–301, 323–324, *331*, *350*, 361, *363*, *383*
dogs, *332*
cotechino, 90, *92*, *101–102*, *113*
cotenna, 102
country sausage, *110*, *134*, *192–193*, *238*, 303, *350*, *352*, 360–361, *365*, *368–371*
couscous, 256, 301
crab, 267, *280*, 322, *340*, *346*, 361, 373
cream (*see also* sour cream), *47*
sauce, 36, 71, 91, 107, 182, *217*, 219–221
Creole food (*see* Cajun)
Creole sauce, 375–376
creosote, 232
crepes, 59, 323
crépinettes, 56, 59, *81*
cucumber, *178*–179, 250, *281–282*
cured sausage, 14–15
currant sauce, *136*
curry, *133*, 250, 268–269, *286–289*
cuscuz, 301
Czech food, 142–144, 146, *147–149*, *168*, 322, 362

dashi, *292*
dates, sausage-stuffed, 190
desserts, 232, 237, 306, *343*
dim sum, 266, *269–272*, 280, *316*
dimugan, 268
Dinkum Dogs, 234
dolma (*see* grape leaves)
donkey sausage, 56
doppa i grytan, 214
dormouse sausage, 90
drisheen, 234
drying sausages (*see also* specific sausages), 14
Dublin coddle, *246*
duck (*see* poultry)
dumplings, 92, *106*, 110, *128*, 266, 269, *270*, 280
Dutch food, 212, 216, *227–228*, 250, 252, 337

edel, 122
eggplant relish, *162–163*, 263
eggs, 94, 172, 197, 216, 251, 254, 258, 262, 331, 361, 367
baked, 191–192, *206*
hard-boiled (*see also* birds' nests; nargisi kofta; Scotch eggs), 36, *49*, 91, 130, *140*, 145, 147, *178*, *199*, 269, *293–295*, 302, *312*, 331, *353*
omelettes (*see* tortilla-eggs)
scrambled, *181*, 250, *311*, 323
eintopf, *137*
elk sausage, 215
embutidos, 269, 302
empadas/empanadas/ empanadillas/ empadinnas/ empanaditas, 191, 269, *304*, *316*
enchiladas, 300, 304, 362
enroladinhos Paulistas, 337
espagueti con salchichas, *317*
estofado à la Catalan, 191
Europe (*see also* specific countries,

34–38, 144, 250–251, 266, 269, 300–302, 322, 329

fabada Asturiana, 191, 302
faggots, 233
farina/farofa, *314*
fat-sealed sausage (*see* confit)
feijoada, *314*, 342
fiambre, 302, *312*
fidget pie, *238*
field mouse pie, 360
finocchiona, 91
fish (*see also* clambake; paella; sauce, fish; yosenabe; specific names): 35, 73, 191, 269, 317
  salad, 92, *312*
  salt cod fritters, *353*
  soups, *47*, *292*, *345–346*, *363*
  stuffed, *46*, 267
fish sausage (*see also* forcemeat; kamaboko; oysters; shrimp; yosenabe), 35–36, 56, 90, 121, 145, 214, 301, 324, 373
  pistachio, 59
  salmon, *344*
  soups, *346*
  tuna, anchovy, cheese, *111*
fleischwurstring, 122
focaccia, 90–92, *114*, *350*
fogoly, káposzta és kolbasz, *152*
forcemeat, 36–38, *40*, *43*, *46–52*, 214, 232, 251, 267
frankfurters (*see also* hot dogs), 122
French food (*see also* andouille; andouillette; boudin blanc and noir; confit; crepinette; pistachio sausage; saucisse; saucisson), 24, 31–32, 35, 37, *43*, 54–59, *59–86*, 92, 122, *131*, 135, 157, 172, 181, 216, 234, 253, 267, 301–302, 314, *353*, 355, 361–362
friandes, 57, *71*
frying sausage (*see also* specific sausages), *20*
Frogmore stew, 361
fruit (*see also* specific names), 36, 90, 92, 115–116, 163, 190, 237, 306
  sausage (*see also* apple; lemon; orange; raisin), 37, 59, 144, *258*, 263, 322, 362
fugu, 268

galantine, 57, *59*, 216, 234, 295, 302, 323–324
game (*see also* specific meats, poultry), *29*, 37, 152, 232, 324
ganseleberwurst, 121
garam masala, *286–289*
garbure, 57, *75–77*
garland, sausage, 38, 52, 216, 324
garlic, 289
  sauce, 41, *94*, *162–163*, 250, 254, 258, 260, *271*, *278*, *288*, 294, *314–316*, *353*
  soup, *196*
garlic sausage, 172
  dried, 58, 92
  fresh, *24*, *29*, *62*, *68*, *71–75*, *78–82*, *92*, *110*, 161–162, *181*, *193*, *237*, *238*, *253*, *256*, *261*, *277*, *284*, *287*, *302*, *314*, *317*, *348*, *352*, *374*, *376*
  smoked, 17, *62*, *84*, *104–105*, *138*, *149–155*, *158*, *173–181*, *192–196*, *201*, *206*, *209*, *295*, *314*, *325–328*, *346*, *353*, *381–382*
gayettes, 56
gazpacho, 192, 309
geraucherte, 124
German food (*see also* blutwurst; bockwurst; bratwurst; himmel und erde; liverwurst; metwurst; weisswurst; wurst), 17, 29, 35–38, *41*, 58, 92, 118–122, *123–140*, 144, 145, 172, 216, 300–301, 322, 360, 362
gilded sausage, 58
ginger, *221*, *271*, *348*
glutinous rice, 268, *270*, *284*
goat, 58, 145, 250, *253–254*, 300
goetta, 362
golden coins, *278*
goose (*see* poultry)
gorditas, 362
goulash, 146, *148*
grape leaves, stuffed, 34, 153,

grape leaves, stuffed *(cont.)*
222, 251, *258*, 263
gravy, *134*, 233, 245, 353, *365*, 368, *371*
green sauce, *92–94*, 198
groene erwtensoep, *227*
gschwollne, 122
gumbo, 71, 174, *345–346*, 353, 375, *379*
gypsy salad, *140*
gyukar, 268
gyuma, 268

hackkorv, 214
haggis, 36, 232, 234, *245*, 250
ham (*see also* jambalaya; paella), 35, 56, *179*, 214, 331, 361
clams and sausage, *210*
eggs and, 191–192, *206*
gravy, *371*
grilled skewers, *278*
pie, *49*, *95*
rice and, 38, *157*, *274*, *381*
sausage (*see also* andouille; forcemeat; galantine; lop cheong), 122, 173, 267, 302
soups, *179*, 191, 214, *227*
stews, 191, *201*
-stuffed pasta, *106*
stuffing, 90, *293*
submarine sandwich, *338*
veal-wrapped cotechino, *113*
hare, 73, 232
harissa (*see* chili paste)
headcheese, *30*, 35–36, 58, 90, 120, 122, 145–146, 173, 214–215, 232, 250–251, 267, 302, 360–362, *367*
heaven and earth (*see* himmel und erde)
herb sauce, 115, 324, 345, 353
himmel und erde, 32, 64, 128, *132*, 135–136, 228, 345
hochepot, 59
hornazo, *199*
horsemeat sausage, 56, 90, 173
horseradish, 144, 182
sauce, *30*, 124, 130, *217–221*
hot dogs (*see also* chili, meat; corn dogs; relish; rolls, bread), 13, 17, 27, 38, 133, 144, 172, 216, 234, 268–269, 300–301, 322–324, 360
beef, 27, 122, *148*, *179*, *328*, 334, 360
casseroles, 27, 324, *179*, 328
pork, 27, 58, *82*, *133*, *148*, 155, *166–168*, *179*, *326*, 328
poultry, *27*, *136*
soups, 27, *137*, *168*, *179*, 187
stews, *137*, *148*, *155*
hot links, 324, 361–362
huevos, 191, *206*, *311*, 362
Hungarian food, 142–145, *147–158*, *165–166*, *253*, 345
"hunter's" dishes, 173, *185*
hurka, 144–145

Indian (American) food, 37, 301, *305*, 322, 362–*363*, 379
ingefarapolse, *221*
involtino di cotechino, *113*
Italian food (*see also* cotechino; Italian sausage; Lucanian sausage; luganega; mortadella; Rome; salami; zampone), 15, 57, 88–92, *92–116*, 122, 145, 194, 234, 301, 317, 324, 338, 361–362
Italian sausage, basic/sweet, *24*, *81*, 90–92, 96, *238*, 301, *350*
chicken and, *100*
clambake, *363*
focaccia and, *114*
onions and peppers, 90, 97, 324
polenta and, 92, *103*
rice and, 90, 92, *116*
sauce, 90, *98*, 317
stuffings, 57, 90, 91, *108*, 340
Italian sausage, hot, 90, *96–97*, *134*, *243*, *340*

jaau ng heungcheung, *277*
jagerwurst, 121
jambalaya, 29, 38, 361, 374, *377*
jaternice, 146
jelita, 146
Jesus sausage, 58
Jewish dishes, *25*, 145, 201, *256*, *328*, 345, 360
Joulumakkara, *218*
Julkorv, *218*

kaalikaaryleet, *222*
kabanos, 173
kalberwurst, 122
kalbsleberwurst, 121
kale (*see also* caldo verde), *228, 314*
kamaboko, 268, *290–292*, 363
karistymakkara, 216
kasha, 31, 36, 121, 172, *183*
kassler leberwurst, 121
kaszanka, 173
kebab (*see* kofta; luleh; seekh)
kefta/keftedakia (*see* kofta)
kielbasa, 17, 172–*173*, 362
  cabbage and, *152–153, 158, 176*
  eggs and, *181*
  meats and, *84, 149, 158, 165, 185*
  rice and, *153, 158, 377*
  salad, *138*
  soups, *84, 175, 178, 187, 209, 379*
  stews, *155, 185*
  stuffing, *295, 340*
kim tien ke, *278*
kishka, 172
klobásy, 146
knackwurst, *133, 137*
knoblauchwurst, 122
knockwurst, 122, 216
kochwurst, 120
kofta, 173, 250–251, *256, 260, 262*, 267–268, *286–289*, 324
kolbásy, (*see* kielbasa)
kolbász, 144
korinthesosse, *136*
korv, 214
krainerwurst, 124
krakowska, 172–173
kvas, *178*

lak jiang, (*see* lop cheong)
lamb (*see also* cassoulet), 59, 153, 190–191, 215, 250, 300–301, 322, 360
  cocido, *201*
  mixed grill, 233, *236*, 301–302
  sausage (*see also* specific sausages), 34–35, 37, 44, 145, 190, 214–216, 233, 250–251, *286–287*, 300–301, 324, 360
landjager, 58, 122
laos, *280*
lasagne, 90, 96
Latin American food (*see also* chorizo), 37, 191, 207, 298–302, *302–317*, 323, 337–*338*, 345, 353, 360–361
Lebanon bologna, 360
leberwurst (*see* liverwurst)
lecsó, *151, 165, 253*
lemon, *258, 281, 314–316*
  sausage, 145, *147, 157*, 233
lemper, *284*
lentils, 57, 73, *101*, 121, 301
  soup, *168*
lettuce, *222, 260*, 267, *278, 281–282, 288, 312, 338*
lime sauce, *278, 281, 304, 314–316*
lingonberries, 172, 215, *222, 226*
linguiça (*see* longaniza)
liquid smoke, 14
liver dishes, 91–92, 295
liver sausage, 35, 37, 56, 58, 91, 121, 173, 215
  beef, 145, 182, *224*
  blood and, 66
  bread, 146
  dried, 266
  goat, 300
  kasha, 172
  lamb, 145, 300
  onion and, 121, *125*, 145, *224*
  pork, 121, *125*, 145–146, *224*, 266, 268, 302
  poultry, 121, 145, 172, 214, 266, 302
  raisin, 214, *224*
  rice and, 145–146, 214, *224*
  sandwiches, 120–121, *125*, 214 *224, 336*
  spinach and, 56
  veal, 121
  -wurst, 16, 120–121, *125*, 173, 269, 323, *336*, 362
lobster, *47, 274, 346, 363*
longaniza, 190, 192, *193*, 268, 300–302, 360
  beans and, 192, *314*, 360
  bread, *199*
  clams and, 192–*193, 210*, 360, *363*
  eggs and, *198*
  mixed grill, 192, 301
  salad, *312*

longaniza *(cont.)*
  smoked, 192–*193*, *198–199*, *207–210*
  soup, 192, *207–209*, 302
  stew, 300–302
lop cheong, 17, 34, 266–269, *269–275*, *278*, *281–284*, 324
lor bok goh, *272*
loukanika, *261*
loukenkas, 57
Lucanian sausage, 35, *39*, 90, 110
luganega, *81*, 90–92, *98*, *108*, *110*, *114*, *116*, 322, *352*, *355*
luleh kebab, 173
Luxembourgian food, 212, 216

macaroni with sausage, *194*, 300, 317
maccarones español, *194*
makkara, 214
  -pannukakko, *225*
manioc, *314*
masa harina, *306*
mazurka, 173
meat cuts, 17
meat glaze, *240*
meat grinders, 16–18, 34, 38, 232
meatloaf, 105, *149*, *240*
meat packers/processors, 13–14, 38, 323, 334
medisterpolse, 215
medvurst (*see* metwurst)
merguez, *71*, 250, *253–254*
metwurst/mettwurst, 58, 122, 215, *219*, *225*, *227–228*
Middle Eastern food (*see also* grape leaves), 17, 22, 30, 34, 57, 95, 144, 153, 163, 173, 182, 194, 222, 248, 250–251, *253–262*, 287, 323, 331
millet sausage, 145
mititei, *161*
mixed grill, 145, 173, 192, *236*, 301, 324
molho de pimenta, *314–316*
moose sausage, 363
morcilla (*see also* blood sausage), 190–192, *199*, 268, 300
  blanca, 190
morcón, *293*, 302
mortadella, 14, 91, *105–108*, 232, 300, *312*
Mostardo di Cremona, *92*
mumbar, 251, *258*
mushrooms (*see also* truffles), 91, 175, 182, 190, 197, 348
  casseroles, *194*, *341*
  chicken and sausage, *100*
  dough and, *49*, *114*, *270*, 272, *350*
  hunter's stew, *185*
  mixed grill, *236*, 301, 324
  rice and, *274*, 348
  sausage, 38, *182*, 266
  sausage and cabbage, *176*
  veal-wrapped sausage, *113*
mussels, 35, *204*, *363*
mustard, 120–122, *129*, 144, 216, 233, *326–328*, *331*
  sauce, 36, 71, 92
  vinaigrette, *68*, 130, *138*, *140*
mutton (*see* lamb)
myma, 251

nabe/nabemono, *292*
nargisi kofta, 251, *289*
New England food, *44*, *193*, 322, 326, 360, *363*
nitrates/nitrites, 15, 362
noodles (*see* pasta)
nor mai shui mai, *270*
nuoc cham, *278*

oatmeal, 240, 362
  sausage (*see also* haggis), 31, 36, 121, 232–234, *240*, *242*
odds and ends, *292*
okroshka, *178*–179
olla podrida (*see* cocido)
omelette (*see* tortilla-eggs)
onion, *162*, 192, 199, 215, *219*, 224, *226*, *289*, *333–334*, 362
  casseroles, *239*, *246*
  clambake, *363*
  eggs and, *198*, *206*
  lecsó, *151*, *165*, *253*
  liver sausage spread, *336*
  meats and, *82*, *92*
  relish, *163*, 325, *328*, *331–333*
  salad, *138–140*, *203*, *281*, *288*
  sauce, *195*, *289*, *316–317*, *365*
  sausage, *26*, *30–31*, *59*, *64–66*, 121, *123*, 125, *127*, 145, 172, 214–215, 233, *242*, 251, *256*, 260, 268, 300, *326–328*

sausage and peppers, 90, *97*, 324
stuffed, *222*, *340*, *348*
turnovers, 269, *316*, *350*
orange sausage, 29, *59*, *66*, 232, 251, *261*, *348–350*
organ meats (*see also* liver; stomachs; tripe), 35, 41, 122, 145, 173, 190, 214, 232–233, *236*, 251, 323
Oxford sausage (*see* bangers)
oysters, 37–38, 40, *44*, 57, 232, *355*, 361, 363, *377*

paella, 57, 191, *204*, 208, 268, 301, 323, 377
pancakes, 59, 191, *225*, 266, 323
panzarotti, 91
parkys, 144, 146, 322
partridge, 57, *62*, *152*
pasta (*see also* specific names), 116, 122, 256, 268–269
alla zampognaro, *98*
fried, 266–267, 363
sausage sauce, 25, 91, *98*, 110
stuffed, 91, 105–*106*, 110
soups, *106*, *201*, *292*
tomato (*see* tomato, pasta and)
vegetables and, 106
pastry (*see also* pies; sausage rolls; toad-in-the-hole), 66, 122, *254*, *304*, *355*
patties, 16, *24*, 37, 56, *81*, *132*, *147*, 233, 266, *274*, *277*, 301, 322, 360–361, 363, *369*, *382*
peas (*see also* snow peas), 62, 91, *140*, *204–206*, *238*, *274*, *312*
soup, 214, 216, 219, *227*
split (*see also* soup), 250–251
"peasant's feast", 146
pemmican, 37, 322, 362
Pennsylvania Dutch food, 38, 360, *365–367*
pepparrotas, *217–221*
pepperoni, 91, 192, *194*, *196*, *203*, *207*, *210*, *293*
peppers (*see also* chile), 250, *261*, 348
calzone, *350*
chicken, sausage and, *100*
eggs and, *198*, *206*, *311*
lecsó, *151*, *165*, *253*
meats and, *92*
pasta and, *194*, *317*, *334*
relish, *163*, 325, 328, *331*, 333
rice and, *352*, *377*, *381*
salad, *312*, *352*
sandwiches, *162*, *328*, *338*
sausage and onions, 90, *97*, 324
perunamakarra, 216, 218
pesto, *115*, *345*
peverada, 91–92
pheasant, 58
pickekorv, 215
pickles, 93, *94*, *140*, *161*, *163*, *179*, *221*, 233, 269, 277, *293*, *295*, *331*, *338*, *352*, 353, *383*
pies, 36, 38, 105, 192, 232, 269, 360, 375, *383*
fidget, *238*
ham and veal, *49*
pizza, *95*
pignoli, *108*, *258*
pigs in the blanket, 216, *337*
pinkel, 121
pistachio sausage, *24*, 58–59, *71*, *78*, *105*, 121, *258*
pitki, 251
pizza, 90–91, *95*, 114, 191, 266, 324, 348-*350*
platio, 361
plockwurst, 122
poaching sausage, *20*
poh pia, 266, *282*, 294
polenta, 39, 92, 100, *103*, 110, 113, 122, 332, 362
Polish food (*see also* kielbasa), 170–173, *173–177*, *185–187*, 362
pollo con chorizo, *309*
polpettone di tonno, *111*
polse, 214
pork (*see also* bacon; ham), 17, 34, 37–38, 56, 91, 94, 144, 190–191, 215, 233–234, 250–251, 266–267, 300, 322, 334, 369
beans and, *73*, *301*, *314*
cake, *343*
chops, 146, *153*, *157–158*, *165*, *292*, *314*, 331
eintopf, *137*
meatloaf, *149*
mixed meat dishes, *84*, 173, 192, *314*

pork *(cont.)*
pasta and, *317*
rice and, *153*, *157–158*
roast, *166*
sauerkraut and, *82*, 146, *157*
soups, *75*, *84*, 191, *201*
stews, *185*, 191, *201*, 216
-stuffed cabbage, *153*, *158*, *222*
stuffings, *106*, *295*
suckling pig, *30*, 37, 302, 371
pork sausage (*see also* specific sausages), 34–37, 56, 59, 91, 120, 122, 173, 190, 215–216, 232–234, 237, *239*, *246*, 251, 266–269, 362, *366*, *372*
crab and, 267, *280*, 322, 340
kasha and, *183*
rice and, *284*
water chestnut and, *277*, 363
porpoise sausage, 35, 90
Portuguese food, 188–190, *192*, *193*, *207–210*, 250, 268, 301, 314, 322, 360, *363*
potatiskorv, 218
potato (*see also* salad; tortilla-eggs), 38, 69, 121, 135, 146, 173, 214, 216, 324
apple and (*see* himmel und erde)
casseroles, *137*, 147, 173, 234, *238*, *246*
choucroute garnie, *82*
clambake, *363*
fried, 77, 122, 168, 172
fritters/pancakes, 324, *353*
mashed, 29, 57, 64, 69, 222, *228*, 233, 237, *245*, 365, 375
mixed meats and, *92*
pastry, 146, 337
sausage, 17, *81*, 214, 216, *218*, *221*, *245*, 322, *352*, 362–363
soup, *75*, 137, *175*, 192, *201*, 206, *209*, 227, 360, *363*
stews, 137, *148*, *201*, 250
stuffed, 360, *366*
turnovers, *304*
potée, *84*, 216
poultry (*see also* confit), 36, 38, 49, 269, 305, 365
beans and, *73*, *77*, 250
boning, *295*
cabbage and, 57, 58, *62*, *152*
capon, 41, *52*, 106
chicken, *39*, 80, *84*, *92*, *100*, *106*, *179*, 190, *201*, *204*, *236*, 250, 266, 269, *274*, *275*, *278*, *282*, *295*, 302, *309*, *312*
cream and celery sauce, *52*
duck, 58, *73–77*, 175, 191, *379*
game birds (*see* specific names)
goose, 38, *73–77*, 147
grilled, *236*, *278*, 301
liver, 91–92
meats and, *84*, *92*, 301
rice and, *204*, 208, 266, 274, 361
salad, *312*
sausage and, *100*, 266, *275*, *309*
sausage garland, 38, 52, 324
skinning, *59*
soups, 41, *100*, *106*, 175, *179*, *201*, 379
spring rolls, 266, *282*, 294
stews, 174, *201*, 250
stuffed, 37, *39*, *52*, 58, *84*, 90, 147, 232, 234, 250, 266, *295*, 300–302, 324, 360–361, *371*, *383*
-stuffed pasta, *106*
turkey, 38, 52, *201*, 300, *312*, 324
turnovers, 269, 304, *316*
poultry sausage (*see also* galantine), *27*, 35, 57, 59, 145, 324
apple, *86*
bread, *26*, *64*, 145, 251, 302
calzone, *350*
capon, 41
caul-wrapped, 266–267
chicken, *26–27*, 37, *41*, *64*, *86*, 190, 266–267, *277*, 302, *373*
cooking, *26*
dried, 266
duck, *27*, 266, 324, *348–350*
dumplings, 266
fish and, 267
forcemeats, 251
game, *29*, *373*
goose, *27*, 121, 145, 172, 214, 360, 362
liver, 121, 145, 172, 214, 266, 302
meat and, *26*, *64*, 145, 266–267, *277*, 302, 324
patties, 266, *277*
pizza, 115, *348–350*
poultry skin casings, 266–267
smoked (*see also* hot dogs), 362

steamed, *27*, *277*, 350
stuffed necks, *41*, 145, 172, 214, 251, 360, 362
turkey, *27*, *41*, 360, 362, *373*
pozhanska kabanos, 173
Prague Powders, 15
preserved sausages (*see* confit)
profiteroles, *355*
prinskorv, 214
puchero, 268, 300
puddings (*see* blood, fish, white and Yorkshire puddings; orange; polenta)

quail, 57, *62*
quesadillas, 300, *304*, 362
queso fresco, 307

rabbit, 64, 66, 216, 324, 373
raisins, 66, *136*, *293*, *295*, *343*, *371*
sausages, 214, 216, *224*, *242*, 251, *258*, 269
raita, 250
rakott káposzta, *157*
red-eye gravy, 368, *371*
red hots, 360
regensburger, 122
reindeer sausage, *29*, 214–215, 363
relish, 97, *162–163*, *325*, *328*, *331*
rellenong manok, *295*
rice (*see also* jambalaya; paella; risotto), 29, 57, 90, 92, 122, 197, 216, 256–257, 266–269, 300–301, 323–324, 361, 363
dumplings, *270*
flour, 272
fried, 267–269, *274*, 323, 342, 348, 363
pork and, *84*, *157–158*, 301
red beans and, *381*
salad, *352*
sauerkraut and, *153*, *157–158*
sausage (*see also* cabbage; grape leaves), 66, 145–146, 190, 214, *224*, 233, 251, *284*, 302, 361, *373*
soup, *84*, *116–117*, *346*, *379*
wild, casserole, *341*
riisimakkara, *224*
risotto, 92, 103, 110, *116*
rohwurst, 120
rolls, bread, *325*, *328*, *329*
rolpens, 216
Romanian food, 142–145, *155–161*
Rome, ancient, 34–35, *39*, 56, *73*, 90, 95, *101*, 105, 110, 131, 190, 245, 345
Russian food, 17, 31, 36–37, 145, 157, 170–173, *173–185*, 215, 362
rye meal sausage, 214

salads, 92, 300, *331*, 363, 382
chick-pea, *203*
green, *281*, *288*, 324
gypsy, *140*
mixed meat, *312*
onion, *138–140*, *203*, *281*, *288*
potato, 57, *68*, 78, 121, 124, 216
rice, *352*
sausage, 58, 172, 269, *281*, 300, 324, 363
sausage-potato, *138–140*, *312*
salame, 363
salami, 14, 34, 57–58, 90–92, 120, 172–173, 214–215, 234, 251, 266, 268, 300–301, 363
beef, *25*, 90, 92, 122, *325*, *338*, 360
boar, 90–91
breads with, *25*, 90–91, *115*, 215, *217*, 324, *338*
casings, 16
dumplings, 92
horsemeat, 90
lamb, *25*, 90, 214–215
pie, *95*
pork, *25*, 90–92, 122, 144, *325*, *338*
reindeer, 215
smoked, 90–91, 122, *140*, *382*
stuffings, 25, 91
veal, 92
vegetables and, 25, 90–91, *140*
venison, *382*
salchicha blanca, 191
sales figures, 13, 323, 326
salsa, *92–94*, *198*, *311*, *353*
salsiccie (*see* Italian sausage)
saltpeter, 15
sandwiches (*see also* spreads), *162*, *198*, *260*, *288*, *325*, *328*, *329*, *338*
sauces (*see also* apple; butter; chile; cream; garlic; gravy; lime;

sauces *(cont.)*
mayonnaise; mustard; sweet-and-sour; tomato; vinaigrette; wine; yogurt)
beer, *134, 136*
celery, *52*
cheese, *98*, 107, 323
chicken liver, 91–92
Creole, 375–376
curry, *133*, 268–269, *289*
fish, 30, *278*
fruit, *136*, 277
herb, *94, 115*, 324, *345, 353*
horseradish, *30, 217, 219–221*
onion, *134, 316–317, 365*
salsa, *92–94, 198, 311, 353*
sausage, 25, 90–92, *98*, 105, 110, 191, *317*
soy sauce dip, *271*, 294
sweet, 37
saucijzebroodjes, 216, *337*
saucisse, 56, *71, 254, 376*
saucisson, 56, 58, *68–69, 82*, 376
sauerkraut, 58, 82, 121, 124, *131*, 215–216, 300, 324, 333, 362
meats and, *82*, 92, 121, 144, 146, *157, 158, 185*
rice and sausages, *153, 157–158*
soup, *83*, 215
sausage rolls, 57, *71*, 78, 146, 190, 216, 233–234, *337*
sauseasons, 216, *337*
saveloy, 233
scallops, *292*
Scandinavian food (*see also* horseradish sauce; potato sausage), *22*, 212–216 *216–225*, 362
schiacciata, 90
schubli, 122
Scotch egg, 233–235, *243, 289*, 301
scrapple, 360, 362, *367*
seekh kebab, *287*
sheftalia, *262*
shrimp (*see also* paella), 266–267, *272, 282, 284, 292*, 300–302, *344, 346*, 361, *377*
si klok, 267, *280*, 322, *340*
smoking sausage (*see also* specific sausages), 14, *21*
snert, *227*
snow peas, *39, 336, 352*
sobrassada/soprassata, 90, 192
solyanka, myasnaya, *179*
sopa, *196, 207, 307*
sosiski, 172
soujouk, 173
soups (*see also* caldo verde; potato; poultry; tomato; vegetable), 29, 36–37, 40, 57, 86, 92, 120–121, *137*, 144, 146–147, 172, 197, 207, 216, 232–233, 268, 300–302, 323–324, 361
bean, *75*, 191, 302, 361
beef, 59, *175, 179*, 268, *293*
beet, *175*, 179, 215
blood, 214
bread, *187*
cucumber, *178–179*, 309
dumpling, *106, 128*
fish, 174, *292, 345–346, 379*
garlic, *196*
lentil, *168*
lobster, *47*
meat, 59, *84, 179, 201*, 214
pasta, *106, 201, 292*
pea, 214, 216, 219, *227*
rice, *116, 346, 379*
sauerkraut, *83*, 215
tortilla, dry, *307*
sour cream, 144, 147–*148, 157–158*, 173, *178*
Southern (US) food (*see also* country sausage), *27*, 361, *368–383*
Southwestern (US) food, 324, *334*, 361–362, *382–383*
soy sauce dip, *271*, 294
Spanish food (*see also* chorizo; longanize; morcilla), 36–38, 57, 75, 84, 188–192, *192–206*, 268, *293*, 300–302, 304, 314, 317, 323, 353, 361, 377
"Spanish" rice, 323
spegepolse, 215
spetsofagi, 261–262
spice mixtures, *256, 286*
spinach, 56, *66*, 175, *209, 292, 314*
spreads, *111*, 120–122, *125*, 216, *224, 336*
spring rolls, 266, *282*, 294
squab, 57, *62*
squid sausage, 35
stamppot, *228*
stews, 29, 36–37, 57–58, 77, 92,

147, 190–192, 233, 250–251, 256, 262, 268, 300–302, 304, 323, 361
  barley, *137*
  beef, *155*, 191, *201*, 268–269
  fish, 361
  lamb, 191, *201*, 233
  mixed meat, *201*, 301
  pork, *185*, 191, *201*, 216
  potato, *148*, 233, 250
  poultry, 174, *201*, 250, 361
stick sausage, *325*
stomachs, stuffed (*see also* haggis), *30*, 34–35, 56, 120, 145–146, 173, 232, 242, 300
storing sausages (*see also* brine; confit), 13–33, 161
stuffing sausage casings, 16–20
stuffings, sausage, 234, 266, 302, 361
  fresh, 37, *39*, *46*, *52*, 57, 90, *108*, 110, 147, 232, 250, *304*, 324, *371*, *383*
  salami, 25
  smoked, *39*, *105–108*, *295*
strata, sausage, *342*
submarine sandwich, *338*
suet, where to buy, 17
summer sausage, 215, *325*, 362
svinjski kotlet sa kobasica, *165*
sweet:
  -and-sour sauce, 37, 121, *136*, *256*, 323
  marag, 242
  potato, 250, *272*, 302, 360
  rice (*see* glutinous rice)
  sauces, 37
sweetbreads, 59, 122
Swiss chard, *209*, *228*, *258*
Swiss food, 58, 92, 118, 122, *140*, 360

tacos, 300, *304*, 362
tamales/tamals, *305*, *383*
tapas, 190, 192, *198*, *203*
teewurst, 122
Thuringer, *325*
tlačenka, 146
toad-in-the-hole, 38, 226, 233, *237*
tofu, *282*, 323, 362
tokány, *155*
töltött káposzta, *153*, *158*
tomatillo, 301, 302, *311*
tomato, 91
  beans and, *73*, *314*
  chicken and, *309*
  chili, *334*, 362
  eggs and, *206*, *289*, *311*
  focaccia, *114*
  lecsó, *151*, *165*, *253*
  mixed grill, *236*
  pasta and, *107*, *133*, *194*, *257*, *317*, *334*, 361
  polenta, *103*
  relish, *163*
  rice and, *204*, *377*
  salad, *140*, *162*, *288*, *352*
  sandwich, *111*, *162*, *260*, *288*, *328*, *338*
  sauce, *81*, 91–*93*, 96, *115*, *133*, *147*, 173, *182*, *210*, *221*, *241*, *242*, *253*, *256*, 268, *289*, *307*, *317*, *353*, 375, 376
  sausage, 91
  simmered with meat, 122, *293*
  soups, *175*, *179*, *207*, *307*, 348
  stews, *148*, *155*, *185*, *201*
  stuffed, 57, 146, *336*, *348*
  stuffing, *295*
  tamale, *306*
  turnovers, *254*
tongue, 30, 121, 269, 295, 314
tortellini, *106*
tortilla-bread, 300, *304*, *307*, *309*, 362
tortilla-eggs, 191, *198*, 301
tostadas, 300, *304*
Transylvanian food, 142–145, *155–158*
tripe, 56, 190, 192
trotter, stuffed (*see* zampone)
trout and chorizo, 191
truffles, 38, 58–*59*, 64, 73, 121, 295, 302, 324
tube steaks (*see* hot dogs)
tuna sausage, *111*
turkey (*see* poultry)
turnips, *62*, *75*, *132*, 137, *272*
turnovers, 91, 191, *254*, 269, *304*, *316*
turtle sausage, 267, 300

uunimakkara, 216
uzenice, 146

Varmlandkorv, 218
veal, 59, 190, 215
  and ham pie, *49*
  mixed meats, *84*, *92*, 301
  stuffed, *43*, 57, *108*, 110, 232, *371*
  -stuffed cabbage, *153*, *222*
  -wrapped sausage, *113*
veal sausage (*see also* specific sausages), 120–122, 145, 146, 214, 324, 361
vegetables (*see also* pickles; specific names), 25, 92, 105–106, *114*, 121, 131, *133*, 144, 146, 190, 216, 267, 280, 301, 304, 374
  eggs and, *206*
  mixed meats and, *84*, *312*
  soup, 57, 59, *75*, 77, 137, 151, 219, 268, 302
  spring rolls, 266, *282*, 294
  stews, *137*, 216, 250, 268, 302
  stuffed (*see also* specific vegetables), 36, 324, *336*, *340*
vegetarian sausage, *258*, 324
venison sausage, *29*, 37, 233, 322, 362, *382*
Vienna sausage, 146, 269, 323
vinaigrette, *41*, *68*, *92–94*, *138*, *140*, *203*, *312*, *338*, *352*
virsli, 144
vitello ripieno, *108*
vogelnestjes, 216

water chestnuts, *272*, *277*, *282*, *350*, 363
weisswurst, 26, 121, *136*, 216, 360, 362
wheat sausage, 268
white hots, *26*, *123*, 360
white sausage (*see also* bockwurst; bratwurst; boudin blanc; white hots), *26*, 36, 120, 173, 190–191, 216, 362
  cooking, *26*, *242*
  pork, 121, 190
  poultry, *26*, 56, 190
  puddings, 26, 232–234, *242*
  sauced, *136*
  soup, 26, *346*
  veal, *26*, 121
wiener (*see* hot dogs)
wine sauce, 59, *69*, *79*, *100*, 135–*136*, *166*, 190, *355*
wurst (*see also* specific names), 38, 92, 120, 144, 146, 232, 234
  -braten, *166*
  -knödels (dumplings), *128*
  -salat, *138*
  -senf (mustard), *129*

yaitsa-boltun'ya z kolbasy, *181*
yogurt, *178*, 250, *258*, *260*, *287*, *289*, 323
Yorkshire pudding, 38, 225, 233, *237*
yosenabe, *292*
Yugoslav food, 142–145, *162–165*

zampognaro sauce, *98*
zampone, 91, 266–267
zigeunersalat, *140*
zrazy, *182*
zupa chlebowa, *187*
zweibelwurst, *125*